Jailed in 'Democratic' Germany: The Ordeal of An American Writer

Copyright ©1997 by Hans Schmidt
All Rights Reserved

ISBN: 0-9654134-0-3

Guderian Books
6223 Highway 90 #190
Milton, Florida 32570

Printed in the United States of America

Second Edition

Hans Schmidt was born in Luisenthal, Germany in 1927. At the age of seventeen, he volunteered for service in an elite German army unit and was twice wounded in frontline combat. Emigrating to the U.S. in 1949, he began a successful career as an American businessman. After his retirement, he founded GANPAC, the German-American National Political Action Committee.

Mr. Schmidt continues to write the group's monthly publications, *GANPAC Brief* and *USA-Bericht,* and to rally German-Americans, who comprise the largest ethnic bloc in the U.S., in defense of the freedoms all patriotic Americans cherish. He resides in Pensacola, Florida with his wife.

The Bützow Prison

The fortress-like Bützow prison, in Mecklenburg, Germany was built in 1837. Hans Schmidt was confined here from August of 1995 to January of 1996.

Author's Dedication

This book is dedicated to the thousands of people all over the world who protested my imprisonment in Germany for articles I had written in the United States; but especially to my wife Roswitha, who so bravely held her own while I was incarcerated; and to Lucile Saunders, my editor, and Carl Hottelet, whose valued advice cannot be overestimated.

Table of Contents

Foreword	6
Introduction	23
The Arrest	29
The Inaction of the U.S. State Department	40
An Involuntary Trip Through Germany	47
Hamburg	56
The Developments in America	64
Bützow	80
With Friends Like These	117
The Hostage Taking	134
Examinations for Continued Reasons of Detention	143
The "East" Germans	150
The Indictment and My Commentary	168
Questions Concerning the Legality of My Persecution	247
The Bonn 'Republic': A System Based on Lies	257
Shenanigans	273
The Trial and Our Defense Strategy	287
Statement to the Court	310
The ADL Report on Hans Schmidt	317
The Sickness	354
Epilog	410

Appendix I: Revisionists and the Internet   **419**

Appendix II: Documents   **424**

Index   **454**

Foreword

For Germans, the month of May has a special significance. For the veterans and survivors of World War II it is a time of reflection and remembrance, of deep mourning for the millions of their comrades, countrymen and family members who lost their lives in the conflict, of sorrow for the immense destruction and permanent loss of cultural heritage the war had wrought, and, not the least, of nostalgia for the *Reich* that is no more.

On the 8th of May 1945, the German armed forces had to capitulate unconditionally after six years of incredible fighting; their people prostrate before the wrath of vengeful enemies.

For those Germans however, who were born after 1940; for the generations whose *Weltanschauung* is the result of fifty years of Allied-imposed re-education and alleged "democracy," those generations that have to bear guilt complexes for historical events (or non-events) that occurred before they were born, are now supposed to celebrate every 8th of May as a Day of Liberation.

The Germans, in their own minds being more democratic than the democrats of the West, and more liberal than the staunchest liberals in Washington, London, Paris and Tel Aviv, (who they love to emulate), these *new* Germans actually believe--in typical German fashion--that it is now up to them to defend not only Germany and Europe, but the entire world from any dangers arising against *what they believe is* democracy. And, since they have also learned from their postwar masters that the end justifies the means, they use any and all means (however illegal, immoral and dictatorial), to suppress political dissent, especially from fellow Germans and others who do not agree with the Allied-imposed version of World War Two history.

Foreword

So it was no surprise to political intimates when in May of 1996 (more than a half century after the cessation of hostilities), the regime in Bonn launched a massive counterattack against political dissidents whose free spirits do not fit into the spiritual mold as formed by the Allied victors; an attack that knows no parallel in the half-century annals of the *Bundesrepublik*, and can only be compared to the wartime methods of the feared Gestapo, or the Soviet secret police (NKVD and KGB). In a single month, the following *well-known* writers, publishers, historians, politicians and revisionists have found themselves in front of judges of the *Bundesrepublik* for transgressions that in the United States would be no crime at all, because the alleged misdeeds fall under the protection of the First Amendment of the U.S. Constitution:

Udo Walendy, historian and researcher, was sentenced to 15 months in prison for publishing findings that contravene the official dogmas of the Bonn Government. For years Walendy's specialty has been the meticulous analysis of WWII propaganda claims which are still being touted as the absolute truth a half century after the war's end. This German historian has also made it his business to discover and publicize World War II *Allied* war crimes, the atonement for which was never undertaken (either at Nuremberg or elsewhere), because they had been committed by the victors. Walendy's extensive archives were confiscated.

Wigbert Grabert, a book publisher, has been fined 30,000 *deutschmarks* ($20,000), for publishing a large volume titled *Grundlagen zur Zeitgeschichte,* an anthology of revisionist scientific writing about WWII concentration camps. The issue was not whether the prosecutor had discovered any errors in this book, but that through the use of qualifying words like "alleged" and "supposedly", etc., its contents expressed skepticism about the official history of the war whose veracity may, *by law,* not be questioned in contemporary Germany. At the conclusion of Grabert's trial in June of 1996, the judge ordered all remaining copies of the book, *Grundlagen zur Zeitgeschichte*, confiscated and burned.

Germar Rudolf, is a young German chemist formerly with the world-renowned Max Planck Institute and the author of *Grundlagen zur Zeitgeschichte*. He was supposed to have been tried alongside Walendy and Grabert. However, for another, similar "transgression", (submitting Auschwitz exhibits to on-site forensic analysis), he had already been sentenced to a jail term, a sentence that is at this time being appealed. Rather than suffer imprisonment and endanger his health and the well-being of his young family, Rudolf fled to Spain. Currently, a warrant for his arrest has been issued by German authorities, and he is being hunted by Interpol. Germar Rudolf has never been implicated in any violence or political activity. His sole "crime" is having used his skills as a Max Planck Institute chemist in double-checking the chemistry claimed for the purported homicidal gassings at Auschwitz. When he published the honest results of his technical research, (which are at variance with Auschwitz dogma), he became an outlaw and a thought criminal.

Hans Werner Woltersdorf, a writer and historian, was fined 24,000 deutschmarks (or four months in prison), for writing *Die Ideologie der Neuen Weltordnung* (The Ideology of the New World Order). The court claimed that this book contained 108 points that could be considered "dangerous to youth". This in spite of the fact that probably very few young people ever had a chance to see this truthful work, which by U.S. Constitutional standards does not contain anything objectionable. Meanwhile, German youth have ready access to the worst kind of printed pornography available on many city street corners, with the full knowledge and approval of the present German government.

Günter Deckert, a former school teacher, and the head of one of the oldest German nationalist parties, has been sentenced to two-years in jail because, at a public meeting, he had translated from English to German what an American lecturer and execution technology expert had said about his discoveries at the former Auschwitz concentration camp. It is doubtful that Deckert will have a chance to be released on probation after having completed two thirds of his term, a courtesy normally extended to common criminals who behave in prison.

Georg Albert Bosse, the publisher of the pro-German magazine *Recht und Wahrheit* (Justice and Truth), received a sentence of one year in jail, and a fine of 4,000 deutschmarks on charges of inciting hate, defaming the dead, and insulting the Jews or other ethnic groups. However, in a break with the usual inquisitorial practice, his sentence was set aside, and he was given four years probation. Mr. Bosse still faces another trial for similar offenses.

The sentences meted out to these German dissidents are merely a small portion of the ongoing repression of anyone who dares to defend the native people, history, culture and traditions of Germany. All of the preceding individuals I have cited, as well as countless others, have suffered house and office searches that may have involved as many as twenty officers and officials of Bonn's "thought police." The confiscation and destruction by fire of *verboten* literature is a common occurrence under the Bonn regime. This author knows of not one instance during the Third Reich when the Gestapo searched the homes of innocent citizens merely for possessing Leftist books (such as Karl Marx' *Das Kapital*). But today, police raids on German homes, in search of forbidden revisionist books, is a common occurrence, perpetrated by the new Gestapo of the Bonn regime's "democratic" Germany.

On the 23rd of March 1995, no fewer than 800 policemen were mobilized to search the homes of Germans who were suspected of having received revisionist literature from the United States.

Statistics released by the German Information Center in New York show that in June of 1996 alone, 37 rightwing (i.e., patriotic) products were forbidden, under the spurious supposition that they "endangered the minds of German youth." [1]

Among these were compact discs, cassettes and brochures concerning the heroic exploits of German soldiers in World War II.

According to the Bundesrepublik office which deals with such matters, there were 16,472 official investigations of so-called "right wing extremists" (i.e. German patriots) in 1994, 2,231 of which led to criminal prosecution, fines or jail terms.

It is safe to assume that in 1995 and 1996 the number of persecuted German patriots was greater than in 1994.

For comparison: the persecution and 'being called to account,' combined with a partial incarceration of the 16,472 top people in politics, media and academia among Bonn's ruling clique, would signal the end of this Allied-imposed

---

[1] German Information Center, 950 Third Avenue, New York, N.Y. 10022. Telephone (212) 888-9840.

system.

One would only have to use their own standards, such as this:

In February of 1996, a teacher in the city of Heilbronn was sentenced to 10 months in jail because he had distributed a flyer in which it was stated that today's Germany is in the grip of a Jewish dictatorship.

But perhaps the most conclusive example of the Orwellian mindset of the Bonn bureaucrats can be found in the official government publication, *Demokratie live* (note the use of an English word in the title, rather than a German one), issued in May 1996 by the German Department of the Interior, which states:

"Wissenschaftsfreiheit ist notwendig, damit sich Forscher entfalten können. Damit neue Erkenntnisse gewonnen werden. Aber sie ist kein Freibrief für Verfassungsfeinde. Deshalb werden auch Hochschullehrer zur 'Treue zur Verfassung' verpflichtet.

"Es fällt auch nicht unter die Wissenschaftsfreiheit, Tatsachen zu leugnen.

"Deshalb können sich rechtsextremistische Geschichtsrevisionisten, die den Völkermord an den Juden leugnen, nicht auf dieses Recht berufen.

"Wer die geschichtlichen Tatsachen des millionenfachen Mordes an den europäischen Juden nicht wahrhaben will, leugnet die Leiden der Opfer und der Überlebenden, und verletzt das Andenken der Ermordeten und Toten - er fügt ihnen sozusagen ihre Leiden noch einmal zu.

"Dagegen steht das Gesetz."

Translation:

"Scientific freedom is necessary so that researchers can develop their ideas without hindrance. Only in this way new knowledge can be gained. But this does not mean that enemies of the Constitution are getting a license to ply their trade. And, this is the reason why (in Germany) high school teachers are asked to sign a loyalty oath.

"To deny facts does not fall under the protection of the freedoms guaranteed to science. That is why right-wing extremist historical revisionists who deny the genocide of the Jews cannot claim the right to scientific freedom.

"Whosoever denies the fact of the millionfold murder of the European Jews, denies the sufferings of victims, dead or alive, denigrates the memory of the murdered and dead Jews--he actually causes a repeat of their suffering.

"And that is against the law!"

Whoever wrote the preceding nonsense is crazy. Is not all research based upon the presupposition that prior knowledge (i.e., "facts") are being questioned and put to test? Isn't that what "right-wing historical revisionists" such as this writer are constantly doing?

If it weren't for people like us, the inscribed, "four-million-dead-Jews" claim would still be on the nineteen memorial plaques at Auschwitz, and historical knowledge would still be in the dark ages of the immediate postwar years.

Thies Christophersen, an agricultural specialist and a magazine publisher, is a former Wehrmacht army officer who, in the latter part of World War II, had been stationed near the Auschwitz concentration camp. He recounted his testimony in the book, *Die Auschwitz Lüge* (The Auschwitz Lie).

Since in this book he articulates his doubts about the gas chamber story, and has good reason to do so, (for he was an eyewitness to the actual events), he was subject to arrest by the German authorities who want to uphold the four-million-dead-at-Auschwitz myth. Christophersen was charged with the usual drivel (paragraphs 130 & 131 of the German law code). [2]

He was forced to flee his homeland and for several years he has been in exile, first in Denmark, and more recently in Spain. In May of 1996 his son died in an airplane crash and was buried in Germany. Christophersen, a man with an unblemished personal life, who has never been convicted of any criminal act, contacted the police in his native Schleswig-Holstein, to inquire as to whether, on humanitarian grounds, they might assure him safe conduct while he attended his son's funeral. The request was not only denied, but he was informed that he would be led away in handcuffs if he dared to be present at his son's burial.

In Thies Christophersen's case there are indications that the Bonn tyrants wish to avoid an open trial since the accused, as an Auschwitz eyewitness, might best his prosecutors and judges. Christophersen is quite willing to return to Germany and face his accusers, if the German judiciary will permit him to call witnesses for his defense, and if the prosecutor will assure him that prior to the trial he will not be locked up in a prison hospital for psychiatric evaluation (something he has been threatened with--shades of the Soviet Union.) Thus far no one in charge of his prosecution has been willing or able to give him these assurances.

---

[2] A French magazine, *National Hebdo* (May 31, 1990) details how the 'sacred' Auschwitz death toll has fallen dramatically over the years: from 8 million (French War Crimes Research Office), to 5 million (*Le Monde*, April 20, 1978), to 4 million (the figure advertised at Auschwitz-Birkenau up until 1990), to 3 million (the "confessions" of Rudolf Höss), to 1.6 million (Prof. Yehuda Bauer); to 1.25 million (Prof. Raul Hilberg), to 850,000 (Gerald Reitlinger, *The Final Solution*), to 75,000 (the Auschwitz archives in possession of the Russians).

Gerhard Lauck, an American writer and publisher of German descent, was arrested in Denmark at the behest of the German Government, and tried in Hamburg in 1996 after he had been extradited from Denmark in violation of all international conventions on human rights.

Lauck's "crime" consists in the fact that he believes (and insists that he can prove) that after 1945 Germany and the Germans suffered an unsung holocaust. Lauck mails nationalist literature stating this opinion, from his office in Lincoln, Nebraska, to people all over the world. Particularly upsetting to the Bonn Government is the fact that Lauck makes extensive use of the swastika, the old European symbol whose public showing is absolutely *verboten* in the new Germany. Lauck's trial opened on 9 May 1996, a date no doubt picked for its symbolic significance.

While initially it was stated that this courageous American faced a five-year jail sentence for his "horrible" crimes, Judge Günter Bertram corrected himself on the second day of the trial and pointed out that due to Lauck's publications, a fourteen year prison sentence (!) was possible.

Since the publisher is "only" a WWII revisionist, and not a Jewish dissident, neither the U. S. Government nor the American media have exhibited any outrage over this reprehensible action by the new heirs of the Gestapo. Hopefully, Lauck's spirit will not be broken by these German traitors who serve foreign masters. But there is reason to be concerned for the life of this U. S. citizen, who has been abandoned by his own government. [3]

The trials and tribulations of yet another U.S. citizen, namely this writer, arrested in "free and democratic" Germany as described in this book, ought to be of concern to every

---

[3] On August 22, 1996, Gerhard Lauck was sentenced to four years in prison.

American. My arrest entails a crisis that is at the heart of many arguments involving one of the most cherished traditions of the United States, namely, freedom of expression as guaranteed by the First Amendment to the Constitution.

At the time that I left Germany on my own recognizance, after five-months' incarceration in a 160-year-old jail, where I had been held for no other "crime" than freely expressing my opinion in my native German language from my home in America, German authorities took it upon themselves to raid the offices of the Munich subsidiary of CompuServe, the American Internet provider.

Ostensibly this was done to halt the transmission of child pornography via CompuServe. However, on January 9, 1996, the German prosecutor in charge of the investigation admitted in a television interview that, in actuality, the real target of the interdiction was the American and Canadian revisionist groups who were sending educational information into Germany by means of Internet (see the appendix).

A few weeks later, German prosecutors in the city of Mannheim attempted to force another Internet service, America Online, into blocking all German access to revisionist material and revisionist organizations, on the grounds that revisionist history constitutes "hate."

At this juncture the question must be asked, what is the definition of "hate material" and who are the "hate groups"? Moreover, who decides what thoughts, opinions and conclusions may or may not be disseminated? Is it hate when a political leader of the largest ethnic group in the United States points out that another ethnic group, consisting of a minority of highly-influential power-brokers, has too much power and influence in vital sectors of this country, and that this all-too-great power and influence of a tiny minority may cause harm to the nation? I leave the reader to be the judge. The contents of this book may provide the requisite, vital information.

It was a German immigrant to North America who first took up the fight for freedom of expression and freedom of the press.

John Peter Zenger (1697-1746), who immigrated as a young boy from the German Palatine, had become a publisher in New York City, and attacked the corruption and ineptitude then prevalent in the British colonial administration. Eventually, he was arrested under a charge of "seditious libel" and jailed for nearly a year, without trial. When Zenger finally got his day in court and tried to defend himself by declaring that he had only published the facts, the authorities replied that, "truth is no defense". Zenger eventually triumphed and his victory laid the basis for the creation of the First Amendment to the U. S. Constitution by the Forefathers of this nation.

Now, more than 250 years later, this writer had to spend five months in a German prison. I too had stated certain unmentionable facts, and again it was said that "truth is no defense," because the truth allegedly caused "mental harm" to others, and supposedly "defamed their dead." In this case it was an American citizen who was imprisoned in Germany, for writing in the United States about ideas that may not be publicly discussed in Germany. As things stand now, matters in Germany will get much worse before they get better, because those holding Germany in their grip are intent on retaining their power, and they can do so only if certain historical (or, semi-religious, such as those pertaining to the "Holocaust") dogmas relating to World War II, can be upheld.

The time has come to expose the charade of the Bundesrepublik as the most free and democratic state that (allegedly) ever existed on German soil.

Foreword

The question must be asked whether the German authorities would arrest American citizens who, unlike the author of this book, were not politically incorrect, and who had no inkling that the Bonn establishment regarded them as political adversaries to be persecuted? The case of Richard Landwehr provides the answer.

Richard Landwehr, a resident of the State of Oregon, is a military historian and the publisher of the magazine, *Siegrunen*, which deals exclusively with the history of the Waffen-SS, the elite divisions of the Third Reich.

Landwehr has authored numerous books relating to individual combat units of the Waffen-SS. He has written only of the military exploits of this elite German army corps. National Socialist politics and ideology, either past or present, do not interest him.

In contemporary Germany, the public display of Third Reich regalia is prohibited by law. This is not the place to explain the incongruity of why Germans may publicly display the Soviet red star, the symbol of the Communist Red Army, at whose hands millions of German civilians were raped, tortured and murdered; but German World War II veterans who fought the Communist scourge, and earned the Iron Cross for doing so, cannot wear their original medals of valor in public.

(For public display, the German veterans are compelled by the Bonn regime's edict to engage in the ridiculous charade of wearing only medals that are postwar fakes--having been manufactured with the politically incorrect symbols of SS runes and swastikas expunged).

In September of 1995, Landwehr received a letter from a German court in Bremen informing him that because a German citizen had been found in possession of a copy of *Siegrunen* magazine, Landwehr had been found guilty of violating German laws against the display of emblems of illegal organizations (in this case, the Waffen-SS). The letter announced that a heavy fine had been levied against the military historian.

Landwehr had not even known that he had been on trial! Furthermore, the German citizen who had been arrested for possession of *Siegrunen* was unknown to Landwehr. The individual was not on the magazine's list of subscribers.

Siegrunen is published only in English and is geared toward American researchers. How can one be expected to publish a magazine devoted to the history of the Waffen-SS without publishing period photographs which contain either the swastika or the double-lightning bolts on these soldiers' uniforms? How can an American publisher know of such draconian modern German laws, or otherwise prevent a copy of his magazine from being circulated in a foreign country?

Ironically, Landwehr would not have been put on trial and fined, if his writings about the Waffen-SS were the usual, grossly bigoted prevarications marketed by the Establishment press. But because Landwehr's magazine includes admiration for the undeniable military prowess and courage under fire against overwhelming odds, that is the hallmark of the Waffen-SS, this makes him, in the eyes of the watchdogs over the hoped-for extinction of the German people--a criminal.

If Richard Landwehr does not pay the fine levied against him (probably several thousands of deutschmarks plus court costs), he will be subject to arrest in Germany, even if he did not know anything at all about the entire matter. This can happen to many other Americans who unwittingly transgress against Germany's arcane laws.

After I had been arrested in August of 1995 at the Frankfurt airport, I discovered that, unbeknownst to me, I had a prior conviction: a court in the port city of Kiel had sometime earlier fined me 3,000 deutschmarks (about $2,000) and never found it necessary to inform me either before or after the trial of this fact! In other words, had I not been arrested in 1995 at the behest of a minister of the state government of Mecklenburg-Vorpommern, I would have been subject to arrest for refusing to pay a previous fine of which I knew absolutely nothing, and the cause of which eludes me to this day.

These weird and arbitrary prosecutions have more in common with the pathological Stalinist show-trials of the 1930s, than they do with a supposedly progressive and "democratic" republic of a "new" Germany. *In such a perverse environment, every American intellectual visiting Germany is now in jeopardy, subject to the prosecutorial whims of the government.*

As time goes by, and as the present political situation evolves, the Zionist-instituted Bonn system (Bonn is the capital of the present regime occupying Germany), will become more and more enervated.

It is already losing the stranglehold that has kept German minds in bondage since 1945 (first by the victorious Allies, and since 1949 by their masochistic German sycophants). It is a fact of political life that regimes which are losing their grip on the population attempt to retain their power by an ever increasing campaign of repression. Bonn has now reached this degenerate stage, as demonstrated by the growing persecution of German patriots.

My case as well as those of Richard Landwehr and Gerhard Lauck, proves that *American citizens are extremely vulnerable to the suppression of their basic human rights at the hands of the clique ruling Germany today, and no assistance can be expected from the U.S. State Department.*

The situation in Germany recalls the terror measures in force when the Communists still ruled Russia. Then, too, Americans were arrested for having "contraband," i.e. books and pamphlets regarded as subversive. Explanations offered by the American visitor, to the effect that he or she could not possibly have known that this or that book or magazine was out of bounds in the Soviet Union, were rarely accepted, and just as in Germany now, heavy fines were levied and sometimes the "culprit" landed in jail.

However, there is a big difference between then and now: Americans ought to be more cautious when visiting Germany at this time, than they ought to have been when they flew to Moscow while the Communists were in power.

Back in the Soviet era, there was no question that, in most cases, the United States Government would try its utmost to free its citizens from Communist jails and harassment.

Today the situation has been reversed. The people in charge of the U. S. Government and especially those handling the German desk at the U. S. State Department, are themselves implicated in keeping the Bonn censors and jailers in power, and they gladly abandon time-honored policies of defending the rights of U. S. citizens, as long as it serves the interests of their peculiar Zionist *Weltanschauung*. We advise American citizens to avoid travel to Germany in the foreseeable future altogether.

In contemporary Moscow and St. Petersburg nobody is being checked for forbidden literature when entering the country, and neither Landwehr, nor Lauck or this writer, have to fear imprisonment in Russia for transgressions against ludicrous, politically-inspired censorship laws that do not belong in the statutes of a civilized nation.

While the bulk of the Germans accept this repression by their own government with the same medieval docility with which Germans once accepted the petty tyranny of feudal rulers, there *is* a noticeable discontent rising among a significant minority of Germans who hitherto could be considered the pillars of the system.

On May 17, 1996, an appeal for freedom of expression was signed by 100 Germans, among whom were many prominent individuals. This appeal was published in the *Frankfurter Allgemeine Zeitung*.

While this number may seem minuscule in relation to the German population of approximately 80 million, it bears remembering that for every one of the signers, there are at least hundreds of key people who agree but who currently dare not voice their opinion because they have a justified fear for their livelihood. Such are the methods of tyranny; even of an allegedly democratic one. The text of this appeal by the one hundred is as follows:

FREEDOM OF SPEECH IS AT RISK!

"We, the undersigned, have recently noted with alarm that in Germany special laws and criminal prosecutions are increasingly directed against publishers, editors, authors--even scientists—on the grounds of justified and documented comments which they have expressed on certain issues of contemporary history.

In particular, the recently established procedure of rejecting, sight-unseen, all new evidence submitted by defendants, on the basis of "judicial notice," borders on a perversion of justice, violates human rights, and is unworthy of a free and democratic nation, under the rule of law.

This practice places intolerable restrictions on scientific and academic research and on the free and open discussion of these issues which are of special significance to Germany, and impedes or prevents the necessary process of establishing the truth. Without wishing to take any position on the controversial issues per se, we--being responsible citizens greatly concerned about freedom of speech, research and teaching as guaranteed by the German *Grundgesetz* (Constitution)--would draw attention to this dangerous state of affairs, and appeal to all those responsible, as well as to the public both at home and abroad, to take steps to ensure that such violations of human rights as well as of the free and democratic order, shall cease."

[The signers of this appeal may be contacted through Prof. Dr. H. Schröcke, Am Hohen Weg 22, 82288 Kottgeisering, Germany].

It is doubtful that the Bonn Government will heed such a reasonable appeal by some of its most distinguished citizens. There are still the bayonets of the American army upon which the vassal regime can depend if its existence were in jeopardy.

It is unfortunate that the expressed wish by these freedom loving Germans of being heard abroad has little chance of being granted. Those who control most of the media of the so-called free West are the very people who are intent on keeping their Bonn servants in power, and the German people in mental chains. (Almost no mention of the appeal appeared in the Western Establishment media).

Yet the significance of this clarion call cannot be discounted. One hundred of Germany's intellectuals and business people defied potential damage to their careers, ensuing police surveillance and perhaps even arrest and prosecution, and spoke from their heart. By giving voice to the passion that motivates freedom-lovers the world over, these Germans have begun to take a first step toward the self-determination that has been denied their people since 1945.

Introduction

"The consequent measures taken by the authorities against the extreme rightists have undoubtedly infringed upon their abilities to be legally active." [1]

This statement was issued by Ernst Uhrlau, an official of the German *Verfassungsschutz* ("Guardians of the Constitution"), a secret police organization not unlike the former German Communist *Stasi*, and similar police agencies in other totalitarian states.

Every American who has the least bit of pride in the republican form of government ought to cringe when reading such utterances. In Germany, "democracy" as it exists today, was instituted by the United States Government after World War II, and has ever since been kept in place by the power of (mostly) American bayonets. The German people never really had a say in the matter. The Bonn *Grundgesetz*, which is little more than an ersatz constitution, was put together in the immediate postwar years, mainly by emigrants to and from the U.S. under the leadership of Jewish professors who had to leave the Reich between 1933 and 1939.

Who are the "extreme rightists" Mr. Uhrlau spoke about? These are people whom we here in the United States would call patriots. Few Americans realize this but in the Germany of today *any* expression of nationalistic or patriotic sentiment is not only frowned upon by a camarilla of political leaders, the media and the academic establishment; but it is brutally suppressed by the Bonn government, as this secret police official's words prove. It is this political atmosphere to which I, an American naturalized citizen for many decades, fell prey

---

[1] *Frankfurter Allgemeine Zeitung*, September 15, 1995.

when I was arrested at the Frankfurt airport on August 9, 1995, just when I was about to board a jet back to the United States. I was charged with transgressions against the notorious statute §130, for allegedly causing "incitement to hate," for having written newsletters in Florida which German bureaucrats deemed offensive. Before I go into detail, I will mention some facts about my incarceration that should make every reader cognizant of the dangerous state of affairs prevailing now in Germany.

For the first ten days to two weeks after my arrest, I was most of the time held virtually incommunicado. Nobody, not my wife, my German attorney, or the American Embassy knew much--if anything--of my whereabouts. While prisoners are supposed to be allowed to make at least one phone call immediately after their arrest, this right was denied to me.

I was merely assured that calls to my lawyer and to the U.S. Consulate in Frankfurt had been made. But I could not be certain until my lawyer visited me for a mere half hour in the Frankfurt jail. Then I lost all contact again for many days.

For five weeks after my arrest I was unable to communicate confidentially by mail with my lawyer (who lived several hundred miles away from the prison). During this period I was forced to hand over to the authorities, unsealed, every letter addressed to my attorney, and this correspondence was probably read by the prosecutor.

After my return to the United States, on January 26, 1996, I received an airmail letter from one of my lawyers that had been posted in Germany sixteen days previously. The letter showed evidence that it had been tampered with. Normally, an airmail letter from Germany to Pensacola, Florida, takes about four to five days.

While I was in German custody, it was six weeks before I

received the first letter from my wife in Florida, bringing among other things, the news of the devastation wrought by a hurricane in Pensacola on August 3, 1995. During these first six weeks, her frantic telephone messages to me were only delivered thus: "Your wife called and said hello." Not a word more.

Almost throughout my incarceration, the mail was delayed for an unconscionably long time. On the average it took more than two months for me to receive answers to questions I posed in letters to friends, even though most of my correspondents had answered immediately after receipt of my missives.

On the day of my release from prison, the presiding judge handed me 150 letters that had not been given to me earlier because, due to a lack of time, it had been impossible for the German judiciary to read and check their contents.

Upon my leaving the prison, I was handed some thirty letters that I had not received in my cell because of their "dangerous" contents.

They had all been withheld by official court ruling. This tampering with mail appears absolutely ludicrous to any American accustomed to free speech.

The pretext given for keeping these thirty letters out of my jail cell was not my personal welfare but the court's alleged concern for "order inside the prison". Little did the court know what the 600 or so prisoners really thought of the German form of "democracy", as proven by my incarceration.

It was fully ten weeks after my arrest that I was finally able to receive permission to make very short weekly telephone calls to my wife, and also talk with my mother in Germany. These phone calls were all monitored and during the remainder of my incarceration I was never allowed to call anyone else.

For approximately two weeks after my arrest, and before I

saw a doctor at the 160-year old Bützow prison in former Communist east Germany, *my daily medicine for high blood pressure (I have a serious heart condition as well as a prostate ailment), was purposely withheld from me. This in spite of the fact that the pills I needed were in my luggage, which was in the possession of the authorities.*

Sometime in August, during my transport from Frankfurt to Bützow across Germany in a prison van (where I was held within a small cell in the van), one day was particularly arduous: not only was it unbearably hot in the nearly airless cabin of the van; during a five hour drive from Hanover to Hamburg, the police vehicle did not once stop either for quenching the thirst of the prisoners; nor did I have a chance to relieve myself during that time. This was an ordeal for a man nearing seventy years of age with major medical problems.

The 29-page indictment contained a biography of this writer, full of errors and scurrilous conjectures which, according to the prosecutor, was obtained from the U.S. Embassy in Bonn, and is allegedly an official report about me by the *amerikanische Behörde* (U.S. governmental authorities).

Since I was certain that the United States Government was prohibited by law from providing such information to a country that did not value basic democratic liberties, such as freedom of expression, my lawyers made it their business to check the real source of the defamatory report in the files of the German court: We were not surprised to discover that it came from the Anti-Defamation League, (A.D.L.) a notorious, powerful, private spy organization based in the United States (though actually, an unregistered agent of the foreign government of Israel).

The German authorities accorded this partisan, private espionage agency, which has been implicated in numerous scandals in the U.S., an official designation as an arm of the

United States Government.² (In the appendix the reader will find a copy of the letter written by the German Ministry of the Interior to the court confirming this fact and also, that this spy agency had supplied much more fictitious material libeling me).

As a former soldier of World War II who in 1945 experienced the privations of POW stockades (one cannot call them camps), after the German surrender, I was able to endure these hardships better than most of the other "first time" prisoners. Yet, I was deeply shocked by the *Menschenverachtung* (disregard for human dignity) proven by the facts as stated above.

At the time of my arrest, at 68 years of age, I had never been in front of either an American or a German judge. The worst transgression one can accuse me of in the past half century are a couple of traffic tickets. In addition, one ought to consider that I had clearly been incarcerated for so-called thought crimes, i.e., not for any criminal actions.

When reading this book, please bear in mind that it is all about our God-given right to free expression for everyone. Our vigilance in favor of the First Amendment must continue unabated. It is constantly under attack. It also bears remembering that those who want to infringe on our rights to free expression always clothe their nefarious demands under the mantle of a battle for "decency" and "tolerance", and against "hate" (whereby we are supposed to use their definition as to

---

² In the course of a 1993 San Francisco police department raid on A.D.L. offices it was determined that the Zionist group had illegally obtained confidential government records such as vehicle registrations and driver licenses as part of the A.D.L.'s domestic surveillance of Americans it regards as too critical of Israeli policies. Some of this intelligence was transmitted to the Israeli assassination bureau, Mossad. Cf. *San Francisco Chronicle,* April 9, 1993 and *San Francisco Bay Guardian,* Oct. 5, 1994.

An article in *The New American,* Sept. 19, 1994, "A.D.L. Campaign Against Tolerance," asserted that the A.D.L. is "engaging in defamation" and using "discreditable techniques such as insinuation and guilt by association." Also cf. "The Jewish Thought Police: How the Anti-Defamation League Censors Books, Intimidates Librarians and Spies on Citizens," *Village Voice,* July 27, 1993.

what constitutes "hate"); words whose real meaning is nothing to them. In this connection I must mention again the Internet/CompuServe/America Online matter making the news at the beginning of 1996, at the time when I returned to America. Before readers judge my actions as a result of prior unfavorable publicity, they ought to verify the actual agenda of those organizations that want to circumvent the First Amendment through the use of eminently false claims.

It bears mentioning that the "ersatz" German Constitution of 1949, cited above, and upon which the Bonn Government bases its legality (but which according to international law is as invalid as was the constitution of that other, now defunct German vassal state, the "East" German Communist Republic), *does indeed* guarantee the right to freedom of expression.

Unfortunately for Germany, those Americans having had a veto right when that "ersatz" Constitution was written, namely, the U.S. Military Occupation Government under General Lucius D. Clay, did not feel compelled to enforce stricter guidelines in conformity with the American First Amendment. Therefore, Article V of the Bonn Constitution has been significantly diluted and its "guarantees" are useless.

Officially, Bonn, Germany is a member of the United Nations, of the European Union, and a signer of the so-called Helsinki Accords, all of which give "assurances" and "guarantees" of freedom of speech and the freedom of the press. Bonn keeps its part of the bargain only in the latter case, in the extra-political realm, whereby pornography is permitted to flourish.

For example, in Bützow prison the most vile pornographic magazines were freely available, while publications extolling German virtues such as thrift, honesty, the work ethic, and morality, were forbidden. Also proscribed was any written material that stated that "Germany belongs to the Germans."

The Arrest

"Herr Schmidt, es tut mir leid, aber ich muß Sie verhaften!"
("Herr Schmidt, I am sorry to inform you that you are under arrest!")

I could see that the young, uniformed German border patrol officer who pronounced these words did not like to say them, but he had a job to do and at that moment there was really nothing either of us could do about it. A few minutes later, after I had been asked to turn in my passports, my airline ticket and other personal papers, I was led into a bare, windowless room that contained only a wooden bench. The waiting began. For the time being, the control over my physical being was in the hands of others.

Just about the time when my plane took off for the return flight to the United States without me, albeit with somewhat of a delay due to the necessity of removing my baggage from its hold, I experienced the first of numerous, thorough searches of my clothes and luggage. (The two pieces of baggage which I had turned in at the airline counter had in the meantime been returned to me.)

When I asked the surly-looking team of special officers who were searching my belongings, what they were looking for, I did not receive an answer. I nevertheless assured them that I carried no contraband, no dope, no weapons, no gold or silver, not even written material that might endanger the existence of the Allied-imposed political system of the German Bundesrepublik.

Thankfully, so far they do not have any technical instruments to measure the "revolutionary" thoughts I always seem to carry in my head.

Flight DL 61 from Frankfurt to Washington, D.C., due to leave at 2 p.m. (14:00 hours) on Aug. 9, 1995, was on time. As

The Arrest

is customary with me, I had arrived at the Frankfurt airport by train from my native city of Saarbrücken, just about 200km (125 miles) to the southwest, early enough to check in leisurely, and also have a light lunch at one of the many airport restaurants, a fortuitous deed since I wasn't going to get anything to eat for quite a few hours afterward.

Even before the boarding announcement was broadcast, I had made my way to the Delta airlines waiting area in the new D Concourse of the airport. But before that I had to pass the passport inspection manned by officers of the German border patrol.

It must have been about a half hour before the plane was to leave, when I presented my American passport to the officer behind the safety glass. Since I had passed a similar barrier when I arrived in *Deutschland* less than twenty days earlier, and had during my brief stay, studiously avoided any controversial activities, I did not anticipate any problem. Usually (but not always) I just get waved through, but now the youthful patrolman put my passport upside down on a scanner connected to a computer and I noticed that he typed a few more keys on the keyboard in order to obtain additional information. After reassuring himself, he motioned me to step aside and walk with him to an office behind the barrier where, after additional computer inquiries, I was arrested. The charge: *Volksverhetzung* (incitement to hate).

An hour later I was in possession of the arrest warrant.[1] On demand, it had been faxed to the airport border patrol office from a prosecutor in the city of Schwerin, the capital of the German state of Mecklenburg-Vorpommern. According to the warrant, in November, 1994, I had mailed a copy of an "Open

---

[1] Copies of the originals of the legal documents will be found in the appendix. See *Haftbefehl* for the arrest warrant. A translation of the warrant begins on p. 34.

Letter" which I had sent to Martin Klingst, a German journalist, to a Mr. Rudi Geil, as well. Mr. Geil is the Minister of the Interior of Mecklenburg-Vorpommern and he was so offended by a passage of about 50 words which did not even concern him (from an Open Letter of more than 2,500 words!), that he personally launched an official prosecution, accusing me of a criminal offense.

Geil is one of the innumerable "carpetbaggers" now holding important positions in the German lands that were the former "DDR" (Communist "East" Germany). Prior to this appointment, Geil had for many years been an elected representative of the C.D.U., Chancellor Helmut Kohl's ruling party, in the West German state of Rheinland-Pfalz. Since Mecklenburg-Vorpommern is currently one of the poorest German states, with among the highest unemployment figures, one could surmise that Geil's transfer to Schwerin might have been an attempt by the Bonn ruling clique to send an overly ambitious junior politician to the boondocks, so to speak, where he can do little damage.

The fact that it took an order from Mr. Geil to effect my arrest seems to confirm this assessment. One can assume that during his tenure as a Rheinland-Pfalz representative he had made valuable contacts with the *Oberjuden* (elite Jews), who rule nearby Frankfurt.

There is the distinct probability that he wanted to ingratiate himself with them by arranging for my arrest and prosecution. Ultimately this scheme backfired, however. "Rudi" has been disgraced and his career has been seriously hurt by my case. It is unlikely that, in the final analysis, Bonn was or still is very happy about the entire episode. Certainly the reputation of Bonn as a bulwark of democracy was seriously damaged by the publicity surrounding my arrest and incarceration, which revisionists and civil libertarians the world over generated on my behalf.

In the few hours while I was waiting in the prisoners' holding room of the Frankfurt airport, to be transported to the city jail, I had time to contemplate my situation. Having been a German and German-American political activist for decades, I was well aware of the fact that my political stance did not coincide with that of the current German Government. As a matter of fact, especially during the last ten years or so it became apparent that the political course of the Bonn regime and that of myself had continuously drifted farther apart, and that no love was lost between me and those whom I like to call the Bonn vassals (of America!).

As the chairman of the GANPAC (the German-American National Public Action Committee), which is thus far, the *only* organization in the United States active *politically* on behalf of the 60 million or so Americans of German descent, I have since 1983 been the publisher and principal writer of two monthly newsletters (one in English and the other in German), espousing political views that are anathema to internationalists and One-Worlders everywhere.

While the English-language *GANPAC Brief* goes to thousands of readers each month, our German language newsletter is regularly mailed only to a minuscule number of nationalist and patriotic publishers and activists in Europe. The objective of my German language newsletter, *USA-Bericht,* (USA Report) is to inform patriotic Germans and other nationalists of "politically incorrect" facts that are purposely withheld from them by the European media.

In achieving this goal, I consistently hark on the over-representation and disproportionate influence of Jews in high office in the United States: in government, the media, entertainment and education; at the top banks and elsewhere (except, for instance, in farming and the manual building trades). According to my thesis, American Jews are currently holding positions of power and influence in the United States that rightfully belong to the Germans (or, rather, German-Americans). However, in opposing Jewish over- representation here in America, I am in conflict with the strict policies of the Bonn Government, according to which Jews are a privileged and protected holy people who are never to be criticized, and whose actions shall always be deemed beyond reproach.

In my letter to Mr. Martin Klingst of the (Leftist) newspaper *Die Zeit*, (this was the missive that had caused Mr. Geil's incoherent action), I had referred to the fact that Jews and Freemasons dominated the Bonn system from the top. I further stated that I considered this domination harmful to the well-being of the German people. Nevertheless, it also bears mention that my Open Letter to Mr. Klingst had been merely my *answer* to an article by him in which he had warned against--in his opinion--the likelihood of right-wing terrorism. As a self-proclaimed German (and German-American) rightist and nationalist I felt unjustly attacked. The essence of my letter was my prediction that it wasn't going to be right-wing terrorism but rather the *Volkswut*, the justified anger of the population, that eventually would drive the Bonn regime out of office.

Obviously, I knew that the Bonn vassals did not like me or my writings. Having investigated and publicized the persecutions and prosecutions of other foreign historical revisionists and nationalists, such as Ernst Zündel, David Irving, Max Wahl, Fred Leuchter, Gerhard Lauck, Jürgen Graf and Günther Vogt, (among others), and German patriots such as Günter Deckert, Erhard Kemper, Christian Worch, Manfred Roeder, General Otto Ernst Remer, Germar Rudolf, Michael Kühnen, and many others, I did not imagine that I was somehow immune to the extra-legal shenanigans of Bonn. Nevertheless, *never* having written anything that could be regarded as unjustified or irresponsible criticism, or even remotely as "incitement to hate", and *always* having argued against the use of violence, I did not believe that my alleged transgressions could fall within the purview of the notorious paragraph 130 of the German legal code under which I was eventually indicted.

Even while being held under arrest at the Frankfurt airport I assumed that on the following day, a Thursday, I would simply have to appear in front of a judge in that city who would open an indictment against me, an indictment that would soon be quashed by my German lawyer whom I had earlier engaged for just such an eventuality. Not having done anything wrong, and with an unblemished record in both Germany and the United States, and due to my age, I seriously believed that I would be on my way to the United States within a few days, after having explained *the meaning of my words,* and after perhaps having paid a fine of sorts.

I couldn't have been more wrong! My ordeal had just begun.

The translation of the arrest warrant:

District Court Schwerin
Dept. 34 28 March 1995
File No. of the Prosecutor: 111 Js 826/95
Arrest Warrant
Hans Schmidt, born 27 April 1927 in Völklingen, U.S. citizen, address in Pensacola, Florida, USA, currently in Völklingen/Luisenthal is to be taken into custody (pre-trial detention).

Schmidt is suspected of having attacked the human dignity of others, (and having disturbed public peace) in the City of Schwerin, on 9 November 1994, through defaming and harmfully ridiculing them.

On 4 November 1994 (date of postage stamp cancellation) the

accused mailed from Burke, Virginia, USA, the newsletter *USA-Bericht* of November, 1994 to state legislator Rudi Geil, C.D.U., Land Mecklenburg, Karl Marx Strasse 1, 19055 Schwerin. Part of this newsletter is an Open Letter of the accused, dated 8 May 1994, to Martin Klingst, a journalist with the newspaper *Die Zeit*, in which he makes reference to an article titled "The new terror" from December 17, 1993 by Klingst. This Open Letter contains the following paragraph:

"...Mein Gott, was haben Leute wie Sie sich eigentlich gedacht? Es waren die Linken, die Chaoten, die juden- und freimaurerverseuchten politischen Systemparteien und die Lizenzpresse, die seit Jahrzehnten Jagd auf alles Nationale machten: Brutal, intolerant, unnachgiebig, haßerfüllt."

("...My God, what did people like you think anyway? It was the Leftists, the anarchists, the Jew- and Freemasonry-infested political parties, and the licensed press which for decades had hunted down all patriots: brutally, intolerantly, relentlessly and full of hate."). [2]

The designations *"judenverseucht"* (Jewish-infested) and *"freimaurerverseucht"* (Freemasonry-infested) are directed against the respective parts of the population, and thereby they constitute a form of defamation, respectively harmful denigration of these groups, and, finally, they are intended to attack the human dignity of the members of these groups. Such a deed is punishable according to §130, No.3 StGB.

It is reasonable to expect that there is a high risk of the

---

[2] This is not an accurate translation, but rather a faulty one published by the Establishment media. It *does not* express my sentiments but rather the mindset of the Bonn stooges who have been trained to think in terms that were unknown to me when I left Germany shortly after WWII. For an analysis of this erroneous translation, see pp. 38-40.

accused becoming a fugitive from justice (§ 112, part 2, No.2 StPo.). The accused is a U.S. citizen, and his permanent domicile is in the United States. He visits Germany only rarely. Therefore we can rightfully assume that the accused will not subject himself voluntarily to orderly court proceedings in this case. An extradition of the accused from the United States is not possible because he is a citizen of the United States. We also cannot expect an American court to either take over the case, or assist us in any way, for instance in subpoenaing him, since this deed is in the United States not against the law.

The punishment to be expected as a result of a conviction due to §130 StGB, namely, imprisonment from between 3 months to 5 years, is a particularly important reason for the accused to become a fugitive from justice, especially so if one also considers the additional §56, part 3 StGB, (Defense of the System of Law and Order) whereby imprisonment *without the possibility of parole* is warranted.

Therefore, the request for pre-trial detention is reasonable.
Signed: Dickmann, Judge. Issued on March 28, 1995.

Later, while I was imprisoned in Bützow and when I attended hearings or the trial in Schwerin, I never came across Judge Dickmann. For all I know, he might have been a phantom.

The paragraph excerpted from my letter to Martin Klingst of *Die Zeit*, deserves more than cursory attention since it provided the Bonn authorities with the pretext (and the spurious legal grounds) for my arrest and incarceration.

Essentially the case hinges only on the four words translated as "Jew-and Freemasonry-infested;" *four words out of a letter of about 2,500 words.*

But, apart from the fact that I could write them in America with precisely the meaning ascribed to me, (in other words, in the U. S. I would not have to think twice about using them in such a way since here freedom of speech is still guaranteed by the Constitution, and neither Jews nor Freemasons would have the slightest chance to accuse me of a crime), the question is, did I really write them? Does the phrase, "*juden-und freimaurerverseucht*" mean "infested," "infected," or even "contaminated," something the *Pensacola News Journal* (and probably other American papers), claimed?

Here I must point out that in both German and English I frequently use expressions that could be considered impolite and crude by my adversaries. I do this purposely because I am sick and tired of the "political correctness" that has been shoved down our throats for decades now, and of the hypocrisy that permeates modern society (not only in the United States).

I still remember when the War Departments of the imperialistic powers of the world were called just that and not "Defense Departments." Yes, I know, the U. S. attack against Grenada was a purely defensive measure, as were all American (and British, and French, etc.) wars in this century. I also still remember when a fag was a fag, and not "gay," when a cripple was a cripple, and not "physically handicapped," and when crazy or stupid kids were just that and not "exceptional students". I also remember when soldiers went on a military campaign and not on a "peace mission." Ah, yes, "affirmative action" really never was that but "special preferences for minorities". But one could not call it that, could one, when one wanted to befuddle the masses?

At any rate, my clear and open, and sometimes impolite expressions were an attempt to circumvent "political correctness", which I deem a handicap to understanding what is really happening in the world. As a matter of fact, I believe that the success of my newsletters (now being published for the fourteenth year), is partly caused by the simple and clear language I use. Like any professor I could clothe my sentences in hard-to-understand words, or multisyllabic, cumbersome sentences, but that would not help my readers to understand what is going on in the world, would it?

So, when in the Klingst letter I wanted to point out that Bonn (i.e., the political structure there which is based on the four parties playing a role, namely, the CDU, SPD, FDP and the Greens) was at the top ruled and dominated in a way harmful to Germany by Jews and Freemasons (something I can document!) I used the words "*juden und freimaurerverseucht.*" Even today I wouldn't know a better way to express clearly what I wanted to say. Someone who knows German well suggested that I could have used "*durchdrungen*" instead of "*verseucht*" but that would not have indicated that I considered the domination harmful.

While I was in prison, many people worked toward my freedom, and wrote letters to officials and others in my behalf. One of these persons, someone to this day unknown to me (the name on this particular letter is a pseudonym) wrote the following pertaining to the "dangerous" paragraph that was used as grounds to have me arrested:

"Criminal" Adjectives, Archaic or Defamatory?

Mr. Schmidt's 6,000-word (sic) polemic, written in rusty German, represents one of his emphatic calls for non-violence in the present and future political life of Germany.

Among these 6,000 words (sic) one finds a single expression of exasperation, i.e., "*die juden-und freimaurerverseuchten Systemparteien und die Lizenzpresse.*"

The phrase is properly translated as:

"witch hunts conducted by the (German) establishment and government-controlled press dominated by Jews and freemasons."

It also might be literally but incorrectly translated as "Jews- and Freemason infested (German) establishment and government-controlled press. "

While in today's Germany the adjectives *"juden- und freimaurerverseuchten"* are definitely derogatory, during Hans' youth they were of neutral connotation.

"Untermenschen," was then the derogatory term for Jews and non-Jews, the word never used in Schmidt's expansive polemic.

Schmidt's "speech-crime" can be compared to an outdated use of English by an American missionary who moved out of the United States in 1949 to the French speaking Tahiti, and forty-five years later, in a letter to United States officials, e.g. asking for donations, used the today derogatory words such as "Negro", or "colored", or "Black" instead of the presently accepted term "African-American."

Thus, for the inadvertent and benign use of two archaic adjectives, in a letter mailed from Florida (sic) to a German bureaucrat in Germany nearly a year ago, German jurisprudence imposed arrest on an American citizen.

By coincidence, the 72-year-old (sic) Schmidt was denied bail by German authorities, on September 5, 1995, the day of the delivery by Hillary R. Clinton, of the impassioned Let Me Be Clear address in Beijing, in the defense of freedom of speech and freedom from political imprisonment.

According to Schmidt's wife, the bail was not granted by the Schwerin Court, despite the fact that Schmidt volunteered to surrender his passport (sic) and remain under house arrest in Germany. Two "nonfighting" words, adjectives, mailed from America to a German official were sufficient in democratic (?) Germany to keep its elderly author incommunicado for two months in prison, without Grand Jury, without bail, and without charges being filed."

The Inaction of the U.S. State Department

"I am sorry to inform you that the U.S. State Department has issued a statement to the effect that it regards your arrest as an internal German matter. In other words, you cannot count on official support by the United States Government to get you free."

I was not really surprised when Hajo Herrmann, my lawyer, said that. I knew that the German (or, rather, Central European) section of the State Department was and had for years been under Jewish control, and since I had been, also for years, one of the staunchest critics of this unhealthy tradition, these people must have been rejoicing to see me put out of circulation.

My thoughts wandered to the tremendous efforts made at that very moment by the U.S. Government, in conjunction with almost the entire Western media, to have the Chinese dissident Harry Wu (who, like myself, was an American citizen) freed from jail in China.

In Wu's case no stone was left unturned to accomplish the nearly impossible, even though the Chinese government had far more justification for incarcerating this man, than the German regime had with me. Wu had entered China with false papers in order to investigate abuses in labor camps. However noble his motives, he did spy on areas that were truly an internal Chinese matter, and, worst of all, he had previously given this sort of information, including video tapes, to the American authorities and media.

I knew that within the American hierarchy there existed two opposing factions. The pro-China faction saw the tremendous business opportunities in the "Empire of the Middle" and had been making incredible profits from it since Richard Nixon opened negotiations with Mao Tse Tung. The other one consisted of an ethnic group that *largely* seems to have been left out of the game, namely, the leadership of the American Jews.

The *Oberjuden* obviously also wanted special privileges in China, similar to those they have gained in other countries of the world, whereas there is evidence that, according to Chinese dictate, Jewish businessmen are welcome, but without the prerogatives demanded by the masters of their group.

It follows that the leading Jews in the U.S. Government and those influencing American public opinion through their power over the American media, are using every means to get the Chinese government to relent in their favor. Harry Wu fitted into this scheme of things. Probably unwittingly he became a tool of the Jewish-American leadership in its battle for special favors in China. In Wu's case this battle was allegedly fought for "human rights," one of the morality wedges frequently used by the elite Jews in the furtherance of their own aims (ironically by the very group that for decades had not only condoned but wholeheartedly supported the worst human rights atrocities against the hapless Palestinians). That Harry Wu was soon freed from prison while I was allowed to languish in one, gives exemplary proof of who in 1995 was calling the shots in the U.S. Government.

Somewhat wryly I also remembered the organized outcry by the American media when not too long ago an American teenager committed some vandalism in Singapore, and was sentenced to a few lashes on his buttocks. At the time it seemed as if the young man was going to be hung by his fingernails, and left to rot. "They" even managed to bring President Clinton in on the matter, and he condemned the (alleged) barbarism in strongest terms. Could it have been because the teenaged culprit was Jewish? Would Clinton eventually come to my aid, I wondered?

Rechtsanwalt (attorney) Hajo Herrmann, a former German World War II pilot of the *Luftwaffe*, and a highly decorated war hero who had spent ten years in Russian POW camps after the war, had been allowed to see me for about a half hour on the Saturday following my arrest.

The acoustics in this particular cell at Frankfurt jail were so poor that we could hardly understand each other. Nevertheless, I did realize the importance of the sentence quoted at the heading of this chapter, and I was certain that without the official support of the American Government, my speedy release from prison would not be possible. I had to prepare myself for a longer stay. Herr Herrmann also informed me of the text of the German law (§130) under which I was being held and prosecuted. He had to laugh when I told him that in my estimation the wording "sounded Jewish".

As a German who after the war had lived most of his life in a Germany almost without Jews, he did not exactly know what I meant by that. I then pointed to the intentional obfuscations and ambiguities in various paragraphs that, to me at least, were definitely un-German and provided evidence of Talmudic thought.[1]

Two days earlier I had been led before a judge at a Frankfurt court house. This judge had merely confirmed that the arrest warrant was in order, and that I was in fact the person for whom the warrant had been issued. He also told me that I would shortly be transferred to the prison of Bützow in the state of Mecklenburg-Vorpommern, the largest penitentiary near the capital city of Schwerin, where the warrant had been issued. Schwerin was also the place where my trial was to take place.

Realizing that a speedy release was not in the offing, certain decisions that had been purposely held in abeyance had to be

---

[1] The full *German* text of §130 and §131 can be found in the appendix.

made now, during Herr Herrmann's visit. First of all was the question of how long my wife was to stay in Europe, (she was supposed to return to the United States a week after me), and furthermore it was up to me to decide to what extent I was to permit the news media and the public to be informed about the intricacies of my case by both my lawyer and the U.S.Government.

As a rule, when my wife had accompanied me during my bi-annual trips to Europe, we traveled together. This time, however, we had altered our plans, and while I had planned to return to America on the 9th of August, she was to stay with friends in Austria for another week or so. It was there that she was informed of my arrest.

Naturally, a wife wants to be with, or at least near, her husband at such a time. On the other hand I realized that she would have very little opportunity to see me. Moreover, I wanted to save her from the embarrassing shenanigans to which some German authorities (especially those with Leftist and liberal leanings), were inclined.

For instance, shortly before my arrest, the wife and adult daughter of a German dissident who had also been accused of transgressing against the stipulations of paragraph 130, wanted to visit him in a West German jail. But before seeing their husband and father, they were told to strip naked for a thorough examination of their bodies and belongings. (Were the authorities afraid these women were going to smuggle an edition of *Mein Kampf*--forbidden in Germany--into the prison?). While the wife acceded to these demeaning requests (she did want to see her husband!), the daughter--utterly disgusted by the demand--declined and was therefore not able to visit with her father. I wanted to spare my wife such ignominy. As a result, I asked my attorney to advise her to return to the United States as soon as possible, and without attempting to see me.

It was not easy to make a sound decision regarding any information to be given out to the media and hence the public about my person by the U.S. Government (which was bound by the privacy act), by my lawyer, and subsequently also by my wife and our German-American, GANPAC organization. I am fully aware of the impact of publicity, and there is little doubt that it was publicity, in conjunction with initiatives by the United States Government, for instance, that had obtained the release of Harry Wu from a Chinese jail, and freed other persons in similar predicaments in the past.

However, the loosening of restraints regarding information about my person would also have opened up a Pandora's box of *misinformation* over which I would have had no control--since I was in prison--and I would therefore have been unable to answer any printed or spoken falsehoods within a reasonable amount of time. At that moment I did not yet have any inkling to what lengths the German authorities were ultimately going to go to surround me with a curtain of silence and isolation.

Since I had not expected to be arrested during this trip to Germany, I also had prepared nothing for such an eventuality (except that, as is normal for me, I had left a slew of written material that could be used for future American newsletters). The fact is, my wife and I had never even spoken about the possibility of my being arrested since I had not seriously considered it.

During the short time I met with *Rechtsanwalt* Herrmann on this Saturday, I also had neither the opportunity nor was I in the proper state of mind to provide him with sufficient public relations information for my wife and our associates. I naturally guessed that the generally internationalist newsmedia (no friends of mine), would use the occasion of my arrest to spread the most horrible lies about my activities, and if it devolved into a publicity battle between the Establishment media and people amenable to me, these lies would increase exponentially.

Remembering the results of arrests, over the years, of people whom I knew fairly well, like the French revisionist professor Dr. Robert Faurisson, and of Ernst Zündel, the German-Canadian publisher and freedom fighter, I was fearful of two things: that somehow persons not belonging to my inner circle of associates would get control of our organization, and that my wife, totally unaccustomed to dealing with the news media, would have to face seasoned reporters of the internationalist press, and be at their mercy. The latter would undoubtedly use every clever means possible to glean confidential information from her. Furthermore, these reporters would not hesitate to use to my detriment any and all utterances made by her.

For the time being at least I decided that a near total news blackout about my person was the best action to take. This would also be a "secret" message to my wife to do likewise, and "stick to her guns." In retrospect I can only say that she got the message, and correctly acted accordingly.

Some people still believe that an immediate, large scale publicity campaign could have freed me earlier. The fact is that this could only have succeeded if both the White House *and* the State Department would have put pressure on the Bonn Government. This was unlikely in my case since I was probably arrested more at the behest of powerful persons in America than of those in Germany. Furthermore, almost all the media in the United States are either owned or controlled by those who regard me as one of their major enemies.

Even if, for instance, my wife had given an extensive interview to one of the better reporters of the *New York Times*, and even if this reporter would have written a rather objective article about my case, the effect would have been nearly nil as long as the Editorial Board of the *New York Times* did not see fit to forcefully come out in favor of my freedom. This could not have happened since I am not only being smeared as one of the major "anti-Semites" in the United States but I am also labeled with such choice epithets as "Neo-Nazi" and "Holocaust denier."

In spite of the appearance they always want to present, the *Oberjuden* have never been known for tolerance and fairness.

An Involuntary Trip Through Germany

At my preliminary hearing, after both the Frankfurt judge and my lawyer had told me that I would forthwith be transferred to the Bützow penitentiary in northern Germany, I was wondering where that could be. I had never heard of the city of Bützow, and prisoners are obviously not allowed any maps.

However, one of the more hardened criminals, a fellow of about thirty whose body was almost wholly covered with tattoos, informed me that Bützow was in the former "DDR" ("East" Germany), somewhere between the Baltic Sea city of Rostock and the Mecklenburg capital of Schwerin.

He added that during the Communist era Bützow prison had been known as one of the most feared detention centers in all of Communist Germany, and that seemingly not much had changed there since then. Personally, this news did not disturb me. I do not easily get excited about things that I cannot change, or of which I know nothing.

I remembered that once before in my life I had been in Rostock, an old Hanseatic port city which, before the Allied terror bombings of World War II (which have gone unpunished to this day), [1] had been renowned for its medieval beauty.

In 1935, when I was a child, seven years of age, and a few months after my home state, the traditionally German Saarland,

---

[1] For documentation of the war crimes of the Allied Air Forces, cf. F.J.P. Veale, *Advance to Barbarism;* Ronald Schaffer, *Wings of Judgment: American Bombing in WWII;* Gordon Musgrove, *Operation Gomorrah* and David Irving, *The Destruction of Dresden.* The genocidal policies of mass murder of German women and children by deliberate fire-bombings of German cities, as ordered by Churchill and Roosevelt, are, by the logic of "victor's justice," crimes that are neither punished, commemorated or even acknowledged. This unsung holocaust against the German people is omitted from the contrived "human rights" agenda, which takes notice of only one "Holocaust"--the troubles of the Jews both real and imagined--which are ceaselessly trumpeted night and day by the Establishment media.

had been reunited with the Reich, [2] many children from the Saar were sent to summer camps deep inside Germany. I had the good fortune to be with a transport to the Baltic Sea spa of Bad Müritz, near Rostock, where we spent a few glorious weeks playing on the beach, sightseeing and eating extremely well. Other memories from that trip which I remember are that I did not have any money with me (our family was extremely cash-poor then); that the postcard I mailed home and which today is still in my possession, is full of spelling errors (definitely no credit for an aspiring writer), and that it was the first time I had seen the open sea. Recently I discovered that during that train trip we had passed--and for a few minutes paused at--the Bützow train station, which was a regular stop for German express trains between Hamburg and Rostock.

While sitting in a dirty, graffiti-decorated cell in the prison in Frankfurt in 1995, I tried to guess what would be the next steps, the German judiciary system would take with my person. Naively I thought that within a day or two I would be on my way to Bützow, accompanied by a lone policeman who would certainly not put me in handcuffs. After all, I surmised, I was really not a criminal, and had caused no harm to either people or property. There was also no likelihood that I would try to flee since I really wanted to get the matter over with.

Most certainly I had no intention of giving up my crusade for

---

[2] After Germany was defeated in WWI, the French coveted the coal-and-steel-rich Saarland for themselves. In order to persuade the other Allies, among them the U.S.A., that a French claim to the Saar had validity, then French President Clemenceau fabricated a claim of 90,000 Frenchmen living in that area populated by about 800,000 Germans. As a result, the Saar was cut off from Germany, economically and administratively allied with France, but placed under control of the newly formed League of Nations, the forerunner of the U.N. 15 years later, in 1935, a plebiscite was held under the auspices of the League whereby the Saarlanders could opt either for France, Germany or the so-called 'status quo,' i.e. the continuance of international control. More than 90% participated in the plebiscite and of these, over 90% wanted reunification with *Deutschland*. It proved to be Hitler's first major foreign policy triumph.

the enlightenment and spiritual awakening of the German people.

As I am writing these lines, I have to work with the extremely sparse notes in my possession that tell of the first two weeks of my incarceration. The officials who more than once went, "with a fine tooth comb" through my personal belongings and luggage, had left me with nothing in my pockets, not even a pencil or a piece of paper. The only things I had constantly in my possession, apart from the clothes I wore, were my watch, my eye glasses and a handkerchief.[3] As a result, I was not able to make notes, (I had also nothing to read) and retroactively I do not even remember exactly on what day I left the jail in Frankfurt for the trip north.

However, at the Frankfurt prison I did receive a thorough medical examination, where the attending doctor was genuinely concerned about the condition of my heart. The EKG showed a highly irregular heartbeat, and the M.D. cautioned me to see to it that I received my blood pressure medication regularly. While a few months' worth of this medicine was in my suitcase, I was not allowed to have any of these pills on my person. Instead, the Frankfurt doctor prescribed me a dose for four days, sufficient, he said, until I would have reached my destination. Little did he know!

The distance by air from Frankfurt to Bützow is about 300 miles. By car or train it would be approximately 100 miles more due to the fact that no straight road or railroad tracks traverse in this direction. I had really believed that I would be in Bützow within a couple of days after I had seen my lawyer in Frankfurt, and that the court proceedings would commence soon

---

[3] Ironically, the hand luggage which I had intended to carry on the plane, also accompanied me on my prison bus tour through Germany, although, except for the perennial searches (at every prison where we stopped for the night), these things were never really in my possession.

thereafter.

On the other hand I realized that my arrest was probably instigated by some of the elite Jews (or should I say, "elite Zionists"?) in the United States, who would have been delighted to see me put away for several years. It was not that I caused them great harm in America; they knew that of the thousands of rightist, nationalist and patriotic activists in the United States, people whom they like to castigate under the collective pejorative of "anti-Semites," I am probably among the more benign.

What alarmed them was the fact that I provided the Germans *in Germany* with information about anti-Christian and anti-Aryan Jewish actions in America, and this ran counter to their aim of brainwashing *all* the Germans for *all* time.

I was arrested on Wednesday, August 9, 1995. I arrived in Bützow exactly two weeks later, on Wednesday, August 23, 1995. During this time I experienced what is perhaps the most un-German, ridiculous and cumbersome prisoner transportation system anyone can imagine.

The things I saw also run counter to the very first article of the (Allied-imposed) Bonn Constitution of 1949 (the *Grundgesetz*) which proclaims,

"The dignity of human beings is inviolable. It is the duty of the authorities to safeguard it. Therefore, the German people recognize immutable and unalterable human rights as the foundation of all human society, and of peace and justice in the world."

There are two fundamental flaws in this German justice system. First, contrary to the basic concepts espoused in the United States, in Germany the accused is not innocent until proven guilty.⁴

It seems that in Germany *everybody* arrested is not only guilty but regarded as an arch criminal. The second, and perhaps most significant point is the (in my opinion) almost total lack of a healthy sense of justice among the prosecutors and judges.

During my transport from Frankfurt to Bützow I had the opportunity to meet and talk to a large and varied group of prisoners, almost all of them in pre-trial detention. There were Germans and foreigners; hardened criminals (murderers among them), and those who had committed only shoplifting.

There were quite a few who had never been arrested before, along with convicted felons with long prison records, who were being transported to court sessions as either witnesses or defendants.

Because I did not want to be prejudiced in my association with the other inmates I made it a policy never to ask anyone why he was in prison. But being the oldest one of the lot, and also because I was *"aus Amerika,"* it was quite natural that the others would want to talk to me, and either tell me their story, or ask my opinion.

Once I was familiar with their situation I often asked to see their arrest warrants, if they had a copy on their person, and I can state without hesitation that, based on these warrants, and again in my opinion, approximately half the prisoners I have met in the *Untersuchungshaft* (pre-trial detention) should not have been in prison at all.

Many of the warrants were poorly written and contained spurious grounds for keeping the accused under arrest. I wondered what went through the minds of the state's attorneys

---

⁴ I am fully aware that there are many cases in the U.S.A. where judicial authorities have violated or merely paid lip service to this concept. But these are *abuses* of a firm tradition of Anglo-Saxon jurisprudence which puts the burden of proof of a defendant's guilt upon the prosecutor, rather than, as in Germany, placing the burden of proving the defendant's innocence upon the accused.

and judges who had to deal constantly with such faulty legal instruments.

One also has to bear in mind that the German people have never before experienced such a crime wave as is occurring right now.

It seems that for political reasons (in the furtherance of the much ballyhooed "multi-cultural" society), the German justice system cannot effectively control the multitude of *foreign* criminals operating on German soil, and is therefore especially vicious against law-breakers among its own people.

The transport from Frankfurt prison to Kassel prison to Hannover prison, and finally to one in Hamburg, took about a week.

It was accomplished with huge, heavy, diesel-powered prison buses whose inside had been separated into a multitude of small cells, some of which were for but one or two prisoners, while one in the very back could hold up to five men.

In place of windows there were small slits that could not be opened for fresh air. Since one could not see much, the travel became extremely monotonous.

Along the way the buses frequently stopped at smaller prisons or court houses to let prisoners off, or take new ones on. It was then that we were able to go to the toilet and receive some food or drink.

But, as I mentioned in chapter one, the trip from Hannover to Hamburg alone took five hours during which we were forced to remain locked in our tiny cells without the chance to relieve ourselves, or obtain some fresh air.

For me personally it was pure torture, due to the prostate problems not rare among men nearing seventy; but I knew that the younger prisoners did not fare much better.

We had longer, overnight stays at Kassel and Hannover. At

each overnight stop, we received another set of bed sheets, a blanket, a towel and eating utensils, which we had to return on the following morning when the next bus picked us up. In the prisons, our cells were nearly everywhere the same: filthy, unpainted and full of graffiti.

When I mentioned this to one of the guards he merely stated that, "with so many foreigners in German jails one could expect nothing better".

But the presence of so many foreigners was no valid excuse for conditions so miserable that I was able to take but one shower in two weeks (remember, this was still August, a very humid month in Germany).

During these long and cumbersome prison bus trips, prisoners were removed from all customary prison privileges, such as receiving visitors and mail, exchanging soiled clothing and--not the least--obtaining medical attention.

In one of the jails I had the opportunity to glimpse a map of Germany with the prison bus routes and their regular schedules marked in. It seems there is an entire transportation system in existence in Germany of which the population at large knows nothing.

When our heavy buses drove through the narrow streets of some of the quaint old cities famous for their history-- for instance, through Lüneburg--I tried to catch glimpses of passers-by. Few took notice of these huge green vehicles with their human freight.

I would not be surprised if this were not the very same people who still chastise their own grandparents for not getting up after midnight during the war, running to the nearest railroad tracks, and there checking into who was in the freight cars taking Jews east (for that is all that a German could know at that time).

People all over the world react the same when they see groups of prisoners in their peculiar clothing or, as was the case recently in Alabama, in a chain gang--they automatically assume that every prisoner is a criminal and deserves what was coming to him. During a war one looks with curiosity at foreign POWs *the very first time one sees them,* but after that one gets used to them and gives the matter little further thought.

To expect from the Germans, the French, the Poles and others that they should have concerned themselves more with the fate of deported Jews than with their own troubles, while the bombs were falling, is nonsense. If the Hungarian Jews (who up to then lived freely in Budapest, for instance), did not know of the existence of Auschwitz in the summer of 1944, why and how should the German population have known, or care, for that matter? *C'est la vie!*

My long, drawn-out prison transport was especially difficult for me because the high blood pressure medication I had received in Frankfurt was depleted after four days. Thereafter all my entreaties to the various guards with whom I came in contact, when I asked to see a doctor, fell on deaf ears. There seemed to be a prevailing mood of, "you are a prisoner, therefore you must be guilty of something, and because you are obviously a criminal, I couldn't care less what is happening to you."

Perhaps not surprisingly, *nowhere* in any of the prisons I saw, or in which I stayed, did I see or was given a copy of the prison regulations. How can someone who has never been in prison in either Germany or the United States discover what to do or what not to do? What were the duties or the rights of the inmates? To this day I don't really know (except for what some of the more helpful prisoners had told me).

Obviously, I do not know what was in my police file that was forwarded from prison to prison, and bus to bus, along with me.

But I am fairly certain that it clearly explained the reason for my arrest. I noticed the impact of its presumed contents on the varied behavior of some of the transport personnel toward me. A few guards (usually those who had no command position) were friendly and polite, and I assume they were basically patriots. But others sought to compound my difficulties, and had likely been taken in by the anti-German propaganda of the Bonn vassals.

Interestingly, during the entire time of my incarceration I did not encounter a single prisoner who considered the infamous paragraph 130 a legitimate law, or who agreed with the Bonn stooges that such nefarious accusations as *"Volksverhetzung,"* ("defaming the [Jewish] dead" or "insulting Jews and Freemasons"), ought to lead to prosecution.

Certainly, prisoners cannot be taken as a typical cross-section of a population, but there is little doubt that the Germans would vote against many of the measures taken by the *Bundesrepublik* authorities, if the system allowed such a direct participation of the people in the democratic process.

For the Bonn rulers to continuously use the term *Rechtsstaat* (government based upon justice) for their own system, is the height of mockery.

Hamburg

We arrived at one of the larger penitentiaries of Hamburg on Thursday, August 17, 1995, more than a week after my arrest.

Catching a glimpse out of the bus, I noticed that the prison was near downtown, not far from a beautiful park and the hotel where I had stayed in the spring.

I was assigned to cell 515 in the block for *Häftlinge in Untersuchungshaft* (prisoners in pre-trial detention).

Immediately after my arrival I demanded to see a doctor, a request that was accepted with a sneer: "Sorry, you will have to wait until tomorrow!"

During the night, I had no choice but to do breathing exercises and lie motionless on my back for hours when I noticed my blood pressure becoming unbearably high, and I had a pounding headache.

But early on the next morning I was taken to the infirmary where once again I received a thorough check-up. Again the physician in charge showed concern about my bad EKG. I received some medication on the spot.

While I was sitting next to the doctor, he wrote a prescription for so-called water pills (for the relief of high blood pressure); enough for the next five days. This was sufficient, he said, to last me through the coming weekend. He then gave the prescription to an assistant male nurse.

On the same day I received my first visit from representatives of the United States Government: two pleasant and truly concerned ladies from the American consulate came to see me. They inquired about my state of health, asked how I was treated, and also wanted to know whether I wanted to lift the black-out about my person that I had initiated immediately after my arrest. Furthermore, they brought greetings from my wife with whom they had spoken earlier in the day.[1]

Unfortunately, the ladies from the Hamburg consulate could not bring me news that the United States Government was going to protest to the Germans about my arrest, and demand my immediate release. All they knew was that I was now in the hands of the German authorities, and that the legalities would have to take their course. As far as the U.S. Government was concerned, my case was just like any other case where an American citizen committed an acknowledged crime in a foreign land, and was to be prosecuted according to the laws of that nation. (In other words, Washington tacitly approved of the flagrant human rights violations of the Bonn regime.)

Having seen a doctor in the morning, and having watched him write a prescription for the next five days, I did not press the medical issue with my American visitors. I ascribed the fact that I was without medicine for a few days to the lack of good organization that seems to be endemic in the German prison system. At the time I did not envision that "they" would withhold medicines from me with malicious intent.

As far as the lifting of my self-imposed black-out was concerned, I stated that certainly, essential information about my arrest could be given out by the government but I still wanted to avoid the printing of "anti-Semitic" horror stories about me that would certainly be the result of unhindered access by the news media. As long as I was not able to talk to my wife by phone and give her some instructions, I considered it best to leave things as they were.

As to the question about my general treatment, I purposely

---

[1] I believe that according to international treaties, American officials are supposed to be able to visit U.S. citizens that have been incarcerated in foreign countries within two days of their arrest. In my case it took nine days. The ladies from the Hamburg consulate told me that for most of the time they didn't know where I was being held, and that the Germans were reluctant to provide better information.

abstained from painting a bleak picture when I spoke to the consular officials. I knew that nothing but a total revolution can change the German justice system as it exists today. The American Government must all along have been aware of how the German judiciary operates, and since they did not insist on any radical changes during the past fifty years while the U.S.A. occupied Reich soil with millions of GIs, they would certainly not try to alter anything on behalf of Hans Schmidt.

Another reason for not complaining even when I had a legitimate reason to do so, had to do with my concern for my family. I saw no reason to cause them unnecessary worry on top of the distress they must have been feeling already. Therefore, my message was always the same: I am okay under the circumstances, and apart from a dislike of being in custody, I had no serious complaints. The consular officials promised to call my wife, my mother and some other relatives and tell them that I was all-right, which they did.

I remember asking the ladies from the consulate for newspapers and magazines in the English language. They mailed me an entire package on the very next day but it was over one month before these things were handed to me in the Bützow penitentiary.

My imprisonment in Hamburg lasted nearly a week for the ostensible reason that only one bus per week traverses the Hamburg- Lübeck-Bützow route. Except for some pornographic magazines, which apparently can be freely obtained in all German prisons (obviously an outward proof of democracy and liberalism), I had nothing to read until August 21st, when I was handed a letter by my attorney that also contained a note from my wife. Personally, I was furious about the tremendous waste of time, and the lack of communication. But it would get much worse.

The days drifted by. There was no sign of the medicine the doctor had prescribed for me upon my arrival in Hamburg. Not a day passed without my experiencing a pounding headache and nausea caused by my high blood pressure. In German jails they have a system whereby everything a prisoner needs or wants has to be requested in writing. In order to do so, one has to have both the properly printed form and naturally either a pen or a pencil. However, to obtain a pen and one sheet of the formal requests, one would need both in the first place, a real Catch 22 situation.

By the time I had discovered how to circumvent all that, the weekend had arrived, and on weekends there was no chance that a guard would accept *any* written request. One of the prison employees was very much insulted when I had written my *urgent* demand for medicine on a piece of toilet paper. By that time I was so angry that I told him he should be glad that I had used a piece from an unsoiled roll.

Finally, on August 22, 1995, the day before my scheduled departure for Bützow (where I anticipated a speedy trial), I was allowed to see a doctor again. In the morning I participated in the walk-about in the prison courtyard for about an hour, then (after nearly two weeks), I had my first shower since my arrest, and shortly before noon I was suddenly told to get all my things together and return the bed sheet and blanket, etc., for I was going to be transferred to the prison hospital.

That sounded very strange to me. Why should I be moved to the prison hospital less than 24 hours before continuing my journey eastward? A week ago such a transfer might still have made sense, but now? I had no intention of staying any longer in Hamburg than necessary. My arrest warrant had been signed in Schwerin, and I had to get at least near that city in order to bring the entire matter to a satisfactory conclusion. Therefore, I was very wary and suspicious when I entered the hospital area.

A male nurse, possibly the very same man who had been given my prescription the week before (but I was not certain), asked me to undress for a thorough examination. While I was sitting there covered by nothing but a hospital gown, the nurse gave me a pen and a preprinted form and asked me to sign it. Not being in possession of my reading glasses, I asked him what it was. "Merely your assent for the treatment you are about to receive." I told him that out of principle I did not sign anything that I had not read, and furthermore, no matter what, I would not agree to any injections or invasive procedures of any kind.

Thereupon the nurse got visibly upset, practically tore the paper out of my hands and, while walking away, muttered to himself, "if they had asked me that *also*, I would have quit on the spot." I wondered what he had meant by that outburst.

I had to wait quite a while until a doctor saw me. He had just come in from the city, and from what I gathered he was not a regular prison physician but a contract doctor who had his own practice outside. When I told him of the missing medicine, he was genuinely surprised. After he had examined me, he mentioned that it was a pity that I had not signed the form agreeing to a more time-consuming check-up.

"How much more time-consuming?" I asked him.

"About three weeks," was his answer. Again he registered surprise when I told him that I was scheduled for transport to Bützow the very next morning. Then his face turned serious and he told me that in his opinion I was not *transportfähig* (i.e., that the condition of my health did not allow the strain of a prison bus trip of many hours duration). The result of my insistence on wanting to go on the transport to Bützow on the following day anyway was that I had to sign a paper relieving the Hamburg prison from any responsibility should I collapse during the trip.

During the following weeks I had sufficient time to think about this odd incident. I came to the conclusion that the medicine had been purposely withheld from me, and that for some malicious reason I was supposed to be held an additional three weeks at the Hamburg prison. Would someone have been very happy if as a result of extremely high blood pressure I had succumbed to a heart attack?

The hospital ward at the Hamburg prison was clean and well equipped. The room I was assigned had eight beds, three of which were occupied. There was a color television set and magazines in abundance. The food was good. One of the prisoners was a former coal miner in his fifties from the city of Gelsenkirchen. He told me that he was imprisoned as a *Schwarzfahrer*. Not being familiar with the term, I asked him what it was. He explained it to me: The transportation system in most German cities works on a honorary system. In other words, there are no turn styles at the subway stations, and several unguarded entrances.

Passengers on most German public transport systems are expected to purchase their tickets from a vending machine, and then invalidate the ticket themselves when boarding the mass transit vehicle. There are infrequent and unexpected inspections by teams of control officers who then ask everybody in the vehicle to show proof that he has a current invalidated ticket on his person. If one does not have a ticket, one is subject to an on the spot fine equivalent to about 60 dollars (although that varies from city to city). The people who use the transportation systems without paying for their trip are called *Schwarzfahrer*.

I asked the coal miner from Gelsenkirchen, whose body was a total wreck from sickness and alcohol, why he was in jail for this relatively minor offense. He told me that he was so sick from black lung disease that he could not work anymore, but that he was not eligible for his miner's pension until about 1998. In the meantime he lived on welfare. Alas, the money he received was barely sufficient for his apartment and the food.[2]

Every time he had to make the trip into the city to go to the social services building he had to take a streetcar. Since he did not have the money to pay, he was a perennial *Schwarzfahrer*. He was in prison because of numerous such transgressions. I asked him whether the social services administration was not able to give him a bus or streetcar ticket to use for his trip to their offices. He said yes, they do give him one for his trips home, once he has satisfied all the requirements of the extensive questionnaires, but they did not make any provisions for his trips from his home *to* the offices. When I inquired how he would get to the social services building after his release from prison, he answered with a laugh, "How else but as a *Schwarzfahrer*."

Talking a bit more about the transportation system of most German inner cities, this man also confirmed what I had long suspected: most of the *Schwarzfahrer* are foreigners, especially those from the Balkans. But--as everywhere in the world--the people in charge of things in Germany are also trying to avoid

---

[2] Foreign asylum seekers (actually, any Third World foreigner who manages to step on German soil and utter the word "asylum"), are more generously treated by the Bonn Government than are native German welfare recipients. Asylum seekers get "everything", so to speak: an apartment, clothes, furniture, free medical care, schooling and a generous monthly cash allowance. It is not unlike the disproportionate generosity and special privileges extended to alleged Soviet refugees (95% of whom are Jews), by the U.S. Government. These "refugees" come to the United States, their airplane fare paid for by Jewish organizations and immediately receive magnificent, subsidized ocean view apartments in Santa Monica, California, and elsewhere in prime areas; apartments that have nine-year waiting lists for native-born American citizens. The Soviet Jews, at least some of whom are undoubtedly Communist war criminals, even receive American Social Security payments and Medicare benefits, although they have never paid a penny into the system. Could there be a method behind this madness?

trouble where trouble is sure to occur, and so it happens that one rarely sees sudden ticket inspections in Germany on subway, bus or streetcar lines that lead to and from districts that are heavily populated by Third World people. It is easier to beat up on the few Germans who do not follow the rules.

I noticed a similar double-standard regarding the usually strictly enforced rules regarding snow removal on sidewalks. The same policeman who will give a ticket to a German businessman who forgot to immediately scrape the snow in front of his store, will bypass the snow-covered sidewalk in front of a Turkish establishment next door. The reason? Ostensibly because "from these people" one cannot expect the sense of orderliness demanded from the Germans. The real reason is likely because the Turks are faster to use their ubiquitous daggers.

The Developments in America

I did not generally discover what happened after my arrest in the United States, and especially in Pensacola, until I had returned home nearly a half year later.

Certainly, I was curious to know all about it while I was imprisoned, but knowing that other ears were listening while my wife and I finally were able to initiate our brief, weekly telephone conversations, or that strangers read our mail, I purposely did not ask for details. The less "the enemy" knew, the better.

While the news of my arrest was broadcast by the international wire services like dpa (German Press Agency), AP and Reuters, most U.S. newspapers did not deem the arrest of an American writer jailed in Germany for what he had written in the U.S., newsworthy.

To most Americans, including the editors of newspapers and magazines, I was an unknown, and besides, unlike in the almost identical Harry Wu story playing about the same time, a catchword like "China" was missing.

U.S. journalists know to whom they owe their loyalty, and at this moment in history it was obviously their duty (in the interest of mighty behind-the-scenes powers), to put the Chinese government on the defensive because of real or alleged human rights violations.

It was not their business to put a similar onus on "America's friends" in Bonn.

Nevertheless, shortly after my arrest in Germany was reported, our house in Pensacola was besieged by journalists. My neighbors told me that the ubiquitous T.V. vans arrived in force, also private cars with press stickers and, redundantly, some perennial press groupies, among whom the agents of such "civil rights"organizations as the A.D.L., Klan Watch, and the spuriously named SPLC (Southern Poverty Law Center) were probably hiding.

Unfortunately for all of them, the Schmidts were still in Europe, and Mother Nature had also provided some cover for my family and myself: less than a week before my arrest, on August 3, 1995, Hurricane Erin had visited Pensacola with force and (among other damage), created havoc in the forest behind our house.

While we had sustained no loss except a few broken trees and torn shrubbery, literally tons of plant and tree debris covered our entire neighborhood, and our front lawn was so covered with a huge mountain of broken branches that it was almost impossible to photograph the house without stepping on our property, something the neighbors were able to prevent.

Unable to speak to any of us, the journalists instead bothered our nice neighbors with dumb questions and ridiculous insinuations.

"Did Schmidt display pictures of Hitler and other high-ranking Nazis in his house?" and "Do you know whether he owns a swastika flag?" or "Does he have secret meetings at his home?"

These were some of the milder questions. But this being what a newspaper called "an upscale neighborhood," in other words, an area where intelligent people value their privacy, the answers the reporters received were not to their liking.

Everybody who was asked confirmed only that we were nice neighbors, that we kept to ourselves, and that I kept my politics generally to myself. Some ventured that, yes, they knew I was a nationalist and active in German-American political affairs, but that I had never tried to impose my beliefs on anybody, and that this was solely my business.

Some reporters seemed really bothered by the fact that I had never mentioned the word "Holocaust" at one of our neighborhood get-togethers.

They obviously cannot understand that there is a fundamental difference between Germans and, for instance, Jews, who seemingly never miss an opportunity to push for what they call the "Jewish agenda". These differences are not only skin-deep.

Obviously that was not what the media's catamites wanted to hear. Sorry, I have to use such strong language, I have no other way but to express my vehement feelings about this.

Almost none of the present-day American journalists make any effort at all to hear the other side of the story, or try to use their God-given sense of reasoning.

Instead, they only gobble up like lap dogs all the garbage that the Leftist propagandists such as the A.D.L., Klan Watch and Morris Dees' SPLC feed them. [1]

Rather than provide too much of my own commentary, I am going to reprint excerpts from an article that appeared in the *Pensacola News Journal,* [2] after my arrest, and following that, the text of the succeeding editorial pertaining to me, that appeared in the same newspaper on August 21, 1995, the very day when I had my first shower in nearly two weeks at the Hamburg prison.

Readers may judge for themselves whether they believe this is objective news writing or the "advocacy journalism" of partisans. Here are the excerpts of the article from the

---

[1] Even honest Leftists hold Mr. Dees in contempt as a profiteer. Alexander Cockburn writing in *The Nation* has described Dees as an exploiter. Dees "Southern Poverty Law Center" (SPLC) is referred to by those in the know as the "Poverty Palace" since Dees has amassed a huge fortune off the backs of the black people he uses in his appeal-letters. Former Dees employee Randall Williams has testified that the SPLC is actually a "super snoop outfit, an arm of law enforcement," citing file-sharing and other cooperaton between Dees and the FBI. Cf. John Egerton, "The Poverty Palace," *The Progressive,* July, 1988.

[2] A newspaper belonging to the Gannet chain.

Pensacola News Journal:

"Apologists like Schmidt make the Hitler regime look like the Boy Scouts.

"In Pensacola, Schmidt's neighbors say he is a friendly man who allows children to play in his yard. However, most of his neighbors were reluctant to comment about him Tuesday.

"We had no idea about his political activities, he never distributed hate literature here," (said one neighbor), "he is very sociable and comes to neighborhood block parties."[3]

"Another neighbor, who would not give his name called Schmidt "a decent neighbor. But he let it be known that he has strong nationalistic views."

"As a result of his radical views, Schmidt has been tracked for nearly 30 years by the New York-based Anti-Defamation League.

He has also been followed for more than a decade by Klan Watch, a Montgomery, Ala., based organization that monitors hate groups.

"Schmidt is a lone wolf, a sole practitioner[4] who probably prints his literature from his home or a small print shop," said Laurie Wood, a Klan Watch investigator.

"We don't believe he has an organized following in the Pensacola area, but he probably reaches thousands of people across the country through his newsletter."

---

[3] I doubt very much that the lady had used the term, "hate literature," but I was not going to trouble her with a query. The *Pensacola News Journal* wouldn't retract their nonsensical statements anyway.

[4] Reading this, I had a good laugh. The Klan Watch people were probably too stingy to order our 1990 and 1995 Position Papers relating to Germany. Had they done so they would have been able to discover the names of nearly 100 persons--people whom I call part of the German-American elite, many of whom have academic degrees--who had contributed to our *common* effort. Ironically, the Bonn government also underestimated the wide-ranging influence of our German-American organization. It is simple as that: if one purposely drives the legitimate opposition underground, then one ought not be surprised if it uses underground means to be able to operate.

"Schmidt has shown no signs of mellowing with age, said Tom Halpern, of the Anti-Defamation League.

"He is well known in the Jewish 'hate community' and recently was in quite a huff over the movie 'Schindler's List,' depicting the Holocaust," Halpern said. "His writing show a depth of hate that he has toward Jews. He is what we describe as an obsessive anti-Semite. [5]

"Schmidt has been maligned by Jewish leaders and he only wants to defend his generation's version of history," according to Ernst Zündel. [6]

"A former German soldier, he is widely known for his nationalistic sentiments and for his outspoken views," Zündel said.

"As he often states, the image of the German soldier has been tarnished by incessant media attacks as part of the liberal agenda.'

"Schmidt has had setbacks in his attempts to rewrite World War II history.

"In 1983, he attempted to create a Werner von Braun German-American University in Huntsville, Ala., with the avowed purpose of counteracting the political philosophy of "10,000 Marxist professors" in American universities.

"The famed rocket scientist's widow disapproved of using her husband's name for the school and it never got off the ground. [7]

"Von Braun headed the Nazi rocket program during World

---

[5] I have never expressed hatred toward anyone. I have often written that I feel sorry for the Jewish masses. In spite of their incredible wealth, I would not like to be Jewish. They are a deeply unhappy and insecure people. What troubles *Oberjuden* like Halpern, is the fact that I do not fall for the Jewish double-talk and manipulation so prevalent today.

[6] For more on Ernst Zündel, see the appendix.

[7] Behind-the-scenes forces powers virtually compelled Mrs. Von Braun to issue a letter of disapproval but that did alter our plans. The fulfillment of the project was delayed due to the entrenched forces of Freemasonry in Huntsville and the lack of a benevolent media, without which no fundraising for such an undertaking can occur.

War II, which used slave labor provided by the SS.[8]

"In 1985, Schmidt's political headquarters in Santa Monica were gutted by fire. Schmidt blamed the fire on the Jewish Defense League (JDL), and said: "That is their purpose. Anything we do to assert ourselves, offends them." [9]

It took me years to realize an important political fact of America, never seen in the establishment media: the political power and influence that rightfully belongs to the German-Americans who constitute nearly a quarter of the population, is *totally* in the hands of the Jewish overlords. They are intent on keeping it that way.

One means they have at their disposal for maintaining control is the media itself.

The newspaper editorial, reprinted on the next page, never once protests the arrest and jailing of an American writer (naturalized citizen), in a foreign country.

Instead, the editorial implies that because I am accused of being critical of a certain "religion," my prosecution is justified. Imagine the howls of outrage if a Jewish writer were to be arrested in Germany for criticizing the Lutherans. So the issue is not really criticism of religion, which happens all the time in the West in anti-Christian polemics, but *exposure* of the *facts* about one enshrined religion, which has rights above all others.

---

[8] Most of the warring nations of WWII used what one could term slave labor. The U.S. government "sold" hundreds of thousands of German POWs as slave laborers to the French, who mistreated them so badly that tens of thousands of them died *after the war and Nuremberg trial had taken place*. Americans handed German prisoners over to the British for toil in mines for years after the war.

[9] From 1983 to 1985 we operated like any normal political organization, with an office, with regular office hours and telephones where we could be reached. This ended in June of 1985 when "arsonists unknown" gutted not only our office but an entire floor in the same building. It was a time when Jewish terrorists were very busy in America. The FBI traced their activities to the JDL, but whether this group was directed by Mossad remains to be determined. Since then our group used a method learned in Germany during the air war, *Auslagerung:* one avoids great losses from air attacks by scattering important resources over many different sites.

Schmidt's 'revisionism' a tool for neo-Nazis

Historical revisionist? That's not the term we'd use to describe Hans Schmidt, the Pensacola resident arrested in Germany and charged with inciting racial hatred.

At best Schmidt is a tool of the pathetic few in the world who still cling to Nazi beliefs. They in turn are a part of the unfortunately larger pool of hate-mongers who find their meaning in hating Jews, blacks, Catholics, you name it.

Schmidt is one of those curious persons who continues to insist that the Holocaust did not happen, that the Nazis in Germany did not carry out the systematic murder of Jews during World War II.

JUSTICE

It's ironic that he makes his adopted home in a nation dedicated to equality for all.

Since the historical facts of the Holocaust are clear and incontrovertible, that makes Schmidt either a liar or abysmally ignorant of one of the most shameful acts in the recorded history of the human race.

Either way, the bigger pity is that there are still people willing to listen to and even seriously consider the ideas of people like Schmidt.

It's ironic that Schmidt lives in the United States and prints his newsletter here. Because this country is one of the few in which he can find the freedom to express his virulent views.

What he has been arrested for in Germany is not, so far as we can tell, a crime in the United States, although we must add that we're not fully aware of everything he might have written or advocated in the newsletter.

Still, how ironic that Schmidt makes his home base a nation dedicated to the equality of all people. Only here can he find the freedom he needs to remain free while he attacks others based on their religion.

The good people of the world must constantly be on guard to reject the dangerous and completely wrongheaded views of people like Hans Schmidt.

Pensacola News Journal, August 21st, 1995

I find it superfluous to comment on the "Holocaust" portion of the preceding editorial. If seemingly intelligent people like the editors of the *Pensacola News Journal* cannot discern the incongruities of the gas chamber tale after the plaques at Auschwitz that touted "here 4 million were murdered," are suddenly removed, and when the alleged victim count is lowered by 3 million, what can we expect from the average American who has no concept of amounts larger than $100,000 (the cost of a single family home)?

Much more interesting is the editorial commentary--that the newspaper finds its ironic that "Schmidt lives in the United States and prints his newsletters here. Because this country is one of the few in which he can find the freedom to express his virulent views."

What is so ironic about the fact that I *have to* write and print my newsletter here, because in Germany I would be arrested for doing so? And why is Germany not free? *Because in 1945 it was "liberated" by the allies, including the United States, and this "liberation," as in most cases of the captive nations (Germany, Poland, Hungary, Rumania, Yugoslavia, Latvia, Estonia, Lithuania) meant loss of freedom, and not the alleged democracy promised.*

Do the Pensacola newspaper editors know that it was a German immigrant, John Peter Zenger, whose battle for freedom of the press eventually led to the formulation of the cherished American First Amendment?

Furthermore, since the seven million Germans that came to this country over the centuries were mostly well-trained farmers and artisans, and since their descendants constitute about a quarter of the U.S. population, can we not assume that it was they, more than anybody else, who cleared the land, built the homesteads, founded villages and cities, and created a civilization that is (today) English by language but essentially German in character?

As a German I consider myself much more rightfully here than any other newcomer of a different national or ethnic background. (I want to here credit the Jewish peddlers who often supplied the farmers with necessities such as yarns and needed kitchen supplies, but they by themselves could not have created a viable culture.)

Regarding the freedoms we still have here, I must ask the question, who is behind most efforts to *curtail* America's Constitutional freedoms through enactment of nefarious laws? The April 4th, 1996 issue of the *Washington Jewish Week* reports that thirteen of the major Jewish American organizations, probably the most powerful combined lobby in existence, had gotten together to fight *for* the passage of the anti-terrorism bill that was finally passed and signed two weeks later.

Does this new law enhance the freedoms of Americans? Will it make their lives more secure? Naturally the answer is no to both points. Why then are the Jewish organizations so intent upon introducing and fighting for laws that hamstring (put in legal chains!) the American population?

The laws the Jewish lobby seeks, as exemplified by such "Israel-first" luminaries as Rep. Charles Schumer (D-NY), include bills to curtail the ownership of weapons, to suppress freedom of speech ("anti-hate legislation") and obstruct the practice of the majority religion in this country (prohibiting prayers in school and preventing a proper observance of holidays like Christmas).

The overwhelming majority of Jewish lobbyists and Jewish legislators can be found in the forefront of all of these efforts, while only a tiny handful of Jews oppose them. This noisy campaign for the curtailment of our cherished freedoms is perpetrated under the subterfuge of "fighting for democracy," of battling for "tolerance" and "diversity", and of creating "equal justice."

But can it be equal justice and the enhancement of diversity when at the Department of Justice there is a special office (the Office of Special Investigations or OSI), almost solely staffed by Jews and exclusively dedicated to prosecuting anti-communist, so-called "war criminals" and never communist or Zionist war criminals?

And, with many Jews having allegiance to, or having been raised in an environment where an alien "moral" code formed their judgment, (the Talmud), is it right that they occupy so many federal judgeships and two Supreme Court seats?

The *Pensacola News Journal* should not find it ironic that I am fighting my battles on American soil. The rights and privileges of Americans have a patrimony that is Germanic, and Americans of German descent comprise the largest single ethnic block in this nation. When I fight "my" battle here, I am fighting America's battle as well!

But since the German *Bundesrepublik* is a creation of the United States, and because Germany has been living with the menace of American bayonets (U.S. Occupation forces), since 1945, doesn't the U. S. Government ultimately bear the major share of responsibility for the conditions that led to my arrest? It is nice and good to proclaim freedom and democracy everywhere, but those who do so must realize that mere talk is not enough.

Remember that stupid sentence connected with the alleged 'Holocaust,' "If only people had not been silent, if only everybody had spoken up against injustice and hate." Well, one does not have to look back to what allegedly occurred fifty and more years ago. *Now* is the time to stop being silent and worry about the present, and what is happening in Germany today is not only America's doing, it is also (still) America's responsibility. Moronic editorials like the one from the *Pensacola News Journal* merely obscure the issue.

Many decades ago, I pointed out shortcomings of the U.S. school system to my American friends. At that time the schools were one element (some of the others being motherhood, religion and apple pie), a foreigner was not allowed to criticize. Then, most Americans sincerely believed that "the U. S. is the greatest and wealthiest nation in the world because of its superior school system." Mindful of the fact that at the time literally millions of people from German lands lived in the United States, most of whom had had excellent schooling in their home countries, I wondered aloud how things would be if millions of immigrants had not come here, since their contribution to this nation's ascent were immeasurable? Thereupon, I usually heard the quick reply, "If you don't like it here, why don't you go back to where you came from?"

Apart from the fact that 1 had never said that I did not like it in the United States, I usually retorted, "I'11 go back on the very day when the last American G.I. leaves the soil of the German Reich."

Little did I think that this day would not have arrived more than fifty-one years after the end of World War II. But in the meantime, West Germany is (really) not Germany anymore. The cultural devastation is incredible. The Coca Cola *Kultur* of Germany's alleged friends has destroyed more of German heritage and tradition than could have been eradicated in a Third World War.

My wife arrived back in Pensacola just in time to read this "nice" PNJ editorial. Thankfully, our neighbors were very understanding and supportive, and they assisted her as much as they could at this difficult time. The political work rested necessarily almost solely on her shoulders. Due to the huge size of the United States, and the fact that GANPAC is an organization spread throughout the fifty states, it follows that the members of the governing board are living far apart, and cannot be assembled in one place on a short notice. Obviously, our moves from California to (near) the nation's capital and then down to Florida, did not simplify matters in this regard. While the directors contributed valuable advice, the actual work still rested mostly on my wife's shoulders. She carried it off beautifully. The story of how she was unnecessarily subjected to mental and moral pressure tantamount to psychoterror, appears in another chapter.

In addition to the inexorable daily concerns of living, my wife faced the formidable task of obtaining my freedom. She started alone, then called a few friends and with them organized contacts with a large and increasing number of people in the United States and in many other parts of the world. It was thanks to their concerted efforts, stimulated and coordinated by my wife and others closely allied with us, to which I attribute my eventual release from the dungeons of the Bonn vassal state.

An example of my wife's accomplishments in this regard came one day in the form of a phone call she received from the U.S. State Department.

A statement of character witness attesting to the general good conduct of her husband was requested. It had to be a statement from a responsible United States citizen in good standing, who knew Mr. Schmidt but was unrelated to him familiarly in any way, and who was not now, nor had been, associated in a business venture with him. In addition, the statement had to be endorsed by a person of similar character.

My wife succeeded--perhaps to the caller's disappointment--in obtaining the required documents, which were duly submitted to our Department of State. I reproduce it here:

In the Matter of Hans Schmidt, of Pensacola, Florida

To Whom It May Concern:

Among my credentials for making this declaration concerning Mr. Schmidt, who was born in Germany, is that I am a native-born American (as is my wife, who agrees in every respect with the appraisal made herein).

I am a U. S. Army officer (volunteer) veteran of World War II. (Pacific Theater). Hans Schmidt is proud to have fought (as a 17-year old volunteer) in the Waffen SS in the last desperate months of the war. I respect him for that, as I respect every man who has fought honorably for his country.

I am trained as an economist, and specialized in international trade. I spent many years, in the United States, and resident in Europe and South America, serving American industrial companies in opening and developing foreign markets for American products. I lived, worked, and dealt with many people of different nationalities and cultures.

I became acquainted with Hans Schmidt in August 1983. He attracted me by his apparent complete honesty and indestructible good humor. In the years since then, I have found Hans Schmidt to be a man singularly free of hatred, malice ,' or rancor.

In his polemical writings he does not attack persons or people," but deeds (and misdeeds).

I have not known him to evince hatred, vindictiveness, or the least hint of violence against even those who attack him most viciously, and unreasonably.

Hans Schmidt has been ready at all times to debate, calmly and rationally, his most fervently held opinions.

I am astonished at the extraordinary breadth of Hans Schmidt's aquaintanceships -- and their evident mutual cordiality and sincerity -- that appears to embrace the whole ethnic spectrum of our society.

I am glad and proud to have Hans Schmidt as a friend.

Endorsed   Toms River   New Jersey 08757

_____
Washington DC 20008   2 November 1995

It was then that the first real disappointment occurred. Ever since our move to Florida in early 1993, we had used the services of a good local printer for our position papers, for our German-language newsletter, and mainly for the East Coast part of the German-American newsletter. Up to my arrest we had never had any difficulties with these printing people. They did a good job and we always paid them when we picked up the finished goods. For a business of that size our regular monthly orders, plus the occasional miscellaneous printing orders, certainly provided a substantial and steady income.

I knew the lady owner of the print shop was a good, Church-going Christian woman, and while our few business meetings were short, they were nevertheless friendly. I always assumed that the lady read some or all of our newsletters and possibly also the position papers in English, so there was no question that she knew of our principles. There was certainly nothing to conceal, for, if anything, I am a stickler for the truth, and I will use no information that I cannot verify from several sources. When I attack the nemesis of the German-Americans, namely, the leadership and the fanatical activists of American Jewry, then I have a good and *legitimate* reason to do so.

One can understand the surprise of my wife when, after the appearance of the *Pensacola News Journal* editorial reprinted on page 70, the print shop owner refused to accept any further business from us.

No reason was given. But with all the anxieties she had already, my wife now had to search for someone else who could print at least a portion of the Florida part of the newsletters, and do so fast and at a reasonable price. In addition, some people who had hitherto helped us stuff envelopes and prepare for mailing some of our mass shipments, suddenly got cold feet, and refused further assistance. One must wonder what went through the heads of these people. Did they think that the Jews are so powerful that they know what transpires in every house or business in America? Such cowardice never ceases to amaze me. [10]

The Christian lady who owns the print shop deserves a special comment. I wonder whether she realizes that in doing what she did, she betrayed her faith. She gave aid and comfort to the very people that are the avowed enemies of Christianity. Certainly, I have heard all the talk of "Judeo-Christianity," and that Jesus was a Jew, and that the Jews are the Chosen People. But those Christians who believe such propaganda must realize that if all that were true, then Jesus' appearance and martyrdom was totally unnecessary. Having a Chosen People as "wonderful" as the Jews are, would it not be sufficient to follow in their footsteps and accept their religion?

Does not the New Testament decree that Jews, "please not God and are contrary to all men"? (I Thessalonians 2:15). Does it not declare that whoever says, as the Jews do, that they can have God the Father without accepting his Son, are the Anti-Christ? (I John 2:22-23).

Why then would the Christian print shop lady want to cooperate with the forces of destruction against those who seek to defend Christian civilization?

In any case, the betrayal by that Christian business owner was a decidedly un-Christian deed. She listened to people (in this case, those of the press), who had never met me, who had never even read any of my newsletters either in English or in German, and who judged me by information provided by such Stalinist outfits as the A.D.L., KlanWatch and the SPLC.

---

[10] This is known as the "Fear of the Jews" syndrome. It was well-described in a book by that title authored by a scion of one of the oldest and most distinguished German-American families, Stanley Rittenhouse. The book is available for purchase for $20.00 from Exhorters Inc., Box 492, Vienna, Virginia 22180.

One must consider that the lady had ample time to get to know me personally, to discover that what I write is the truth, or, if it is opinion, that this opinion is well-founded and--according to the First Amendment of the American Constitution--certainly legitimate to express. For an American citizen, any American citizen to act as this woman did, is simply a shame.

Bützow

I arrived at my "final" destination, namely, the Bützow penitentiary, in the evening of Wednesday, August 23rd, 1995, exactly two weeks after my arrest. Incredibly, it had taken the German "justice" system that long to ship me the 500 kilometers or so from Frankfurt to this place near the Baltic Coast. The transport from Hamburg had been tedious, with numerous stops on the way, but uneventful.

In the prison bus I had shared a cell with a man from Hamburg, not much younger than myself, who months before had committed a traffic offense in the State of Mecklenburg-Vorpommern (of which Bützow is one of the more important jails), and he was now hauled before a court of that jurisdiction. I assume that his offense had been alcohol-related (but no person had come to harm), and there is a possibility that the miscreant had not heeded a Mecklenburg summons. At any rate, to his (and everybody's) surprise he was arrested at his place of business in Hamburg, and willy-nilly transported across state lines to Bützow. It seems that in Germany the individual states do not have as much independence as have the various states of the American union, where prisoners have the right to fight extradition.

Later I discovered that this Hamburg native had probably received a sentence of one year. After his trial he told me that he assumed he would be released (with good behavior) around March or April of 1996, which would mean that he had to serve two-thirds of the sentence. Since I never did find out the exact nature of the man's offense, I cannot be too quick with my judgment, but I do believe that it would make more sense if in such cases the culprit could be sentenced by a court in his home town, so that he could more easily be visited by his family and friends, his lawyer and, as in his case, even attend (by phone) to absolutely necessary business affairs.

When I arrived at Bützow I had the choice of a single cell to myself, or of sharing a small 'suite' of three cells with two other occupants. Normally, I would have taken the single occupancy option--I have no difficulty in getting along by myself.

But a brief reflection on another of the innovations, unknown in the previous history of Germany, introduced by the "humanitarian democrats" in Bonn, gave me pause. Too many political prisoners, embarrassing to the regime, or to its alien masters, have died strange and sudden deaths in its prisons. Men (and more than one woman) in the prime of life and health, died from "internal afflictions" never experienced before, or from grotesque "accidents" in the dead of the night, or committed "suicide" in unlikely circumstances.

In a multiple cell, with two others, the risk of having my food poisoned was diminished. The risk of three people dying in the same cell of the same 'gastric disorder' at the same time is still too much even for Bonn. In a few years, seeing the way events are going against them, perhaps they will resort even to those tactics, but not just yet. At the same time, the chance of being 'suicided' was equally diminished; an attempt at it would have been awkward even for the Teflon-skinned Kohl and his Klowns.[1]

Of course, I might have been murdered outside my cell and

---

[1] A month or so after my arrival at Bützow I was not only generally known to most prisoners at this penitentiary, but I had also made the acquaintance of young, politically aware German inmates who viewed the Bonn vassals as I did--with disdain. We discussed the methods used by the alien masters to eliminate such 'dangerous' persons as myself. The young prisoners assured me that they would watch over me and they made it clear that, if in spite of every precaution, something bad were to happen to me as a result of the malfeasance of the government, they would avenge me. I was very moved by the loyalty of these young men who--despite whatever their previous offenses--saw in this writer a reflection of the true Germany they longed for and were willing to defend.

out of sight and hearing of any other prisoners, but that is an occupational hazard, as it were, that I face anyhow, anywhere, and all the time.

At all events, and while I may never know to what extent my decision for multiple occupancy may have contributed to my having survived my prison ordeal, I shall remain ever thankful that I made the choice I did.

Cell 313 was in the B block, where pre-trial detention prisoners were held.

The number 300 indicated the third (and highest) floor, which was better than the ground floor, where usually the more intransigent prisoners were being confined.

Although B313 was probably planned to hold only two men, three were now assigned to it.

It had a total area of about 10 by 25 feet, and consisted of three cells of about equal size that were interconnected with door openings.

The center cell was merely the entrance way, and contained a large locker in which the prisoners kept their belongings.

The door leading from the hallway into our entrance cell had a narrow opening, akin to a mail slot.

We generally used it to find out what was happening "outside," when there was any commotion of any sort, by surveying the entire floor with a small mirror that had been glued to a toothbrush handle, and held through the mail slot.

I did notice that some of the older doors in this cell block still had large trap openings that years ago must have been used as reach-throughs for food, etc.

The cell to the left of the "entrance hall" was both toilet and washroom, and it could be closed with a door. Apart from the W.C. (which was behind a room divider) there was only the sink, and a small wall cabinet for our toiletries.

Unfortunately, there was no hot water faucet. Whosoever needed hot water for washing, or even for making a cup of coffee, had to call upon one of the guards who would then take the prisoner with his water container one floor below where hot water was always available from a big electric kettle.

In order to get the attention of the guards, each cell had something like a nurses' light above the cell door, which was activated by a button inside the entrance cell.

It goes without saying that one could not overdo its use. Those who did so couldn't even gain the guards' attention in medical emergencies.

The third and largest cell of our compartment, a room of about 10 ft. by 10 ft. with a 9 ft. ceiling, contained three steel cots similar to the ones used by armies all over the world; one single, and a bunk bed, one above the other.

There was also a table, three chairs, a one-man locker, and below the window a small cabinet that functioned as a television table.

In the course of the renewal or repair of the entire infrastructure in "East" Germany after the reunification, attempts were also made to improve the prisons, and thus it happened that we received new furniture about two weeks after my arrival at Bützow.

I was happy to be able to exchange my worn-out, sagging mattress for a new one made from thick foam rubber. It worked wonders for my back.

Each of our three rooms had a high window (starting about six feet above the floor) that was made escape-proof by heavy steel bars. Looking out (by standing on a chair) one could see first, a bit of the prison yard, then the 12-foot high walls topped by razor-wire, and beyond that, toward the east, a large lake and part of the old city of Bützow.[2]

At the corners, where the walls came together, one could see towers that reminded me of those I had seen at the Dachau concentration camp a few years ago. At Bützow it seemed that

---

[2] Not knowing anything at all about my new and temporary domicile, and always eager to obtain every scrap of knowledge I can, I asked my relatives in America to do some historical and geographic research. They consulted the new *Bertelsmann Encyclopedia* in my library at my home, after my arrest, under the category of Bützow.

This is what they found:

"Bützow, county seat in the district of Schwerin, between Warnow and Bützow lakes, population 10,400 (1981). City church from the 13th Century.

"Hydrogen and furniture factory, food industries and agriculture. Bützow is a planned city from the 13th century. It received its patent in 1236. From 1239 to the reformation it was a bishopry, and in the 18th century it was for a time the seat of the University of Rostock. There is also the Dreibergen penitentiary."

When I returned to America, I went back to my old and trusted *Brockhaus Lexikon* (Encyclopedia) from 1908 (!) which I had once bought at a surplus sale of the U.S. Library of Congress. Not unexpectedly, the information I was able to garner there was much more extensive, albeit somewhat outdated:

"Bützow, city in the grand-duchy of Mecklenburg-Schwerin, formerly the principality of Schwerin, near the confluence of the Warnow and Rebel rivers, and stops of the railroad lines from Berlin to Rostock, and from Lübeck to Strasburg.

Bützow is one of the nicest and most prosperous cities of the area. It has a district court and is also a county seat, and has an office of the forestry administration.

"In 1905, the population was 5,886, mostly Protestants. It has a postal office first class, and regular steamship connections to Rostock via the Warnow river.

"Worthy of mention are the Lutheran City (formerly Catholic) church built in Gothic style between 1239 and 1248, a reform church (the only one in the dukedom), a synagogue, a new and beautiful city hall, a former castle that is now being used to house officials, a central jail, a hospital, a Latin school, a trade school, a high school for girls, several breweries, two paper mills, and a factory for machine tools.

"Bützow also transacts much trade, especially grains. Near Bützow is the Dreibergen penitentiary holding 265 prisoners. Bützow was founded in 1302 by the bishops of Schwerin, and was made a bishopry thereafter.

"In 1648 (after the Thirty Years War, HS) Bützow became, along with the Schwerin bishopry, a possession of the grand-duchy of Mecklenburg.

"At the beginning of the 18th century, many (Hugenot) refugees from France settled in the area, and started factories. Between 1760 and 1789 Bützow was the seat of the university that had up to then been in Rostock."

(Younger readers of my book are advised to also have an old encyclopedia, preferably from the time before World War I, on hand. Almost every subject is more extensively treated. Modern encyclopedias seem to be published with the intention of keeping people uninformed.)

the towers were often not occupied by guards. There was a serious shortage of prison personnel. Mecklenburg is a poor state.

Beneath each cell window was a heating unit fed by a central steam-heating system. This was overhauled while I was there, and it kept the cells warm throughout the winter, although at first I did experience a few chilly weeks in September and October. I must also mention that the cells were generally as clean as the prisoners kept them, obviously an impossibility for cells used only for transients, who had neither pails, nor detergent nor other means to scrub the painted cement floors and walls. I was fortunate in this regard since both of my roommates were themselves tidy and saw to it that we lived in decent surroundings. Furthermore, nowhere did I notice an infestation of lice, bedbugs and similar critters, although one of the prisoners who worked in the ancient kitchen at Bützow told me of cockroaches that seemed rampant there.

I met my new cell mates, a West German in his mid-fifties who was being held for grand larceny, and a 25-year-old "East" German who, in a family squabble, in a moment of passion, had killed his younger brother, and had received a seven and one-half year-sentence.

A few weeks before I arrived in Bützow, a gang of seven Rumanian criminals [3] (Gypsies, but the German press has

---

[3] In 1995 and 1996, Germany was besieged by well-organized criminal gangs from Rumania. Hardly a day passed without a robbery of a supermarket, gas station or post office. These "Rumanians" (actually Gypsies) specialize in removing safes and stashing them in forests. They also steal items that have high cash liquidity, such as cigarettes and postage stamps. These gangs are heavily armed and very brutal when cornered. They are also an escape risk once in custody, often carrying diamond-tipped files in their shoes for sawing through steel bars. These professional criminals have a command structure in Rumania and are reputed to learn their "skills" in crime schools there. Neither the police or population in orderly Germany can cope with such an onslaught. The leaders of the Bonn vassal state are too occupied with toadying to the Israelis to safeguard the borders of Germany against this floodtide of brutal criminality.

followed the example of its American co-propagandists in suppressing the racial identity of any criminal minorities), had managed to saw their way through the steel bars on one of their cell windows on the ground floor, and had made a clean escape.

It is assumed that they had outside help since they were never recaptured. This mass break-out was reported all over Germany, and it reflected badly on the politicians in charge of the Mecklenburg prison system (there had also been other successful escapes).

The man most often prominently mentioned for incompetence in this regard was Rudi Geil, the interior minister (Secretary of the Interior), of the State of Mecklenburg-Vorpommern, the very person who had been responsible for my arrest.

Immediately after the Rumanians had made their get-away, Geil must have known that it reflected badly on his career, and being the ambitious politician that he is, it was to be expected that he would take some spectacular action in order to show his ability and resolve. This occurred precisely on my first weekend in cell B313.

A *"Generalrevision"* or *"Filzung,"* as the prisoners called it, namely a thorough search, combined with the issuance of more stringent measures, occurred at Bützow penitentiary on the weekend of August 24th through August 27th, 1995.

While we had to spend hours on end in dirty, practically empty hell holes on the ground floor, Geil sent a large detachment (probably an entire company) of riot police to the jail, whose order it was to search all the cells for contraband (files, knives, dope, alcohol, broken mirrors, maps, money, etc.)

The regular guards of the Bützow prison could do nothing but unlock the cell doors when the green uniformed riot policemen began their search. In an area of Germany where the unemployment rate is as high as 14 percent, people always have to fear losing their jobs, and therefore it was best for them to keep their mouths shut.

Nevertheless, on the faces of the Bützow guards I could see that they did not agree with the measures implemented by Geil. They knew that the outcome would entail future troubles with the prisoners after the riot police had long gone.

When we returned to our cells, we were greeted by havoc: the furniture stood in disarray, the mattresses and the bed linens had been thrown into a corner, and there were boot prints on some of the sheets, pillows and towels.

All pictures and calendars had been torn from the wall, and were lying on the floor. The lockers had been emptied of their contents (foodstuffs, writing and reading material and clothing) and had been dumped into one giant heap on the floor.

The policemen had even opened store-sealed packages; for instance, packages of oatmeal, and checked them for contraband.

The floor in front of the cells was arranged similar to the open style apartment house hallways of southern California. They were not enclosed and there was a relatively narrow, U-shaped balcony on each floor that was fenced by a waist-high railing.

The center was open, and one could see from the third floor down to the ground level.

However, in order to prevent prisoners from committing suicide by jumping through this opening, chain-link wire fencing had been stretched from side-to-side on each floor. It looked like the safety net in a circus.

As we returned to our floor after the general inspection, we noted that the chain-link fencing in front of our cells was filled with things that over time had been accumulated by the prisoners, but which according to the new rules could not be kept: surplus clothing, surplus books, shelving, bedding, old magazines, large bottles of detergent, soap, toothpaste, curtains, even medicines--you name it.

Obviously, everything was to be thrown into trash containers. All complaints by the prisoners that many of the items thrown out had been their private possessions were to no avail; only rarely was the permission given to retrieve this or that piece of property.

I suppose what really upset most prisoners was the callous disregard of the (obviously idiotic) riot policemen for their innermost feelings.

Most of the imprisoned men had few consolations. The photographs of their loved ones hung or glued above their bedsteads were one of these.

When the policemen (obviously on orders) tore them off, they not only did not take precautions not to damage the pictures, but in many instances they threw them on the floor and stepped on them either purposely or through neglect.

Only the calm attitude of the regular guards prevented a riot then and there.

They assured us privately that within a week or two everything would be normal, and one could see that there was no fraternization going on between them and the riot police.

I did not have many possessions to be concerned about. Up to that point, I had not been able to purchase anything in the commissary and I had not had a chance to obtain any prison clothing.

I still wore the same clothes I had worn when I was about to board the plane at Frankfurt.

Thankfully, some of the prisoners had lent me detergent with which I could now wash my underwear everyday.

But I did have an accumulation of legal papers, for instance the arrest order and an instruction booklet from the American embassy in Berlin, and some mail I had received from my attorney, Mr. Herrmann.

It was obvious, in my estimation, that someone had snooped through my files during the *Filzung* (riot-police raid).

One letter from Dr. Frey, the head of one of the three major, constantly harassed, German rights' parties, the DVU (*Deutsche Volks-Union*) bearing a colorful letterhead--a letter that had not been addressed to me but to someone else I knew--had been purposely torn in half by one of the goons.

This leads me to believe that most of the policemen of this riot squad had been West Germans who were garrisoned in former Communist Germany (Mecklenburg) in order to keep an eye on a population that was lacking in loyalty to the Bonn regime. In other words, these were "political" police.

It is doubtful that a young "East" German policeman would have known either who Dr. Frey or his DVU was, and that both had been labeled enemies of Bonn's "anti-Fascist" dictatorship that masquerades as a democracy. [4]

The main part of the aging Bützow penitentiary was erected in

---

[4] The repression by the Bonn Government of every patriotic, nationalist sentiment in the German population by wholly undemocratic means justifies the designation of dictatorship. There are other things that point to the fact that the "BRD" (Bundesrepublik Deutschland) is now really turning into a leftist "Gross-DDR" (Greater Deutsche Demokratische Republik: "Communist" Germany). For instance, for decades it has been Communist usage everywhere in the world to misname Hitler's National Socialism as "fascism". This is not the place to explain the substantial difference between the two, but the Communists were loath to use the correct, "National Socialist" designation for the Third Reich system, because it would have shown that another socialism besides Marxism was not only possible, but could be successful, as far as it concerned the social welfare of an entire people. Other evidence of Bonn's leftward tilt can be seen from the fact that now the day of Germany's WWII surrender, May the 8th, is celebrated as a Day of Liberation (as the Communist 'East' German "DDR" had also designated it), and that old German Bolsheviks still receive their *Ehrensold* (honor pension), for their past activities on behalf of Josef Stalin and against the German nation. Moreover, some alleged German "war criminals" that had been sentenced in Communist show trials have not been freed. Also, a 1950 border treaty concluded between the "DDR" and Poland has now also been accepted as legal by the *Bundesrepublik*.

1836.⁵ It consists essentially of three wings, A, B and C, and some buildings that had been added during the past one hundred and sixty years, including modern "containers" (manufactured housing), holding some of the long-term prisoners who had work permits.

My personal observation was that the entire Bützow prison complex should be put out of commission, with the oldest buildings perhaps being preserved as a museum or for an archive, and that an entirely new prison should be built nearby, using the knowledge gained in the last century or so in the field of criminology.

Certainly, it costs huge sums to build a new prison but I estimated that the several hundred million *deutschmarks* the Bonn vassals give every year to the Israelis, above and apart from the regular World War II, "restitution payments" which run into the billions of *deutschmarks* ("tribute"), could be used for this purpose. Besides, for a new prison fewer guards and administrators would be needed.

I have never given much thought to these cages for humans that are called prisons or penitentiaries. Certainly, one needs jails in cities and near court houses for short term offenders, or for the holding of pre-trial detention prisoners. But there ought to be the caveat that *all* trials must be held swiftly, and strict guidelines should rule the period in which a prisoner may be held without trial.

---

⁵ The architecture is typical of the post-Napoleonic era in Prussia and northern Germany: twin towers frame the entrance to the old main building that should give the appearance of a very old fortress, and there is an extensive use of red bricks. I can imagine that the prison in the Ruhr valley, in which my great grandfather Hannes Schmidt had been incarcerated for four years after the failed 1848 revolution, had a similar look. Interestingly, my ancestor had been on trial alongside his acquaintance and neighbor Friedrich Engels (the benefactor of Karl Marx). While Engels was acquitted, Schmidt got four years, and his family was dispossessed by the Prussian Government.

In my case the five-months' waiting period was already unconscionably long. After all, I did not deny writing the Open Letters that eventually constituted the essence of the indictment, and the question of whether my words could be construed as "incitement to hate," ought to have been settled within a week or so. As far as pre-trial detention in Germany is concerned, the judicial system seems to act according to medieval standards. I heard of prisoners who had waited as long as five years until their trial commenced.

Decades ago, business interests had made it mandatory that I frequently drive from Southern California to Las Vegas. On the way I had to drive past a modern, large penitentiary near the California-Nevada border (belonging to the state of Nevada, if I remember correctly), that struck me as the epitome of inhumanity. There, in the middle of nowhere, in the brutal desert, totally out of sight of trees and meadows, far from any civilization, sat this highly guarded prison, brightly lit by artificial light at night, and relentlessly tormented by the sun during the day.

How difficult it must have been for the families of the prisoners to visit. How demoralizing it must have been for criminals who wanted to better themselves. Often I was wondering what these men and women were doing all day long: watching stupid television shows, reading the sports pages of the newspapers with their transient "news," or just sleeping and wasting their lives away?

I am not and never have been a "do-gooder." Criminals ought to be punished severely and swiftly. But above all, the punishment should fit the crime. Mass murderers like Speck, Dahmer and Gacy, or those young criminals who years ago tormented an entire family at a roadside business in Utah by raping the girls and, among other things, driving a screwdriver through the ear of a young boy, should have been executed while their crimes were fresh in the minds of the public.

I regard executions less as "punishment" than as the necessary elimination of such miscreants from society. However, I am also mindful of miscarriages of justice where innocent people have been put to death. Bruno Richard Hauptmann, the German immigrant to the United States who had wrongly been implicated in the kidnapping and murder of the Lindbergh baby in the early 1930s comes to mind. To this day I am convinced of Hauptmann's innocence. Based on the injustice meted out to him, I believe that the strictest standards have to be adhered to before a man or woman is strapped to the electric chair. If there is even the slightest doubt, no death sentence should be pronounced.

In Bützow I had ample opportunity to talk to real criminals. Until then I was under the erroneous impression that most people in prison would proclaim their innocence. Amazingly, this is not true. Even the worst culprits admitted to having committed this or that crime, and in a number of cases I noticed the common denominator of all *real* criminals, namely, a lack of conscience.

An added surprise was the way criminals acted or reacted when reading of crimes that had been committed on the outside. Seeing newspaper and magazine articles concerning murders, robberies and similar offenses in a newspaper, I often asked criminals, during our one-hour walk-abouts in the prison yard, what punishment *they* would mete out in such instances, once the offender was caught. Their judgment was often close to mine.

What irked prisoners the most was the callousness of the system. While we all agreed that it is not the purpose of a detention facility to provide "country club living" to criminals, it was the petty, unnecessary chicaneries inherent in the system that annoyed all of us: the lack of visiting hours; the fact that in one year only three small parcels could be received; the long, unnecessary waiting between hearings and the trial; all this and more created friction. In Bützow the age of the facility made for additional problems. For instance, due to the fact that there was only one telephone room with but one telephone for so many prisoners, telephone calls were a rarity.

Here is an excerpted translation of an article about the Bützow penitentiary that appeared in the local newspaper (the *Schweriner Volkszeitung*), on October 10th:

"Finally we can present a clear picture of the conditions inside the JVA (*Justizvollzugsanstalt*) penitentiary at Bützow. It was generally known that there are about 600 people incarcerated in this prison but it may help the situation if everybody realizes that among them are only forty to fifty criminals that have been sentenced to very long stretches.

"Asked why there are any hard-core criminals at all incarcerated at Bützow, the current director of the prison explained that under Communist rule such people had been sent to prisons in the south of the country but that now, after the reunification, each state is responsible for its own prison system, and this leads to the facts as they exist now. The director further stated that this 160-year old institution had originally been built to have the prisoners almost exclusively in one-man cells but that in later years this had been changed, and after that even necessary accommodations, such as the infirmary, had been neglected. The director also said that according to present usage, prisoners who had been sentenced to life imprisonment cannot be put permanently in chains, nor can they always be kept in one-man cells.

"It seems that at the moment there are about 600 prisoners in

Bützow.

"This means about twenty to thirty over the planned quota. Of these 600, about half of the prisoners have already been sentenced, more than 200 are in pre-trial detention, and the rest are in transit. There are twenty-five to thirty female prisoners in a special building. Of the approximately 300 prisoners who have been sentenced, only about 230 to 240 are working.

The others either do not want to work, or else there is not enough work for them. About sixty of the prisoners are taking part in the schooling that is being offered."

When I was assigned to cell B313, I did notice that the person in charge, obviously a well-intentioned professional with many years of experience, took great care in placing the new arrivals in the appropriate cells.

The idea was not to punish people but to avoid unnecessary trouble and friction. In our case for instance, our cell was about as far away as possible from the room where the guards (who worked 12-hour shifts), spent most of their time. This meant that I was in a cell where little or no trouble was expected.

Prisoners from foreign lands were usually placed with their own countrymen: Poles with Poles, blacks with blacks, Rumanians with Rumanians.

(In the case of the latter this was obviously to the detriment of the prison since there had been up to eight men in one cell, and it was easy for them to hatch escape plans).

But one must concede that this commonsense segregation along ethnic lines generally promotes harmony and it is a tragedy for all involved that such benign segregation practices are now illegal in American prisons.

Bützow also has its share of characters. "Sergeant Klinger," is a male who dresses in female clothing.

Calling himself, "Jana" he is heavyset, rather coarse looking and could usually be found in a large, separately enclosed area that is traversed by the ordinary prisoners only when going to the commissary, the telephone room, or to the outside of the cell block.

It was Jana's duty to keep this area clean but I personally believe that she/he had been placed there in order to avoid unnecessary contact, and therefore trouble, with others.

Someone told me that Jana had been convicted of murder, and had a long sentence ahead. I did not have any reason to disbelieve the story.

Once, when I was waiting to make a telephone call, Jana asked me whether it was true that I was an American.

"Well, to state it better, I am a German who has lived in America almost since the end of World War II," I answered.

Then Jana wanted to know why I had been incarcerated. I gave her/him the same answer I gave to everyone:

"I am a journalist in America. I had written there that Germany is now ruled by the Jews of the world, and that I did not think this is right. I was arrested in *Deutschland* because one of my writings in this regard ended up in the hands of Rudi Geil."

Jana was aghast.

"But *everybody* knows that the Jews have too much of a say in Germany!"

At any rate, after that I was always greeted with friendliness and respect by her/him. I did not fail to note that it was a rare instance when a prisoner made fun of this (in my opinion) unhappy creature.

Our days in Bützow were long and boring.

The situation improved however, thanks to my allies--I began to receive the many letters from family, friends and supporters all over the world. But at first there was always the waiting and killing of time.⁶

Around seven o'clock in the morning there was the first counting of the prisoners (whereby the guards came into the sleeping cells to take note of prisoners still in their beds), and at the same time breakfast, usually three slices of white bread with a sufficient slab of margarine (they called it butter), one of the tiny restaurant containers with jam, and, if you wanted it, something called coffee that probably wasn't.

Then, depending upon what day it was, and following an uncertain schedule, there might soon have been the one-hour *Freistunde* (walk-about) in the prison yard. For this exercise the cell doors of about 12 to 15 of the prisoners were opened and the prisoners could then proceed past two separate iron gate enclosures and two usually locked doors, to the yard below which had been made into three large units separated by chain-link fences. The prison officials wanted to avoid ever having forty to fifty prisoners together in one place. The guards usually were *not* armed. In other words, in case of a riot they would have been at the mercy of the prisoners.

In all my time in Bützow, I missed only one or two *Freistunde(n)*. Once because I had a visit by my lawyer, another time because I had a persistent cough, and I didn't want to miss the call to the infirmary. In general I felt that for the sake of my health it was absolutely necessary that, rain (or snow), or shine, I should get some fresh air and move about, even if only in large circles.

As a rule, I walked around the perimeter of our yard enclosures with one or two of the prisoners with whom over the

---

⁶ This "killing of time" business was probably the worst part of my incarceration. Someone like myself who is always busy, doing things for what I hope is the betterment of mankind--for such a one--the wasting of even one hour is horrible. (Don't think I don't know how to relax. In normal life I take a regular, afternoon nap). Therefore, it is no wonder that in Bützow I was less angry about any personal deprivations than about the fact that I could do so much more if I were free.

time I had developed a friendly relationship. These were people I enjoyed talking with.

There was a Bulgarian, a very intelligent fellow, who had worked in Germany for years, all the while sending enough money home to his family so that they had been able to erect a rather nice single-family house. Stanislaw was the type of guy who would take any and all jobs in order to be able to send enough of his savings to Bulgaria. But this had been his undoing. A businessman had asked him to drive a truck from Holland to Germany, something quite normal and legitimate. At a border checkpoint it was discovered that the truck had been stolen. Because he was a foreigner without permanent residency in Germany, Stanislaw was being held as a material witness. Never having been in jail before, he took his imprisonment very hard. His predicament was exacerbated by the fact that around Christmas 1995 his wife (who had remained in Bulgaria) expected another child. I saw no reason to disbelieve Stanislaw when he told me that he was innocent in the matter.

A relatively young German, also a family man with whom I spoke often, was a native of the nearby port city of Rostock. Immediately after the reunification of Germany he had realized the pent-up demand of his "East" German countrymen for hitherto forbidden travel to the west, and he was one of the first organizers to send charter busses full of Mecklenburgers to London, Paris and Italy.

He also managed to sign a ten-year contract with his home city, whereby he provided extra buses should the city-owned transportation system require additional vehicles. But it was this contract which would prove to be his undoing.

What he had not contemplated was the vehemence and callousness with which the Bonn vassals took over "East" Germany, and particularly its entire infrastructure. Comparably, the 1938 *Anschluss* of Austria to the Reich was an exercise in virtue. [7]

It did not take long after the reunification until almost all the important positions in Rostock, as well as in the state of Mecklenburg-Vorpommern, were in the hands of people from West Germany.

They naturally saw to it that all lucrative contracts went to their cronies back home.

So it was no surprise when this young Rostock travel manager one day received a note from the city informing him that it was unilaterally canceling the ten-year contract it had with his business.

Not knowing of the Western adage that you cannot fight city hall, he threatened to take legal action if the city did so.

The result of this step wasn't long in coming.

Shortly before Christmas he found himself arrested for allegedly cheating the German tax system out of millions of *deutschmarks*.

He was also accused of having absconded with the down payment "East" German people had deposited for future trips, and with other assorted petty crimes.

In conjunction with his arrest, not only was there a thorough search of his office but also of his home and of that of his

---

[7] In the course of reestablishing German sovereignty after the defeat of World War I, Hitler also fulfilled the will of the Austrians who, in 1919, had opted for unification with the Reich, but were prohibited from doing so by the victorious allies. The *Anschluss* of March 1938 turned into one of the most equitable unifications of two separate states on record. The exchange of the money, the interchange of the various authorities and the integration, for instance, of the two armies, took place in an atmosphere of good will and with a minimum of friction. The Austrians gained by becoming an important part of the Greater German Reich. However, when the "democratic" and "free" *Bundesrepublik* took over the insolvent Communist part of Germany in 1990, it was more like the victorious American North taking over the South after the Civil War, when countless carpetbaggers plundered their way to wealth.

mother. [8]

Speaking with him I noticed that he had no idea what had hit him. Obviously he had no concept how "democracy" works and what can be expected in such a society.

Being a basically honest, good-hearted and politically naive German, he could not believe that "democrats" could go to such lengths in order to eliminate their competition.

When he first told me of his case, he thought that it was all a mistake, and that he would be out within a few days.

Later he related that he had arranged numerous bus trips for his loyal customers to some German cities. It was in these cities that the forthcoming New Year's Day was going to be celebrated in particularly festive ways. I predicted that, no matter what, he would not be freed before that date, since in my opinion it was the intention of his enemies to completely ruin his business.

What better way to do that than by creating hundreds of disappointed customers for him?

I was proved right.

The prosecutor had to reduce the claim of alleged tax misappropriations down to a figure of less than 100,000 *deutschmarks* ($60,000).

It was also proved that he had never left Rostock at the time when he was supposed to be spending stolen millions on the Riviera and in America(!).

These facts came out before Christmas, and justice would have demanded that the man would be released into freedom.

Yet he was not let go.

---

[8] Thorough house searches in which often ten, twenty or more detectives and ordinary policemen participate, seem a specialty of the Bonn system. Personally I assume that it is done in order to terrorize the population. In political cases the police are very liberal as to what evidence to take along. Even books that can be bought in every bookstore, for instance World War II memoirs, are often seized in order to prove the culprit's intransigent nature.

They didn't even permit bail to be considered in his case. [9]

Sometimes during my walks I was approached by other prisoners.

Since I still remembered some cursory Spanish and French, and because after October 20th I was in possession of a manual typewriter, I was asked to help these prisoners write letters to lawyers, judges, politicians and prosecutors.

At other times my opinion was needed about political events taking place in the world.

One day a prisoner of about 24 years of age, by his dialect an "East" German, asked whether it was true that I was "a high official of the N.S.D.A.P. (the *National Sozialistische Deutsche Arbeiter Partei*), the Hitler party?"

"Well, no," I answered, "there hasn't been an N.S.D.A.P. since 1945!"

He looked surprised and said, "Really? But why not?"

"Because the Allies forbade it at that time!"

He shook his head. "Why would they do that? They must be crazy!"

Now it was my turn to ask him some questions.

Why did he come to me? Why his sudden interest in the "Nazi" party?

He explained that on the evening before he had watched a

---

[9] In order to discover whether there was any substance to the allegations of the prosecutor, I questioned this young man extensively about his standard of living. Since the authorities and the newspapers had based their actions on "millions" of dollars with which the culprit was supposed to have fled abroad, I believed that I would discover some proof of greed or inordinate materialism in the man's life. This is what I found: he drove a medium-priced BMW, he and his family hadn't had a real vacation in years (although he naturally had to travel abroad on business), and they lived in a middle-class, and by no means luxurious, apartment. They had no large savings account, and owned no stocks, jewelry or real estate. If bail had been granted he would have had difficulty raising a larger sum. In short, he was only the owner of a relatively small travel business with absolutely no means of amassing the larger sums of which the prosecutor had spoken.

program about Hitler on TV, and that he was so impressed with Hitler's accomplishments that he immediately wanted to join the N.S.D.A.P.[10]

For most of the time while I was at this place of confinement, about a dozen black men from Africa were also incarcerated there.

I assume they were so-called asylum seekers who committed illegal acts, such as peddling dope or selling untaxed cigarettes, and since all were in pre-trial detention, I believe that eventually they will be sent back to Ghana, Nigeria and Rwanda, from whence they had originally come.

It follows that I was soon asked to act as an interpreter between these English-speaking blacks, and either the prison employees, or the other prisoners.

Since I have always had a good relationship with African-Americans, I also had no difficulties in getting along with these unfortunates, and I was soon their favorite German.

(Many blacks like to banter. It was easy for me to associate with them and help them overcome their language difficulties.)

---

[10] Beginning with November 9th, 1995, the major German government-sponsored TV channel broadcast a series of six half-hour films on Hitler. The various segments were titled, "Hitler, the Seducer", and "Hitler, the General", or "Hitler, the Criminal." The series was planned to eliminate once and for all any lingering sympathies average Germans may yet still harbor for the Führer. Unfortunately for the modern film makers, no Goebbels is among them who has a deeper understanding of the psychology of the masses.

I also watched this series, and I found the propaganda so crude and stupid that I immediately realized that Hitler's aura could only gain from this idiotic portrayal. On the days following the showing of each segment of the series, I made it my business to ask as many guards and prisoners as possible whether they had watched this show. Not surprisingly, most of them had done so since, during the Communist era, they had had little chance to view authentic German newsreels of World War II on TV.

It is the availability and the necessity of this Third Reich movie material that always and everywhere kills all the chances of the "anti-Fascists" to misconstrue the idea and the spirit of National Socialist Germany. What white person is not uplifted by seeing the happy faces of the Germans when they greeted their leader, or when they contrast the demoralized youth (of whatever race) of today with the high-spirited boys and girls of the Hitler Youth, the *Arbeitsdienst,* and the Waffen-SS!

One day when the Africans had their *Freistunde* at the same time we did, I saw them congregating in a corner of the separate court yard enclosure, next to ours.

When they asked me to come nearer their chain link fence, since they had some political questions to ask, I kidded them that I was unable to talk to them since I had just read in the German news magazine *Der Spiegel* that I was one of the eight or nine worst racists in the United States, and that, after all, I had to live up to this reputation.

Hearing this, the blacks couldn't stop laughing. They knew that I was a white nationalist and separatist, and that I did not believe in any inter-marriage between the races, yet they declared that whoever wrote *Der Spiegel's* stupid assessment of me didn't know what he was talking about.

The question these allegedly primitive men asked me was quite interesting.

They wanted to know how I assessed the fundamental differences between Whites such as myself (i.e., Aryans) and themselves on one hand, and Jews and their Aryan and African lackeys on the other.

It was not easy to provide the proper answers in less than an hour, and we dealt with this theme for several successive days.

The black men told me that by themselves (and without the necessary background knowledge) they had come to the same conclusion as I had, namely, that Aryan whites and African blacks are spiritually closer to each other than are Aryans and Jews.

We agreed that it was the Jews themselves who set themselves apart and above everybody else.

Lunch, the main meal of the day, was served shortly before noon. As with all the meals, we ate it in our cells.

There were great differences in the quality of the various meals served but having gained many years of experience in the hotel and restaurant business, and also having had service in the armed forces, I know how difficult it is to prepare and serve institutional food.

I can therefore state without hesitation that whoever was in charge of the food preparation at Bützow, did his best under the circumstances.

Here are some of the menus that I jotted down:

Stuffed cabbage with mashed potatoes. Jell-O with whipped cream (factory prepared) for dessert.

Pea soup with knackwurst, and an apple.

Deep fried fish, with boiled potatoes and celery salad, and a kiwi fruit.

Pigs' knuckles with sauerkraut and mashed potatoes, chocolate pudding.

Two boiled eggs with mustard sauce, mashed potatoes and creamed spinach, one pear.

Meat patty with potatoes and mixed vegetables (peas and carrots), ice cream.

Half a roasted chicken with rice, and factory packed pudding for dessert.

Beef roulade in gravy, boiled potatoes, Brussels sprouts, and an orange.

This last dish is one of my German favorites, and I have to say that it was well prepared. The point is that the sauce (which I have purposely termed "gravy" for the benefit of my American readers), has to be well prepared with onions, and whoever cooked this meal knew his business.

The portions were always more than ample for me, and should have been sufficient also for the younger prisoners who worked. At any rate, I could rarely eat everything on my plate.

Regrettably, the food was rather quickly dished out on three-compartment plastic dishes, and this did not enhance the look of the meals.

I was surprised how rarely we were served typical German meals that had been the staples of the poor even while I was a child: heavy soups, such as those made with lentils, beans, peas and barley served with sausage or a piece of bacon.

Actually, I personally would have liked to see more of that.

One meal I didn't like, and which I tried only once was some kind of oddly tasting vegetable soup made in a way unknown to me, probably a specialty of Mecklenburg.

I was glad to see that the other prisoners felt about it as I did.

The evening dinner was served rather early, at about 4:30 in the afternoon.

The reason for this was the perennial shortage of sufficient guards at the institution.

Obviously, the day shift wanted to make certain that all the necessary daily tasks were accomplished before they went home.

It always consisted of what I would generally call cold cuts, with other food stuffs for variety.

There were three different kinds of bread--dark, white and what the Germans call *mischbrot*--where the dough is made from different grains.

This is my favorite. The portions were large enough that I was able to save two slices of the *Mischbrot* for my breakfast, rather than eat the wheat bread which I did not care for.

We usually received something like this: 2 slices of ham and 2 slices of salami plus a one-portion chocolate drink, or one can of sardines, plus two slices of cheese, and some other pre-packed drinks.

The quality of the ham, sausage, cheese, etc. was excellent, and the variations were great.

While the portions were ample, I am sure that most inmates would have liked to have received additional slices of cold cuts or cheese, for instance. Again, as in the morning, everyone received a slab of margarine for additional bread spread.

Did the other prisoners complain about the food?

Yes. But, just as in the army, that was to be expected. My main concern was that nobody should be hungry, and I do not believe that this occurred.

Earlier I had mentioned the matter of the cash that is taken from the prisoners upon their arrest, cash which is then ostensibly transferred to a central office of the German jail system in Bonn or Berlin, and only after a while placed into an account at the place of detention where the prisoner can draw from it.

Although I had more than 1,400 *deutschmarks* (somewhat less than $1,000) on my person at the time of my arrest, in prison I was without money, and therefore without the opportunity to purchase even the most necessary items such as writing paper and postage stamps.

This went on until September 13, 1995, exactly 5 weeks after my apprehension at Frankfurt airport.

In our part of the prison, one day every fortnight was set aside when each prisoner who had money in his account was allowed to go to the downstairs commissary and do his shopping.

There was an upper limit to the purchases however: 100 *deutschmarks* for each buying spree (200 *deutschmarks* per month). In anticipation of the arrival of my money, I had made a list of the things that I wanted or needed:

postage stamps, writing paper and envelopes[11]

vitamin juices, vitamin tablets

skim milk

oatmeal and muesli

chocolate bars

jam and honey

chocolate covered almond cake

German sugar beet syrup (a bread spread that is a favorite in the Saarland)

laundry detergent

apples

mustard

Nivea cream

herb tea

decaffeinated coffee

and tobacco with cigarette paper to give to others who had no money.

Soap, tooth paste, tooth brushes, shavers and shaving cream were supplied by the prison.

Apart from the times when the meals were served, and the *Freistunde*, the most important event of the day occurred (on weekdays only) in the afternoon, when the mail was delivered.

---

[11] Most letters I wrote were sent to America. For a German to mail a simple, one-half ounce airmail letter to the United States, will cost him 3.00 *deutschmarks*, or about $2.00. One must compare this with the fact that Americans only have to pay $0.60 for a one-half ounce air mail letter or about $1.00 for a one-ounce airmail letter from the U.S. to Germany. Why do the Germans have to pay more than three times as much? It is not generally known, but I have it from a good source at the U.S. Postal Service HQ in Washington, that the Bonn Government has *voluntarily* assumed to make the hard cash payments for such "poor" countries as Israel and Poland at the supra-national post office institution in Switzerland, where the international settlements for postal services between the nations are made. As a result of this nonsense, I had to spend a considerable part of my monthly allowance for stamps until we found other ways to get additional stamps to me.

Usually, one of the guards came into the cell, gave the prisoner a larger envelope with mail destined for him. The prisoner then had to open it in the guard's presence in case there was a notation on the outside of the envelope that money, stamps or photographs were inside. All cash was then withheld and placed into the prisoner's account and a receipt issued.

As far as I was able to notice, in Bützow all monetary matters were properly transacted.

Twice a week we were able to take a shower. We were brought to a special shower room below the center of the prison, where an array of water pipes were suspended from the ceiling. In regular distances there were simple openings (i.e., no normal shower heads) through which the hot water came flowing down on us. It reminded me of the shower rooms at the German World War II concentration camps of which I have read. Oddly, I had no fear that somehow poison gas would come through the pipes instead of water. I know that many Jews were miraculously saved from certain death when such a normal event occurred at Auschwitz.

Jewish *Kapos* (Jewish police in the employ of the Germans), as a cruel joke, had told many concentration camp inmates to expect poison gas from the shower heads. This, in addition to the *Kapos* pointing at the smoke-spewing chimneys of the distant Buna factory and exclaiming, "Just look, there go your relatives...", created many a "gas chamber" rumor.

Having read innumerable stories by "Holocaust survivors," I was always amazed how much they remembered, and claimed to have seen, of the goings on in such "death camps" as Auschwitz.

One would assume that the Germans in charge of the "death camps" would have been very secretive, or at least would have been more fearful of prisoner uprisings (remember, these were allegedly all prisoners facing certain death), than were the guards at Bützow. At any rate, many Jews were able to tell in detail what occurred at their camp on a certain day in an area that was literally miles away from their own bunk. Were they that free to move about?

The fact is that although I was incarcerated in Bützow for about 4 1/2 months, I know very little of what occurred outside of my cell--in the other wings--of this relatively small penitentiary.

Certainly, there were times when I was able to walk, accompanied by a guard, either to the visitors' room, or to the rear entrance of the jail, where one boarded a vehicle to be brought to the court house, or to the infirmary. On such occasions I sometimes had to pass the cells of the long-term prisoners, but if the prison personnel had really wanted to keep events from us (for instance, the purposeful mistreatment of prisoners), they could have done so. Therefore it seems incongruous that Jewish Auschwitz "witnesses," to name but these, were so extremely well informed. Either they had more liberty than we had at Bützow (which I suspect), or they made everything up (which I also suspect).

I am fully aware that the bulk of the inmates at the Bützow penitentiary were true criminals who had transgressed against the very normal laws every human society has to have in order to assure the well-being and safety of the people. Yet, I still pitied many of them. Often, they had slid into a life of crime, or committed a single crime, through only partial fault of their own, and listening to many stories I came away with the sense that many prosecutors, judges and legislators are performing their jobs too mechanically, without consideration of the fact that both the culprits and their victims are human beings. How can judges mete out heavy prison sentences without having spent time in jail themselves? That some judges also see a victim in the criminals can be glimpsed from the following story:

Bodo, a naive but not unintelligent young man in his late twenties, arrived at Bützow with a prior conviction. He had now been arrested a second time, this time for stealing a bus and cashing stolen checks. Since he absolutely did not seem the criminal type (yes, there is a criminal type!), I asked him what he had done. He related that he had been an illegitimate child, born to a teenage girl who never forgave him for (allegedly) ruining her life.

When he was about six years of age, his mother broke both his arms in a fit of rage. Bodo was taken from her and sent to an orphanage. The mother was incarcerated for a couple of years. (This happened during the rule of the Communist regime in "East" Germany). Later, the mother married and had other children but the relationship between Bodo and his mother remained one of intermittent love and hate. In spite of what she had done to him, Bodo always felt the need to return to her.

Bodo learned a trade, and worked at a large company. His dreams were (and, incidentally, still are) *"die grosse Welt"* - the greater world - outside of the confinement of his hometown and its surroundings.

He loves everything that is connected with large hotels of what he imagines are the world-class: the aura, the elegance, the never-ending activity, and not the least, the constant coming and going of so many different people. He told me that he would take any job, even the lowest one, as long as it could be in a hotel such as the Waldorf-Astoria in New York City, about which he had read in a book

One day, still in the Communist era, Bodo took his vacation, and traveled to the sea port of Rostock. There, the large, high-rise Neptune Hotel was the best in town. It had been built by a foreign consortium, and was alleged to be one of the most elegant in drab "East" Germany. Bodo dreamed of staying a few nights at the Neptune, but since he had only a low-paying job, the room rates were completely out of his reach.

Having increased his appetite for the better things in life by admiring the Neptune Hotel from a distance, Bodo finally went to the nearest telephone cell, called the hotel and, pretending that he was an official of the well-known factory for which he worked, asked to be connected to the person in the hotel who was in charge of dealing with large companies.

He then asked this person whether they had a room for one of the company officials who was coming to Rostock for a few days, and whether it was possible to charge the company for the stay. Needless to say, the answer was yes. Incredibly (and naively), Bodo gave his own name, and when a few hours later he checked in at the Neptune, he also did so under his own name. For a few days he fulfilled his dream of being in a "world-class" hotel, and, as he told me, in retrospect it had all been worth it.

Months later, the Neptune billed Bodo's company, and as a result, our hero saw the inside of Bützow prison for the first time. If I remember correctly, he had to spend a year there before he was released.

Our meeting in the B-block of the prison in the fall of 1995 was caused by an incident that is not unlike the story just related.

Although Bodo was now living by himself, he could not stay away from his mother who lived with her family in a nearby village. As so often, his visit to her ended in an argument and with her showing him the door. Although Bodo is not an alcoholic, and rarely drank too much beer, he did so on this occasion. He only stopped after midnight, when the bars closed. Not being near the place where he had his apartment, and owning no car, he decided in his drunken stupor, to find a place to sleep. He found it in the wooden shed that served as a temporary office of the city transit company; that he had to crawl through a window to get inside, didn't bother him.

In the morning, Bodo awoke before anybody entered the office. Looking for a cigarette to smoke, he rifled through some drawers, and there found two signed checks in the amount of 1,500 *deutschmarks* (about $1,000) each, on which so far no recipient had been designated. He took them.

It was still so early in the morning that no buses were running. Bodo, who never in his life had driven a bus before, went into the first one he saw next to the building, found the key, and started it. But having no idea how the gears worked, he had to read the instructions first. After he thought he had learned enough, he drove the vehicle from the lot.

To his surprise, people who had been wanting to board the first bus of the day were already waiting at the regular bus stops, and when he had to stop for a traffic light, some tried to enter it. Someone asked, "Are you going to Anklam?," a city some ten miles away. Bodo answered yes.

"You had better change the sign in front!" was the answer.

Bodo went out to see what it said. Anklam was only half visible. He changed the sign so that the destination was clearly visible. While climbing back again into the bus, he put on the driver's cap that was lying next to the seat.

A problem arose with the collection of payments. Having taken the bus only to get home, and without any larceny in mind, Bodo could nevertheless not refuse to accept the fares the passengers offered him. On the other hand, he had no change on his person. But people were both honest and helpful. They thought Bodo was a new bus driver who merely didn't know the ropes. So, without really wanting to, he collected quite a few *deutschmarks*. Reaching Anklam he parked the bus near the railroad station and went on his way.

Later that day, he went to the bank on which the "found" checks had been drawn, and cashed one. Then he again checked into one of the better hotels in the area, and lived it up for a week or so. When the money ran out, he went back to the very same bank to cash the second check, and was promptly arrested. That is how I met him in Bützow.

In the meantime, I have been informed that Bodo has been released from prison. A wise judge who is familiar with his life story put him on two years probation, with the obligation to stay away from his mother. I believe he will.

Earlier, I had mentioned that during our purchases in the commissary I had bought tea bags and honey, and I also had noted that we had no hot water in the cells. How were we able to "brew" tea or coffee for our afternoon siestas when no guards could be called for hot water? Well, the prisoners of almost every cell had hidden somewhere a device that for some reason was called a "*Fuchs*" (fox). It consisted of a piece of electrical extension cord with the plug still attached, and the other ends of the two wires cleared of insulation. Then the prisoners manufacture (without tools!) a device consisting of two small metal plates tied together with thread pulled from bed sheets and between which a piece of plastic, usually part of a throw-away razor, is sandwiched (so that the plates do not touch). Then, all one has to do is to drill one hole (again without tools!) into each of the metal plates, pull a blank wire of the extension cord through each hole, fasten them somewhat by twisting, and an immersion water heater for immediate use, is ready. Depending on how well the device is made, and upon the quality of the metal, one can bring a cup of water to boiling heat in less than a minute.

The prison employees obviously knew that most of the cells "owned" one of the "foxes," and they made it their business to discover the ingenious hiding places the prisoners had discovered. When a "fox" was found it was confiscated and thrown into the trash. I found this childish game stupid. Would it not have been better for the prison to allow the inmates to purchase such *"Tauchsieders"* as they are available in the German stores, and thereby prevent the frequent power outages that occurred because "foxes" had been improperly made and blew the fuses?

During my stay at Bützow our cell lost about two or three "foxes" through confiscation, usually because one of the prisoners was careless in hiding it before we went for our daily walk. But as a rule we were not without boiling water for more than half a day. The metal for the "foxes" usually came from the top of cans. Extension cords were widely used for radios and television sets, and could be bought in the commissary.

For reasons never clear to me, we were not able to own nail clippers. Myself being very fastidious about having my finger nails relatively short, it bothered me that I had not been able to cut them for several weeks. Later I requested unnecessary visits to the infirmary, using the excuse of a headache as a cover story, so that I might ask one of the nurses for the use of a pair of nail clippers.

Sometime in December, anticipating my release, I asked for new underwear during our weekly exchange of these items. The prisoner in charge of giving out the laundry wondered aloud why it had to be new underwear.

I laughed, "because I am going to take it back to America!"

"Why would you want to have this in America?" he asked in

return.

"As a souvenir!"

"You'll never get it out of here," said he, while he gave me a new set of long cotton underwear of good quality which had formerly been used by the Communist "East" German Army. Well, I now have these pieces of clothing in Pensacola, and in cold winter months that lie ahead it will come in handy; a reminder of the deep freeze cold that I experienced in the German state of Mecklenburg-Vorpommern in late 1995.

In the future, when the Schmidts have guests over for dinner, the *Kaffee und Kuchen* (coffee and cake) afterward will be served for them on what we now call our "prison china." Shortly before I was going to return to America, my wife and I had visited the famous Villeroy & Boch porcelain factory, whose original plant is located in a former Benedictine Abbey in the Saarland, not far from where I was born. There we purchased a beautiful china set to be used for coffee, tea, and dessert, that would match the dinner china we had already.

Since the factory doesn't ship abroad (except to their own representatives all over the world, obviously), we had no choice but to package the china as well as we could so that I could take it with me aboard the plane. And it so happened, that this china set was in my baggage when I was arrested, and accompanied me during my involuntary travels through the various German prisons. Idiotically, there were numerous times when I had to unpack the china piece by piece when some overzealous (West) German policeman or woman thought that I might smuggle dope, guns, or files into their prisons.

While the heavier part of my luggage made its way across Germany as railroad freight, I saw to it that most of the time I personally carried the china from prison bus to cell and vice versa, and when I finally arrived in Bützow I was certain that not a piece was broken.

And so it happened that the box with the china was among the ten (!) pieces of luggage which I had to stow in my attorney's car when in the evening of the January 4, 1996 he picked me up from the gate at Bützow penitentiary. This inordinate amount of luggage (that had grown to such proportions while I was imprisoned, and among which was the typewriter, radio, and the boxes with hundreds of letters I had received), was also the reason why I could not just take a train when I made my way back to the Saarland, and instead had to rent a car.

A week later I was on a plane back to America, and as was intended from the start, the Villeroy & Boch porcelain that had 'survived' the German prisons was safe and sound in the overhead compartment of the Boeing 747. Not a piece was broken or damaged when we unpacked it in Pensacola. Is it any wonder that henceforth we call this set our "prison china"?

Before I close this chapter on the conditions inside Bützow, I would like to mention the books available through the prison library.

A prisoner was allowed two books a week, which he first had to select from a list of all the books available that "made the rounds" so to say, in the prison. It was wise to request a much larger number of books since there was no assurance that the volumes one really wanted were still available.

It is my guess that the the Bützow prison library consisted of approximately 4,500 books, most of them paper backs, and the bulk of them were novels. There were relatively few books in foreign languages; some of them in English, but not one title that interested me.

Among the non-fiction books in the catalog, I discovered numerous works by Communist authors that seemingly were never requested by inmates, but to my great surprise I found some works pertaining to German-America; for instance, the biography of probably the most famous "1848 immigrant," Carl Schurz, and also the memoirs by Curtis B. Dall, president Franklin Delano Roosevelt's one-time son-in-law.

My most interesting observation about the Bützow books had to do with works pertaining to the heroism of German soldiers in World War II. No matter how often I asked for one, I never was able to get one of these war books. They always seemed to have been in transit or having been requested by another prisoner.

Toward the end of my incarceration, one of the prisoners with whom I had had more personal contact than with others, was appointed the librarian, and I asked him about these perpetually unavailable books.

His answer was surprising. It seems that prisoners liked these German war stories and documentary books (for instance, *The History of the German Navy in World War II*), so much that they had managed to take them along while being transferred to another prison, or upon their release. At any rate, almost none of the World War II books were still in the library system. I take this fact as evidence of the subconscious patriotism of the "East" Germans. In forty years of Communist rule they had not been able to read such books, and now they were making up for it.

With Friends Like These...

I had been in Bützow penitentiary for about three months when a prison official whom I regarded as the most professional and incorruptible of all those I had met at the prison, asked me to come to his office when we returned from our daily *Freistunde*. I could see that he was visibly upset.

After I had closed the door, the good man showed me printed matter (by the looks of it a fax message), which I immediately recognized as an information letter coming from the HSDC, the "Hans Schmidt Defense Committee." The date on the letter was November 14, 1995, and it was written under the byline of someone named "Danylo Dyatel," obviously a pseudonym.

I noted that some of the sentences on the HSDC-letter had been highlighted, and reading them, I was not surprised that the official was angry and upset, for in his hand he also held a German translation of the most pregnant one of these passages:

"The 29-page-long charges against H. Schmidt were slipped under his prison cell door two weeks ago...."

(*"Die 29-seitige Anklageschrift wurde H. Schmidt vor zwei Wochen zugestellt, indem man sie ihm einfach unter der Zellentür zuschob"*).

Reading this nonsense, I was flabbergasted. Why would anybody write such an untruth? As was his duty, the official asked me whether I had anything to do with the invention and broadcasting of this claim. Naturally, I could only tell him that I had had no prior knowledge of it and that it could not have come from me, although technically it was possible to smuggle messages out of the prison.

The warden was visibly relieved when he heard that, and I knew that he believed me. But he still was curious to know what could be the reason for someone in America to relate such foolishness.

Since he was in possession of the entire November 14 letter (that seemingly had been faxed to a great number of people, and especially the news media, in the United States), I was able to translate some other sentences for the official that proved to both of us that the writer of this message was either crazy or mean-spirited. There was for instance the claim that I had "extolled" prison life, and that I had said "life (in prison) is good." Both this warden and I knew that I would never utter such silliness, since we had held a private conversation on the matter several weeks before, during which we both had agreed that in the future, better ways ought to be found to deal with professional criminals, and average citizens who had merely transgressed against the law.

Re-reading the two page information letter of November 14th 1995, I came to the firm conclusion that the entire matter was not *"kosher."* I could only envision what would have happened if instead of this nice, highly professional official I dealt with in Bützow, there would have been one of the holier-than-thou fanatics that sometimes can be found in responsible positions in a prison system (including in the United States). What if for some reason someone like that would have taken a dislike to me due to my principles and politics?

The delivery of letters and especially of official papers was always very properly handled at the Bützow penitentiary. The guards bringing such things to the prisoners *always* unlocked the cell doors, and *always* called the name of the prisoner to whom the letter or document was addressed. Reading the translation of the HSDC claim, a prison official could easily have assumed that I was the originator of the lie and that it was my intention to besmirch the reputation of all the people working at this penal institution.

But for my good relationship with most of the officials and guards at the prison, it could have transpired that, as a result of this letter by "Danylo Dyatel" of the HSDC, I might have ended up in the "hole" of the prison, a dark, cold cell on the ground floor where intransigent prisoners were placed, and where all privileges were withheld. Because of some stupid, malicious statement written in America, there was the distinct possibility that for weeks I could have received and written no letters, that I would have had no reading matter at all, and no radio, no television, no company, no showers, no fresh underwear and bed linen and towels, no daily *Freistunde* so necessary for my health. But perhaps that is what "Danylo Dytel" really wanted?

Who is "Danylo"?

Returning to the United States, I found a mountain of letters and faxes that to this day I have been unable to wade through. But it did not take me long to discover that the November 14th HSDC information letter had been written by someone whom I shall henceforth identify only as "Dr. X."

Before I go into this dismal subject matter, I must emphatically state however, that all the other good people and volunteers of the "Hans Schmidt Defense Committee" had nothing to do with the shenanigans perpetrated by one (malicious?) individual.

They could not possibly know what had transpired behind the scenes. For sure, some had noticed that something was wrong, but there was always the honest concern for my personal welfare (I am grateful to all people who worried about my fate and prayed for my well-being), and since it *looked* as if the HSDC was *the* only organization fighting for my freedom, many of these good persons put their doubts to rest, while the battle for my release was waged.

Due to the fact that I was (purposely) prevented from

communicating at any length with my wife and other relatives for several months, and because I could not even exchange confidential letters with my lawyer for the first five weeks of my incarceration, I could not get a clear picture of the developments in America, and what was being done on behalf of my release. I knew that time was on my side, but I also realized that it would take weeks or months before the groundswell of demand for my freedom would gain such a momentum that the pressure would be felt by both Washington and Bonn.

I assessed my situation thus: immediately after my arrest, Jewish officials at the U.S. State Department had proclaimed to all the world that my case was an internal German matter. This meant that no speedy release (i.e., within a few days or a week) could be anticipated. And, once the *Haftprüfung* (examination for continued reasons of detention) of September 5th had passed without any hope of discharge, I definitely had to consider a longer involuntary stay.

I knew that by the time most of my friends and co-fighters in the United States, in other words, the entire *true* right-wing of the American political spectrum, would hear of my arrest, their September magazines and newsletters would either be at the printer or being readied for mailing. I also surmised (correctly) that the American news media would, due to Jewish influence and control, try to prevent wide-scale reporting of my arrest.

In other words, there was not going to be any officially orchestrated outrage such as we have seen in similar cases when the arrested person was a Jew or someone beholden to Zionist interests.

An American Jewish boy who in Singapore painted graffiti on buildings and was sentenced to a few lashes on his behind, received the wholehearted verbal support of the President of the

United States, but a former German soldier named Hans Schmidt, who in the name of freedom of expression had written skeptically about Allied propaganda tenets of World War II, surely deserves everything that is coming to him. (Imagine what would happen, if it were otherwise!)

At the earliest, I could expect widespread mention of my situation in the essentially clandestine "right-wing" press in the October issues of their publications, and that meant a *beginning* of concerted efforts in my behalf about the middle of that month, and with an ever widening circle of patriotic Americans who had become sufficiently upset to write to newspapers, to the president, the State Department, their Congressman and many international organizations. Later I discovered that people from all over the world had written to German officials such as Chancellor Kohl, President Herzog, the Bonn minister of justice, and others. In the end it was this avalanche of protest letters that showed the German vassals of Washington and world Jewry that my arrest had backfired.

But before the letters by American (mostly Christian) patriots were written, there were the actions by the HSDC to contend with, and some of these actions undoubtedly had also made an impact. At any rate, they had undoubtedly caused the Bonn stooges to reconsider their foolhardy decisions about my person. For instance, relatively soon after my arrest, a few stalwart American defenders of liberty had gotten together and distributed so-called "Travelers Alert" flyers at a few of the major American airports (New York, Newark, NJ, and others). Leaflets such as the one reproduced on p. 122.

These activists had made it their business to concentrate on people whose planes were just leaving for Germany. Needless to say, they caused great consternation among the travelers and the airplane crews.

With Friends Like These...

! TRAVELERS ALERT !
all travelers to
GERMANY

Travelers to and from Germany are now being arrested at German airports if they have expresed themselves, even in the remote past, in speech or in writing which is construed as "illegal" according to German Federal Penal Code Statute 130, Article 3, regarding "defamation." This retroactive statute does not define this crime either explicitly or exactly. It's interpretation is subject to the whim and biases of the German Prosecutors.

!BEFORE YOU ENTER GERMANY!

Call the German Embassy at 202-298-4000 for a list of words, thoughts and literature now forbidden in Germany. Demand that all forbidden words and ideas be posted at both German airports and foreign airports with departures to Germany.

THE PENALTY FOR IMPORTING PRINTED MATERIAL CONTAINING ILLEGAL WORDS AND SUBJECTS IS THREE MONTHS TO FIVE YEARS IMPRISONMENT. THERE IS NO BAIL AND NO PARDON IN GERMANY FOR FREE SPEECH PERPETRATORS.

President Clinton will not intercede on your behalf as he did with Harry Wu! Americans are now being imprisoned in Germany for speaking or writing on politically incorrect topics or using forbidden words.

LATEST ARREST

U.S. citizen, Hans Schmidt's name was entered in European airport computers because of his use of two proscribed adjectives; that's right, illegal adjectives! In a letter of November 1994 which he wrote while in America and which subsequently ended up in the hands of government authorities. Retired businessman Hans Schmidt, 68, from Pensacola, Florida, while returning from a family reunion was arrested at Frankfort airport on Aug. 9, 1995 and will remain in jail without bail until his trial in Schwerin, formerly East Germany. Contact the German embassy at the above telephone number and also contact the U.S. Department of State, Country Desk, Germany at 202-647-2155. Refer to the Hans Schmidt free speech case.

THIS INFORMATION IS PROVIDED BY THE
INTERNATIONAL COALITION FOR A DEMOCRATIC GERMANY
FUNDED BY THE HANS SCHMIDT DEFENSE COMMITTEE

At one time a head stewardess of Lufthansa, the German airline, stormed out of the plane shortly before take-off and berated the pickets for inconveniencing the airline. To this day I am very grateful to such brave activists.

Ironically, since at first we had no direct and speedy communication with each other, (even when the letters arrived "normally," it never took less than two months for me to receive an answer to my questions), I could only assume that my wife had given approval for the "Hans Schmidt Defense Committee" to operate.

The name certainly indicated that it was the sole and official organization working on behalf of my freedom. On the other hand, almost all my relatives and friends who heard of the HSDC or had been contacted by it, assumed that it was created with *my* assent.

Learning of the "Travelers Alert" action, and similar efforts, I at first did not notice anything wrong until I received faxes mailed out under the HSDC auspices that indicated erratic behavior.

Some of these fax messages claimed things that were absolutely untrue, as the November 14th fax message by "Danylo Dyatel" demonstrates.

Being a stickler for the truth, I was wondering from whence these people (by that I meant the persons whom I assumed to be in charge of the HSDC) had received their facts.

Still, being the eternal optimist, I ascribed certain shortcomings to the pressures of time and other circumstances under which everyone had to operate.

I would never have imagined that someone would go to such lengths and *purposely* create such mischief as I discovered when I returned to Pensacola. To this day I wonder what *really* motivates such people.

My first alarm bells went off when I discovered that the person who was (seemingly) solely responsible for all the HSDC faxes and messages I had received at the prison, had been demanding that my lawyer withdraw from the case. [1]

"Dr. X," who to this day I have never met, had taken it upon himself to claim that Mr. Herrmann did not defend me in the right way, and he demanded (!) therefore that another attorney, someone from the United States (!) should be hired.

Throughout my ordeal I had the greatest confidence in Hajo Herrmann's abilities. He always did his best under the circumstances, and in my case he often went beyond the call of duty on my behalf. I knew that due to the great distance between the city of Düsseldorf, where Mr. Herrmann's office is located, and Schwerin, where the trial was to be held, eventually another local attorney would have to be called in on the case, but I had left both the timing of this event, as well as the selection of the co-defender eventually chosen, (Dr. Günter Eisenecker, a lawyer who has offices in Central Germany), entirely up to Hajo Herrmann.

Dr. X's (alleged?) dissatisfaction with both Mr. Herrmann and my wife, practically the only persons with whom I had direct contact once any permissible contact was possible, derived from the fact that news about my case was so extremely sparse. For weeks there was no news to report. The mills of justice (or, in my case, I should perhaps write "injustice"), did grind slowly. Not only here in the United States but more so in Germany. The prosecutor, for instance, had promised my attorney on September 5th that he would have the indictment

---

[1] The matter of the faxes sent to me at Bützow prison shows how far removed from reality "Dr. X" really was. He ought to have realized that they would not be given to me on arrival. The translation and censorship of all incoming and outgoing mail was the task of the court. Sometimes I was advised by a prison official amenable to me that a fax had arrived, but then it would still be three weeks or more until I received it.

ready in three weeks, and that the trial could commence soon thereafter.

However, it took this official exactly twice that time to finish the document, and a few days more to get it to both myself and to my attorney.

At any rate, the interference by strangers like Dr. X into the relationship between my attorney and myself bothered me greatly. At the time I did not realize that the nice and well-meaning volunteers and supporters of the HSDC had absolutely no control or knowledge of the behind-the-scenes maneuverings that occurred surreptitiously in their name. (After my return I discovered that Dr. X had also used the names of other volunteers without their consent.)

In a previous chapter I have told how in Pensacola my wife suddenly stood practically alone when she had her hands full with the production of the newsletters, the multitude of new contacts, and her constant worries about me. For months she was under immense pressure, and there was hardly a day when she did not work fourteen or more hours.

It was then that the malice of Dr. X came to the fore. I have read numerous faxes which Dr. X mailed to my home during the most critical months after my arrest. They are insulting, demeaning and downright obnoxious. On some days when my wife had just gone to bed at 2 a.m., she was awakened at 4 a.m.(!) by a call from Dr. X who ordered her to get up and immediately duplicate one of his ubiquitous faxes and mail these messages to a slew of newspapers, news services or officials. It was psycho-terror in its worst form.

What, in my opinion, upset Dr. X most was the fact that my wife had refused to turn over to him the mailing lists of our German-American organization.

He claimed that the HSDC had a right to get these lists

because it was--in his words--absolutely necessary for the committee to contact all of our readers and supporters directly. Writing these lines in the safety and tranquility of our home in Pensacola a few months after my release from prison, I am convinced that our *entire* German-American effort would by now be destroyed had our address lists fallen into these wrong hands.

One thing is clear: Dr. X would have written similar outrageous letters to all our friends and supporters as I discovered in our files recently. He would be claiming things that had no factual basis, telling untruths such as the ones mentioned before, and creating further dissension wherever he could. [2]

There is nothing worse for a political organization than lack of leadership and commitment at the top. (And that is what it would have looked like to our friends. Unless they read this book, even the best and most generous volunteers and supporters of the HSDC will have no idea what really happened).

I have mentioned that I have never met Dr. X personally. I also never saw a picture of him. But reading his letters and knowing of his behavior, I am able to come to some judgment. I know that the man is not a German. This fact itself should have been cause for his *not* wanting to try to play a major and *public* role in my affair. Instead, he seemed a man possessed-- pushing himself into the head position--to take credit for actions that had

---

[2] As a result of being active in politics for years and having observed similar destructive developments in other organizations, I was adamant in frequently voicing my intent that nobody was ever to get their hands on our mailing lists. We are in a political fight. We are the minority battling the people in power. We cannot afford to have our trusted friends and supporters harassed by the system or its agents. Immediately in the wake of my arrest, I stated emphatically that only essential information was to be given to the news organizations. I did so mainly to impress upon my wife the importance of not speaking with reporters (for reasons cited earlier) *and to guard the privacy of our mailing lists.* Thankfully, she understood.

been initiated and accomplished by others, and to invent stories that had no basis in fact.

Indicative of what transpired behind the scenes, but of which few people were (or could have been) aware, is this letter faxed by one of my brothers to Dr. X on 26 October 1995:

Dear Dr. X:

My wife told me of your phone call, and I received your fax for translation. Unfortunately, your unprofessional behavior toward my brother's wife Roswitha leaves me no choice but to ask you to refrain from contacting me. Although I understand that your intentions may be honorable, in my opinion your work is ineffective and counterproductive. Your behavior toward Roswitha is despicable.

I request that you immediately stop writing, faxing or calling Roswitha. Writing to her, "you do not want Mr. (the name of an American lawyer suggested by Dr. X, -HS), to take over the defense because you hope that Hans gets the full five years, while you enjoy life," was just the icing on the cake in a multitude of such comments. [3]

You should be ashamed to put Hans' wife under such psycho-terror. You are entitled to your opinion but it is not your place to

---

[3] The story of this famous American lawyer Dr. X *allegedly* was able to interest in my case, deserves special mention. The gentleman in question is a former high-ranking U.S.Government official, and known for his espousal of liberal causes. I was totally flabbergasted when I heard that he might want to assist in my case. Dr. X however asserted that the firing of Mr. Herrmann was a prerequisite to this lawyer coming to my aid. Obviously, I could not accede to this demand. I had no objection to the American attorney co-defending me with Mr. Herrmann, but I preferred to deal with the latter. Not having close enough contact with me to hear my opinion, my wife and daughter made numerous calls to this lawyer's office in New York and asked to speak with him directly. He was never in, and did not return their calls. When once he inadvertently answered the phone himself, he could not even remember receiving Federal Express mail from my wife, and asked her for more information. He promised to let her know the following week whether he would take the case but no call from him ever came. So much for this "excellent" contact of Dr. X.

call Hans' lawyer a 'nobody', or his behavior 'criminal.' Your comments about Mr. (the American attorney, HS) 'taking over the case' shows me that you know very little about the ability of an American lawyer to operate in Germany. Your letters are always based on lots of money that Roswitha is supposed to have received. Another one of your letters, threatening the halt of activities of the "Defense Committee" if Roswitha does not send $4,500, is psychological extortion. When you started this, I supported you and you implied that people will be there to pay and do the fundraising. Now you are talking about being $4,500 in debt, and you want to put pressure on the wife of Hans to part with the little money she has for a 'debt' that no one authorized! I don't want a committee organized in the name of my brother Hans associated with any debt.

Unless you immediately start acting in a professional manner, I request that you refrain from any activity in behalf of Hans. I will forward a copy of this letter (and of your letter to Roswitha) to Hans, and will recommend to him to distance himself from you and your activities.

Again, I request that you refrain from any contact or communication with Roswitha Schmidt and myself immediately!"

Thus my brother's letter. Note that it was faxed to Dr. X almost three weeks *before* the latter sent out that notorious fax message of November 14th. The good doctor surely did not give up easily, did he? Dr. X did not only imply that my wife wanted me to stay five years in prison "so that she can enjoy herself," but in one of his messages to her he also referred to Mr. Herrmann, one of the most honorable persons I have ever had the pleasure to meet, as her "sugar daddy." All this at a time when Roswitha was under almost unbearable pressure anyway.

One of Dr. X's brainstorms was to ask my wife to drop everything in Pensacola (among other responsibilities, Roswitha had to see to it that the readers of our organization's publications received the monthly newsletters regularly and on time), and come to Washington. There, she was supposed to visit all the Senators and Representatives, (plus the offices of the major news organizations) and plead on my behalf.

Dr. X obviously has no idea how things in Washington really work. He must have been under the impression that just because Mrs. Wu, the wife of the Chinese-American dissident Harry Wu who at that time was also making news, had found open doors wherever she went (even at the White House), the same courtesy would be extended to the wife of a German-American freedom fighter. [4]

Later, by the time my wife and I had our brief, weekly telephone conversation, she asked me what I thought of the

---

[4] Having been active in Washington between 1985 and our move to Florida eight years later, I had no illusions as to what one could accomplish there. At one time, both my wife and I had been invited to a German-American affair at the White House. Shortly before the event, I received a telegram informing me that there had been a mistake--we were summarily disinvited.

At another time, there were Congressional hearings on the relations between the U.S. and Germany. Immediately upon being informed, I requested that two men of our organization (the only organization in the land politically fighting for German-American interests), be allowed to testify. This request was turned down because there were allegedly too many speakers already. We went anyway. And who were those who had been permitted to testify? All Jews! The story of the German-American Friendship Garden is even more laughable-- few people know of it, but it is located on Constitution Avenue, in a direct line between the White House and the Washington Monument. It was supposed to have been dedicated by President Reagan on German-American Day, October 6, 1988. Although this had been planned far in advance, suddenly the head of an obscure African republic arrived, and the U.S. President was needed that day for an official state dinner.

The Germans-Americans, accommodating as always, then agreed to move their ceremony a day ahead. For a little while everything looked fine, but then with so short a notice that no further changes were possible, the *Oberjuden* suddenly needed Reagan on that particular day for the laying of the cornerstone of the Holocaust Museum--at a time when there was nothing but a huge hole in the ground and the actual construction was months away!

idea. I was adamantly against it.

To this day I am certain that not one of the important Congressmen or newspeople would have dared to see her. I am certain that everybody in the capital knew at whose behest or in whose interest I was locked up.

Dr. X also claimed to have made tremendous progress with such organizations as Amnesty International and the Human Rights Watch.

Before she knew better, my wife had sent fax after fax to such groups not only in the United States but also in Europe, asking for their help.

The polite but declining answers sometimes took up to three months to reach Pensacola. Some arrived even after I was back in the United States.

Certainly, these organizations profess to assist freedom fighters and political dissidents wherever they are, but absolutely *not* if their "crime" is in any way connected with any criticism of Jews; that is, if it was connected with alleged "anti-Semitism." Everybody in the world who at this time in history has any position of influence knows who is "the sacred cow."

Since I am always forward looking, and I am also the type of person not to try to alter things that happened in the past (obviously an impossibility), I had no intention of wasting too many hours on the schemes of Dr. X.

It struck me that his actions were entirely commensurate with someone who is Jewish: the tremendous need to be in the foreground; the telling of tall tales; the taking credit for the accomplishments of others; the conviction of his own superior intelligence, and last, but not least, the methods of psycho-terror he used against my wife. I had seen it all before.

There was one factor that interested me greatly in this regard. Just as Dr. X had claimed fantastic victories in the battle for my freedom that either were nonexistent, or I knew for sure that the credit must go to others who must remain unknown, so had he also asserted that he had been influential in obtaining the freedom of John Demjanjuk. [5]

Having personally met a person whom I knew had done more for Demjanjuk's freedom than almost anyone else, I asked this individual's opinion of Dr X. The answer did not surprise me: "That guy did more harm than good."

Hopefully, this book will be read by many American patriots and defenders of the endangered Aryan peoples. The detailed account of this matter in this chapter may prevent some unnecessary grief and consternation for some other dissident in the future. There is more than one Dr. X waiting for an opportunity to sow confusion, and destroy what others have built up over the years.

In the beginning of December 1995 I had been incarcerated for four months. Virtually everybody at the Bützow penitentiary was getting ready for Christmas (although most of the inmates and probably also the guards had never seen the inside of a church, they nevertheless celebrated Christmas in the traditional German way). Both my lawyers and myself tried our utmost to arrange for a *Urlaub auf Ehrenwort*, a short leave of absence

---

[5] John Demjanjuk was the hapless Ukrainian-American auto worker from Ohio who, during World War II, was a Soviet soldier, and had been captured by the Germans, only to be impressed into the Wehrmacht. In the 1980s the OSI, the notorious, Jewish prosecuting office within the U. S. Justice Department, fingered Demjanjuk as "Ivan the Terrible," a brutal guard at the German-run Treblinka internment camp in Poland, where allegedly 800,000 Jews had been murdered. Demjanjuk was stripped of his U.S. citizenship, delivered to Israel, and there sentenced to death in a show trial. He would have been hanged but for some brave defenders in the United States and Israel, who at the last minute were able to prove that "Ivan the Terrible" was someone else. John Demjanjuk is now back in the United States, a free man, but still being harassed by fanatical Zionists, and it is doubtful that he either received an apology or financial compensation from the United States Government for his Israeli imprisonment.

where I would give my word of honor to return, so that I could celebrate Christmas with my mother in the Saarland. She had just turned 91 years of age, and with all her six children being residents and citizens of the United States, she was quite alone. Moreover, she had recently been released from a short hospital stay that had been necessary due to a recurring heart condition, possibly aggravated by what had happened to me.

There was a slight possibility that I might spend about ten days at my ancestral German home beginning just before Christmas, until the day after New Year's. Unfortunately, "friends" or a "friend" in the United States thwarted these plans. Here's how the chance for my Christmas leave was sabotaged:

Early enough so that our enemies could act upon it, a notice appeared in the *Spotlight*, a populist weekly newspaper published in Washington, D.C. and widely read among right-wingers.

The *Spotlight* announced that I was to be released on bail before Christmas! Needless to say, the *Spotlight* is also diligently read by the enemies of freedom, and it did not take long for them to put pressure on the Bonn Government and its judiciary to refuse me a Christmas leave as well as any possibility of my full release into freedom. The *OberJuden* are fully aware of the profound significance Christmas has for the Germans, and these top Jews demonstrated their power and vindicative hate by preventing my humanitarian release at that time.

To this day I am certain that but for the erroneous notice in the *Spotlight*, I could have celebrated Christmas with my mother in my boyhood home in the Saarland, and thereby have given her the joy of having one of her children with her on this greatest of all traditional German holidays.

The *Spotlight* is not entirely to blame. This newspaper had printed numerous helpful articles about my case soon after my arrest, and did not relent until I was back safely in the United States. A large number of people who had written to the various governments and international organizations (and also to me in prison) were *Spotlight* readers. The paper's editors, having been notified by a "good" source (and seemingly close ally of mine) of my supposed, impending release before Christmas, fell for the story and printed the "good news" without checking with my family first.

Needless to say, I was more than upset about the idiotic or malicious person who had initiated the *Spotlight* report. As far as this person was concerned, the message had been pure invention since my lawyers and myself had kept our efforts to ourselves.

The minor German judicial civil servants who would have permitted the leave of absence most certainly did not have any contacts in America. Upon my return to the United States I tried to discover who had given the *Spotlight* the phony story. I was not surprised when all the indices pointed to Dr. X.

There is only one question to be answered regarding this dismal chapter: did this individual act on his own, driven only by the demons within himself, or had he from the start been an agent for our enemies? His actions obviously point to the latter, but in the end I will have to concede that we may never discover the truth. Gratefully, the damage done by this one man has been overcome, and somewhat the wiser, we can all work toward a better and more sane future.

The Hostage Taking

After the politically inspired *Filzung* (general inspection and thorough search) on the weekend of August 25th, 1995, the mood of the Bützow prisoners experienced a noticeable downswing.

It was not that the inmates had objected to the search as such. They knew where they were, and why they were imprisoned, and most of them realized that it was the duty of the prison personnel to prevent escapes, to remove items from the cells that could be used as weapons and to see to it that there was neither alcohol or dope present.

But according to everybody to whom I had spoken in the aftermath of the search, the green-uniformed policemen had gone too far in invading the privacy which prisoners seem to cherish more than people on the outside.

The gratuitous defacing of family pictures and the groping by the policemen into legitimately purchased food containers for contraband, made everybody's blood boil.

But slowly things began to get back to normal. A month after the *Filzung,* the relationship between most of the prisoners and the regular guards seemed to resume its previous state of mutual respect. Each tolerated the other and here and there I again saw bantering going on, whose main purpose seemed to be to show that "look, we are humans too."

During the days while the riot policemen were occupying Bützow on Geil's orders, everything was in disarray and abnormal. Visiting hours were curtailed or had been called off altogether; we could take no showers, nor were we able to exchange our bed linens and towels. All these things are *very* important to prisoners.

The escaped "Rumanians" did not have any assistance from

any of the German prisoners at Bützow. The latter therefore resented the fact that they should suffer because of some foreigners whom they had not even known.

The October 3rd holiday is the newest one for the Germans. It was proclaimed in the aftermath of the reunification, when the Bonn Government thought that such a day was necessary so that those who never before had done anything to see Germany reunited, could later brag about their efforts.[1]

In 1995, this day fell on a Tuesday. As was to be expected, we were on a holiday schedule, and except for the morning and evening roll calls, our three meals a day and the daily *Freistunde,* nothing else happened; no mail, no newspapers, no visitors, no showers, no visits to the infirmary, and for those who had been scheduled to go there, no purchases at the commissary. Furthermore, the prison personnel were on a holiday schedule and that meant fewer guards on duty than normal.

It was already dark and some hours after the evening meal on October 3rd, when we heard shouting and screaming outside, just below our cell windows. Mike, the younger of the three of us, immediately climbed high up on the window, and gave us a running account of what he saw happening.

It seemed that several prisoners, fellows unknown to us, and possibly hard-core criminals from cell block A, had two or

---

[1] By all means, November 9th should have become the most revered German holiday since it was on that day in 1989 when, by what I consider divine intervention, the Berlin Wall fell. This set not only German reunification but a world-wide change in motion. Alas, Nov. 9 had been a holiday during the Hitler era (to commemorate the 1923 *putsch*). Furthermore, on Nov. 9, 1938 the so-called *Kristallnacht* occurred, when synagogues and Jewish businesses were attacked. It was for this reason that the leaders of the present, *very tiny* Jewish minority in Germany vetoed declaring Nov. 9 a holiday. Instead the Bonn vassals selected Oct. 3, the day in 1990 when the reunification agreement between the BRD "West" and Communist "East" Germany was signed. Unfortunately for the people in power, this date has no deep meaning for the German people. The day is largely regarded as just an extra day off from work.

three guards on the ground, and were assaulting one of them, using some kind of hatchet in the process. This guard was bleeding heavily.

Throughout the commotion the strong search lights remained lit and after a time the guard was so motionless that Mike insisted the man had been killed. (The rumor that a guard had been killed lasted throughout the following day).

After a while we heard the assembly of forces outside of the prison walls, sirens of arriving ambulances and squad cars and the motor noise of heavy equipment that was brought into position. One could also hear the chatter of unseen men talking on walkie-talkies. Outside of our cell doors nothing moved at all. There was dead silence. It was a complete lock-down.

My own fear was that a German "Attica" was in the making. I remember that situation of about a quarter of a century ago clearly, when a few hardened criminals had taken over Attica prison in upstate New York, and in the ensuing counterattack by state police forces, which was ordered by then Governor Nelson Rockefeller, many guards and inmates were killed.

My concern was that here in Bützow, like then in Attica, the activist prisoners would open all the cell doors, force everybody out, and thereby make all inmates accessories to a crime. While the situation was deteriorating on the outside, we three cellmates spoke about such a possibility, and what we should do should it come to that. We prepared for the worst.

The entire episode lasted about five hours. Later we found out that two of the prisoners had taken several of the guards hostage during the evening roll call (about 7 p.m.), had grabbed their keys and then unlocked several other cells in order to free other prisoners. It was also rumored that the hostage-takers had asked for a get-away car, money and a helicopter, but I was never able to confirm this assertion. Prisons (and concentration camps) are

The Hostage Taking

virtual breeding grounds for the most incongruous rumors.

About fourteen days later, five Bützow inmates were brought before the court in Schwerin, where they were accused of taking hostages and causing serious injury to others. The accusation of attempted murder was dropped at the behest of a court-appointed doctor who stated that none of the injuries sustained by the guards were life threatening. All of the hostage-takers were transferred to other prisons and received additional prison time. It was related to us that the most heavily injured guard did not return to his job at the Bützow prison after he was discharged from the hospital.

I discovered that on the weekend when the *Filzung* occurred, one of the hostage takers had earlier been involved in a serious altercation with one of the injured guards. According to my information, at that time the prisoner had to be taken to the infirmary. However, I never found out whether this incident had a direct relation to the searching of the cells by the riot police. After everything was over, prison officials told newspaper reporters that the former incident had nothing to do with the latter. Few inmates would agree with that.

The hostage situation ended when a special team of riot police was brought to Bützow and with military precision and without the use of firearms, overwhelmed the hostage-takers in two minutes. For a few days afterward I noticed bloodstains on the concrete and near the doorways when we took our morning walks.

As a result of the Bützow hostage-taking, the name of this prison almost became a household word in Germany. Few newspapers failed to mention that it had been one of the most brutal places of incarceration during both the Third Reich and the Communist era. As a matter of fact, both regimes had used Bützow as a place of execution, and long-time prisoners told me that the *guillotine* that had been used to execute men condemned to death had been dumped into the nearby lake (seemingly after 1989). To this day one can see in front of the prison a monument to the Communists executed at Bützow during World War II (for treason, desertion, sabotage, etc.), but to the best of my knowledge there is no memorial stone for those (mostly innocent people) who lost their lives *after* the war, at the hands of the Communists, just because they were patriotic Germans.

My relatives and many friends in Germany were rightly concerned about my well-being when they heard on the evening news of the hostage episode and the (allegedly) dismal conditions at Bützow.

One of my co-fighters called the lady handling the *dpa* (Deutsche Presse Agentur, the German AP), and asked her why in conjunction with her report on the hostage-taking it was not mentioned that "an important German-American journalist" was being held in Bützow prison. Her answer? She doubted that this was of interest to the German population.

(Similarly, my very own hometown German newspaper, the *Saarbrücker Zeitung* never mentioned either my arrest nor later my "escape" from Germany. I wrote to them from Pensacola and asked sarcastically whether they are really afraid that I might take away the governor's [*Ministerpräsident's*] job from their crony, Oskar Lafontaine.)

Of the many reports on the Bützow penitentiary I have read in conjunction with the attack on the kidnapped guards, perhaps the most interesting was the one I discovered in the *Schweriner Volkszeitung* dated October 18th, 1995. It was written by their reporter, Michael Brackmann. Following, I will translate excerpts from Brackmann's article. I would like to caution readers however, to take some of the statements of this reporter

The Hostage Taking

with a grain of salt: it is a newspaper's business to paint a bleak picture. The very first lines provide the best indication of that:

A ghost wanders through Dreibergen prison (the local name of the Bützow penitentiary), a ghost of fear and uncertainty. Even after more than two weeks, the everyday life at the prison is under the spell of the hostage-taking that occurred on October 3. The guards tell us that they are still extra cautious; each one of their moves is well calculated. And the prisoners admit: "In here the mood gets hotter day by day." Here is the first report by any newspaper of what goes on inside the Bützow prison - - - this report was written with the assistance of both guards and prisoners.

The sirens call. It is six o'clock on a Monday morning. The guards are receiving orders from their superiors. Some do not wear ties as the regulations demand. They refuse to do so because a tie can be easily used to strangle a person. A drunken prisoner who is supposed to be put into Building 2, the jail inside the jail, does not have to wear his leg chains, the officer in charge decides. But the handcuffs remain.

Officer Diel is assigned to the A-block, where the hostage taking began, and where, according to the prison administration, too many hardened criminals are in one place. "

For us every day is like playing roulette with our lives," says Diel. All guards are working in two shifts of 12 hours each. There is a shortage of personnel everywhere.

The guards enter the cells equipped only with walkie-talkies. The count begins. On this day, all prisoners are in their cells and there are no holes in walls, nor missing steel bars on the windows. Breakfast follows.

Then the working details leave their cell blocks, some walk to the carpentry shop, others go to work on the plumbing. However, of the 130 inmates in A block, 80 do not work at all, some because they do not want to, others because there simply is no work available for them.

Somewhat later, all cell doors are opened, and many prisoners congregate in the hallway and talk to each other.[2]

Others ask for mail, still others want to make contact with their attorney or demand to be taken to the infirmary. One man, his face and hands full of tattoos, walks along the hallway carrying a chessboard on his head. "That fellow is ready to die," says one of the prisoners. "He is a goner."

One of the prisoners asks a guard to open one of the iron gates which intermittently hinder free access to other parts of the B block. These special enclosures are necessary in order to prevent larger congregations of prisoners, but it is precisely the sort of thing that creates bitterness among the inmates. One is never without the loud noise of heavy iron doors being locked and unlocked.

Geritt W. is in his cell. He has three more years to go until he can be free again. He is eating his main meal of the day: cabbage with sausage. "All the crap began with the *Filzung* in August," he exclaims. Before that the Rumanians had escaped. "They emptied all of our cells, removed the pictures from the walls, threw the bookshelves out, destroyed the houseplants, and broke an aquarium. Things like that create bad blood between inmates and the guards."

One official in charge of the prisoners agrees that during the search some of the policemen went too far, but then he added that some of the cells had been so filled up with furniture and personal belongings that the prison personnel had lost all overview. But after the removal of everything that had made the surroundings somewhat human, the four man cell now looks like a miserable hole. Four primitive cots, four lockers and the paint peeling from the walls - - - in spite of the color television set there is no resemblance to the hotel room atmosphere politicians like to complain about. Most of the other cells look like that also. Geritt adds: "In surroundings like that it is no wonder when some of the inmates turn crazy."

After lunch the prisoners in cell block A will be locked again in their cells for two hours. Gerrit knows that once in a while inmates come to blows. I can see that in the well-equipped sports center some

---

[2] This was not possible in the B block or wing, since the justice system sought to avoid the possibility of pre-trial detention prisoners exchanging information, if they were being held for the same crime.

of the inmates are steeling themselves for just such an eventuality. Their muscular, tattooed biceps provide a warning to those who want to tangle with them. It is no wonder that in Bützow muscle-building equipment is in great demand. "The stronger an inmate looks, the higher he moves in the prisoner hierarchy," explains one of the guards. After their exercises, the inmates go to the shower room which the prisoners have sarcastically named the "gas chamber." From twenty-five openings in the pipes along the ceiling spurts a steady stream of hot water. Everything smells old and moldy. I see lots of mildew. This is where all the inmates take their showers.

Fred K., a convicted bank robber, complains that the hygienic conditions at the prison are a catastrophe. He works in the laundry room. "Imagine, prisoners can exchange their underwear but once a week," he says. "I think that is a joke." He also complains about the prison personnel, most of whom held their jobs before the reunification (under the Communist regime). He admits that there is no physical mistreatment but if one complains then one gets punished psychologically, nevertheless. One of the persons in charge of an entire block doesn't accept that. "It is a lie!" he states flatly.

The boss of the B block told me that he fears for the worst if the stronger measures instituted after the escape of the Rumanians (and in conjunction with the *Filzung*) are not soon reversed. Another official states that over 65 more employees are needed to run the prison properly.

In one corner of the C-block I talk to a group of hardened criminals. One looks like he is drunk. Someone told me that the prisoners are brewing their own alcohol. There is nothing the prison administration can do about that.

"Here you can have anything," one of the inmates brags, "male prostitutes, marijuana, heroin -- you name it. Every second guard can be bribed."

As I talk about this to one of the officials, he finds these allegations absurd.

Later, after their twelve hours are over, the men of the day shift are preparing themselves to go home. They are happy that on this day nothing bad has happened. Their colleagues taking over for the night are now equipped with firearms, something that was not necessary before."

Reading the preceding German media report, one has to consider the source. Certainly in a prison with more than 600 prisoners and about 240 personnel there is some minor corruption, but I doubt that in Bützow it is as rampant as is depicted here. All the other allegations brought forth in the last part of the article read much worse than I believe it to be,. even in the A-block. Yes, I am sure, that some of the inmates, as wily as they are, and with lots of time on their hands, manage to brew their own alcohol. And certainly, with so many men thrown together, there must be some homosexuality going on. But pot and heroin freely available? I just don't believe it. I know that (in the absence of money) there was a constant trading of items and the greatest demand was for tobacco and coffee.

The idiocy of the *Filzung* of late August, and its repercussions is what needs to be emphasized. The *Filzung* took place all because some stupid politician wanted to enhance his own stature and further his own career.

As of this writing, the legislators of the State of Florida have voted to remove all weight-lifting equipment from Florida's state prisons *against the advice of many of the penal experts*. The stupidity of politicians (everywhere) never ceases to amaze me.

Examinations for Continued Reasons of Detention
--Haftprüfungen--

"HAFTPRÜFUNG" is a repetitive procedure, actually a judicial ruse by which, under the pretense of legality, a prisoner can theoretically be held, without trial, until he dies. (The German justice system does not know the writ of *habeas corpus* which in the United States is widely used to prevent illegal imprisonment, and to keep the judges on their toes.) Perhaps a better and somewhat more cynical translation of the term *Haftprüfungen* might be "judicial interrogation of a prisoner to decide upon pretext what would appear to warrant his continued detention."

My first experience with *Haftprüfung* took place in the Justice building in Schwerin, about thirty miles southwest of Bützow, on September 5th, 1995. I was sitting in a small court room next to my lawyer, facing a female judge, Frau Freitag. Behind us were chairs for the prosecutor, Herr Kollarz, and a couple of guards who were there to insure that I did not escape. Behind the judge were a few rows of chairs for the press and visitors. They were sparsely occupied. The only other official in the room was the judge's assistant, a woman who seemed to take notes, but does not keep a verbatim record of the proceedings.

Judge Freitag: I looked at her. She was very young, surely not yet 30 - - - much too young, I thought, for her position. She was conventionally pretty. Her bland countenance was unrelieved by any trace of intellectual concentration, or of experience outside the juridical cocoon of the "Federal Republic." It offended me that a person so immature --- and necessarily amateurish--- was placed in judgment over a man well above twice her age, with far longer, and infinitely better, knowledge of the ways of men and the world--a young woman, not long out of school, empowered to render decisions that could affect him, and his family, for the rest of their lives!

Knowing the conditions in Germany, and being familiar with the mis-education Germans of Frau Freitag's generation have received at their universities, she could not possibly know what my story was all about, or realize that paragraphs 130 and 131 of the German law under which I was being held, were illegal statutes used to further the interests of the enemies of our people.

I was only half listening while Judge Freitag read the accusations against me as described in the arrest warrant. I knew it all by heart, having had a month to study it. At this moment I am much more interested in guessing the woman's first name. The Germans have a very curious system whereby civil servants sign and type only their surnames even on the most important documents, or, more often than not, permit only the typing of their surname under the text of a letter, and have some underling sign the paper simply as "i.A." (*"im Auftrag"*: in other words, "by order of..."), again only with a last name.

Note the letter by the Bonn Ministry of the Interior dated August 23, 1995 reprinted in translation in my chapter on the A.D.L., and published in the original in the appendix, for example.

A certain Judge Siegfried Meier for instance, will only sign "Meier," and nothing else. I wonder how this custom crept into the German bureaucracy. Could it be that the important people of the *Bundesrepublik* realize the illegality of their system and are already trying to pave the way to disavow responsibility for misdeeds for which many of them will be called to account someday?

Not having the slightest idea what could be Frau Freitag's first name, I wondered what first name would be suitable. She was blond and blue-eyed, and had a straight bearing. Naturally, a few old Germanic names came to my mind: Krimhild-- Gertrud --Edda--Helga--Kunegunde--Thusnelda? No, they couldn't be it. But looking at her good figure and envisioning her hair somewhat longer, I thought that Godiva would fit her best. Godiva Freitag. Not bad, and so I referred to her in conversations with others throughout my imprisonment.

The *Haftprüfung* of September 5th, 1995 was a sham. From the very first minute, my attorney and I realized that no matter what arguments we brought forth in order to effect my release on bail or on my own recognizance, they would be futile. My age; the fact that I had no prior conviction of any kind (either in Germany or in the United States); the state of my health; my having also a steady domicile in Germany (and being officially registered there); the fact that my "transgression" was no crime in the usual sense *and* had been "committed" on American soil: each point was denied as irrelevant by Frau Freitag. Both my lawyer and I noticed that there was quite an interplay of glances between the judge and the prosecutor, leaving the impression that both acted on higher orders. The aim was to keep me in prison. Judea had spoken!

Almost as soon as the charade had begun, I realized the uselessness of our efforts. But after about fifteen minutes into the procedure, I decided to try yet another tack. I asked Mrs. Freitag whether it would help if I gave her my *"Ehrenwort,"* (my word of honor), that I would definitely be in Schwerin for the trial. She looked at me as if she didn't have the slightest inkling what I was talking about. Terms like *"Ehre"* and *"Ehrenwort"* were probably not in her vocabulary.

It deserves reporting that both this judge and the prosecutor (as were most of the other judges with whom I came in contact), were West German carpetbaggers who had been

Examinations for continued reasons of Detention--Haftprüfungen--

assigned to "East" Germany after the partial reunification. The mind-set of most of these people is decidedly un-German.

In an earlier chapter I had mentioned that Herr Herrmann, my lawyer, lived several hundred kilometers from Bützow and Schwerin, and that it was rather difficult for him to travel from his office in Düsseldorf, to Mecklenburg. In each and every instance when my lawyer had to make the trip, it took more than a day of his time, sometimes even necessitating an overnight stay at a nearby hotel.

The *Haftprüfung* of September 5th had been arranged for 9:30 a.m. In theory, Herr Herrmann arrived early enough to speak with me, and, if possible, develop some sort of strategy in order to procure my release.

But since the German judiciary sought to prevent this, I was probably purposely delivered from Bützow to the court house in Schwerin, about 50 kilometers away, with but 5 minutes to spare. This was not enough time for me to confer with Herr Herrmann.

The only actual result of the September 5th hearing was the promise by Mr. Kollarz, the prosecutor, that we would be in possession of the indictment within 3 weeks. (Being a German of the old stock, I really believed him. Little did I think that it would take more than twice that long.)

Under ordinary circumstances, an examination for continued detention takes place in Germany only about every three months. Therefore, I was very much surprised when but one month after the *Haftprüfung* above, I was again bundled into a smaller prison van and transported to the court house in Schwerin. This happened on the morning of October 5th, but two days after the Bützow hostage situation had made headlines all over the nation.

Being the sole prisoner in the van as it moved speedily over the narrow, two-lane highways of a Wisconsin-like landscape, I had no idea what was happening.

"*Herr Schmidt, bitte machen Sie sich fertig. In fünf Minuten müssen wir Sie nach Schwerin bringen!*" (Mr. Schmidt, get ready, in 5 minutes we have to take you to Schwerin), was all I was told.

I wondered whether the hostage-taking was the cause for this transport. Could it be that someone of the higher-ups in Bonn had realized that my life had been in danger because of the hostage situation, and that it would have harmed Bonn if the headlines in America were to proclaim, "U.S. citizen murdered in German jail," and that therefore my release was contemplated?

At the courthouse there was a repeat of the *Haftprüfung* of exactly a month earlier, except that my lawyer was not present, and another woman had taken Frau Freitag's place as judge. There were also no other observers. Since my lawyer couldn't possibly attend on such short notice, I refused to say anything of importance. But soon the reason for this session became clear: in the meantime the prosecutor had realized that he needed more time to finish the indictment, and, obviously, no trial could take place before that was accomplished. So he used the legal subterfuge of an extra "examination for continued detention" to gain at least another month. If he had not done that, the court might have been forced to release me on my own recognizance in early December. It again became apparent that my continued incarceration, "come what may," was the main aim.

While the ladies in the court room typed a new and larger arrest warrant, I was told to wait outside in the hallway of the justice building. Mister Kollarz, the prosecutor, also had nothing to do, and came to ask me whether I had any complaints about the treatment in Bützow, or if he could do anything for me. He was pleasant enough, and I asked him for some news magazines which I had not been able to purchase in the Bützow commissary. (He subsequently mailed me a stack.) Thereupon we had an interesting conversation of about a quarter of an hour, touching on many subjects except anything pertaining to my case.

Kollarz, a man of about fifty years of age, was smoking and rather nervous. I tried to guess his ethnic background, and intuitively came to the conclusion that he was not of German stock. I always do this by trying to envision the person in question in a German WWII uniform; so to say, as my comrade-in-arms. Just by judging his looks and demeanor, in Kollarz' case I was not able to picture him as a German soldier. But perhaps only the (obviously) different *Weltanschauung* made the difference.

While Kollarz and I spoke, "my" guard remained discretely in the background but I did notice that he was avidly listening in, and I made sure that he understood every word I said, especially when I predicted the eventual demise of the Bonn system. Later, on the drive back to Bützow, this officer came to me and merely said that he had found my conversation very enlightening, leaving no doubts that he had enjoyed my ideas.

The new arrest warrant dated October 5, 1995, was basically the same as the one issued at the time of my arrest in Frankfurt. The difference was only that the same nonsensical accusations were repeated twice. Still everything revolved around the fact that in today's Germany one may not criticize the Jews, question the "holy" tenets of the "Holocaust," and otherwise delve into the taboos imposed upon the Germans by the 1945 victors.

Interestingly, it was at this second *Haftprüfung* when I was for the first time informed that a year earlier I had been fined DM 3,000 *in absentia,* by a court in the city of Kiel, probably for similar offenses. The Schwerin court then "graciously" informed me that this fine had been erased, since I was now on trial for much more serious "offenses."

The "East" Germans

Ever since Roman times, and their entry into history, the German tribes occupying Central Europe had to guard themselves against foreign invaders. Germany's almost indefensible borders necessitated the development of several character traits that still seem inherent in the Germans today - - - even in their off-spring living in America, namely, the German-Americans.

One of these characteristics was the *modus operandi* of withdrawing into the deep, dark German forests when danger arose. It happened around Jesus' time when the Teutons under Arminius beat the legions of the Roman general Varus.

Again several hundred years later, when the Huns rode in from the East, and much later during the incursions of the Mongols, or the French, or even the Swedes and the British, the Germans proved to be slow to react to hostilities. They preferred to withdraw rather than defend their--what they considered-- indefensible positions.

But when forced into battle, Germans usually bettered their enemies. German-Americans used the same method of avoiding danger and inconvenience after the 1960s, when non-German elements in the U.S. population voted for laws that brought forced integration, bad schools, crime, corruption and decay to the inner cities. As a result, in time-honored fashion, the American Germans left everything, their homes, their schools, their churches and their *Turner Halls,* to others and rebuilt anew in the suburbs. (The Poles, the Irish and the Italians followed suit, but the German-Americans led the so-called white flight. They did this not because of what others call racism, but because they wanted to live in an orderly society.)

Another trait the Germans and German-Americans have in common is an abhorrence of politics. They do not mind being active on a local level. As a matter of fact, the centuries' old democratic charter of German cities was, and still is, the model for city charters all over Eastern Europe. But what Germans do not like is the abstract politics in which Jews particularly are so adept. This abhorrence of politics can have serious drawbacks, as we can see in the United States, where the largest ethnic group (German-Americans), is also politically the most insignificant one. Whoever heard of a German lobby in Congress?

The Germans being masters of creating long and cumbersome (but also pointedly clear) words, have recently formed a new one: *Politikverdrossenheit*, the disgust of the general population with politics. This revulsion manifests itself in many ways; in some places through the people's boycott of the voting booths, in others by an overemphasis on the diversions of sports or travel, or even by a general damnation of all politicians. Nowhere is this more apparent than in so-called "East" Germany.

Ever since the 1990 reunification of the two small remnants of the German Reich, it has become apparent that the populations of these territories have grown more apart, rather than together as had been anticipated. Although they look alike, speak the same language, and probably still have the same desires, the Germans of East and West, who since the end of World War II have been separated by the Iron Curtain, have developed very different world views (*Weltanschauungen*), and the future will show that from this chasm a spiritual conflict will arise which may be as deep and as long lasting as the North-South division of Germans between the northern Protestants and the southern Catholics.

Hopefully, it will not lead to an internecine conflict such as the Thirty Years' War that caused the deaths of the majority of Germans in the seventeenth century due to these religious differences.

But, unfortunately, the current crop of politicians in the German *Bundesrepublik* is so far removed from the mass of the people that from these political hacks no relief can be expected. The ineptitude begins at the very top, with people such as President Roman Herzog, Chancellor Helmut Kohl, Finance Minister Theo Waigel and the feminist Speaker of the *Bundestag* (parliament), Rita Süssmuth.

Not surprisingly, it doesn't look any better with the members of the *Bundestag* itself, or in the governments of the various German states. All one observes is greed, corruption, abuse of power and a general disdain for the population at large. The German traditions of thrift, discipline, honesty, honor and sacrifice are eroding, along with the old standard of Prussian incorruptibility.

Even to use these terms is considered obsolete, or even dangerously *Deutschtümelei* (sentimentally German-patriotic), by these "representatives of the people." One thing is certain: as the world's economic and political situation worsens, few of the current politicians in Bonn, Berlin and the state capitals will have the ability to provide the necessary leadership for the German people.

I was not long in Bützow prison before I realized that it was very fortuitous for me to have been sent to a prison in so-called "East" and not in West Germany. Obviously, I am using quotation marks to show my disapproval of calling this area of the Reich, "East" Germany. It isn't! I am quite certain that this intentional misnaming of German territory, i.e. calling this part "East" instead of "Central" Germany, (what it had been for many centuries), was ordered by the enemies of Deutschland. Ironically, Bützow in alleged "East" Germany, is about 100 kilometers *west* of the West German city of Passau. [1]

For more than four months I was incarcerated in that part of the Reich that had for forty years been the *Deutsche Demokratische Republik,* (the "DDR" as it was called for

---

[1] A similar scam is afoot regarding the term "Central Europe". For centuries, people all over the world thought of Germany first when reading "Central Europe" in English, or, *Mitteleuropa* in German. Some time ago, I had noticed that internationalist writers, especially those connected with the Trilateral Commission, the CFR and the Bilderbergers, had begun to refer to the *East Central* European states such as Poland, Slovakia and Hungary, or even Rumania and Yugoslavia, as "Central Europe". At first this didn't bother me. But then I discovered that Jews in charge of the European section of the U.S. State Department (Holbrooke, Kornblum, etc.) had asked the major outlets of the American news media to henceforth use the designation "Central Europe," for the newly freed "democracies" of Eastern Europe, thereby relegating the remnant of the Reich, namely, the German *Bundesrepublik*, to Western Europe. Soon thereafter I learned of the appreciation the State Department expressed to the *New York Times* for following suit. In such matters it bears remembering that they are never happenstance. There is always method behind the madness.

For millennia the German Reich was the *Ordnungsmacht* (the power that kept order) in Europe. It was the core of the *Abendland* (Western Civilization). In order to destroy Europe and the hated white race, one had to destroy the Reich. 800 years of German history beyond the Oder-Neisse rivers have been eradicated with the suppression of the term East Germany. Now, terming the genuine Central Germany (that seemingly has ceased to exist), "East" Germany, the enemies of the West assume that by merely changing the designation of Central Europe to Western Europe (for, that is what it is all about!), one eliminates Germany as the natural center of Europe. "They" know that Poland, politically and economically backward as it often has been and is even now, is an unlikely candidate to become the new *Ordnungsmacht* envisioned by some. Putting Poland in the forefront, would almost certainly guarantee the continued subjugation of Europe by non-European usurpers.

So far the German news media have *generally* not embraced the dishonest scheme of naming *East* Central Europe, "Central Europe," as the *Oberjuden* have decreed.

short), namely, the Reich provinces that were ruled by the Communists.

This provided me with a unique opportunity to get to know and study my *Landsleute* (compatriots), who for so long had been cut off from the non-German fountainheads of European culture, such as, Italy, France, Spain and Great Britain, and its traditional German centers such as Trier, Cologne, Aachen, Vienna, Frankfurt, Munich and Nuremberg.

Both the personnel as well as the inmates of the Bützow penitentiary were almost exclusively former citizens of the ex-DDR.

The psychological differences between them and their Western brethren are deep. Undoubtedly, it will take decades or even centuries to overcome them, unless such an aberration as the twelve years of the Third Reich occurs again (because in that era, a determined effort had been made to bring the Germans of the different tribes together, and create, *for the first time in German history,* real cohesion among them).

It is no coincidence that after the 1990 reunification, new designations arose through popular usage that express the East/West German differences clearly: "Ossies" for people from the former "DDR", and "Wessies" for West Germans.

And these are not terms of endearment. While they do not denote enmity, a certain sarcasm or disdain is quite noticeable. For example, the "Wessies" consider themselves superior to the "Ossies". They point to the dismal state of the entire "East" German infrastructure that became apparent after the reunification. Rather than hold the Communists *and the Bonn rulers* responsible, they blame the ordinary "Ossies" who had slaved and sacrificed beyond endurance for four decades.

The "Wessies" allege that those who grew up under Communism are lazy and do not have the drive to succeed; that they are not punctual, and furthermore, that their education in the trades and professions is not up to par. [2]

The Westerners complain that it is they who have to pay exorbitant sums for the rebuilding of the dilapidated "East" German infrastructure. One fact which few of the West Germans realize, and no newspaper dares point out, is that the worth of the infrastructure "captured" (stolen) by the West in the old Central Germany since the reunification, was far in excess of the 500 billion deutschmarks the *Bundesrepublik* claimed to have spent in the last five years in order to bring that part of the nation up to Western standards. A relatively few people ("internationalists") of the West (not all of them Germans), were able to enrich themselves tremendously when Bonn took over the possessions of the former DDR. Only recently it was reported that the number of millionaires in West Germany has risen greatly since the reunification.

Then, in turn, the West German taxpayer had to foot the bill for the rebuilding. It reminded me of the American Savings and Loan scandals, where U.S. taxpayers ultimately had to make good for the swindles of the monied elite.

Even five years after the collapse of the system under which they grew up, most of the "Ossies" have not found their bearings. While they are grateful that *materially* things are now better for them and that they travel to such exotic places as

---

[2] When I visited "East" Germany in 1985, I was shocked by the extent of the unnecessary destruction of German cultural heritage and the deterioration of such things as highways. Most of the medieval cities that survived the war looked ready for demolition. It was quite obvious that for more than forty years, nothing had been done to preserve the architectural beauty of what had once been the heart of Europe. The Bonn vassals must have also known this. But they never used their power and influence with the Soviets to save such well-springs of German culture as Erfurt, Eisenach, Wittenberg, Quedlinburg and Potsdam. Instead of hastening the demise of the communist regime in the DDR, when it was nearly bankrupt, Bonn propped it up with generous loans, thereby prolonging the destruction. Meanwhile the allegedly "free" German media, never reported the extent of the damage perpetrated by the Communists. The West German press found it more expedient to bash Hitler.

Paris, Rome, London or Cologne, or even the United States (one of their very favorite destinations), they are not quite certain about their own future.

They regard their West German brethren as money-hungry, callous and brash.

They do not dislike them (there is more of that the other way around), but having lived all or most of their existence in a society where there was always a shortage of some daily necessities, this forced them to be nicer and more comradely to each other, a courtesy lost in West Germany due to excessive materialism and an overabundance of goods.

(Older Americans may remember how during the Depression neighbors helped each other more than in later years, when there was less suffering.)

I think that the "East" Germans are the better Germans. There exists among them a certain goodheartedness combined with simplicity and the typical German (political) naiveté that cannot be found in West Germans.

One would think that people who all their lives had suffered under Communism, with its constant propaganda for forty or more years, would be totally brainwashed, and bereft of any independent political thought.

The truth is that the Red propaganda was by and large so ham-handed that it was largely ineffective among the masses.

During visits to "East" Germany in the last five years, I have certainly met some staunch Marxists who, in spite of the obvious failure of the Communist system, still adhere to their failed pipe dream.

But such people are found almost exclusively among the intelligentsia.

Most "East" Germans I have met since the reunification have told me that they always viewed the world through German eyes and regarded the Russians as occupiers (no matter how friendly their personal relations with individual Russians might have been). Not so the West Germans. The brainwashing in the *Bundesrepublik* was and is far more pregnant and insidious than that of the Communists.

It ought to be clear to most Germans that their so-called "friends" among the "Allied nations," namely, the governments of the United States, Great Britain, France and Canada (and smaller nations like Belgium and the Netherlands), have their troops on German soil not because they love the German people, but because they want to keep the German nation subservient and on a leash. Yet few West Germans seem to grasp this simple political reality. Only a scant minority of West Germans acknowledge that the aforementioned nations are still occupiers, left over from a long ago war. An inordinate number of the Bonn Germans actually believe the hypocritical talk of "eternal friendship" between some nations that are bound by treaties such as NATO, the EU, and those signed at Maastricht. [3]

Living among "East" Germans for these months, I noticed how they viewed their Western brethren with slight bemusement. I was surprised that so few DDR-Germans were

---

[3] I am not denying that a sincere friendship between the German population at large and most Americans exists. I am only referring to the fact that *nations* can only have their own interests, and never base their foreign policy on some sentimental alliance with other countries. For instance, the American "friendship" with Israel will eventually cost the U.S. dearly, because it is based upon emotion and not on *Realpolitik*. The genuine affection Germans feel for "America" predates Hitler and can partly be attributed to the fact that so many millions of Germans helped create the United States. The United States is an off-spring (albeit an unruly one) of Europe, and especially of Germany. For me it was never a foreign or strange country. In this context it bears remembering that since 1945 millions of American GIs have served their tours of duty in Germany. Besides Japan, Germany has been the favorite assignment of the U.S. Army since the end of World War II. This mutual good will, generated on a personal level by the unintended beneficial effects of an otherwise hostile, 50-year (!) occupation of Germany, undoubtedly has created a long-lasting friendship between the German people and many segments of the American population.

upset that almost all the major positions in their part of Germany were now occupied by Westerners. Almost all the important people with whom I came in contact in the "East" German system, were carpetbaggers from the West: judges, prosecutors, ministers of state governments and even many of the elected representatives.

The wholesale theft by the West German capitalistic system of almost the entire "East" German infrastructure deserves more than a cursory notice, but in order to explain the true extent of the thievery, I would have to write a separate book. In the interim, I will sketch the basic details.

Under Stalin, there was hardly any private enterprise possible, and after 1949, when German Communist puppets were allowed to fill top posts previously occupied by the Soviets, they confiscated every corporation, factory, and almost every farm, home and single-proprietor business, with the exception of very small, "Mom-and-Pop" stores.

In 1990, at the time of the reunification, the state owned almost everything save for some single-family homes. The Communists naturally claimed that "the people" were the true owners of everything, but for the sake of clarity it is more correct to state that East Berlin was the seat of one giant enterprise of state-run, monopoly capitalism, with a gang of nincompoops managing everything.

Once the reunification occurred, almost the entire wealth of the former DDR came into the possession of the West German *Bundesrepublik*. This allegedly "freest state that ever existed on German soil," loudly proclaims its adherence to the free enterprise ideals promoted in the West. One should have assumed that it would approach the difficult question of ownership in "East" Germany, in a manner consistent with the age-old justice of European tradition. Certainly, many of the farms and businesses whose owners were still alive should have been returned to these rightful owners forthwith.

Some of the newer and better run Communist enterprises, such as the factories that had huge contracts with the Soviet Union and other Eastern European states, should have been turned into *Aktiengesellschaften* (corporations) where the long-time workers ought to have become at least part-owners.

Nothing like that happened. Declaring the entire "East" German infrastructure virtually bankrupt, the West Germans created an outfit which they called *Treuhandanstalt*, which was an "Escrow Company" headed by a woman with alleged connections to the secret society of Freemasons. She obtained her position shortly after the first executive of *Treuhandanstalt* had been murdered by persons unknown, soon after he had assumed his duties. [4]

After his death, a "fire sale" of incredible dimensions was initiated, resulting in the wholesale impoverishment of the population of "East" Germany. They were entirely at the mercy of the West German carpetbaggers and their foreign business associates.

This is perhaps the place to point out that the seventeen million "East" Germans never had the opportunity to acquire any significant valuables such as stocks, bonds, gold, silver, and jewelry, under Communism rule. The only possession of value that these people could bring into the reunited Germany, was, in some cases, their single-family home. Obviously, they will be severely handicapped by this one-sided distribution of wealth.

How did the *Bundesregierung* deal with the huge assets of Central Germany which came into its possession after the 1990

---

[4] To this day the murder of the first head of the *Treuhandanstalt* has not been solved. This writer is not the only one who believes that this able German manager was killed in order to make the large-scale thievery which occurred after his death, possible.

reunification?

Here is but one example: assume for an instant that a Belgian manufacturer had for years fought his major competition, a well-run "East" German company producing the same product for the world market.

With the promise that the Belgians would guarantee to keep the several thousand "East" German workers of his former competitor employed for a predetermined number of years, the *Treuhandgesellschaft* then "sold" the "East" German company to the foreigners for the nominal sum of one *deutschmark* (all such deals were made with the claim that otherwise "millions" of jobs were going to be lost).

More often than not, it happened that in such a case the foreign or West German company would take a year to remove all the best "East" German machinery, steal patents if there were any, and then sell all the valuable real estate that could conceivably be sold.

Then, after the year was up, *Treuhandgesellschaft* became the owner again of the gutted remnant, swindling the German taxpayers by means of a huge debt, while the Belgian not only had made a good profit but had also "forever" eliminated his major competition in the world market.

Travesties like that happened in nearly every branch of German business and with every imaginable nationality. All the while hundreds of thousands or even millions of "East" Germans lost their livelihood.

I know of "East" German factories that were shut down and labeled bankrupt, even though they had the best products of their kind in the world, and in spite of the fact that they were sitting on orders that would have kept them busy for years. This occurred, for instance, to the makers of fine hunting weapons in Suhl.

While in Bützow I read of a clear-cut case of such theft which took place on the border between the German states of Hessia and Thuringia.

Straddling the inner-German border that for decades constituted the Iron Curtain separating East and West, are huge deposits of potash, a much sought-after fertilizer. The same field of potash deposits was mined by a West German company located in Hessia, and by a "VEB" (a designation for a supposed, "people-owned enterprise") in "East" Germany's Thuringia.

I do not know the respective volume of potash these two mining firms had shipped in the years before reunification, but I discovered that the VEB was, with about 10,000 employees, the larger one of the two. I also know that the latter had a steady clientele and had no worries about selling all the potash they could mine.

After the reunification, the VEB fell into the hands of *Treuhandgesellschaft*, and was declared bankrupt. When word came that a West German company was going to buy its assets for peanuts, and intended to mine potash from only one site in the West, thereby making the firing of all "East" German workers necessary, the workers took over their mine, and did not permit the transfer to take place. (This is something I would have expected to happen in nearly every large company in the former "DDR," but it did not.)

It took long negotiations and many promises, to get the striking workers to vacate the mining facility, but finally a contract was signed that would have assured continued employment of about 2,000 of the "East" German workers.

The area in Thuringia where the mine is located is practically bereft of any other industry. In other words, people there are dependent on working at the mine, or else they will have to move away.

In Hessia, the situation is not as bad. For decades the border region near the Iron Curtain had been heavily subsidized by the Bonn Government, and this had enabled many small manufacturing firms to locate there.

It was not long after the agreement between *Treuhandanstalt*, the "East" German VEB miners and the West German mining company was signed, that it was unilaterally broken by the latter. Now, a couple of years later, potash is only being mined from western Germany, and most of the workers in Thuringia are on welfare.

Before the Bonn regime's cronies withdrew from the agreement, they did not hesitate to disassemble and take to their location the best and largest pieces of the mine equipment of the former VEB, equipment that was far better and more modern than the Bonn vassals had possessed.

As I mentioned before, stories like that could fill a book. Viewing these rip-offs from a distance, I am amazed at the docility and tolerance the "East" Germans exhibited at such criminal behavior by Bonn's corporations. The question remains, whether this docility is permanent or may turn into its opposite, into political resistance that may eventually topple the *Bundesrepublik?*

I predict that the spiritual confrontation between Wessies and Ossies will grow in time, and it will be the Ossies ('East' Germans) who will become the driving force behind this conflict.

Frankly, I do not regret this development, since the complacency and crass materialism of the West has nearly destroyed whatever one might consider traditionally German. There is little if any pride in either the nation or in its thousand-year-old culture, visible among the West German population.

The "East' Germans

While being held as a political prisoner in Bützow penitentiary, I studied the German unemployment statistics carefully. I was amazed to see the inability of the Bonn politicians to cope with this crisis. In Mecklenburg-Vorpommern, for instance, the state where I was incarcerated, the unemployment rate is alleged to be 14 percent, but I believe it is in fact much higher. However, many "East" Germans had been granted a Social Security pension much earlier than usual (some at age 55 or younger), and many others are on "workfare" programs paid for by the state and this distorts the unemployment figures.

At any rate, now the entire world seems to have entered a period of economic downturn recently, and a few months after my release from prison, the unemployment statistics from Germany show a steady rise. I assume, things in Mecklenburg have also gotten worse.

After Germany was reunited, numerous old-line German companies from the West opened new plants and warehouses in the former DDR. If the current world-wide economic recession deepens, these companies will also have to "downsize."

Will they close their older plants in the West, or the newer ones in "East" Germany? Knowing the Germans, many business owners will be guided more by tradition and loyalty to their longtime employees than by a strict business sense.

I would say that they will close their "East" German branches first. Therefore, my prediction is that with the ongoing recession, ever more "East" German workers will find themselves on the street, with the unemployment rate in some areas rising to 40 percent or more. And, if that happens, Germany may have entered a revolutionary period for the first time since the ascent of Hitler.

Due to its central location, large population, scientific prowess and potential military might, Germany is and will always be of special interest to its direct neighbors as well as to its international enemies. Germany's border adjoins nine different countries (twelve if one includes Austria as part of the Reich).

Currently, it is the playground of the secret services of the world, with the CIA having more German agents than any other nationality. The American embassy in Bonn is supposed to have a larger staff than any other in the world

Even a small country like Czechia (a stripling since its founding as "Czechoslovakia" in 1919), is actively spying on Reich territory, especially regarding German intentions toward Eastern Europe, and the rise of German nationalism.

It follows that other nations are also attempting to influence German politics. Some directly, as the French are wont to do, others, like the United States, through a military presence and still others, such as the Israelis, through terrorist acts that keep German politicians and media people intimidated and in line.

It is not too far fetched to assume that sometime in the future, a more independent-minded Russian ruler than Boris Yeltsin (General Lebed?), may want to disturb or cut the strong ties that bind Washington and Bonn, and will use illicit means to accomplish his goals.

Certainly, a strong discontent in "East" Germany concerning untenable circumstances, could be manipulated by the Russians to sow discord and bring about a collapse of the Bonn regime. Whether the Russians would use the ever growing (and deep-seated) nationalism that still exists in at least a third of the German population, as a springboard to further Moscow's aims, remains to be seen. But the possibility is there.

Recently, a 41-year-old "East" German legislator from Mecklenburg-Vorpommern, Eckhardt Rehberg, issued a 34-page declaration, detailing the justifiable grievances that exist in the former Communist part of Germany.

In his declaration, Rehberg accused his own party, Chancellor Kohl's CDU (Christian Democratic Union), of neglecting "East" Germany and plunging its population into "disappointment, despair, anger and bitterness."

Rehberg confirms everything I had discovered during my frequent trips to *Mitteldeutschland* in the last five years, and during my incarceration in Bützow. He wrote:

"Five years after the German reunification, a serious discussion of our needs and hopes is more urgently necessary than ever. These years have shown how inflexible our society is when it faces serious political problems. It has retreated into an encrusted and outmoded form of thinking.

"If you take away 'workfare' programs, we have a 50 percent unemployment rate in 'East Germany,' said another politician from that area.

"For many people, times are very difficult and there is an undercurrent of anger everywhere. Many people think that Karl Marx was right after all. Certainly, they do not see the free enterprise system [5] as a more humane form of society for dealing with their problems. They view the West German capitalist system as a swindle."

Representative Rehberg's office has had to print 6,000 copies of his declaration to meet the demand for it among the population. Many newspaper columnists and other prominent figures from Central Germany have endorsed his views.

Some say that the gains of the reunification are being undermined because of the way Bonn treats the "East Germans," not as equal partners in a new Germany, but almost as a conquered people.

No thought is given to the fact that this part of Germany has

---

[5] In other words, monopoly capitalism.

always been different and independent, and certainly ought not to be treated as a newly annexed colony without any heritage or roots.

Social and political tensions in "East" Germany are reaching explosive levels. One newspaper reported that some people fear "East" Germans may take to the streets if their demands are not met, or if there is no other way to get the attention of the Bonn rulers.

Most "East" Germans abhor the intensely competitive nature of the West German social and economic system, an *Ausbeutersystem* (exploiters' system), as they call it, which they believe has been transferred lock, stock and barrel to the newly acquired territories.

There has been a sharp rise in crime as well, and the complex legal system of West Germany has also created havoc. Some "East" Germans have begun to boycott elections, others are supporting the successor party of the former Communist party. [6]

Newspapers report that Bonn party leaders have berated their cousins in the "East", and warned them that such protests as Mr. Rehberg's manifesto are only deepening the gulf that already exists between the two unequal parts of the former Reich.

I welcome this growing resistance in the "East," since it may bring about the needed reforms in Germany, hopefully without civil war.

If matters continue to decay in West Germany, as they have since 1949, then this would definitely lead not only to the destruction of the sovereign Germany so necessary for the

---

[6] This phenomenon bears watching. The East German Communists are under the leadership of the Jewish party boss, Gregor Gysi. The Communists naturally claim that people who vote for them are still true believers in Marxism/Leninism. I can state without hesitation that most of the new voters for this party are probably "protest voters," who see no other way to show their dissatisfaction with the Bonn *Anschluss,* and its ramifications.

rebirth of an independent Europe, but it would also destroy the last vestiges of German culture and traditions, and, not the least, of the German people, through planned *Umvolkung*.[7]

Recent reports demonstrate that all four of West Germany's traditional political parties are fast losing support in the former DDR." As far as I am concerned, this is a wonderful development.

---

[7] *Umvolkung:* To alter the ethnic composition and nature of an entire people through the planned introduction of large populations of aliens. This has been happening to the Germanic stock of *Deutschland* since the 1960s and to the Germanic and Anglo-Saxon stock of America, also since the '60s.

The Indictment and My Commentary

On the following pages you will find a translation of the 29-page indictment that was handed to me on October 26, 1995, almost exactly eleven weeks after my arrest. I had anxiously awaited this document, since it was the most important legal instrument necessary to finally bringing about the judicial proceedings.

I must admit that I laughed aloud when I had finished reading it. The prosecutor could not have been doing me a greater favor than to have included, intact, more than twelve pages of my own writings.

Didn't he realize that this overabundance of my own writings would not only broaden my defense strategy but also strengthen my case? I certainly had no reason to be afraid that the words I had consciously written could be used as a potent weapon against me, for there was one thing I was certain of: I had only told the truth, or explained an opinion based upon facts.

On the pages following this translation, I shall present a page-by-page commentary. Many of these comments would have been presented in court had the proceedings lasted four days or more, as planned, instead of just one, as it finally transpired.

Prosecuting Attorney's Office, Schwerin

Ref.: 111 Js 826/95
To: Schwerin, October 18, 1995
District Court Schwerin   ko-eh
Criminal Division 3
Demmlerplatz 1-2
10953 Schwerin
Review of Remand in Custody

as per §§ 121, 122 StPO
set for February 8, 1996

Indictment

Hans Schmidt,
Businessman,

born in Völklingen (Luisenthal) on April 27, 1927, resident at Pensacola/Florida/USA, American, according to his own statements also German citizen, married, arrested in this matter on August 9, 1995 (v. I p. 74 enc.), in detention awaiting trial since that same date on the basis of the arrest warrant issued by the County Court of Schwerin on March 28, 1995 (v. I p. 33f. enc.) - 34 Gs 350/95 - presently detained in Bützow, Prisoners Log Book No. 1708/95; arrest warrant revised, decision of the County Court of Schwerin, October 5, 1995 (v. II pp. 152ff. enc.).

Defense Counsel:
Attorney Hajo Hermann,
Friedrichstraße 11, 40217 Düsseldorf (v. I p. 83 enc.) -

is charged as follows:

In Schwerin and elsewhere, between December 23, 1993 and April 25, 1995, in the form of 12 criminal offenses, in Counts 1 and 5, the accused did attack the human dignity of others in a manner likely to lead to a breach of the peace by slandering, maliciously belittling and libeling them, and, in this same act, did produce, introduce into the spatial jurisdiction of the German Criminal Code, and disseminate, writings inciting race hatred or describing cruel or otherwise inhuman brutality against persons in a manner glorifying or trivializing the cruel and inhuman nature of such events in a manner injurious to human dignity,

in Counts 2 - 4, 6 - 8, and 10 - 12,

in a manner likely to lead to a breach of the peace, did attack the human dignity of others by slandering, maliciously belittling and libeling identifiable groups, in each case, concomitantly, producing, importing and disseminating writings inciting hatred against identifiable groups or against a religious group and attacking their human dignity by slandering, maliciously belittling and libeling them, while the offense in

Counts 2 - 4 and 6 - 8,

related in each case to such writings in which an act committed under the National Socialist regime, and of the nature specified in §220a Section 1 StGB, was denied or trivialized,

and in Counts 1 - 9,

in each case concomitantly, disparaged the memory of persons deceased.

The accused is the author and publisher of the publications "USA-Bericht," "GANPAC-Brief," as well as of the writings he titles "Open Letters," which he produces in the United States and mails from there in unknown numbers to destinations including the Federal Republic of Germany.

Where publications as well as letters of indictable content are concerned, the accused is charged with the following:

Re. 1.: (Main Files v. I):

From Burke, Virginia (USA), the accused mailed the

publication "USA-Bericht, November 1994", postmarked November 4, 1994, to the address "Land Mecklenburg, Bundesrat CDU: Rudi Geil, Karl-Marx-Straße 1, 19055 Schwerin.

The mailing was received by the Mecklenburg-Vorpommern Ministry of the Interior on November 9, 1994. It contained an "Open Letter" dated May 8, 1994 and addressed by the accused to journalist Martin Klingst in response to the latter's article *Neuer Terror* which had appeared in the weekly newspaper *Die Zeit* of December 17, 1993. This "Open Letter" includes the following content:

"But every time I sat down at my computer to discuss the matter in detail, the American Top Jews thwarted my plans. Clearly the doubts spreading through the USA regarding the Holocaust-story and the open, polemical attacks directed at them by the Blacks have put them into such a panic that hardly a day goes by now without their inventing yet another 'Holocaust'-tale, which of course must be corrected by someone like me who has actively represented the interests of our German people and our nation in the USA for almost half a century.

"In reading your letter one notices that you too are worried, perhaps subconsciously. Right at the start of your article you mention with obvious consternation that a small right-wing magazine published a list of fully 250 persons - politicians, lawyers, writers, mayors, social workers, journalists, teachers, businessmen - whom the right-wingers should eliminate, since their 'courageous support of liberal policies regarding foreigners' and their 'staunch resistance to radical right-wing activities' had shown them to be enemies of Germany.

"I had to laugh when I read that. Do you know how many Germans, in my opinion, will have to be removed from the public life of our nation after the coming revolution in Germany?

Close to 100,000! And particularly in the professions you mentioned (though professors and television liars were missing from the list). I am basing this figure on the corresponding number of French collaborators murdered by the Allies and their accomplices - the French collaborators who were killed in 1944/45 for the sake of their friendship for or cooperation with Germany. But to forestall any misunderstandings: I am not suggesting that the approximately 100,000 worst German henchmen of our enemies should be executed.

"Rather, I feel that only a very few of the worst traitors to our Fatherland should lose their heads, and when such an execution takes place, then - while being one hundred percent justified - it should also be of considerable symbolic impact due to the prominent position of the person in question.

"The main reason why I oppose a great many executions has nothing to do with any feeling of reverence - I lost that after the War, when I saw how the Allies treated our people.

"But I think that for decades after the revolution (until 2033, since this is an equal time removed from November 9, 1989, the day the Communist regime collapsed in the German Democratic Republic, as May 8, 1945 is), we will have to hold trials in which all those who have so grossly violated our people and our nation will be called to account, both in the interests of ascertaining the truth as well as for the sake of Germany's mental and spiritual recovery. And in order to serve the cause of truth, such trials require living witnesses. Whom do I mean?

"I mean those politicians who have lied to and cheated our nation ever since the end of the War. There is no need for me to name any of those yet living; the 'secrets' that recently came out about late politicians such as Brandt, Wehner and Strauss should suffice.

"Are there really any Germans who still believe that the enemy vassals currently reigning in Bonn are different? As usual, we will learn of their lies and misdeeds only after their arrest or death. It is my hope that this will happen soon, under the aegis of a decent and proper German (Reich) court.

"I mean public prosecutors and judges who violate and disregard their own Basic Law, introduced by our enemies, in order to trample all over the right to free expression of opinion. Particularly in the context of the Holocaust they hand down verdicts citing the alleged 'self-evidence' of the events in question - verdicts that make a mockery of justice. This practice seems to be due to religious reasons which, however, clearly conflict with being German. Later, once these people are called to account, it will be fitting to recall the fates of German patriots such as Ernst Zündel, Erhard Kemper, Günther Deckert, T. Rudolph etc. and to take as much pity on the perhaps elderly jurists as these had for General Remer, a German hero."

And further:

"(...) Historians such as Eberhard Güchel, the so-called Holocaust expert who assiduously strives to maintain the six-million-tale in the interests of our enemies."

And further:

"... my God, what were people like you thinking of, anyhow? It was the leftists, the anarchists, the political parties loyal to the System and infested by Jews and Freemasons, as well as the licensed press, who have spent decades shooting down anything and everything national: brutally, intolerantly, obstinately, full of hatred."

Re. 2.: (Case File 1):

From Burke/Virginia (USA), the accused mailed the publication "USA-Bericht, November 1994," postmarked December 19, 1994 and with the same contents as specified under 1, to the Prosecuting Attorney's Office of Kiel, where this mailing was received on January 9, 1995.

Re. 3: (Case File 2):

The same publication was mailed by the accused - again from Burke/Virginia (USA) and postmarked December 19, 1994 - to the address "Staatsanwaltschaft, Westring 8, 4630 Bochum 1," where this mailing was not stamped with the date of receipt but was received by December 29, 1994 at the latest.

Re. 4: (Case File 3):

The same mailing, also postmarked December 19, 1994, was sent by the accused to the address "Staatsanwaltschaft Bochum, Reitzensteinstraße 17, 4350 Recklinghausen", where the missive - also not stamped with the date of receipt - was received on January 4, 1995 at the latest.

Re. 5: (Case File 4):

On a date not known precisely but falling between May 8 and June 8, 1994, the accused sent a letter dated May 8, 1994, with contents as described in 1, to the address "Martin Klingst, DIE ZEIT, Postfach 10-6820, 2000 Hamburg 1."

Re. 6: (Case File 5):

On a date not known precisely but falling between March 9 and March 21, 1995, the accused sent Professor Dr. Michael Wolffsohn, Munich, a letter with the following content:

"Hans Schmidt, P. O. Box 11124 Pensacola, FL 32524-1124 March 9, 1995 USA FAX (904) 478-4993

(1) Professor Dr. Michael Wolffsohn

(2) Professor of Modern History

(3) Bundeswehr-Universität

(4) Werner Heisenberg-Weg 39

(5) 85579 Neubiberg, Germany

OPEN LETTER

Dear Michael!

"I hope you don't mind that, in American fashion, I am using the familiar form of address ["Du"], in writing to you. After all, we have already met once, in Washington - we even spoke - and besides, we have a good number of mutual acquaintances (on both sides of the Atlantic). Perhaps using the personal form of address will persuade you to set aside your innate reticence and to respond to this letter, which is the eighth I have written you

"After all, I am dealing in this letter with what is doubtless the most important problem of our era, namely the German-Jewish or Aryan-Jewish relationship. For someone as familiar with the situation as you appear to be, it ought to be child's play to expose any errors in my views.

"I receive many of your articles that appear in German newspapers and can see from these how 'admonitory' you can sound when you address the anonymous and (in this specialized subject area) largely ignorant German masses. The main thing for you is to defend the Jews!

"I am sorry that nothing came of your plans to move to the United States. Our mutual acquaintances here in the States still cannot understand what ultimately kept you in Germany. Especially after certain people in Neubiberg had made life so unpleasant for you.

"Your (German) pension claims were settled, and as far as I knew you even already had a good job lined up in the States. Still, something kept you in the 'Reich of Murderers'. Was it an express order from your more senior co-religionists in Tel Aviv or New York, directing you not to give up your position in Germany - a position which after all is of vital importance to international world Jewry?

"I cannot imagine that the rather uncertain quiet that now surrounds you in Neubiberg could have prompted your decision to remain at the Bundeswehr-University. You and I, we both know better than most that the friendliness which your colleagues express to you now is largely fake.

"Now that you have even succeeded in effecting the removal of a University President disagreeable to you, and because it is common knowledge at the University that Germans who write you honest but, in your opinion, insulting letters can expect to be severely punished, Neubiberg has been invaded by the peace of the graveyard. But how much longer will it last?

"Reports which were sent to me indicate that it is particularly your newer, younger colleagues and many of the current students who (as was to be expected) make fun behind your back of you and your unctuous words and solemn mien. All the laws in the world, and even psycho-terrorism, are ineffective against something like that. But I know, you gladly endure all that for the sake of Israel.

"Even though you are frequently unclear in what you write (typical Jewish obfuscation), reading your articles does always leave one with the impression that, for you, the entire Holocaust charge against the German nation has become an inviolable religious dogma.

"By virtue of this attitude you have practically become a priest of the new Holocaust Religion, who pronounces anyone who doubts (even slightly), a heretic. Therefore you cannot possibly be such a 'German-Jewish patriot' as you yourself may perhaps believe you are.

"Someone for whom truth does not come first is not a good history professor. Such a person has made himself a dark agent of a more than dubious Cause. What was the motto of the British in their ruthless expansion of their racialist Empire that Hitler admired so much? 'Right or wrong, my country!' Yes, it is very easy to fall into this moral trap (out of love for a Cause). The day will come when you will slap your forehead and cry: How could I have been so stupid?

"By the way, you acted in true Jewish fashion when you reported those German letter-writers to the police. Before I mention something similar that happened here in America, I just want to point out that I would never dream of doing something like that. But no doubt that is because we (Germans and Jews) are of completely different genetic predisposition. And therefore it is our respective genetic make-up that prevents me from ever becoming a Jew or you from turning into a real German.

"(I am aware that there are presently quite a few true-blue Germans, especially in important positions, who have fallen for the Holocaust Faith and who act typically Jewish in other ways as well. Disregarding for the moment the fact that this is due chiefly to opportunistic motives, I dare say that the Jewish philosophy of life espoused by these Noahites is only whisper-thin and will disappear the second the Jewish world power does.

"If I were a Jew I would not count on the loyalty and steadfastness of these characters: they will be the first to turn against their present Jewish patrons and 'friends'.)

"In Germany people have no doubt read about 'Proposition 187', a referendum in which the voters of California decided with an overwhelming majority that illegal immigrants (in other words, such that break the law by sneaking into the country) should no longer enjoy social benefits such as welfare, public education for their children, and free hospital care. The reason was the fact that by now millions of Mexicans have pitched their 'tents' in California and have burdened the people living there with immense expenses.

"(In Los Angeles there is a district hospital whose maternity ward has become off-limits for 'normal' American women because it is always occupied by Mexican women. If a White mother-to-be happens to stray into this ward, the brownskins proceed to deliberately rout her out.)

"We never doubted for a moment that 'liberals' under Jewish leadership would do everything in their power to annul this referendum decision by means of laws either passed or perverted by Jews. And that was what happened. At present the matter is still up in the air, and if things continue as they have been going to date then it will take years before the issue is settled to the satisfaction of the majority.

In the meantime, the Jewish attorneys for both sides pocket astronomical fees for their shadow-boxing, while the majority must foot their bills.

"Not a month had passed after the referendum, and already the Jewish Judge Mariana Pfaelzer (well, who else?), wife of Hollywood producer Frank Rothman, declared the referendum decision invalid. Shortly afterwards, a legal immigrant from Argentina wrote the judge a letter, asking her 'how is it possible that lawyers like you can dare to support illegal immigrants, whose very presence constitutes a breach of the law?'

"The Argentinean also mentioned that he had had to wait two years for his immigration papers. The letter did not contain threats of any kind. What did dear Mariana do? Believing, as you do too, that Jews must never be criticized (doing so is always anti-Semitic!), she gave the letter to the authorities, and one fine day the Argentinean immigrant was visited by two officers from the 'US Marshal's Service', one of the Federal American police authorities, and was interrogated by a woman named Aschbrenner...

"The reason why I am writing to you today has to do with the surprising and, for me, gratifying election results with which the

American voters put an end to Jewish power over the American Congress this past November 8 (which, by the time the last polling station closed in California, was already the heavily symbolic November 9 in Germany!). You with your hypersensitive Jewish antenna will certainly have recognized the implications of this day. But since you are not living here you will have missed some of the signs of this 'revolution', and so I will briefly describe them for you.

"American and German patriots in the USA are not deceiving themselves that this election has changed everything for the better for the American people (i.e. the Aryan Americans). As yet your co-religionists in the Clinton Administration have a tight grip on the reins of power, and there is no doubt that the media as well as the national finances are completely in their hands.

"Even the chief spokesmen of the 'revolution,' Newt Gingrich (who, incidentally, is not of German descent, since he was born a McPherson), and Robert Dole, are loyal servants of Internationalism and of God knows whom else, and they have proven this more than once since November.[1]

"But that doesn't matter. We of the right wing in both the USA and Germany consider the present state of affairs to be merely an interregnum which may already end in 1996. In other words, Gingrich especially may be regarded as an American Gorbachev, who merely facilitates the transition into the new age. It is quite possible that he will lose his great influence as early as 1996.

"Personally I suspect that the generally conservative White American masses have now tasted blood, as it were, and will not be content until the predominance of the American democratic

---

[1] In mid-1996, Gingrich's wife was given a position with a Jewish firm striving for improvement of trade relations with the Israelis. There is some speculation that the company is a Mossad front. Furthermore, Newt Gingrich's closest advisor is Jewish and he recently hired another political aide who previously was a high-ranking functionary of AIPAC, the Zionist lobbying group.

dictatorship, to which the power of Jewry is indivisibly linked nowadays, has been broken. The last election statistics reveal what is yet to come: 37% of those entitled to vote actually did so.

"A mere 2% of these 37%, almost all of them White men, were the decisive factor in bringing about the surprising election result. 78% of the Jewish and 90% of the Black voters voted for the losers, putting themselves out of the running in the process. What I am most interested in are the 63% of voters who stayed at home.

"Since for various, usually racial reasons the conditions in the United States are often completely different from those in Germany, I assume that there are approximately 20% eligible voters (mostly Blacks) who simply never vote. Therefore one must ask who makes up the 43% of non-voters who did not participate for other reasons this time.

"I believe that they are Aryan Americans, many of them of German descent, who were sick of the whole 'democratic' mumbo jumbo (to date).

"The above example of the Californian 'Proposition 187' which has been temporarily derailed by the Jews should suffice to prove that the displeasure of the voters is justified. But now the events of November 8, 1994 have shown, for the first time in more than 40 years, that elections can indeed effect fundamental changes. This is why I would expect a considerably greater voter turn-out in 1996, constituted largely by people who think like we do.

"In other words, the Democratic Party (which is known as the Jews' party because, as has been conceded, more than 50% of its funds come from Jews and their organizations), not only has no chance of regaining the Congress, it will also lose the White House. However: in the wake of the tremendous and unexpected defeat of November 8, the elite Jews will do everything they can

The Indictment and My Commentary

to bring about a change in their favor.

"This is why the final candidates of both parties, and of any third party that may perhaps be created at the last minute, will almost certainly be loyal followers of Israel. Someone like Patrick Buchanan will not have any chance yet to become President in 1996. The demise of Jewish power, and the consequences that may be expected, will not be clearly apparent for everyone to see until after 1996. At this point I'd put my money on Dole as the Republican presidential candidate; he and his wife, the President of the American Red Cross (an Internationalist pay-off position), belong to the ranks of our opponents.

"One of the best examples of how much has changed since November 8 was the collapse of the Mexican peso. In December 1994 this currency suddenly dropped sharply in value compared to the dollar, which hurt American investors badly. Clinton, quite unsuspecting, went to the Congress and requested guaranteed loans of 40 billion dollars for our southern neighbors, allegedly in order to back their currency and to preserve that nation from an economic catastrophe.

"There can be no doubt that before the November election everything would have gone smoothly and that the President would have received the requested guarantees within days. But suddenly everything was different.

"In the Congress as well as in the media it was openly suggested that the loan guarantees were first and foremost a rescue operation for the 'Wall Street financiers,' and some went so far as to hold Alan Greenspan (of the Federal Reserve Bank) and Secretary of the Treasury Robert Rubin responsible for the fiasco, leaving no doubt in the process that they actually meant the 'Jews.'

"In any case, the almost unbelievable happened: after nearly two weeks Dole and Gingrich (who naturally supported the issue, since after all the bosses in the back rooms were to profit from it), had to inform Clinton, that in light of the stubbornness of especially the new members of Congress, it was impossible to win enough support for the project.

"Clinton was left with a perhaps unlawful and definitely dangerous step as his only recourse. He took 20 billion dollars from a fund dating from Roosevelt's time and which was earmarked for backing the dollar if ever it were to drop too low in value in international trade. He also promised the Mexicans enormous sums from the International Monetary Fund (IMF) and from other international agencies over which he does not have sole right of disposal, which led to disagreements especially with Germany and France. The missing $20 billion will of course hasten the collapse of the dollar.

"If this collapse does come about, then the United States will see an economic catastrophe of undreamed-of proportions. The American people will remember the names Greenspan and Rubin, which may mean dreadful repercussions for the whole of American Jewry since particularly the Jewish associations stand almost unanimously behind these two and avenge any and all criticism of their dirty machinations, as anti-Semitism.

"(In this context it should be pointed out that the wide distribution of computers in the United States has already broken the Jewish monopoly over the media. Even 80-year-olds in retirement homes are connected to the rest of the world via the Internet and other programs. A few keystrokes suffice to inform one's Representative that 'one' does not endorse financial support for Israel, or the rescue of Jewish Wall Street financiers. People are also becoming better informed than ever before. Radio talk shows also contribute to these changing conditions.)

"The fact that the ultra-rich Jews were deeply involved in the peso affair from the start was demonstrated by the eagerness with which all the prominent Jews (including the great many Jewish journalists), strove to push the loan guarantees through Congress.

"It is also no secret that it was primarily Jewish investors and investment companies who had invested most heavily in Mexican companies of late. I assume that your fellow Jews, sticking together like burrs as they always do, were hoping to manage for the second time within one decade to massively feather their nests at the expense of the American taxpayers, even more than they do day in, day out anyhow, (or perhaps more money was needed to stuff the craw of The Parasitic Nation).

"The first great fleecing, reminiscent of the 'German' trust company's misdeeds, was pulled off via the Savings and Loan scheme which robbed the American people of nearly 500 billion dollars. There are indications that the course for the Mexican fiasco was already set more than a year ago, prior to that surprising November election.

"It was done on the assumption, therefore, that the Congress which was still in the pockets of the 'financiers' at that time, would 'of course' approve the loan guarantees, and then everything would have been set for the big rip-off.

"(I don't believe it is commonly known in Germany that the major investors in Mexican loans received up to 23% interest; with a few even receiving as high as a 50% per annum interest. And this for amounts running into the billions. This money was to be guaranteed with US taxes. No wonder, since Mexico was going bankrupt.)

"It is also likely that there were plans to buy up Mexico at rock-bottom prices after the peso had collapsed.

"Only this time with the difference that the Mexican state was also to have 'privatized' PEMEX, the national oil company - a goal which the Internationalists (One-Worlders) in New York have been pursuing for decades. (The deals worked out between the US and Mexico in February remind me vividly of American 'generosity' towards the German Reich after the First World War [the Dawes-Young Plan], where practically the whole of Germany was mortgaged to the crooks overseas. It is certain that the Mexican peons will now be even poorer than before.)

"The defeats of November 8, 1994 and of the peso affair - defeats which are the writing on the wall for the Jews and which cannot be reversed even with the greatest exertion of all resources yet available - prompt me to point out that the leadership of at least the American Jews is entirely on the wrong track.

"Instead of finally doing what I had suggested as early as 1987 or so, when Jews had attained the greatest possible extent of their power in this country - namely to tighten its collective belt and be content with the booty it already had - the Jewish leadership has continued to expand its power base, and has drawn ever more attention in the process.

"In my opinion there is nothing worse for a Jew than 'exposure,' regardless of whether it is brought about by Aryans or by themselves. It's too late now to turn back, and the awful fate will run its unalterable course. The fact, whether one likes it or not, is that no people, no nation, can afford to be ruled indefinitely by a small, fanatical racial-religious minority ever intent on its self-ordained segregation but wallowing in special privileges.

"That the elite Jews have now realized, at least subconsciously, that their power is waning, is demonstrated by a phenomenon currently in evidence all throughout the world, whether it be after liberation festivities in Auschwitz, terrorist attacks on Jewish institutions in Argentina, England and elsewhere, 'kamikaze' attacks on Jewish soldiers in Israel, or American 'Holocaust' events, the press and TV assiduously show pictures of weeping Jews. Since the same is not done with pictures of Bosnians in Sarajevo, women in Grossny, survivors of Israeli attacks in Lebanon or mangled people in Rwanda, one must assume that there is a specific intent behind this sob campaign. But what intent?

"I am reminded of children who have done something naughty for which they know they will definitely be punished. They already start to cry even before they are spanked - sometimes out of fear of the expected pain, but usually in order to arouse sympathy.

"Could it be that the propagandistic exploitation of weeping Jews is intended to revive the sense of pity that no longer exists today in the collective breast of the Aryan masses? Maybe. In any case, at least in the United States, the Jews managed long ago to erode the post-1945 good will of the people. Even the day-in, day-out exhibition of weeping, mourning, helpless and oh-so-sensitive ('human') specimens of your racial fellows will no longer suffice to change the facts. We have seen through Judaea...

"In this respect, Jews like you, Bubis, Friedman, Gysi etc. are doing your people a great disservice by infiltrating Germany, the nation that belongs solely and exclusively to the Germans of true German blood, in positions where (in my opinion, and under the prevailing conditions), you simply have no business being. And even if it is no more than 60% of all Germans who think 'Jew' every time they see one of your sort on TV, this can yet turn out to be dangerous to you later on.

"It is not that I expect a pogrom-like reaction to the (present) abuse of Jewish power; there was no such reaction even during the Third Reich. But what did happen back then, and what is already happening in the States today, will also happen in Germany: there will be very few people willing to place themselves protectively in front of threatened Jews (and the heroes of protest-candle fame will wisely stay at home and keep their blinds down).

"The reason is simple: whenever Jews (as we have seen since 1945), have the power, their presumptuousness knows no bounds. Not a day goes by without their making new enemies for themselves (what you did at the Bundeswehr-University is a good example). But one fine day the scales tip, and as has been the case time and again for millennia, the dream of Jewish omnipotence is suddenly no more.

"In one of my earlier letters I already pointed out that nothing bothers me about your people as much as their frequently apparent, profound dishonesty.

"Today I have another classic example of this. On the occasion of the American 'Days of Remembrance' in January of this year, the January 26, 1995 issue of the *Washington Post,* a Jewish-owned newspaper, published a long article by Jewess Sharon Waxman, who commented on the now disavowed figure of 4 million casualties in Auschwitz: "The West had never believed this figure anyhow."[2]

"What audacity, what impertinence, what a lie! How many people have been punished in Germany for decades now because they presumed to publicly question the mendacious claim of 4 million in Auschwitz (and the '6 million' directly related to it)?

"How many Americans have been branded as 'anti-Semites' and deprived of their positions and their honor by that allegedly so defenseless little nation, merely for pointing out the impossibilities connected with the 4-million-figure?

---

[2] Our research has shown that *every single one* of the approximately 1,600 American dailies and almost all weekly papers and other publications carried a report on Auschwitz at that time.

"And now this Jewess comes along and coolly claims that 'the West' had never believed this nonsense anyhow. Will she perhaps soon make the same insolent claim with respect to gas chambers in Auschwitz?

"In connection with the 'Holocaust' story, I must reproach you personally (but I will gladly take it back if you should actually have dealt with the matter publicly). In the *Washington Jewish Week* of February 2, 1995, there was a brief report about the 'American Red Cross Holocaust Tracing Service,' that was established a few years ago in Baltimore, Maryland, after the two chief Allies (the USA and the former USSR), had finally released the detailed and carefully-kept German concentration camp registers (giving names, transport, casualties, work details etc.)--lists that were already used in 1945-46 in the Nuremberg Trials. In any case, according to the newspaper article 260 families were reunited in the past couple of years.

"And after almost 50 years! But what could have persuaded the Americans, for example, to keep these immensely important records secret for almost half a century?

"I have only one explanation: the more Jews were unable to locate their loved ones after 1945, the easier it was to maintain the 'Holocaust' tale.

"In other words, it was for politically motivated reasons that millions of Jews have died all over the world ever since 1945, never knowing that their parents and siblings, grandparents and other relatives had survived the chaos of war, starvation and thirst, typhoid, cholera, and blanket bombing by the Allies.

"I myself can swear to it that as early as 1949 the Zionist associations in the United States routinely told Jews searching for their loved ones that these had been gassed in Auschwitz. Only a very few continued searching after that. Can one blame them?

"(According to a report that appeared in the *New York Times* on February 19, 1995, there are still 70,000 'Holocaust-survivors' living in the States today.)

"But you, a Jewish history professor who is also politically very active, ought to consider it your duty to look into this matter at long last and to denounce those who are guilty of this crime that is truly unparalleled in the history of mankind. I think you owe it to your people and to the actual victims among them. Even the Jews cannot indefinitely maintain a state built on a foundation of lies. The telephone number of the Tracing Service in Baltimore is 800-848-9277 (toll-free in the United States).

"Do you recall that in one of my letters I wrote about the OSI, the Office of Special Investigations of the American Ministry of Justice, which almost committed the judicial murder of innocent Ivan Demjanjuk?

"As you know, the OSI was created by an Act proposed by Jewish groups, introduced by the Jewish Representative Elizabeth Holtzmann, and passed by the then Jewish-controlled Congress.

"Well, according to the *Washington Jewish Week* of January 26, 1995, it is still in existence fifteen years later. The Office has a staff of thirty-two mostly Jewish persons (including at least 12 Jewish lawyers) and an annual budget of 3.5 million dollars, and in the past year it instituted proceedings, in all, for seven new trials, mostly of simple ex-soldiers of Eastern European nations who had fought on the German side.

"In my opinion it would have been easier simply to give each of these old men half a million dollars on the condition that they return to Europe. But of course that would not have quenched the Jewish thirst for revenge, would it?

"Neil Sher, the Jew who was Chief of the OSI for many years and is now the head of AIPAC, the Israel Lobby, suggested that the OSI is very important for American Jews and has taken on particular significance now that there are so many Revisionists who no longer believe in the Holocaust.

"In concluding this letter I want to return briefly to a topic that surely interests you as well: the controversy still surrounding the murder of American President John F. Kennedy, now more than 3 decades ago.

"At the time of the murder I never believed for a second that it was the act of one individual assassin, one who at first was always portrayed as a little crazy. I also remember very well that 'they' (assisted by the media under 'their' thumb), initially tried to make American right-wingers appear to be the ones chiefly responsible. This fact alone ought to have tipped me off even then as to who the real powers-behind-the-scenes were that desired Kennedy's removal. In any case, I never believed the story of the lone assassin, and I left the question as to the real culprits open.

"On January 31, 1995, in the *Washington Times* (a paper which I do not think is under Jewish control; it belongs to the Rev. Moon sect), I found - in this paper and nowhere else - an article about one Dr. Charles Crenshaw; according to this article, the *Journal of the American Medical Association* as well as the *Dallas Morning News* had to reach a legal settlement with this former physician from the Parkland Hospital in Dallas, where Kennedy as well as Oswald were treated after being shot.

"Thirty years after the murder, Dr. Crenshaw had written in a book that in his capacity as attending physician he had realized right away that Kennedy had been shot from the front, and thus not by Oswald. The AMA and the DMN (both of them Establishment institutions) had responded to his observations by publicly questioning his medical abilities.

"That the subsequent settlement awarded Dr. Crenshaw

amounted to several hundred thousand dollars, speaks volumes. Interestingly enough, a Jew was involved in this matter too, David Belin. In 1963-64 he was one of the lawyers of the Warren Commission, whose aim it was to see the 'lone wolf theory' (Lee Harvey Oswald as sole assassin) officially established.

"A lot of water has flowed under the bridge since then. After so many years there is a much better perspective on the whole matter, and I think I now have a better idea of who - or which group - wanted or needed Kennedy to die. In any case, since November 8, 1994 it is chiefly the Jews who complain time and again that 'the Republicans now aim to destroy the entire American social structure that was so carefully built up during the Lyndon B. Johnson years.' What these Jews mean are those dreadful laws that destroyed the system that had existed since our nation's infancy.

"In other words, what happened under LBJ was a Revolution favoring Jewish interests. If Kennedy had lived, this would not have happened. Another indication that Kennedy had perhaps been murdered on Jewish initiative, has been right before my eyes all these years, but I recognized it only recently. Ever since 1964, a tremendous number of books have been written about the Kennedy Assassination, many of them by Jewish writers, each of them proposing a different theory as to who might have been behind it.

"Since in the United States almost no book running counter to Jewish interests is published by a 'reputable' publisher, is reviewed in important newspapers, or finds its way into the selection offered by most bookstores, one must assume that the spouting of all these theories has been in the interests of Jewry. In other words, Kennedy's real assassins wished to cover their tracks by means of the common technique of obfuscation and to confuse the masses in their search for the truth.

"At any rate, there is no doubt today that the assassins of JFK opened the doors for Lyndon B. Johnson (who, I think, was not involved in the assassination but who did 'sense' that he would come to power soon), and this in turn allowed for the Jewish revolution in America which changed this nation beyond recognition.

"I know that this is a serious allegation against your people. For this reason, and due to your prominent position in Germany, you ought to consider it your duty to find and expose any potential errors in my reasoning and my expositions. If you do not, then I will know that deep down you agree with me, but have chosen to withhold the truth out of loyalty and a sense of duty to Jewry.

"Greetings,

"[signed] Hans

"P.S.: According to the *Süddeutsche Zeitung* of January 20, 1995, the French Jew Michel Friedman, presently the token Jew in the CDU Federal Council, commented on the infiltration of Germany by people of foreign race: 'No one has ownership claims on this country. And national identity, a priori, is the right of the individual, not of the nation... ' Does this also apply to Israel ? I wonder...

"Re: the Kennedy Assassination. I want to add the following: I already mentioned once that a Jewish couple by the name of Krim were permanent residents in the White House during LBJ's time in office. And in February of this year, the Jewish Judge Irving L. Goldberg passed away in Dallas, Texas --the same Jew who, according to the *N.Y. Times* (February 13, 1995), "was called (from Dallas!) to the White House for consultation on November 22, 1963, only a few hours after Kennedy had been shot." During the Second World War, Johnson, then a Member of the House of Representatives, had summoned Irving L. Goldberg from the US Navy to the Capitol."

Re. 7.: (Case File 6):

On a date not known precisely but falling between May 1995 and June 27, 1995, the accused sent the publication *USA-Bericht* Nr. 6-95, authored and published by himself and consisting essentially of the letter to Professor Dr. Michael Wolffsohn as reproduced in point 6. above, to the pensioner Werner Schulz in Bonn.

Re. 8.: (Case File 7):

On a date not known precisely but falling into the second half of March 1995, the accused sent *USA-Bericht* 4-95 to the District Council in 82140 Olching. This publication contains, inter alia, the following:

"(...) Naturally, the Jewish leadership exploited the Auschwitz and Dresden remembrance days and the upcoming anniversary of the dropping of the first large atomic bomb on Hiroshima for their own purposes - as usual. Considering that the brainwashing of the Germans has worked so well that the mere mention of the word 'Auschwitz' by a Jewish activist produces the same effect as the 'Open Sesame' of fairy-tale fame, opening all the German treasure vaults like magic, they are now trying the same here in the States. (...) Besides, there are now even more millions of people in the whole world who know that not everyone believes in the dogmas of the new Holocaust Religion."

Re. 9.: (Case File 8):

From Burke/Virginia (USA), the accused mailed the publication *USA-Bericht* 1-94, postmarked December 23, 1993, to *Bundestag* Member Siegfried Vergin in Bonn. The mailing was supplemented with an accompanying note handwritten by the accused, containing the following:

"Dear Herr Vergin -

"I read your letter to the editor (MA Mo Dec. 12, '93) about Leuchter.

"Do you know anything about freedom of speech?

"Incidentally, Leuchter is anything but a propagandist, but he did help smash the 'H'-myth.

"Keep it up.

"Yours, H. Schmidt"

Re. 10.: (Case File 9):

From Pensacola, Florida, the accused mailed a newsletter of the GERMAN AMERICAN NATIONAL PUBLIC AFFAIRS COMMITEE [sic] (GANPAC), dated November 1, 1994 and postmarked December 21, 1994, as well as an "Open Letter" dated November 10, 1994 and addressed to the Chief Council, County Court and Prosecuting Attorney's Office Arnstadt, Thüringen, 99310 Arnstadt, Germany. This open letter, which was received by the Prosecuting Attorney's Office of Bochum on December 28, 1994, contains the following:

"In view of the overwhelming evidence for their self-ordained segregation, is it possible that the Jews (as an entity, as religious, racial, cultural and ethnic community) might be pursuing goals other than those they profess, to promote race mixing and to subvert other nations and peoples from inside by means of the introduction of unassimilable ethnic groups?

"(Note the refugee problem in modern Germany.) It really looks that way, and I would be much obliged to you, dear Prosecuting Attorneys and Judges of Arnstadt, if you could suggest other motives for the Jews' actions in this regard.

"(...) Only the truth (about themselves) can set the Jews free from their vicious circle, but you will never get close to this truth as long as there are ignorant Prosecuting Attorneys and Judges who seek to prevent public discussion of the subversive behavior of the Jews and of other dangerous (collective) characteristics of these strange people."

(Case File 10):

From Pensacola, Florida, the accused sent the writings described in point 10, postmarked December 21, 1994, to the address "Prosecuting Attorney's Office Bochum, Reitzensteinstrasse 17, 45657 Recklinghausen." This mailing was received by the joint Letters Department of the Recklinghausen Judicial Authorities on December 28, 1994.

Re. 12.: (Case File 11): From Karlsruhe, the accused sent Bundestag Representative Peter Conradi, Bonn, a copy, postmarked April 25, 1995, of a letter dated July 5, 1994 and originally addressed to Foreign Minister Klaus Kinkel.

The copy of this letter bears the following additional comment: "Attention: Herrn Peter Conradi! Maybe now you will realize who has the say over us again?"

And contains the following text:

"Dear Herr Kinkel!

"On May 31, 1994, the German-language Californian newspaper *Neue Presse* ran a dpa article about you after you had commented that 'the German image abroad is dreadful, enough to make one weep.' The report also mentions that your Embassy in Washington had wired you that (in the USA) 'all the media were horrified' by the Magdeburg race riots.

"Other high points of the dpa article included that German diplomats and other representatives abroad had noticed "a worldwide outcry" (after Magdeburg) and that anxious attention was reported even in cities such as Singapore, Budapest, Copenhagen and Sophia. 'The greatest concern was revealed, (however), by an American investigation - commissioned by the Foreign Office --of all the country's television channels.'

"This last sentence prompts me to ask whether you as 'German' Foreign Minister really don't know that not only the

American press, but almost all other media as well, including television, are in Jewish or Jewish-dominated hands? And do you not understand that race mixing and the destruction of the individual peoples is part of the Jewish agenda, as the elite Jews themselves have admitted? That any German attempt at self-defense a la Magdeburg is therefore in violation of Jewish interests, and will be avenged accordingly? Just look at the actions and listen to the words of the chief representatives of world Jewry in Germany, i.e. of Bubis, Friedman, Wolffsohn, Cohn-Bendit etc., and you will clearly recognize in them the Jewish line. (...)"

Indictable offense under §§ 130 Nos. 1 and 3,
131 Sec. 1 No. 1 and 4 (old ea.) StGB;
§§ 130 Sec. 1 No. 2, Sec. 2 No. 1
ltr. a) and d), Sec. 3,
Sec. 4 (new ea.) StGB;
§§189, 194 Sec. 2, 52, 53 StGB

<u>Evidence:</u>
I. Statements of the accused
II. <u>Witnesses:</u>
1 Martin Klingst, to summon via: Pressehaus Speersort 1, 20095 Hamburg

2. Professor Dr. Michael Wolffsohn, to summon via: Historisches Institut der Universität der Bundeswehr München, 85577 Neubiberg

3. Werner Schulz, Im Weiler 5, 53123 Bonn (Case File 6, p. 1R)

4. Frau Ruhle, to summon via: Gemeindeverwaltung Olching, Rebhuhnstrosse 18, 82140 Olching

5. Siegfried Vergin, Member of the Bundestag, to summon via: Bundeshaus, Görresstrasse 15, 53113 Bonn

6. Peter Conradi, Member of the Bundestag, to summon via:

Bundeshaus, Görresstrasse 15, 53113 Bonn

III. <u>Material Evidence:</u>

1 USA-Bericht No. 11/94 also envelope with return address: P. O. Box 10600.

(Case File 7, p. 3); (Case File 8, p. 2); (Case File 1 1, p. 1)

Burke, VA 22009-600, USA, addressed to: Land Mecklenburg, Bundesrat: CDU: Rudi Geil Karl-Marx-Strasse 1. 19055 Schwerin

USA-Bericht No. 11/94 in 2 pieces with 2 envelopes with return address: P. O. Box 10600, Burke, VA 22015, USA, with 2 envelopes addressed to: Staatsanwaltschaft, Schützenwall 3 1, 2300 Kiel 1

(Main Files v. I, p. 4ff.). (Case File 1, p. 2ff.)

3 USA-Bericht No. 11/94 also envelope with return address: P. O. Box 10600 Burke, VA 22015, USA, addressed to: Staatsanwaltschaft, Westring 8, 4630 Bochum 1

4 USA-Bericht No. 11/94 also envelope with return address: P. O. Box 10600, Burke, VA 22015, USA, addressed to: Staatsanwaltschaft Bochum, Reitzensteinstrasse 17, 4350 Recklinghausen

5. Letter to Martin Klingst in Hamburg dated May 8, 1994

(Case File 2, p. 2ff.). (Case File 3, p. lff.) (in photocopy form)

6. Letter of March 9, 1995 to Prof. Dr. Michael Wolffsohn, Neubiberg

7. USA-Bericht No. 6-95

8. USA-Bericht No. 4-95

9. USA-Bericht No. 1-94 with a handwritten note affixed thereto, directed to Member of the Bundestag Vergin, also an envelope with return address: P. O. Box 10600, Burke, VA 22015, USA

(Case File 4, p. 4ff.) (in photocopy form) (Case File 5, p.

2ff.) (in photocopy form) (Case File 6, p. 4ff.(Case File 7. C

10. *GANPAC-Brief* dated November 1, 1994 as well as an "Open Letter" to the Chief Council, County Court and Prosecuting Attorney's Office Arnstadt-Thüringen, dated November 10, 1994 also one envelope with return address: P.O. Box 11124, Pensacola, FL, 32524-1124, USA, addressed to: Staatsanwaltschaft Westring 8, 44787 Bochum 1

11. *GANPAC-Brief* dated November 1, 1994 as well as an "Open Letter" to Chief Council, County Court and Prosecuting Attorney's Office Arnstadt-Thüringen dated November 10, 1994 also one envelope with return address: P.O. Box 11124, Pensacola, FL, 32524-1124, USA, addressed to: Staatsanwaltschaft Bochum, Reitzensteinstrasse 17, 45657 Recklinghausen

12. Letter to Member of the Bundestag Peter Conradi, also one envelope without return address, mailed on April 25, 1995 in Karlsruhe.

IV. Supplementary Files:

1 1 Special Issue with photocopies of the proceedings in 11 Js 10471/92, Prosecuting Attorney's Office München I and 11 Js 14651/95, Prosecuting Attorney's Office München II

2. 1 vol. documentation 11 Js 10471/92, Prosecuting Attorney's Office München II

3. 45 Js 352/91 Prosecuting Attorney's Office Freiburg, to obtain from thence.

Summary. Results of Investigations:

I. Re. the Accused:

The accused was born on April 27, 1927, in Völklingen (Luisenthal) on the Saar River, the second of his parents' six children. He grew up with his parents in Luisenthal, where he attended public school from 1933-1941.

He subsequently apprenticed as merchant, until in 1944 he

volunteered for the Waffen-SS and served in this capacity until the end of the War, serving last in Austria. After the end of the War the accused fell into American captivity for a few weeks, but was able to escape. He subsequently completed his apprenticeship in Saarbrücken and began a career as a businessman. From 1947 to 1949 the accused remained in hiding because he had reason to fear that, being a former member of the Waffen-SS, the French military authorities in the Saarland would abduct him to forced labor.

In 1949 he left Europe and emigrated to the United States. According to his own statements the accused received American citizenship sometime after a five years' residence, while also retaining his German citizenship. According to his own information, the accused has been an independent businessman, with his own company, since the late 1950s. Since 1978 the accused has been retired. Since 1975 he has been married to his second wife Roswitha (Case File 4, p. 54ff. enc.).

According to the District Criminal Police Office of Mecklenburg-Vorpommern (p. 2f. enc.) the accused has been known for some time as the author and publisher of publications with indictable content. According to the above Department, he is Chairman of the "German-American-Political-Action-Comitee" [sic] (GANPAC) headquartered in Santa Monica, California (USA) and, as such, also the author and publisher of the *GANPAC-Brief,* Publisher of the *Amerika-Briefe,* P. O. Box 27566, Washington DC 20038, USA;

Author of various open letters published under the return address "P. O. Box 10600, Burke, VA 22015, USA."

Publisher of the *USA-Bericht,* P. O. Box, Burke, Virginia 22009-600, USA, which in part also appeared later under the return address P. O. Box 11124, Pensacola, FL 32524-1124.

In the course of the trial 45 Js 352/91 / Prosecuting Attorney's

Office Freiburg, the Federal Criminal Police Office sent an inquiry to the American Embassy, which provided the Criminal Office with the following information held by American authorities (v. I, p. 12ff.):

In 1988 the name Hans Schmidt came up in the trial of a man who was convicted of distributing hate propaganda in Canada. It was ascertained that a post office box which had been used by the person involved in this trial had been rented by one Hans Schmidt, 1411 U Street, NW, Washington DC. It was found later that the address 1411 U Street did not exist and that the man who had rented the P. O. Box had used a forged driver's license. The file also contained an article by columnist Jack Anderson, dated July 24, 1985 and titled 'PAC Lives Off Its Proceeds'. In summary, the article stated that a group from California that called itself the only 'political action committee' (PAC) 'defending the interests of 52 million Americans of German descent' had received US $55,000 in donations in the course of two years, but had used none of the money to support candidates running for any public office.

Most of the money had been used to disseminate 'information' which the Chairman of PAC believed would further the interests of '...good American... and Western civilization...'. Formal financial disclosure proved that much of the money had been used for offices rented by Schmidt, for credit card payments, and for other personal expenses.

The article claimed that Schmidt published a monthly information newsletter and that his statements therein are 'full of skepticism regarding the butchery of millions of European Jews by the Nazis during the Second World War.' The article did not mention the title of this information service.

The article further stated that Schmidt described himself as 'former member of the Hitler Youth and the Waffen-SS, who had fought for Germany, not for Hitler.'

In a further case in 1988 it was determined that one Hans Schmidt was the author of an *Amerika-Brief*. The *Amerika-Brief* was a regular column in the German right-wing extremist publication *Sieg*. Schmidt was brought to the attention of the FBI because he had written an article for *Sieg* which the Federal Office for the Protection of the Constitution (in Germany) deemed to be racist and directed against the predominance of the 'Jews' in the United States.

Schmidt is described as male, White, born on April 27, 1927.

The Hans Schmidt in question was born on April 27, 1924 [sic]. In light of the similar birth dates the two persons may be identical.

In 1988 Schmidt (*Amerika Brief*) had used post office boxes in Washington, DC as well as in Virginia. It was determined at that time that Schmidt lived in Fairfax, Virginia.

Fairfax is located near Burke, Virginia, where the Hans Schmidt currently at issue has a P. O. Box.

According to statements made by the accused to the District Criminal Police Office of Saarbrücken on March 21, 1995, he maintains a second residence at the address of his mother, Hilde Schmidt, at 66333 Völklingen-Luisenthal. He also stayed there on occasion while visiting Germany (v. I p. 53 enc.).

According to a statement given by his mother to the police in Völklingen, the accused stays at her home only "sporadically" (v. II p. 149 enc.).

II. Re. the Case at Issue:

Regarding the individual offenses, reference is made to the main of the indictment.

With the exception of counts 5., 6., 10. and 12., the offenses with which the accused is charged are matters of press content. However, since the publications disseminated by the accused do not originate within the spatial jurisdiction of the German Criminal Code, the particular court of jurisdiction of the press (§7 Section 2 StPO) does not obtain. The court of jurisdiction is determined by the principle of the scene of the crime (§7 Section 1 StPO).

This means that in the case of printed matter published abroad, a court of jurisdiction is warranted at every site of dissemination (cf. Kleinknecht/Meyer-Golssner, StPO §7 MN 7).

So far as the misdemeanors at issue are matters of press content, the statute of limitations is determined by the District press laws in force at the respective places of distribution. With the exception of the Land of North Rhine-Westphalia, where offenses as per §130 Sections 2 and 4 StGB are not subject to lapse under press law, the statute of limitations is set at six months in every Land of the Federal Republic of Germany.

So far as this statute of limitations would have expired for the individual offenses, the lapse period has been recommenced by the initiation of appropriate judicial measures.

The following is supplementary to the review of the individual offenses: Re. 1:

Lapse was prevented by the issuing of the arrest warrant of March 28, 1995 (v. I p. 33 enc., §78c Section 1 No. 5 StGB); by the August 10, 1995 decision of the County Court of Frankfurt am Main, supporting the further detention of the accused (v. I pp. 84 and 114ff. enc.); and finally by the revision of the arrest warrant and the order for further detention issued by the County Court of Schwerin on October 5,1995(v.IIp.151ff. enc.).

In denying the deliberate mass murder of the Jews in the concentration camp gas chambers during the Third Reich, which is reflected in the Charge and has been manifested by his disputatious statements regarding the self-evidence of this historical fact and by his description of this fact as "six-million-tale, maintained in the interests of our enemies", the accused has committed the crime of incitement of the people, concomitantly with incitement of race hatred and disparagement of the memory of persons deceased (§§130, 131 Section 1 No. 1 StGB in the form in force until November 30, 1994).

Insofar as he strives thus to give the impression that the Jewish minority in Germany exploits the Federal Republic by means of lies, he portrays Jews as inferior beings undeserving of the respect of other citizens, and in this way evokes in the recipients of his writings an emotionally greatly enhanced, hostile attitude towards Jews (cf. BGH NStZ 1995, 1 28f).

At the same time he disparages the memory of those who lost their lives in the gas chambers of concentration camps during the National Socialist mass murder.

Insofar as the accused describes the Federal German political parties, which he calls "parties loyal to the System," as being "infested by Jews and Freemasons," these descriptions are directed equally against the corresponding population groups in Germany and represent a particularly vicious form of slander ie. malicious disparagement of these groups, intended to deny them their full right of existence in the national community ie. to portray them as groups of inferior worth

(cf. OLG Hamm, NStZ 1995, 136ff.).

The various incendiary and disparaging aspects expressed in the publication combine to create its discriminatory overall character and complement each other naturally as components of the crime (§52 StGB).

The range of sentence will be determined by Section 2 of §130 as revised by the Crime Control Act of October 28, 1994, in force as of December 1, 1994. §130 Section 4 also obtains for the denial of the deliberate mass murder of Jews in publications

(§ 11 Section 3 StGB).

Insofar as the publication described in point 1 was in each case mailed by the accused with postmarks of December 19, 1994, then in view of its receipt by the Prosecuting Attorney's Office of Kiel on January 9, 1995, the period of lapse under press law was initially recommenced by the order issued on May 11, 1995 for the interrogation of the accused by the Prosecuting Attorney's Office of Saarbrücken (Case File 1, p. 24R, cf. also note ret No. 1 on p. 28 of Case File 1).

The period of lapse was again recommenced by the decision of County Court of Schwerin, of October 5, 1995, which expanded the arrest warrant to include the offense relating to the subject of Case File 1.

Counts 3. and 4. concern offenses whose period of lapse is determined by the provision of North Rhine-Westphalian press law, whose §25 Section 1 Subsection 2 specifies that for offenses under §130 Section 2 and 4 StGB the limitation provision set by the Criminal Code for the institution of proceedings apply.

Count 5. pertains to a letter sent to a newspaper editor and which, due to the incendiary nature of its contents, constitutes an attack in the sense of § 30 StGB (old version) that is likely to lead to a breach of the peace.

A letter to a newspaper (or to an editor) lends itself to provoking a breach of the peace even if the sender does not expect that his letter will be printed as "letter to the editor" without comment, but rather --as was to be expected in this case under the circumstances--expects only a report expressing critical rejection of his incendiary statements and, possibly, emphasizing the danger inherent in the political endeavors they express (cf. BGH 29, 26ff.).

In the absence of publication, this "original letter" addressed to the journalist Martin Klingst is not an offense of press content, so that in this regard the limitation provisions of the Criminal Code [StGB] obtain.

Re. 6. and 7:

The object of proceedings is the text - reproduced in its entirety in the indictment - of a letter to the historian and journalist Prof. Dr. Michael Wolffsohn in Neubiberg, whose nature as a publication suited to public incitement as discussed in §130 Section 2 No. 1 (new version) becomes apparent from the countless defamations of people of Jewish faith expressed in, and to be considered in the overall context of, this letter.

These defamations culminate in the denial of the deliberate extermination of Jews in gas chambers during the Third Reich and in the way in which the murder of the American President John F. Kennedy is blamed on "the Jews".

Re. 8.:

From the overall context of the publication described in the Charge, and the description of the deliberate extermination of Jews during the Third Reich as "dogma of the new Holocaust Religion", together with the claim that "the mere mention of the word 'Auschwitz' by a Jewish activist produces the same effect as the 'Open Sesame' of fairy-tale fame", it becomes evident that this too is an instance of the so-called "qualified Auschwitz-Lie", an account intended to dismiss the mass extermination during the Third Reich as an untruth concocted for purposes of facilitating material demands to be made on the Federal Republic of Germany.

This constitutes concomitant violations of §130 Section 1 No. 1, Section 2 No. 1, and Section 3, Section 4.

Re. 9.:

The description of the deliberate extermination of the Jews during the Third Reich as "Holocaust myth" ("H-myth")--an expression made prior to the revision of §130 StGB--constitutes disparagement of the memory of those Jews who fell victim to the mass extermination under National Socialist tyranny (§189 StGB).

Re. 10. and 11.:

The letter--reproduced in its essence in point 10 of the indictment--in which the accused charges "the Jews" with "subverting other nations and peoples from inside by means of the introduction of unassimilable ethnic groups" and with exhibiting "subversive Jewish behavior and other dangerous (collective) characteristics", serves the purpose of inciting hatred against a religious group and of attacking the human dignity of this religious group with the particularly vicious slander contained herein (§130 Section 1 No. 1, Section 2 No. 1 StGB rev. ed.).

Re. 12.:

The description of the racist excesses in Magdeburg in April 1994 as "German attempt at self-defense" that violated Jewish interests and would therefore be "avenged" by the media that are "in Jewish hands" also serves the aforementioned purpose and constitutes an offense under §130 StGB (rev. ed.).

III. Determining the Sentence:

In determining the sentence it should be considered that according to the Federal Supreme Court's ruling on determining sentence in cases of incitement by political criminals of conviction (cf. BGH NStZ 1995, 128f), the imposition of a severe term of imprisonment not subject to suspension in favor of probation should be considered.

In this context the other offenses of the accused which have already lapsed (cf. Supplementary Files) ought also to be considered as compounding the crime, thus warranting a sterner sentence (cf. BGH StV 1994, 423; Foth in NStZ 1995, 375f.).

IV. Competence

§24 Section 1 No. 3 GVG indicates that the District Court is the court of competent jurisdiction to pass sentence with regard to the offenses charged herein. That these are particularly significant offenses becomes apparent from the extent to which the law has been contravened, as well as from the consequences attendant on offenses of the kind the accused is charged with, which - aside from stirring up the public - have consistently lent themselves in recent times to setting the stage for racist, anti-foreigner and religious discrimination all the way up to acts of arson and murder.

Furthermore, the offenses committed by the accused, as well as his arrest, have evoked a particularly vigorous response in the press, both domestic and abroad. As well, the fact that the trial may be expected to be a lengthy one further warrants its being held before the District Court in light of §24 Section 1 No. 3 GVG (cf. Kleinknecht/Meyer-Gossner, StPO 42nd ea., §24 GVG MN 6).

I move a) to initiate the main proceedings, b) to expand the arrest warrant in accordance with the indictment, and to order the continued detention of the accused.

Kollorz
Prosecuting Attorney

Author's Comments
Regarding the Preceding Indictment

The sentence in the first section stating that I am an American citizen, but (only) "according to (my own) statements also a German citizen," is absolute nonsense, since at that very time the court was in possession not only of my valid American passport but also of my equally valid German one.

In other words, there is absolutely no ambiguity about it, as the indictment seems to indicate; it was not just my word for my German citizenship, but there was also the evidence of my German passport.

Patriotic Americans and persons wishing to visit Germany in the near future ought to take special notice of the accusation that I committed 12 criminal offenses while a) only expressing a benign opinion, and b) never writing anything at all except non-political postcards while I was on German soil.

I also never uttered my political opinion in public in the *Burndesrepublik*. In other words, I committed all these "crimes" in America.

And what were they? The indictment claims:

"The accused did attack the human dignity of others in a manner likely to lead to a breach of peace by slandering, maliciously belittling and libeling them, produce, introduce into the jurisdiction of the German Criminal Code, and disseminate, writings inciting race hatred or describing cruel or otherwise inhuman brutality against persons in a manner glorifying or trivializing the cruel and inhuman nature of such events in a manner injurious to human dignity; producing, importing and disseminating writings inciting hatred against identifiable groups or against a religious group and attacking their human dignity by slandering, maliciously belittling and libeling them, related in each case to such writings in which an act committed under the National Socialist regime, and of the nature specified in §220... was denied or trivialized, and disparaging the memory of persons deceased."

Apart from the fact that a free nation should never have such tyrannical and unethical laws as those used against me in this indictment, I would like to state that my newsletters never reached the German people, nor even a noticeable part of it.

These letters were mailed only to politically open-minded persons who used the information for the furtherance of their own knowledge.

Therefore, in any case, one can never accuse me of "breaching the peace." It didn't happen, and could not have happened. Reading the typical "Wolffsohn letter" reproduced in this chapter will prove to Americans whether I slandered others, belittled their sufferings, or defamed their dead.

I can also flatly state that I never preached or promulgated racial hatred against anyone or any group.

While I never made a secret of the fact that essentially I am for racial separation (in other words, I was always against the forced integration of the races as it was attempted in America), my personal relationship with persons of other races was always good, and was never clouded by my political views.

As a German I am fully aware of the talents and the shortcomings of my people, and I do not hesitate to point them out. On the other hand I am also not afraid to write about the characteristics of other groups that hinder their mutual progress.

If I point out that there is a huge numerical disparity between the original (Allied) death figures for the concentration camps at Dachau and Auschwitz, from 238,000 and 4 million respectively, in 1945 (and long thereafter), to 32,000 and about one million now, and I call the earlier propaganda numbers just that, then this cannot be taken as trivializing the cruel and inhuman nature of war.

As a matter of fact, the Jews ought to be happy that many more of their brethren survived the war than earlier anticipated. It also follows that with the "official" lowering of the Auschwitz death toll by about three million victims, the claim of "six million Jews killed in the Holocaust" has become untenable.

I have never delved into the matter of the Jewish religion.

The Indictment and My Commentary

Therefore, the prosecutor ought not to have used the religious factor in his indictment. As far as I am concerned, and I have abundant evidence of it, the Jews are the politically most active group of all ethnics or peoples on record, and as such they are not above scrutiny.

They themselves may certainly regard their community as being mainly guided by religion (and their current propaganda seems to be geared toward this view), but the very fact of what one may call common physical characteristics, points toward genetic rather than religious cohesion.

I did not deny writing the letter to Martin Klingst, a journalist for the leftist/liberal newspaper *Die Zeit*. However, I cannot be certain who mailed a copy of this letter to the CDU politician Rudi Geil. It doesn't really matter. Our offices mail thousands of letters each month, albeit most of them in the English language.

Klingst's article was an unwarranted attack on the German Right, of which I count myself, and he deserved a coherent answer. He got it from me. There was absolutely no reason for Geil, who may or may not be Jewish, to feel insulted or defamed.

The very fact that for a long time he has been an active politician and that as such he bears some responsibility for the untenable circumstances now plaguing Germany, should bar him from accusing someone like this writer, or any other German nationalist of such "criminal offenses" as telling the truth.

Further on in the indictment there are several specific points that undoubtedly raised the dander of people like Geil.

For one, I used the term *Oberjuden* (elite or 'Top Jews'), to point out that there is a vast difference between the Jewish leadership and fanatical activists on the one hand, and the great mass of Jews in America, on the other.

The elite Jews regard my term *Oberjuden* as defamatory. But it is not intended to insult, but to accurately describe a segment of the personnel within the hierarchy of Jewish power in America.

It may be quaint, but how can one defame someone in elevating him above the mass of his people? If someone describes me as an *Oberdeutschen* (Top German), will I feel insulted or defamed? No! I'd laugh.

To convey to the Germans (even only a few Germans), the truth that many Americans do not believe the gas chamber story anymore, is obviously *verboten*.

Yet, in April of 1993, just in time for the dedication of the taxpayer-funded U.S. Holocaust Museum in Washington, D.C., the American Jewish Congress (AJC), published the results of a poll showing that approximately 23% of Americans do not believe the "Holocaust" (gas chamber) story, and 30% doubt that it could have happened as told.

The AJC was severely criticized by fellow Jews for publishing the truthful results of this accurate poll. To repair the damage, the Roper organization was shortly thereafter commissioned to poll a different group of people (presumably residents of Beverly Hills, Brighton Beach, Brooklyn and Skokie, exclusively), and now the claim is that only 3 to 5% of Americans are "Holocaust deniers," and 10% are doubtful. (Isn't it wonderful to control the mind-manipulating industry?)

An awareness of American doubts may induce some Germans to also question the dogmas of this "Holocaust" semi-religion and if such ideas spread, they would eventually cause the remnant of the Reich to curtail its financial largess for the Jewish state.

In this conjunction, my term "Holocaust' tale" (in German, "Holocaust' *Mär*") is considered a grave sin; the assumption being that everything connected with the gas chamber claims is absolutely true and beyond reproach, as befits a religious dogma.

The Indictment and My Commentary

Yet no one in the corporate media asks how this word "Holocaust" was so quickly and uniformly imposed as a supposed precise description of the fate of the Jews during the war. This word "Holocaust" wasn't widely applied in this regard until more than thirty years after the end of WWII, around 1978. Such imposition of new words which generalize particular details into a distorted composite, was predicted by the English writer George Orwell, in his prophetic novel, *1984*. He called it "Newspeak" and said that it "was designed not to extend, but to *diminish* the range of thought..."

The fact is that I was specifically referring to *the new Holocaust-tales* that continuously flow out of the vivid imagination of the *millions* of "Holocaust survivors." [3]

Incidentally, my letter to Martin Klingst consisted of six single-spaced pages. It is interesting to take note of those of my statements which both the prosecutor and Mr. Geil found so offensive as to consider them a criminal offense.

Pages 171-173: For Americans who are used to seeing Democrat party bureaucrats and officials losing their jobs when a Republican administration takes over (and vice versa), that which I have written here will look like a statement of a political fact. Not so in Germany. There my words constitute a threat. In spite

---

[3] One of the best examples of such hallucinations by "Holocaust survivors" was a cover story published by the *New York Post* on November 6, 1988 (just in time for the fiftieth anniversary of the Kristallnacht). According to the article, German-Jewish survivor Clara Feldman is making the rounds of the New York City schools, and telling the mostly African-American students that during World War II "the Nazis" had killed one million blacks. Nobody seemed to have noticed that at no time during the war did any such remarkable number of blacks fall into German hands, nor was Germany's struggle with Africans. (Similarly, an article in the *Washington Times* of April 18, 1996 suddenly claimed 1.2 million Gypsies murdered by the Germans, 700,000 more than the already incongruous 500,000 figure.) American newspapers never hesitate to print such fabrications. But when we proposed ads in such publications as the *Washington Post*, the *Washington Times* or the *New York Times* some years ago, we had to provide absolute, documentary proof for every single one of our statements.

of my very clear disclaimer that I did not mean that 100,000 of the worst German collaborators should be executed, one German newspaper claimed just that. Personally I think that those who have a bad conscience may already feel that their lives are in danger, and that is why they were so adamant in prosecuting me.

My reference to trials that will have to be held at a later date (when Germany is again truly free and sovereign), has to do with the continuing hunt for alleged "Nazi war criminals" all over the world.

I cannot strongly enough express my feelings about the travesty of justice that more than a half century after a lost war, soldiers of the defeated nation are still being arrested and put on trial (or otherwise persecuted) for alleged war crimes.

For example, a German officer, former *SS-Hauptsturmführer* (Captain) Erich Priebke, 82 years of age, was seized in Latin America, transported to an Italian prison in Rome, and put on trial in 1996, for his participation in the legal execution of 335 Italian hostages in 1944.[4] Priebke had been living an exemplary life in Argentina since the end of the war, and was delivered to Italy mainly at the behest of the leaders of international Zionism. Acquitted by an Italian court (to the credit of a courageous judiciary), he is, as of this writing, scheduled to be retried, in dutiful obedience to the demands of Italy's Israeli lobby.

This is against all moral and ethical traditions of Western Civilization. I am fully aware that the hunt for old enemies is

---

[4] In the summer of 1944, Italian communists planted a bomb that killed 33 German soldiers. According to the international laws of war then in force, it was standard to shoot 10 enemy captives for every soldier murdered. Further, it is very doubtful that Priebke could have refused the order to lead the execution, especially since it came from Hitler's HQ. The hostages had been convicted of various criminal activities (including terrorism), and according to a British newspaper account, after the execution of the terrorists, "the partisan movement in Rome was devastated and unable to function." Unfortunately for Priebke, there were seventy-seven of "the Chosen" among those executed, and this explains the howls of vengeance for his punishment fifty-three years later, even as Jewish communist perpetrators of atrocities enjoy 100% immunity from prosecution.

allegedly being conducted in the interest of justice, but anybody who has any sense of European history knows that this persecution of old men has nothing to do with justice or setting the record straight. It is a clear expression of Jewish hatred, vengeance and power.

One of the travesties of these "war crimes" show trials has always centered on the question of why German and German-allied military personnel are the targets for these prosecutions, since the policies of the war were devised by the leaders in Berlin, not by the soldiers.

I am surprised that American veterans' groups have never come out and spoken against these immoral persecutions. It is obvious that they can only backfire against American soldiers in the future.

Even Americans without any military background should wonder why only German and German-allied veterans are being hunted, while so far nobody has been called to account for the atrocities at Dresden, Katyn, Hiroshima, the murders by deliberate neglect in Eisenhower's death camps, or for the unnecessary destruction of, for instance, the ancient monastery of Monte Cassino. Justice is only served when it applies equally, to everyone.

Far worse atrocities (by all sides) in the Pacific theater of war are not even an issue. Could this be due to the fact that there were no Jews involved?

I am certainly not happy that these continuing hunts for alleged war criminals are still taking place. I feel sorry for all of the persons involved. The average person cannot imagine how, for instance, the spectacle of the innocent Ukrainian-American John Demjanjuk, shipped in chains to the Israeli state, with U.S. government connivance, made his family suffer.

Nevertheless, these political persecutions at the hands of the present oligarchy will likely serve as a precedent for the revolutionaries of a new era that is sure to come, when they need a pretext for eliminating vestiges (i.e., "personnel") of the criminals who run the current System, in the not too distant future. I surmise the world will see trials of the bosses of the current ruling clique extending far beyond the year 2033, which I predicted in my letter to Martin Klingst.

As of this writing, fifty-one years have passed since the cessation of the open hostilities of World War II. The hunt for old enemies of the Jews (for, that is what it is all about!), continues unabated, and it will probably not cease until the present world order is near total collapse, or even until shortly before the dawn of the new era that is sure to come soon.

If we assume that this great turning point of world history will occur shortly after the beginning of the new century (which is also the start of a new millennium), say around the year 2002, that would mean that the Jewish quest of hate and revenge had lasted 57 years. Using this measure for the future, this would mean that those in power now and their underlings would be hunted and persecuted and executed up until the year 2059, for the havoc their system will undoubtedly cause within the next few years!

I am bringing this to the attention of the reader so that you may see how asinine it is for normal, Western societies to permit themselves to become accomplices in the execution of the Talmudic philosophy of unremitting hate and vengeance.

Will the age of one of the current Establishment stooges be a determining factor in obtaining clemency as late as 2059? Not if we apply the yardstick of Allied vengeance in the post World War II years.

I remember when, a few years ago, a former minister of the National Socialist (N.S.) German-allied Croatian government,

The Indictment and My Commentary

the anti-communist statesman Artukovic, was at a very advanced age and near death, forcibly taken from his home in California on a hospital gurney and extradited into the blood-drenched hands of his old Communist enemies. He promptly died in captivity.

And, just in time for Hitler's 107th birthday, and the almost concurrent "Holocaust Memorial Day," the Jewish-dominated Office of Special investigations (OSI) at the U. S. Justice Department, announced that it has begun proceedings against an 86-year old former Hungarian writer, Ferenc Koreh, a longtime U.S. Government employee at Radio Free Europe. It seems that more than 53 years ago, he had written some critical comments about the Jews. Koreh has already been stripped of his citizenship, and the Jews are now trying to have him deported from U. S. soil.

The last paragraph on page 173 was the pretext needed by Rudi Geil to sign the arrest warrant for me. You may note that the translator of the indictment put the very meaning into these words that I have disputed in chapter 3 of this book.

Obviously, the translator is a younger person and she could only interpret the words in the present sense. However, through her erroneous assumptions, as well as those of others, the subtle changes have become apparent that occurred in our languages in the last fifty years. Many words have gained different meanings.

It is similar to the common and at one time, only rarely defamatory use of the epithet, "nigger" in the American South as little as forty years ago. Now that word is probably the worst insult one can direct at a black person.

At any rate, since I know what I wanted to say, I can unhesitatingly state that I did not mean "infested," but rather "dominated in a malignant way," by both the Jews and Freemasons who dominate the German political system.

The indictment also contains an excellent translation of an Open letter I wrote to Professor Michael Wolffsohn, who teaches modern history at the German Army college (i.e. the German "West Point"), near Munich.

Wolffsohn was born in Palestine in 1947, and claims dual German and Israeli citizenship. Although he has lived in Germany since age 7, and went to school there, he voluntarily joined the Israeli Army, and fought in the 1967 war against the Arabs. It is not known whether Wolffsohn participated in the atrocities of that war, in which Israeli troops killed thousands of Egyptian prisoners in cold blood, allegedly because they had no way to transport them to the rear. [5]

I do not think a committed Israeli Zionist can teach modern German history objectively at the German war college, and without thereby indoctrinating young, impressionable future German officers with myths and false values.

How can someone like Wolffsohn teach Third Reich history objectively? That is impossible! Would the Israelis permit a Syrian who fought against Israel to teach modern Jewish history to the future officer corps of the Israeli Army?

Michael Wolffsohn claims to be a German-Jewish patriot. He alleges that he has the best interests of the German nation and the German people at heart. But the fact is that he never ceases to beat the hateful "Holocaust" drum, defaming the parents and grandparents of Germany's upcoming generations.

If all of Wolffsohn's subversive proposals and ideas concerning the fate of the German nation came to fruition, this

---

[5] The story of these executions became public in late 1995. When the Israeli Government was asked whether the surviving commanders of the Israeli Army responsible for these massacres were now going to be put on trial, Jerusalem answered with the short comment that there exists a "twenty year statute of limitations for such 'transgressions". No American newspaper dared to point to the double standard evident in this limitation on the prosecution of Israeli war criminals, while at the same time persecuting alleged German ones from a war that ceased a half century ago.

would mean the end of Germania! Yet Bonn idolizes this destroyer.

Besides his important position at the *Bundeswehr* military college, Wolffsohn is also a prolific writer and lecturer. He is the most insidious as well as the most effective of all Zionist writers influencing German life today. Wolffsohn writes a weekly column for a German magazine in which he relentlessly promulgates his Zionist *Weltanschauung*.

He is also the most prominent litigant in Germany, having hauled more German critics of his utterances before the courts than anyone else. The notorious statute §130 seems tailor-made for him.

In January, 1995, the prestigious *Frankfurter Allgemeine Zeitung*, the daily newspaper which in the *Bundesrepublik* occupies a position of eminence similar to that of the *New York Times* in America, printed a long "op-ed" essay by Wolffsohn underneath the title, *Deutsche und Juden sind aneinandergekettet* (Germans and Jews are forever tied together).

In an essay full of Talmudic hairsplitting and sophistry, he explains his view of the relationship between Germans and Jews, that ought to drive all healthy Germans to the barricades.

Unfortunately for Germany, few people seem to have grasped the ramifications of Wolffsohn's poisonous, anti-German agenda.

Here are a few sentences from this remarkably racist treatise:

"Every German is liable (for the "Six Million"), because he is a German.

"He has no choice in the matter.

"The guilt for which he is responsible is known to him.

"Even if he absolutely doesn't like it, and while his innermost being battles against it, he nevertheless bears this liability.

"This (subconscious) knowledge forms the identity of the

German, even if he does not acknowledge it to himself." [6]

"The political and moral deliverance of the Germans depends upon their relationship to the Final Solution.

"The postwar Germans obviously do not bear any responsibility for what their grandfathers did. But one can inherit guilt even without being responsible for it, and therefore one can be held to account.

"The Germans that were born after the war also carry the Mark of Cain. They carry it because they are Germans, because the first thing that comes to the mind of anybody else (in the world) when being co-opted by a German is 'Auschwitz,' namely, the millionfold murder of the Jews.

"This will remain so forever, and especially so after November 9, 1989, because this date is to the entire world, and especially the Jewish one, connected with November 9th, 1938, the so-called Kristallnacht, the beginning of the Final Solution.

"In conclusion: without the Jews there is no German identity, and without the Germans, no Jewish one. Jews and Germans are forever tied together--and after Auschwitz and the murder of millions of Jews, more than ever."

--Michael Wolffsohn.

---

[6] Wolffsohn is not alone in attempting to impose a destructive concept of self-hate and artificial guilt upon the Germans from this ridiculous angle. The Nobel Peace prize winner Eli Wiesel, a "paragon of virtue and tolerance," in the eyes of the mainstream media, wrote the following sentence in his book *Legends of our Time*: "Every Jew, somewhere in his being, should set apart a zone of hate--healthy, virile hate--for what the German personifies and for what persists in the German." (Holt, Rinehart & Winston, New York, 1968, page 142). One must wonder, did Wiesel receive the Nobel Peace Prize because he wrote this message of "love"?

Economist Daniel McGowan, a professor at Hobart College in New York, has approached Wiesel about lending assistance with a holocaust memorial on behalf of helpless Palestinian villagers slaughtered at Deir Yassin by Israelis in 1948. Despite repeated overtures, Wiesel wants nothing to do with the project. Wiesel's "human rights" campaign is just a front for the promotion of Jewish supremacy. Atrocities committed in the Jewish holocaust against the Palestinians are never acknowledged by Wolffsohn and Wiesel. Yet such people dare to lecture the Germans on the need to "take responsibility" for "guilt."

The views expressed here are insane, but so are a lot of other nonsense written in the same vein here in the United States.

That Wolffsohn hasn't changed since he wrote the preceding malevolence, can be seen from a sentence he uttered in an interview published in Germany in the spring of 1996:

Interviewer: "You (Professor Wolffsohn), really expect to see German uniforms in Israel, in the country that was created as the result of the Holocaust?"

Wolffsohn: "Especially because of the Holocaust! Germany can never again accept that the lives and the existence of Jews, in Israel and elsewhere, will be endangered. *The peace with Syria will be difficult, but the presence of German soldiers (on the Golan heights) will assure Israel's security. And that is what matters.*" (Emphasis supplied).

Thus spoke a self-styled "German-Jewish patriot."

Unfortunately, Michael Wolffsohn is not alone in trying to retain the false and unnecessary guilt complex that has been imposed upon the Germans, due to allegations of having gassed Jews in World War II. [7]

The two worst propagators of mythological gas chamber guilt are Germans: former President Richard von Weizsaecker and Roman Herzog, the current president of the German *Bundesrepublik.* Both of them miss no opportunity to degrade the spirit of the German people. They insist upon a "special

---

[7] While there are now fewer Germans in the world than there were at the beginning of World War II, the Jews, who were allegedly exterminated, seem to have miraculously recovered. The *World Almanac* of 1931 puts the Jewish population of the world, just before Hitler took power, at 15,630,000. The same publication in 1995 gave a figure of 18,153,000 for the Jewish population worldwide. Personally, I don't believe either figure (I have sound reasons for questioning them), but such a gain, after a loss of "6,000,000" is truly a miracle.

responsibility" toward the Jews because of the "Holocaust". In doing so they commit high treason.

Not all German or other Aryan intellectuals accept the theses propagated by Jews like Wolffsohn, and German collaborators like the two high German officials cited.

Occasionally the prestige of a dissident letter writer forces the German media to print letters that counter the prevailing premise of German collective guilt. One of the best of these was published in the *Frankfurter Allgemeine Zeitung* (F.A.Z.) on February 14, 1996.

It was written by Professor Kenneth Lewan, a man who obviously knows whereof he speaks, and whose thinking is still influenced by the traditional ethics of Western Civilization, and not by the new *Zeitgeist* originating from the Near East:

"On the occasion of the Day of Remembrance for the victims of National Socialism, President Herzog stated that Germans bear an especially great responsibility because so many Germans had made themselves guilty (of genocide).

"It is a generally accepted principle of the ethics of Western Civilization that a responsibility to make restitution exists only when we, through our own negligence or due to other motives, cause harm to others. In such a situation the question is asked what we knew, and what indemnification is possible.

"In other words, we cannot demand from an individual that he accept the burden of responsibility for the damages caused by others. There is no such a thing as a responsibility without concomitant guilt. It is part of our (Western) civilization that children are not supposed to bear the burden for wrongdoings of their fathers or their compatriots. Thereby it is totally unimportant how great is the guilt or how horrible was the crime.

"On February 9th, 1994 we were able to read in the F.A.Z. that most Russians do not believe that they ought to feel guilty or responsible for Stalin's crimes.

"Yet we know that the Stalinists have, among other things, caused the deaths by hunger of millions of Ukrainians.

"In the United States there is never any talk of *all* Americans accepting a feeling of responsibility for black slaves and the Indian victims of ethnic cleansings and genocide. The same is true for France and England and all the other nations that had a colonial past.

"Only in Germany is it customary to hear politicians, journalists and theologians speak of the responsibility of all Germans for the misdeeds of the National Socialists. Former President von Weizsaecker expressed himself more than once in a similar vein.

"These people seem to have accepted the following thesis for Germany: 'There is no collective guilt, only an individual can be guilty for his own wrongdoings. However, all Germans are responsible (for what happened during the Third Reich).

"To hold a human being responsible for the misdeeds and the sins of omission of others means that this person has to be imbued first with a bad conscience, until he is willing to make restitution for something over which he had no control.

"The never-ending repetition of the accusation that all Germans bear a special responsibility for National Socialist crimes is clear evidence that this (the continued payment of monetary restitution), is the intent of the accusation.

"As far as we know, not one person who uses the moral sledgehammer of never-ending responsibility against the German people has tried to give a sound reason for this demand.

"However, for such an artificially created responsibility to retain its value, it ought to be measured against the age-old principles of our civilization. Only this assures that the Germans receive the equal treatment that must be accorded to them.

"If we judge according to the principles of our civilization, then it becomes clear that in spite of all the talk to the contrary, no special German responsibility exists.

"This does not mean that we cannot make good when someone close to us has done wrong and harmed others. We can voluntarily accept responsibility for misdeeds of relatives or of our government. But for such a voluntary action on our part there exists the term *Ehrensache,* a Matter of Honor, because it concerns something that goes beyond our customary duties as citizens.

"The attempt to imbue innocents with the feeling that they somehow are responsible to make good for the crimes of others is amoral and irresponsible. Those who claim that all Germans bear a special responsibility for the crimes of the National Socialists are acting against the principle of equality: they do great harm to those Germans who bear no guilt."

Obviously, there is a great difference between the *Weltanschauung* of Professor Lewan, and that of Professor Wolffsohn.

The former bases his arguments on the ethical principles of our great civilization, the latter is not honest enough to admit that his whole thinking --his entire being-- is based upon the culture of the Talmud.

Obviously, there is nothing wrong with a Jew being a nationalistic Jew, and if Michael Wolffsohn had stayed in Israel, and there assumed a teaching post at the Israeli Military Academy, that would be fine with me.

But a German-hater like him has absolutely no right to be a professor at the German military college.

The letter to Michael Wolffsohn is the eighth of a series of Open letters that I wrote to this Jewish professor.

As in all previous letters, I merely replied to those musings

The Indictment and My Commentary

which Wolffsohn had *first initiated* and published in Germany, either as articles or in book form.

A number of years ago I had attended a lecture by Prof. Wolffsohn arranged by the German Historical Society of Washington, D.C., a group financed by the Bonn Government. Wolffsohn's speech was short but full of the usual deceit about German-Jewish "togetherness."

Having made notes, I intended to question Wolffsohn on some of his ideas, during the question and answer period following his speech.

I was not alone in my surprise when the Jewish academic stepped down from the podium immediately after he finished reading his prepared text.

It would seem that he is afraid of an open debate. I managed to exchange a few cursory words with him one-on-one, but he refused to go into any depth on the significant issues on which he had lectured.

It was then that I decided to use the Open Letter approach.

As I wrote these missives, I certainly did have Michael Wolffsohn and his inane statements regarding Germany, and the German-Jewish relationship in mind, but I wrote them from the outset with an eye toward the other readers (mostly Germans), who eventually would read them.

Having assessed Wolffsohn correctly during our brief meeting in Washington, I did not think that he would answer me, and so I was not offended when he never did.

As a rule I waited several months to hear from him; not surprisingly, always in vain. After that interval, I felt free to make my "Letters to Professor Wolffsohn" available to a wider circle of readers.

Having good contacts in Germany, I discovered that at least some of my letters upset Wolffsohn greatly. I knew that at times they were copied in greater numbers, and I was told that at least on one occasion, someone had placed a stack of these copies in various places at the *Bundeswehr Universität* so that military professors and students could help themselves.

Needless to say, they had the impact I desired.

I am not certain whether it was due to my writings or as a result of some criticism of Wolffsohn originating from some other quarter, but in the beginning of the 1990s this conscious agent of Greater Israel went to the authorities with the complaint that "anti-Semitic" literature had been placed on campus, and that the president of the university had done little or nothing to stop the "abuse."

Wolffsohn's special complaint was that the head of the school had not come out forcefully enough to defend him, the Jew. As a result, the president of the university was fired!

The eighth letter to Wolffsohn is typical of the series. I tried to retain the framework of seven or eight single-spaced pages, and without exception all of those Open Letters concern matters of importance to Germans and Jews.

Having naive, uninitiated Germans as the final recipients in mind, however, it was my intention to tell them as much as I could in these few pages of the doings and shenanigans of the *Oberjuden* and other Jewish commissars in America.

Since I stuck to easily corroborated facts (deriving much of my information from Jewish newspapers, which I read diligently), I knew from the start that Michael Wolffsohn could not defend his brethren.

In using this method of transferring much needed information to Germany (information which the German newsmedia would never print), I also managed to give hope to my unfree and demoralized compatriots in the German lands of Europe.

Commentary on my Eighth Letter to Michael Wolffsohn:

According to information that was sent to me by an anonymous, but well informed source, Wolffsohn at one time had the intention of leaving his position in Bavaria and emigrating to the United States. Among friends (?) he was supposed to have stated that he was totally exasperated with the Germans and Germany.

However, he is undoubtedly one of the most important assets of "Judaea" in the former Reich, and I assume that somebody from Israel or New York appealed to his sense of loyalty to the greater Jewish cause, noting how important his high profile position in *Deutschland* was for all Jews. Thus he chose to remain in Germany.

It is doubtful whether Wolffsohn will ever "see the light of day," so to speak, in spite of my expressed expectation that some day he may realize how wrong he has been. His entire existence is geared toward the furtherance of the Jewish agenda.

He is not the only person who is acting as if the "Holocaust" business can be the foundation of a new religion. But by virtue of his influential position in Germany, Michael Wolffsohn is certainly a high priest of that pseudo-religion.

I do not know exactly how many Germans have already been fined or incarcerated because of legal actions launched by Professor Wolffsohn. But of the five of which I'm aware, none wrote any differently than I did.

Certainly, it was not the intention of these good Germans to insult Wolffsohn, attack his religion, or defame the (real) Jewish war dead.

Nevertheless, they had to undergo costly court battles just because of one thin-skinned Jew who doesn't hesitate to continually defame and insult the German nation and people.

Undoubtedly it is Wolffsohn's genetic make-up that is so vastly different from that of the Germans that makes him act this way. I am amazed that according to German law, celebrities like Wolffsohn seem to have the freedom to do and to say anything they want publicly while on the other hand the average German is not allowed to answer in kind.

Most Jews will consider my statement in the Wolffsohn letter alluding to the 'tight grip of Jewish power in the Clinton Administration' as evidence of the "virulent anti-Semitism" cliche´. That my statement is true does not matter for these people; it is *verboten* to mention it.

The facts stated in the Wolffsohn letter are gleaned from establishment papers and magazines. Certainly, as they are written here they are my interpretation but that makes them not less true.

Obviously I write in a non-P C. (politically correct) fashion and that will undoubtedly offend many people. It may also cause others to henceforth read everything more critically.

Contemporary journalists have been indoctrinated since they first entered kindergarten, and one must assume that they conform to the norms and expectations of a fixed, Establishment agenda.

To state that a Jew is a Jew is already a sin. On the other hand, I personally have never taken offense or felt insulted when someone "exposed" me as a German. Why should Jews be treated differently?

The matter of the "weeping Jews" in my letter deserves special attention. I am not the only one who has noticed the fact that when something tragic happens to Jews, in Israel or elsewhere, or when alleged "Holocaust Survivors" meet, the tears not only flow profusely, but no American newspaper or television show will fail to display or broadcast pictures of this weeping.

The Indictment and My Commentary

On the other hand, photographs of Lebanese or Palestinian civilians who cry over their children murdered by the Israelis are infrequently shown.

Seemingly, only the Jews are such *"Menschen"* (a German word meaning a human being) that they really can cry over lost loved ones, or over other losses.

To this day I have never seen a photograph showing the grief of a German-American farm family who, due to some bankers' shenanigans, has lost their homestead of a hundred-fifty years, and now faces an uncertain future.

Before Hitler's *Machtergreifung* (ascension of power), there were about 600,000 Jews in Germany.

About half of them emigrated before the start of the war on September 1, 1939. Even during the war, German Jewry was not totally removed from German society as is now claimed.

The Berlin telephone book for 1941 (two years into the war), showed more Jewish organizations in the German capital than German-American organizations can be found in all of America's major cities together in 1996.

The Jewish groups (among them synagogues, schools, cultural societies) still had more than 110 different telephone lines operating. A Jewish hospital existed throughout the war, including during the last hours of the Reich. [8]

Although Germany is now under greater Jewish-Zionist dominance than it ever was, the number of *Oberjuden* whose names are known to the German population is very small indeed.

Offhand I could come up with but a handful of names. This proves that Jewish power is exerted by other means than demographics.

For years it was claimed that the Jewish population in

---

[8] For comparison a researcher should check how many Japanese-American organizations (of any kind) were still allowed to function in either Los Angeles or San Francisco by 1943. Personally I doubt there were any.

227

Germany was only 40,000. Now there is a considerable immigration of Soviet Jews from Russia to Germany, where they live like drones. [9] It is anticipated that their numbers will swell to about 150,000 by the year 2000. The German people have no say in the matter.

Near the end of the Wolffsohn letter I cite an important fact that is seldom mentioned, and that few people know. Except for the Zionist-originated November 9, 1938 Kristallnacht, there was no pogrom against the Jews or anybody else in N.S. Germany before or during the war. In other words, Jewish and other individuals could and did walk the streets of the Reich unhindered and without being accosted by anyone. I would say they were much safer then than we are now, when walking through our darkened American cities.

During World War II, Germany was host to more than seven million foreigners, many of them Polish and French POWs who could walk the streets (within their designated towns), freely. In addition, there were the voluntary or involuntary workers from the Ukraine and other countries, who had their distinctive patches with their origin sown on their clothing. If there were Jews among them, we Germans would have known it, and it would not have mattered. I know of no instance where German civilians attacked any of these foreigners out of pure hate.

The matter of the German concentration camp records that were "lost" for fifty years troubles me; especially because no one in the Western world has to my knowledge ever delved into this miserable and dishonest Allied scheme, which prevented innumerable Jews from finding their missing relatives after the

---

[9] According to *This Week in Germany* (April 12, 1996), a publication of the Bonn Government, 40,000 Jews have already immigrated to Germany since the reunification. Only 14 percent of these 40,000 are gainfully employed (and of these, a number have Social Service positions taking care of their own brethren). All others live a dependent life on the backs of the German social system, to which they have not contributed a penny.

war.

Reading newspapers, magazines and post-combat reports of Allied military units carefully, it becomes apparent that at the end of the war, when the concentration camps were opened by the Allies, the records of every major camp fell into the hands of the conquerors.

From the documents relating to the Nuremberg trials it is also known that these records were used to obtain the convictions of German officers and officials. After that they disappeared into Russian and American archives for nearly half a century. Why?

In my view it was to give the Allied propagandists time to concoct the "Six Million" tales in the totality of their absurdity.

In doing so, the postwar Allies prevented the newly freed Jews from finding their family members; which didn't seem to bother the leaders of the "free world" too much. For them it was much more important to put the onus of a criminal nation on Germany, and especially on the leadership (and ideology) of the Third Reich; or as Michael Wolffson stated, the "Mark of Cain."

Soon after the collapse of the Soviet Union, Mikhail Gorbachev opened the Kremlin archives, and permitted scrutiny of the Auschwitz death lists, according to which about 74,000 people succumbed in that camp in the approximately five years of its existence.

This is a very high number but it certainly bears no comparison to the "4 million dead at Auschwitz" proclamations carved into plaques at Auschwitz, in front of which the Polish Pope (who should have known better since he lived but 30 miles away during the war), paid homage in 1979.

The "four million dead" inscriptions on the plaques have since been removed, Orwellian-style, but the merchants of the Shoah business industry still insist that more than one million people had been killed at that camp; also a preposterously high figure.

Regarding the OSI in my letter, (Office of Special investigations of the Justice Department), no major American newspaper has ever written an *investigative* article about this "ethnic" office.

The story of Dr. Crenshaw and the Kennedy assassination in my letter was also omitted by the mainstream American media, although I think it would have warranted extensive commentary.

This concludes my commentary on the letter to Professor Wolffsohn.

Commentary on the Indictment (Continued)

The name Werner Schulz does not appear on our address lists. It is doubtful that he received a copy of the Wolffsohn letter from us. If he did, and he asked us for it, he certainly has no reason to complain about its contents. I am sure someday we shall find out who "Herr Schulz" is.

It is doubtful that our offices mailed a letter to a small farmer's village named Olching in Bavaria. The correct quote however is from the *USA-Bericht* April 1995. I still stand by what I wrote then, and I cannot see what would have upset the Bavarians.

I am aware that it is *verboten* to mention in Germany that the German largess toward Israel and the Jews (amounting to about $100 billion since the end of World War II), results from the guilt feelings imposed upon the Germans (to quote President Reagan) because of the "gas chambers."

At first I did not remember it, but since it is in my handwriting, I obviously did mail a note to the German parliamentarian Siegfried Vergin, and I also mailed him the latest *USA-Bericht*. My comment regarding Fred Leuchter and the "Holocaust" was factual. There was no reason for this politician to run to the prosecutor.

In Germany one may not state without being accused of inciting racial hatred that the Jews, respectively the *Oberjuden,* are the major propagators of race mixing, while they themselves try to keep apart from all others.

Another portion of the indictment refers to a letter I wrote to the German Foreign Minister Kinkel, but I do not recall mailing a copy to Representative Conradi. The text of the note does not read as it would have, had I written it. My terminology is different.

One must wonder why Herr Conradi should feel it necessary to go to a court and independently of Mr. Kinkel, accuse me of all the "crimes" mentioned on the bottom of this section. It bears remembering that Mr. Conradi is an elected representative and he most likely believes that he is a staunch defender of "democracy" These people surely have an odd belief about what constitutes freedom and democracy.

My letter to Herr Kinkel (p. 194), is factual and needs no comment. I am certain that most Americans who read this book will agree with me that the artificial outrage by the American press after such incidents as occurred at Magdeburg and elsewhere in Germany did not affect the (generally sympathetic) feelings of the American people for my home country. Kinkel is simply falling for Jewish propaganda.

I must also correct the statement that I merely feared that the French would abduct me for slave labor after the war, due to my having served in the Waffen SS.

In the spring of 1947, two years after the war, and a year after the Nuremberg trials, as a result of which German leaders were hanged for using "slave labor" during war time, the French re-arrested almost all the former members of the Waffen-SS in the Saarland, whether properly discharged from POW captivity or not, and shipped them as slave laborers to the area of Lille, in

Northern France. I was able to avoid this fate only because a day before the French action I got wind of it, and I left home.

When my family and friends received a copy of the indictment, they saw that the alleged facts about me as emanating from "American authorities," were such nonsense that they refused to include a translation of this page in mailings to our American supporters.

As for myself, I merely smiled when I read this report by "American authorities," for I recognized these lies as coming from the notorious A.D.L. (Anti Defamation League of B'nai B'rith), an unregistered agent of the government of Israel, which spies on American citizens, and strives for the release of dual Israeli-American citizens who betray the U.S. (such as Jonathan Pollard).

On the following pages I shall reprint the assessment about the A.D.L. interference by one of our supporters who knows both this writer, and their underhanded tactics, well.

But before I do that I have to make a confession. Some of the erroneous "facts" were my invention, and my supporter could not know that when he wrote his evaluation of what he believed was information coming from the U. S. State Department (as stated in the indictment), and, ipso facto, the columnist Jack Anderson.

In the chapter on the A.D.L. in this book I am presenting evidence that the false information actually was transmitted by the A.D.L. to the Germans.

Apart from a secret A.D.L. agent within the State Department illegally telling the Germans whom to contact for information about me, I doubt that this part of the U. S. Government had anything to do with the matter.

About ten years ago our German American organization used a Washington D.C. post office box as our mailing address.

The Indictment and My Commentary

Although this particular post office was located not far from the White House, all employees there, were, without exception, African-Americans.

As usual, I soon established a very friendly relationship with these pleasant people, and we had much fun together.

One day when I picked up our mail, one of the Black ladies told me that "one of my friends" who works within the U.S. Postal Service, but not at this location, had inquired about our post office box, and what names, addresses, etc. we had provided when applying for it. By the term "one of my friends" we both knew that she was referring to a Jew.

The Black lady also told me that so far she had not given out the information, but that it was only a matter of time until someone in the Postal Service hierarchy would obtain it.

It was then that she made a photocopy of my application blank for the box number and I was able to make some slight, belated, "befuddling" changes, the very changes that are now stated as 'facts' about me in this indictment.

For instance, while originally I had given our correct street address in Washington of that time as 1411 K Street, I changed the copy that would inevitably be faxed to the inquirer, making a U out of the K; an address that didn't exist.

If I remember correctly, I didn't leave anything of importance unaltered on the copy of the application card that was to be faxed. On the copy I changed a number here, or a letter there, including data from the driver's license. That is also the reason why the year of my birth was transformed from 1927 to 1924, an easy thing to do.

My black friend and I had a good laugh about this some weeks later, when she told me that she had finally been required to fax the contents of the photocopy to the investigator, who was obviously also one of the ubiquitous A.D.L. agents.

(I find it truly regrettable that one has to go to such lengths in "free" America to guard one's privacy, possessions or even life. I'd much rather live in a society where such a ruse is not necessary. But the actions of the Stalinist A.D.L. in my case prove that my skepticism about these obnoxious fanatics was justified.)

Analysis of the State Department's Jack Anderson Deposition by C H

Jack Anderson crops up early as the co-(or sole) author of the State Department's disgraceful submittal to prejudice German jurists against Hans Schmidt.

Anderson is infamous as the country's most notorious --and maybe its most venomous-- gossip columnist. As such, he has become an Establishment figure. Some informed sources consider him a deep cover government agent, as well as a purveyor of misinformation and an all-round snoop.

Anderson's specialty seems to be character assassination. Certainly, he employs an extensive repertoire of calumny, including innuendo and insinuation, for which, on numerous occasions, he has been brought into libel court.

That the State Department should engage Jack Anderson to cook up a malignant, dirty tricks 'backgrounder' on Hans Schmidt, serves to expose the State Department's character and its intent toward him. It demonstrates, too, that it lacks anything in the least adverse to bring against Schmidt.

No knowledgeable American takes Anderson seriously. But the State Department's Jack Anderson is not for knowledgeable Americans. His ruminations are intended for the benefit of dupes in Germany.

The name Hans Schmidt didn't merely appear in 1988, it 'surfaced,' as though he had been in hiding, or otherwise a fugitive.

The record shows, however, that Schmidt has been consistently as candid and open with people of good will as is humanly possible. He frankly identifies himself as a former member of the Hitler Youth, and of the Waffen-SS. Anderson calls attention to this because he believes it to be derogatory. [10]

It is beyond the moral make-up of furtive characters like gossip columnists, and other professional sneaks, to recognize that everyone who fights honorably for his country merits respect.

At age 17, knowing the cause to be lost, Schmidt nevertheless volunteered for the toughest outfit in the German armed forces. During the last desperate months of the war this teenager fought in the front lines, where he was wounded several times. Based on a record like that, Mr. Schmidt has earned the respect of any veteran or patriot. These are qualities all decent people admire, in friend or foe.

The State Department slyly conceals the identity of the man with whose case, in 1988, it says Hans Schmidt was 'involved.' That is because the man, and his case, are known in Germany. Providing his name and the details about him and contrasting them with Anderson's, and Anderson's whole case would be penetrated on sight.

The man is Ernst Zündel. He was not sentenced for 'spreading hate propaganda' but 'for publishing false news.' He was absolved and acquitted by the Supreme Court of Canada, a fact suppressed by the State Department report.

Hans Schmidt was not a witness, either for the prosecution or

---

[10] The Waffen-SS was the fourth arm of the German Wehrmacht during World War II, the other three services being *Heer*, *Kriegsmarine* and *Luftwaffe*. Throughout the war, about 900,000 soldiers served in the Waffen-SS, many of them volunteers, and a total of about 250,000 either died in combat, were missing after the war or succumbed in POW camps. The Waffen-SS divisions were an elite fighting force of unparalleled courage and tenacity. As a rule, the Waffen-SS saw combat only where the fighting was most fierce.

for the defense. He gave and showed moral support for his friend, Ernst Zündel. What is a natural, often instinctive gesture in every true friend, becomes 'involvement' for those to whom this is incomprehensible.

Jack Anderson continues: 'A post office box used by the person involved in the case was rented by a Hans Schmidt, 1411 U Street NW, Washington, DC.'

Anderson states neither the post office box number nor its Zip code. He asserts 'it was ascertained later' --by whom, how, when, or why, is not divulged -- that 1411 U Street didn't exist, and that the man who had rented the post office box used a fraudulent driver's license to do so.

We thus have a situation in which 'a Hans Schmidt' rents a post office box under a fictitious address that eluded the Postal Service, and that 'the man who rented the post office box' used a fraudulent driver's license.

But the 'fraudulent driver's license' obviously contained a correct name, Hans Schmidt, under which the post office box was rented.

This infantile, malicious witch hunt is in tandem with the other deceptive drivel the State Department was feeding the German officials.

'Also found in the file' according to the July 24, 1985, Jack Anderson article captioned, 'PAC lives By Its Revenues.' Anderson had been told of the existence of a small California group that claimed to be the only political action committee that defends the interests of 52 million Americans of German descent... and that, over two years, it had received $55,000 in contributions.

Like a hyena sniffing carrion, Anderson leaps at the $55,000 figure. He tries hard to magnify this into an enormous sum from which the PAC chairman (Hans Schmidt) --like a Hurwitz or a

Millken in a billion dollar junk bond swindle-- enriches himself, illicitly.

Yet Anderson, better than most, knows that $55,000, over two years, or $27,500 a year-- which is a trifle more than five hundred dollars a week-- ten years ago--hardly amounted to petty cash even to a poverty line PAC.

Anderson reports in his article that Schmidt publishes a monthly information letter that is 'full of skepticism about the slaughter of millions of Jews by the Nazis during WWII.'

Then follows the curious sentence: "The article does not name the information service."

As a matter of common fairness the State Department could have offset Hans Schmidt's skepticism about the slaughter of millions of Jews' by pointing out that numerous authoritative Jewish scholars, from Israel (Yehuda Bauer, Hebrew University) to the United States (Arno Mayer, Princeton University) display skepticism about certain aspects of the so-called "Holocaust" story as well.

Bauer has debunked the soap-from-Jewish-fat claim and Mayer has said that Hitler's government was motivated by a profound fear, not of the Jews *per se*, but of Bolshevism.

More from Jack Anderson: In a further case in 1988 'it was ascertained' that a Hans Schmidt was the author of an '*Amerika-Brief.*' This was a regular column in the extreme right periodical '*Sieg*' (Victory). Schmidt was reported to the FBI because he had written an article that the 'BfV' (Bonn's secret police, *Bundesverfassungsschutz*) regarded as racist and as against the predominance of Jews' in the United States.

Who, or what, is the BfV? In the original English of the State Department's Jack Anderson deposition is it 'ADL?'

What other organism has the obsession and the means to ferret out an obscure foreign language publication unknown to more than one American in a million, to spy massively on the citizenry, and to report to the FBI whomever it perceives to be unsympathetic to its extreme-Zionist objectives?

German jurists may not be aware that anyone--frivolously, spitefully, stupidly, wrongfully-- can report anyone else to the FBI. Such reports, regardless of their quality, become inexpungable parts of the targeted individual's record.

The 'extreme right' smear is not lacking. To rabid Marxist Socialists anyone to the right of Mao Tse Tung is not merely 'right', but 'extreme right.'

Much of what goes into a Jack Anderson gossip column is 'ascertained.'

The same trick is employed in his State Department deposition. 'Ascertained' implies that what is imparted by Jack Anderson is not something that was just laying around where it might have been picked up by anybody.

No, it is a Jack Anderson exclusive, discoverable, and discovered solely by his ingenuity and diligence--though sometimes also through privileged access to private sources.

Thus, when he uses the term in reference to Schmidt--as in having 'ascertained' that Hans Schmidt is the author of something he signed, and did his best to publicize-- the fellow is operating under a false pretense.

Anderson has a fixation on post office boxes. They must attract his spy complex as objects of potentially ominous significance, and their tenants are sinister. The libel and slander of Hans Schmidt in Anderson's State Department tract begins and ends with post office boxes.

Anderson scoops the sensational news that Fairfax, Virginia is near Burke, Virginia. Hans Schmidt may have lived, or rented post office boxes --in the one or the other-- or both.

The State Department sets forth: 'Schmidt is described as a

white male born April 27, 1927.'

Then, in the following paragraph, it states: 'The questionable Hans Schmidt has as his date of birth April 27, 1924. In the light of the similarities in the dates of birth there could be an identity of persons.'

So, at the end, we are astonished at being presented with a 'questionable' Hans Schmidt!

Have Anderson and the State Department been talking about two Hans Schmidts? They don't tell us which is the 'real' Hans Schmidt.

How are we to tell the 'questionable' from the 'unquestionable' one?

It doesn't matter. The entire Jack Anderson - State Department joint venture into character assassination, to destroy a dissident writer by misinforming German justice, is far worse than questionable. --C.H. Nov. 30, 1995.

Even though my friend C.H. criticizes the U.S. State Department, possibly unfairly as far as their report is concerned, this agency of the U S Government still deserves to be chastised. "State" having received the indictment about the same time as I did, could and should have immediately disassociated itself from Bonn's false charges.

Readers should take note of the fact that according to the indictment 'the (German) Federal Criminal Police Office sent an inquiry to the American Embassy, which provided the Criminal Office with (this) information.'

As long as the State Department does not issue an official dementi, we shall regard this German contention as true.

In 1988 Jack Anderson wrote a couple of derogatory columns about me and our German-American organization, and I was then already certain that one of the major Jewish organizations was behind the campaign. [11]

Since Anderson had been known to do yeoman work for the A.D.L., I believed that it was this group that had paid him for his services. Anderson deserves C.H.'s critique even though we now know that neither the Germans or the State Department received the information from him.

In another section of the indictment it is stated:

"In denying the deliberate mass murder of the Jews in the concentration camp gas chambers during the Third Reich, which is reflected in the charge and has been manifested by his disputatious statements regarding the self-evidence of this historical fact and by his description of this fact as the 'six-million tale, maintained in the interests of our enemies,' the accused has committed the crime of incitement of the people," etc.

Ironically, I only deny what is not true and logically cannot be true. If the original "four million Jews exterminated at Auschwitz" figure is now acknowledged to have been false (i.e., war propaganda), it follows that the 'six million Jews exterminated' figure is also not true.

But in Germany it is *verboten* to argue the point since in questioning these things one insults the (integrity of the) Jews and "defames their dead." In relation to this last word, I am not certain whether it refers to the actual dead or the "living dead" (i.e., the millions of 'Holocaust survivors' who receive or have received indemnification from the German government).

I can also state emphatically that I have never regarded or called the Jews 'inferior beings undeserving of the respect of other

---

[11] At the time Anderson tried the usual tricks of unfounded accusations and ridiculous assertions. He had one of his underlings call me, who then warned me of dire consequences if I did not play along with them. I merely used some cuss words (for me a very abnormal thing to do) and hung up. It was clear from the beginning that Anderson was acting in behalf of the *Oberjuden*. We had nothing to lose.

citizens.'

During my half century stay in the United Stated I have usually had good relations with what I call "normal" Jews, namely, those outside of the realm of politics and other activism and it would, in retrospect, constitute a betrayal of these people, if I were to state otherwise.

I apply the designation liars to the many Jews who are deserving to be called liars.

It is possible that only liars and cheats have a chance to rise in the Jewish political hierarchy, and that the multitude of Jews are innocent in the matter. But if they are innocent then it is their duty to speak up and defend the truth.[12]

For example, *The Chicago Tribune* printed an interesting article relating to Julie Salamon, the daughter of "Holocaust survivors" who became a film critic for the *Wall Street Journal*. She had been wondering about the "secrets" her parents had kept from her for forty years, and therefore arranged to travel with her mother to the set of *Schindler's List* in Poland.

Seeing the female Auschwitz inmates (movie extras) in their shapeless dresses, the mother exclaimed: "We never wore that kind of dress, we were different from those Poles." In Auschwitz, the mother mentioned how lucky she had been in a particular barracks, how "delicious" was the black bread she was given upon arrival.

Mrs. Salamon's parents evidently are honorable people, not to be counted among the horde of "survivors" who made exceedingly lucrative and pleasurable careers recounting their

---

[12] I have long held the belief that the mass of the Jews suffers more from the psychoterror from fear of their *Oberjuden* brethren, than we do. For instance, one can frequently read the lament of the offspring of Jewish "Holocaust survivors" who complain that their parents never speak of their experience in the camps, including Auschwitz. As a rule, this silence it taken as confirmation that the elders can't speak about this time because everything was so horrible. But couldn't it just be the opposite: they do not talk about it because it was a relatively normal experience associated with a horrible war'?

concentration camp horror fantasies and, having been granted *a priori* immunity against prosecution for perjury, "testifying" at the countless trials of Balts, Germans, Poles, and Ukrainians around the world. These lying "survivors" plague us to this day, having sent, deliberately and malevolently, untold numbers of innocent people, men and women to life, and death, in prison, and others to the hangman.

Paul Rassinier, the distinguished French scholar, Socialist, member of the "Resistance," and an inmate in the camps, draws the parallel in which he recounts his experiences, and those of other concentration camp inmates he observed.

He does so in a ground-breaking work titled *Les Mensonges d'Ulysse* (*The Lies of Ulysses*). At first sight, the title is odd, even puzzling. But the book shows it to be marvelously appropriate. It took Ulysses ten years to return, alone---perhaps with some reluctance --- to Ithaca and Penelope. When he was asked to account for the inordinate length of his voyage, and what happened to him, he could not answer truthfully. "Nothing much ... I was just dragging my feet..."

He saw that his interlocutors were avid for sensation. He was aware that their chagrin at being told only the humdrum truth could get him killed (as has been the fate of so many others since then).

So he regaled them with wondrous tales of gods, and spirits, and beasts, and monsters, natural and unnatural marvels, a race of giants with just one eye in the center of their foreheads, lovely maidens whose singing lured sailors to their death and a great sorceress who turned men into swine.

He also spoke of a six-headed monster whose long necks whipped out of its lair on a mountain top, seizing six of Ulysses' compatriots as he steered his ship too close in order to avoid a whirlpool that would have sucked them down into a bottomless chasm in the sea, and so on. Read Homer for the details. His listeners were well content. His tales have become classic.

So it is with the "Holocaust survivors." They served up stories no less bizarre and incredible than Homer but, unlike Homer, ineffably disgusting, the revolting effluvia of putrefied minds. But that is what is wanted. It forms the "Holocaust," the most astronomically profitable swindle ever conceived. It threatens to also become an immortal classic too. Like *The Old man of the Sea*, this Big Lie will be on our backs as long as there are Jews.

Mrs. Salamon's parents on the other hand, felt a natural and decent reticence about elaborating on their internment in Auschwitz. It must have been dreary and unpleasant, but essentially uneventful, except when punctuated by the sadistic actions of the guards known as *kapos*--invariably Communist POWs, often Jews--or by Anglo-American bombing, or the true horror of typhus brought in from the east.

They kept their integrity; they did not, as did hundreds of thousands of others, succumb to the compulsion to furnish luridly embroidered fantasies to dramatize themselves during a bleak and banal period of existence.

I know that everything I wrote in my letter to Professor Wolffsohn is true, and can be proven with information from Establishment sources.

Reading this letter it becomes evident what I have been stating so frequently in this book: Jews are a specially protected class in "the new Germany," and Professor Wolffsohn makes the most of it.

The reference to the Jews as 'people of Jewish faith' is interesting. Naturally, this is pure malarkey. Here in the U.S. the Jews are an ethnic group just like the Germans, the Irish, the Blacks, and the Asians. When I criticize them for their over-representation and misuse of power (and, yes, for their lies), then it is as members of an ethnic group, "of a separate and distinct people," and not solely because of their religion; even though I know that religion does form the basis for the moral and ethical values of a society.

Reading my words about the Kennedy assassination carefully, I am not blaming Jews for the murder of the president, I am posing a question: whether or not a line can be drawn because of some new facts which became recently available, and as a result of some quotes discovered in American newspapers, such as the *New York Times*.

Do the Zionists (Israelis, the major Jewish organizations, and millions of individual Jews), use the Six Million swindle as a means to extort billions of dollars and *deutschmarks* from the United States, Germany and other countries? Or, are we to believe that all this wealth is given to Jews voluntarily, just because everybody loves them? At any rate, that is what the Bonn Government insists the Germans ought to believe.

Tall tales about homicidal gas chambers are not their only racket, however. In one of the longest-running scams ever to victimize Americans, cryptic symbols are inserted onto the labels of food and other products to mark them for synagogue-network insiders as "kosher."

The marks usually are a tiny "U" or a minuscule "K." They are placed so inconspicuously, not to say surreptitiously, as to be detectable more or less readily only by an instructed buyer.

The quasi-clandestine nature of the racket is due to the fact that the manufacturers (and "the Jewish community"), want to conceal from the public the fact that their producers, in order to get their merchandise onto supermarket shelves, must pay tribute--including high fees and opulent perks--to the rabbis who "bless" the food and authorize the tiny emblems. The cost of this tribute is added to the prices paid by the great all-American consumer. (My indication of a "K" Street address to a "U" Street address is mere coincidence).

Are the *Oberjuden* in the forefront of race-mixing everywhere? Who pushed "forced busing" on America with the result that the inner cities were destroyed and the American school system deteriorated in many places into Third World levels?

Who introduced legislation to forbid segregation (i.e., racial separation) everywhere except in Israeli-occupied Palestine? Who is now decrying the demise of affirmative action (while seeing to it that their Jewish brethren retain their inordinate influence at the top universities)? Are not the Jewish legislators in the forefront of those Congressmen, such as Rep. Charles Schumer (D-N.Y.) who pass legislation that destroys the last vestiges of the old, Constitutional United States?

Was it not New York's Rep. Emanuel Celler who introduced and--along with all his Jewish colleagues in the House of Representatives--agitated for the passage of the 1965 immigration law that created havoc with American society, and opened the door for a flood of Third World persons to come to this country? All in the name of doing good, naturally.

Both the U.S. and Germany face these problems. Foreigners in Germany (less than ten percent of the population) commit an extraordinary number of crimes. In 1995, in the State of Hessia, 86 percent of the pocket thieves, 60 percent of street robbers, 55 percent of burglars, and 51 percent of murderers were of non-German origin. At times things get too much for the more honest Germans, and they attack the ghettos where most of the foreigners live. I call that self-defense; the Bonn prosecutors believe the German patriots are always "Neo-Nazis", and that anybody who defends them acts against §130.

On the last page of my indictment the prosecutor asks for a

prison sentence *without the possibility of parole.*

This request is made against someone of nearly seventy years of age who has never in his life stood in front of an American or German judge, and is fighting for the continuing existence of the German people in its God-given heritage, and the German nation.

Note that my other "offenses," which in the meantime have lapsed due to a statute of limitations, are supposed to be taken into consideration also.

The very last sentence stating that my offenses as well as my arrest have "evoked a particularly vigorous response in the press, both domestic and abroad," is quite indicative of the mentality of the rulers who pretend to act in the best interests of the German people. Here the Bonn vassals openly admit that their prosecution of a German-American dissident writer, and their having threatened me with a possible sentence of imprisonment without parole, is beholden to the hype and propaganda issued by the international corporate media.

This is an admission that traditional German courts, which were based solely on justice, are now dead and that the modern Bonn court system is hostage to corporate newspaper bias and opinion.

Perversely, considered grounds for my imprisonment, is the automatic "outrage" that came from abroad, namely, from Jewish-dominated newspapers and other media.

A reprint of the indictment in the original German language is in the appendix.

Later, I will delve into the matter of the dual citizenship and why I insist on retaining a German passport.

Questions Concerning the Legality of My Persecution and Imprisonment in Germany

In the indictment, the now notorious, and often used paragraph No. 130 of the German *Strafgesetzbuch* (Criminal Code) is most frequently used. This paragraph (and the associated §131) concern, *Volksverhetzung,* namely, the alleged *attempt to incite the public to hate.*

Before we try to prove that no attempt to incite anybody to hate has ever been made, the very legality of these laws has to be established, especially since every year thousands of Germans fall prey to their stipulations.

Freedom of expression is explicitly guaranteed in the United States and in Germany, *as well as through international conventions to which both of these nations are signatories,* and it is interesting to note how differently these treaties are applied.

Under international law, freedom of expression and the right to associate without fear of improper governmental interference, are considered fundamental human rights. These rights are guaranteed by Articles 1(3), 55(c) and 56 of the United Nations Charter (October 24, 1945), as further defined and clarified in Articles 19 and 20 of the Universal Declaration of Human Rights (December 10, 1948).

It is instructive to note that Article 25 of the German *Grundgesetz* of 1949 demands that in the case of doubt, all national domestic law should be interpreted in conformity with international law. Moreover, public documents such as the United States Constitution and its accompanying Bill of Rights are recognized as valid documents by foreign governments pursuant to international law. The texts of the German paragraphs 130 and 131 are as follows:

§130. Public Incitement of Hatred.

(1) Everyone who, in a manner likely to lead to a breach of the peace 1. incites hatred against parts of the public or urges violent or arbitrary measures to be taken against them, or 2. attacks the human dignity of others by slandering, maliciously belittling or libeling them, is liable to imprisonment for a term from three months up to five years, without the possibility of parole.

(2) Everyone who 1. a) disseminates, b) publicly exhibits, posts, displays or otherwise renders available, c) offers, gives or makes available to anyone under the age of 18 years, or produces, obtains, supplies, keeps in stock, offers, announces, advertises, or engages in import or export for purposes in accordance with a) to c) or to enable another person's use of them in such a manner, or 2. disseminates by means of broadcasting, any publications (§11, section 3) that incite hatred against parts of the public or against identifiable national, racial, religious or ethnic groups, that urge violent or arbitrary measures against them or attack the dignity of others by slandering, maliciously belittling or libeling parts of the public, or a group such as defined above, is liable to imprisonment for a term not exceeding three years, or to a monetary fine.

(3) Everyone who, publicly or in an assembly, and in a manner likely to lead to a breach of peace, endorses, denies or trivializes any act committed under National Socialist rule and of the type specified in §220a, Section 1, is liable to imprisonment for a term not exceeding five years, or to a monetary fine.

(4) Section 2 also applies to publications (§11, Section 3) with contents such as described in Section 3.

(5) In cases of Section 2, also where concomitant with Section 4, and in cases of Section 3, §86 Section 3 applies accordingly.

§131. Depiction of violence. (1) Whosoever does the following with writings (see §11, section 3) that either glorify or belittle such violence (crimes), or depicts such acts in a manner that harms through slandering the dignity of others, namely, 1. disseminates, 2. publicly exhibits, shows or otherwise makes them available to the public, 3. offers them to persons under 18 years of age, or makes the writings in any other way available, 4. produces, subscribes to, delivers, keeps on hand, offers, announces, imports or exports, in order to use these writings in concordance with sections 1 to 3, or any other usage, is liable to imprisonment up to one year, or a monetary fine.

(2) Whosoever broadcasts such material as the writings mentioned in section 1 via the radio, shall also be punished.

(3) Section 1 and 2 shall not be enforced when it is a matter of straight reporting that serves the depiction of current or historical events.

(4) Section 1, part 3 cannot be used when it concerns a personal matter.

I am going to show on what basis not only paragraphs 130 and 131 but the entire German legal system are now grounded, and I am going to prove to the satisfaction of most (I hope), that ever since the reunification of Germany in 1990, the "Bonn" judiciary has been part of an enemy system operating on German soil, with the major aim of continuing the plutocrat's 20th Century wars of fratricide against the German people by other means.

From the onset it has to be understood that so far no peace treaty relating to World War II has been signed between Germany (or, the German Reich), and its enemies in these wars, the Allies. Technically, the armistice signed on May 8, 1945, has merely been carried over into the present. As a rule, the passage of time does not alter legal circumstances.

There is no question that it is the right of victors-occupiers to pass and enforce laws that make an occupation bearable for all, victor and vanquished. Therefore, it is reasonable to expect that occupiers organize a civil administration which establishes rules and regulations so that normal life can proceed. It would be ludicrous to assume, for instance, that today's automobile traffic could function without laws regulating it.

Since the various victors had agreed even before World War II had ended that there would be four different zones of occupation, it follows that at first also four different military governments were formed, out of which, due to further political developments, eventually "West Germany" (the Bonn "Republic"), and Communist Germany (the "DDR"), arose.

Pending a peace treaty, the eastern part of Germany was put under Polish and Russian administration, the Sudetenland was incorporated into reconstituted Czechoslovakia, and Austria was again separated from the Reich, and made a separate state.

As a result of the collapse of the Soviet Union in the 1990s and in the aftermath, the collapse of its Communist client state of "East" Germany (up to then so named only by the Allies), the remaining parts of the Reich that remained under German civil administration, namely, the Bonn "Republic" and the "DDR" were reunited in 1990, forming present-day Germany.

On the next page we are reprinting a letter written in June 1994 by an official of the German Ministry of the Interior in Bonn, that was an answer to an inquiry regarding the present status of the Reich. Then I am going to reprint the Reich German answer to these allegations.

Reading the Bonn letter, it is important to note that at no time since 1945 did the German people either in its entirety or in part, have a chance to vote either on a Constitution, on the continued existence (or abandonment) of the Reich, or on any other form of government it desires, or on a peace treaty (or any other treaty which Bonn claims took the place of a proper peace treaty).

The assertion that Bonn is a "representative Republic," and that therefore the legislators are empowered to act in such vital matters in the name of the German people, is ridiculous at best.

BUNDESMINISTERIUM DES INNERN
Postfach 17 02 90. 53105 Bonn
Translation: June 16, 1994
Re: Decision by the Constitutional Court of July 31, 1973

(Since the end of the war) the German Reich continued to exist within the meaning of international law as an inactive object within the borders of December 31, 1937. This was confirmed by the London Protocol of September 12, 1944, as well as by the Potsdam Agreement of August 2, 1945. Neither the Görlitz Agreement between the former "DDR" and Poland of July 6, 1950, nor the Moscow Treaty of August 12, 1970 negated or altered these international agreements. This confirms the numerous judgments of the Constitutional Court, one of which, namely the one of July 31, 1973, you have quoted. According to these judgments it had been the duty of all officials of the Republic to strive toward the goal of reunification.

As of now, the legal situation is as follows. With the signing of the "Treaty Concerning The Final Solution Concerning Germany" of September 12, 1990, the so-called "2+4 Treaty," occurred the final solution to the German problem, since it not only made the reunification possible but also concluded the rights of the occupiers, and re-established German sovereignty.

With this act (due to the reunification), the German Reich within the borders of 1937 has ceased to exist. Questions regarding unsolved problems, or matters of succession, have been assumed by the *Bundesrepublik Deutschland* within the present borders.

With the Unification Treaty of August 31, 1990, the stipulations regarding the joining of the German states according to Article 23 of the *Grundgesetz* have been satisfied. This concludes the legal requirement that all German officials had to work toward German reunification, and with it the constitutionality of the process. (A decision by the Constitutional Court dated September 18, 1990 was used as final reference).

Sincerely, *Baumann-Hendricks*

Reading the Bonn letter, one cannot help but notice the emphasis on the West German Constitution of 1949 (the *Grundgesetz)* that was essentially written by Americans or by persons who had emigrated from the Reich to America before the war.

These persons returned to Germany in the *entourage* of the Allied troops, *and* upon the enactment of the *Grundgesetz* that was made the law of the land, only after the American Military Government under General Lucius D. Clay had made use of its right to veto or object to certain passages.

In other words, the post-war, Bonn (now, all-German) Constitution in no way constitutes authentic German law. In many of its articles it is decidedly un-German in spirit. That is why the Germans using this law for their new republic in 1949, wisely named it a *Grundgesetz* (basic law) and not *Verfassung,* namely, constitution.

It is also a fact that for decades its temporary (provisional) character had never been questioned. The truth is, in 1949 Germany had already a constitution, one that had been in force since 1919, (and throughout the Third Reich and the war years), the so-called Weimar Constitution.

In retrospect it seems that certain behind-the-scenes groups among the Allied occupiers did not like the Weimar Constitution because it did not contain such dangerous articles as the revised paragraphs No. 130, 131 and 220, and others. These are the pseudo-laws that make the current persecution of German patriots possible, permit the inundation of Germany with unassimilable foreign immigrants ("asylum seekers"), and otherwise run counter to everything that is truly German.

The Bonn Government is in the process of forever relinquishing German sovereignty to bureaucrats in the European Union (EU) offices in Brussels, Belgium. [1]

Not once since the end of World War II, have the German people been allowed to participate, through a plebiscite, in deciding the fate of Germany or its borders. It seems the present rulers are not very certain of the projected results. The reluctance of the Bonn stooges to permit the people to decide anything of importance is further evidence of the regime's illegality and usurpation. A referendum can only backfire, not only for those in power now but also for their allies across the Atlantic.

On the occasion of the signing of the previously cited "2+4 Treaty," a German constitutional lawyer, the late Professor Dr. K. Muench of Heidelberg, authored a learned treatise regarding the legal situation of the Reich. Here are excerpts from this essay:

---

[1] In late 1996 Jörg Haider's Freedom Party won several seats in the European Parliament, based on voters' opposition to an Austrian merger with the EU. The Austrians are supporting Haider in ever greater numbers. Haider is on record upholding the heroism of WWII German veterans, including Waffen SS veterans.

1. The German Reich continues its existence under the name *Bundesrepublik Deutschland.* This is, however, only a partial successor. But, *no partial successor may act in the name of the Reich.* (West German Supreme Court judgments of 1973, 1975, 1 987).

2. Since 1945, the right of self-determination has been part of international law (*ius cogens*), and it was incorporated in the Vienna Convention of May 23, 1969. Therefore, no present German Government is in a position to relinquish German rights to such annexed German territories as the Sudetenland (or Silesia, Pomerania, East Brandenburg, Danzig or East Prussia); as long as the right to self-determination of the expelled Germans (or their heirs), and that of the Germans still living in these areas, has not been taken into consideration.

Every treaty which does not recognize the right to self-determination of the German population expelled from these territories, and does not address itself to the legal right of these people to be part of the Reich or its successors, according to the above-cited Vienna Convention (to which the United States also was a signatory), is null and void.

The rights granted by this Vienna Convention cannot fall under any Statute of Limitations (UN Convention, November 27, 1968), nor be unilaterally abandoned (Geneva Convention of 1949, Article 8).

3. The internationally binding borders of the German Reich are those of August 1, 1914, plus those of 1 September 1939. [2]

A) Because the Treaty of Versailles was formulated without the contribution of the German Reich, and was created to the detriment of a third party (*res inter adios acta*), and was signed under duress (Vienna Convention of 1969, Article 52); hence, it

---

[2] However, the Czech Republic was a protectorate and not part of the Reich.

was from its inception, null and void.

B) The unilateral delineation of the legal borders of the German Reich under the declaration of December 31, 1937 as proclaimed by the Berlin declaration of the four powers on June 5, 1945, is, according to international law which prohibits unilateral agreements to the disadvantage of third parties, null and void. (Vienna Convention of 1969, Article 34). In fact, only the occupation zones were legally established at that time.

4. The rights and obligations ("supreme power") which the Allied victors assumed in 1945 could only have been those of occupation powers, according to the The Hague Laws of War of 1907, of which the 1945 victors were signatories. Therefore, the following actions by the victors were transgressions against international law:

A) The arrest, captivity and incarceration of the members of the Reich Government on May 21, 1945.

B) Military tribunals which were convened with complete disregard for the most basic judicial principles and which led to death sentences resulting from forged documents. The London Agreement of August 8, 1945 is null and void since it created hitherto nonexisting legal principles on which the judgments of the International Military Tribunal (IMT) at Nuremberg were based.

C) Interference in internal affairs of the Reich - for instance, the eradication of the State of Prussia.

D) The annexation by others of German Reich territory.

E) The expulsion of the Germans from the annexed territories and the confiscation of their private property (Geneva Convention of 1949).

F) The resettlement in occupied or annexed German territories of non-Germans. The latter have no permanent rights in these areas (UN agreement regarding the British-organized elections at Gibraltar; Geneva Convention of 1949, Article 49). [3]

5. Local treaties are only valid insofar as they pertain to agreements to prevent the use of force, but not if they concern any renunciation of German territory (West German Supreme Court, July 17, 1975).

6. The elimination of the German people as the *Staatsvolk* of the *Bundesrepublik* through massive immigration of non-Germans, and the granting of German citizenship to aliens, as well as the right of domicile (anywhere), as a result of the "European integration," is unconstitutional. The Basic Law (Constitution of 1949) upholds fidelity to the continued existence of the identity of the German *Staatsvolk* (West German Supreme Court, October 21, 1987).

Here we conclude Dr. Muench's expert treatise on the bogus status of the Bonn regime.

The four Allied victor nations that were signers of the "2+4 Treaty" seem to acknowledge these finer points of international law.

For instance, they cleverly used the term "United Germany" in order to circumvent the rights and obligations (and the name) of the German Reich.

Will this subterfuge help the anti-Germans to retain the present status in the future? Time will tell, but we seriously doubt it.

---

[3] The Hague Convention of 1907, at which the Laws of War were promulgated, was convened by U.S. President Theodore Roosevelt and the Russian Czar. This is more reason for the U.S. to abide by it.

The Bonn "Republic"
A System Based on Lies

It is generally known or assumed that politicians lie in order to stay in power and it would be surprising if the leaders of the Bonn "Republic" were any different from their counterparts elsewhere in the world.

But when we generally speak of the lies of politicians, especially of those active in the "Democracies," we more often than not mean their election promises, their utterances in campaign speeches, and their excuses as to why they had to compromise on some specific issue.

But what sets the leaders of the Bonn "Republic" apart from all others in the industrial nations, is their absolute dishonesty relating to fundamental questions of the German nation.

For instance, since the end of World War II, the Bonn rulers had only given lip service to the quest for German reunification, a quest which had never been extinguished in the hearts of the German people. For decades the major politicians of the Bonn regime actually swore that the re-establishment of German unity was their first priority, while in fact they did *absolutely* nothing to promote this goal.

Former Chancellor Konrad Adenauer, the political Godfather of Helmut Kohl, was actually *opposed* to the reunification of the Fatherland, for "religious reasons" which he never divulged. With Chancellor Kohl it was similar. Only after the Berlin Wall had fallen and after reunification was actually a *fait accompli*, did Kohl take the necessary steps to incorporate the "facts on the ground" with the infrastructure of the Bonn regime. Yet with hindsight, he now calls himself the "Chancellor who made the reunification possible."

Viewing the occurrences connected with the opening of the Berlin Wall from the vantage of America and with a world view (*Weltanschauung*) that was essentially formed in the United States, one should have assumed that the various departments of the Bonn Government would all have had plans for "Day X," the day of the eventual reunification, in their drawers. This was especially incumbent upon them, since all government officials had to swear to uphold the 1949 constitution which admonished all Germans that it was their duty to work toward the *unity* and freedom of Germany through insistence on self-determination.

But when November 9, 1989 arrived and the Berlin Wall fell without the active assistance of the Bonn bureaucracy; and when immediately after that the reunification of at least the West-German and Communist-occupied German parts of the Reich became feasible, it became known that *nothing,* absolutely *nothing,* had been prepared for such an eventuality.

This purposeful neglect was not some minor malfeasance of office, it was downright criminal. While their German brethren to the east were hostage to the Soviets, suffering under the Communist yoke, Bonn never so much as formulated a contingency plan for the day of their freedom, because Bonn was content with the status quo of Communist occupation. Those responsible for this criminal complacency should be called to account.

Another lie of the Bonn regime concerns the question of the eastern German borders. Ever since the Bonn government was established soon after the war, its officials not only claimed to work toward the reunification of Germany, but they also always maintained that the question of the final settlement of Germany's eastern border with Poland and Czechoslovakia, had to be regarded as an open one, until a peace treaty between Germany ("The Reich") and the Allied victors was possible.

Implied in this Bonn doubletalk was the escalation of false hope for the remnants of the fifteen million Germans expelled from the east at the end of the war, whose ancestors had for many centuries lived in the true east Germany, beyond the Oder-Neisse line and the Sudeten Mountains. [1]

These peoples hopes that someday most of them could go home again, were falsely and cruelly exploited by Bonn.

Politically astute Americans have *always* known that the Allied powers would *never* assent to a return of the Germans to their ancestral homelands in east central Europe, since the "cutting down to size" of the Reich had been one of the major Allied war aims.

The Bonn rulers also knew that, but they were dishonest enough to keep this knowledge from their people.

Then occurred an act by the Bonn bureaucrats that I consider the height of infamy.

Soon after the West German *Bundesrepublik* and the former DDR (Communist part of Germany) were officially reunited in October of 1990, somebody gave the order to the entire German media to henceforth name the territory that had been the DDR not *Mitteldeutschland* (Central Germany), as many editors had still been (correctly) wont to do, but to use the designation *Ostdeutschland* (East Germany) instead. And, Germans being Germans, Bonn received near 100 percent compliance.

Consequentially, the real East Germany--and with it, its

---

[1] This forced deportation of millions of civilians by the Soviets, with the full approval--and even applause--of the western Allies--resulted in the deaths by starvation, abuse, rape and murder, of upwards of two million eastern German civilians. This is yet another aspect of the unsung holocaust *against* Germany, which we must memorialize and commemorate and in which Hollywood and the Establishment media have no interest. Though a comprehensive English-language history of this horror has yet to be written, the reader will find a groundwork in Alfred DeZayas' *Nemesis at Potsdam*. For an interesting and moving historical novel of the fate of Germans in Ukraine, written by an eyewitness, cf. Ingrid Rimland, *The Wanderers*.

thousand year history—was spiritually eradicated.

With a stroke of a pen, Bonn wrote off centuries of German history and cultural achievements. For example, Königsberg in the authentic "East" Germany (east-central Europe), was founded in 1255 by the German Knights.

Bonn eliminated the memory of this and other lands of the true *Ostdeutschland,* paid for with the blood and sweat of our ancestors, from the consciousness of the modern German people.

In the long term, the result of this betrayal will be, for instance, that future American history books may claim Immanuel Kant as having been born in Russia (East Prussia), and the poet Eichendorff in Poland (Silesia).

In due time then, they will become Russian and Polish respectively, just as the German (by ethnicity and language), Nicholas Copernicus, is now universally acclaimed as a Polish astronomer.

For many Americans (including this writer), the 200-year-old Constitution of our nation is sacrosanct. It is unthinkable that an American administration or even the United States Congress would dare to alter the wording of the Constitution without first executing the proper procedures (for instance, in the way amendments are enacted into law). Not so the Bonn vassals of the Allies.

I have before me two identical booklets issued by the Bonn government titled *Grundgesetz,* namely, "Basic Law" or "Constitution."

One is from October 1988, the other from October, 1990. In other words, one was issued before the fall of the Berlin Wall, the other in the very month of the official reunification.

The preamble is an integral part of this constitution, and I am herewith translating these paragraphs from both booklets:

1988: "Being conscious of our responsibility toward God and mankind, and being imbued with the will to retain its national and administrative unity, and furthermore to serve world peace as an equal member of a united Europe, the German people living in Baden, Bayern, Bremen, Hamburg, Hessen, Niedersachsen, Nordrhein-Westfalen, Rheinland-Pfalz, Schleswig-Holstein, Württemberg-Baden and Württemberg-Hohenzollern, have decided to create a new, albeit temporary administrative order which resulted in this basic law of the German *Bundesrepublik*.

"We also acted in the name of those Germans who currently are not in any position to cooperate in this endeavor.

The entire German people are asked to work toward the reunification and the freedom of Germany through the means of self-determination."

1990: "Being conscious of our responsibility toward God and mankind, and being imbued with the will to serve world peace as an equal partner in a united Europe, the German people have decided to give themselves, according to their constitutional rights, the following basic law.

"The Germans in the states of Baden-Württemberg, Bayern, Berlin, Brandenburg, Bremen, Hamburg, Hessen, Mecklenburg-Vorpommern, Niedersachsen, Nordrhein-Westfalen, Rheinland-Pfalz, Saarland, Sachsen, Sachsen-Anhalt, Schleswig-Holstein and Thüringen have, through their free self-determination, completed the unity and the quest for freedom of Germany. With this act, the *Grundgesetz* is the basic law for all Germans."

Note the striking differences between these two preambles. They are no doubt an integral part of the German constitution. But would you believe that in spite of the claim of the people's participation, absolutely no referendum or plebiscite on the alteration of the *Grundgesetz* was allowed?[2]

I would not be surprised if the wording of the preamble was simply changed in some back room, even without the input or a vote of the elected representatives. The treachery of the Bonn rulers is incredible.

They declare, without the valid vote of the people and without a constitutional congress, that this is "it," and no German has a chance to say a word against it. If you do, you will quickly come to the attention of one of the German secret police agencies that is quite aptly titled, *Verfassungsschutz*, namely, "Guardians of the (ersatz) Constitution."

It also bears remembering that with this new instrument of law, the Bonn rulers have accepted all the dictates by the 1945 victors without asking the German people first. The final settlement of the postwar borders, the elimination of both the Reich and of the State of Prussia; even the theft of much of the German cultural heritage, is acknowledged without a murmur of protest from Bonn. [3]

One of the most flagrant examples of Bonn's deceit has to do with the private *German* properties which the former Communist rulers of so-called "East" Germany had confiscated in the immediate post-war years.

Communists being Marxists, they believed that all land and all methods of production had to be in the hands "of the people."

---

[2] The Bonn regime, in typically dictatorial fashion, does not allow any referendum by the entire German nation on such fundamental questions as the abandonment of German sovereignty in favor of the European Union (as codified in the Maastricht Treaty), or the forced imposition of a single European currency accompanied by "austerity measures" decreed by the International Monetary Fund, which can only result in a lower standard of living for Germans.

[3] Recent reports of the vast wealth represented by the German art treasures stolen by the Russians in 1945, which remain to this day in mainly Russian museums and libraries, has not troubled the current German government in the least. Bonn continues to bankroll the Russians with billions of *deutschmarks*, seemingly without any demands or preconditions.

So they confiscated, *without compensation,* the farms of those who had for centuries provided Germany with its basic foodstuffs, and the factories and businesses not only of the anonymous corporations but also of the many small and middle-sized entrepreneurs for which Germany has always been famous.

This did not result in a true "ownership of the people," but a kind of state capitalism of the worst sort, that was never able to satisfy anything but the most basic needs of the population.

I have given a lot of thought to this Communist injustice against the farmers and businessmen that had lost their properties in the land between the Elbe and the Oder rivers. Being a firm believer in the sanctity of private property, I assumed that shortly after the disappearance of the "East" German Communist regime, and after the resulting reunification of these parts of the Reich, the rightful owners could take possession of their ancestral farms and businesses.

I anticipated that problems would arise, for instance in cases where the Communist regime had sold or given away former farm acreage for the building of houses.

One could not expect that suddenly the former farmer would become the owner of the homes that had been built on his land in the last forty years. But these problems could be solved, with all parties being willing to wade through the legal entanglements, and come to *just* conclusions.

How wrong I was! Elsewhere I described how the *Treuhandanstalt* (a Bonn instituted escrow company), criminally stole the entire "East" German infrastructure, and often gave it away to enemies of the German people. But what got me most was the unethical and dishonest way in which the Bonn stooges of the Allies dealt with the formerly independent land owners of that part of *Deutschland*.

With the signing of the reunification treaties (both inner-German agreements and the 2+4 Treaty of Moscow), the West German government became the "legal" owner of all properties formerly held by the Communists; namely, almost everything in that part of Germany.

(The ownership of mostly small private homes was still permitted, and, although rarely, there seem to have been apartment houses still in private hands, where the rents were so low as to make the normal upkeep impossible. This contributed to the destruction and neglect one could discover after the Berlin Wall went down).

After the Communists had disowned the German *kulaks* (large and middle class landholders), most of them left the Red "paradise," and settled either in West Germany or on other continents. Believing in the legality and orderliness of the Bonn system, most of these people imagined that with the reunification, and the ensuing radical changes occurring in their former homeland, they could soon again take possession of what was rightfully theirs.

However, it did not take long for them to experience the disappointment of a lifetime. Chancellor Kohl and other Bonn bureaucrats declared at the signing of the 2+4 Treaty in Moscow, that the Russians had demanded assurances that the Communist property confiscations of the immediate postwar years would not be reversed, and that they, the executives of the present German Government, had no choice but to abide by this demand.[4]

In other words, generally no outright return of the stolen property was possible or even contemplated.

Few people in Germany considered that Bonn had not told the

---

[4] No one ever explained why the Russians would want such assurances. Once they had withdrawn their troops from German soil--a step that was planned and implemented in 1994--why should they care who owned the "East" German farms?

truth about the matter. After all, was it not in the all-German interest when legality prevailed, and when the true owners of farms and small industries could return to their former "East" German holdings with the expertise gained in the West?

It took years for the truth to filter through, but one day a reporter asked Mikhail Gorbachev, the Russian leader at the time of the signing of the 2+4 Treaty, why his nation had insisted on not having the 1945--1949 confiscations reversed. Gorbachev, who had already made waves in the case of the murdered Rudolf Hess, Hitler's party deputy, when he countered Western allegations about Russian intentions and actions in the matter, thereupon explained that Russia had made no such demands on Germany!

To put it bluntly: Helmut Kohl and his then foreign minister Genscher had swindled the owners of the ancestral farms of "East" Germany and told a blatant lie in order to pull off the swindle.

Now Bonn was in a quandary, albeit not necessarily insurmountable. The Kohl Government immediately reversed itself and maintained that it was the *American* Government that had insisted on retaining the post-war status quo regarding the landholdings. In the meantime, Bonn did not keep the situation in abeyance until perhaps some high courts could decide either on the legality of the alleged Allied stance, or for the rights of the disenfranchised real owner. The ironically named *Treuhandanstalt* continued to sell or give away properties to which it had no legal title.

Some time passed, and one day the matter of the alleged U. S. insistence on upholding the Soviet confiscations was settled abruptly by George Bush, the former president of the United States. During an interview nearly five years after the German reunification, Bush was asked by a German reporter whether he recalled the negotiations leading to the 2+4 Treaty, and whether the United States Government which he headed at that time had insisted upon retaining the status quo as established by the Soviet Union, and in particular, regarding the "East" German land holdings.

Bush's answer was to the point: "No, the U S Government had made no such demands on Germany."

One would assume that the Bonn Government would be awfully embarrassed by this disclosure and might have come forth with another explanation. The fact is, nothing happened. Nothing at all.

In the meantime, the most valuable holdings had changed hands (i.e. from the Bonn Government to others), and one could discern the attitude that "in the interest of internal peace in Germany, everybody had better accept the situation as is." Those (relatively) few old and true owners who managed to retake possession of their land often had to pay an arm and a leg to Bonn in order to see that justice was done.

This entire episode points to one of the very serious faults in the Bonn system, a fault which eventually will cause the collapse of this edifice built on lies: if such a development as the one mentioned above had occurred in the United States, we can be sure that a number of the betrayed landholders (farmers) would have gotten together, sued the government, and eventually fought their case to the United States Supreme Court.

Whatever we may think of the Supreme Court now (especially after the anti-*Staatsvolk* [anti-populist] decisions of the Warren court in the mid-1960s), it still retains a semblance of independence.

No American administration can ever be one hundred percent certain that the U. S. Supreme Court will support its policies, either domestic or foreign. This fact alone forces the highest American executives to watch their steps, and consider the ramifications of their actions.

Not so in Germany. The German high court in Karlsruhe is highly politicized and would never really act against the policies of the Bonn administration. This leaves the entire German people at the mercy of the bureaucrats holding the power. Justice is continually being subverted!

Now the question arises as to why Bonn went to such lengths to keep the dispossessed "East" German farmers off and away from their holdings. To this day I have never read a reasonable explanation but, as is usual for me, I try to reach a conclusion that is based upon both logic, and my background knowledge.

It is likely that most of the farms in former "East" Germany that had been confiscated by the Communists, had been owned by the *Junkers,* the minor Protestant aristocracy that had formed the backbone of the Prussian state for centuries.

The state of Prussia was one of the two empire states of the German Reich, (the other one being Austria) and, as could be seen from recent German history, Prussia was without doubt the engine behind the resurgence of the German Reich since the Bismarck era.

Prussia was also the best run German state, with a reputation for an incorruptible civil service that was the envy of the entire world. These were reasons enough for Germany's enemies not only to eliminate the state of Prussia by Allied dictate in 1947, but later to keep insisting that the Prussian *Adel* (aristocracy), remain disenfranchised and relatively poor.

The fact that the bulk of the "East" German farmers had been Protestants, probably also played an important role in their dispossession. Ever since Adenauer, an arch-Catholic devotee of Rome, had become the first Chancellor of the

Bundesrepublik, and ever since he had insisted that the Catholic university town of Bonn become its "temporary" capital, one had to regard the *Bundesrepublik* as an essentially Catholic state.

The CDU, (Christian Democrats), the party of Adenauer and Kohl, was little more than a rerun of the Catholic political party that had existed before the Hitler era.

The closeness of some of the more important Bonn politicians to Rome assured that all of West Germany had *ipso facto* become an instrument of the Counter-Reformation which had been one of the mainstays of the Papacy ever since Martin Luther tore the Roman Catholic Church asunder.

It has been Rome's strategy for the past five hundred years to negate the successes of the German Protestant Reformation, an event that had culminated in setting the minds of many Europeans free, and laying the groundwork for the technological progress of our age.

Bonn's tacit acknowledgment ever since 1945 that the expulsions of the mostly Protestant Germans from East Prussia, Pomerania, Silesia and the Sudetenland were both legal and irreversible and the never-ending support of the Kohl Government for Catholic Poland--the very nation that is holding most of the East German territory now in foreign hands--point to the likelihood of the correctness of my assumptions.

Additional evidence may be glimpsed in the fact that the government of the Bonn Republic seems actually too intimidated to move to Berlin, the rightful capital of Germany. Berlin was also, after all, the capital of the state of Prussia, and since the Reformation it has been a Protestant, rather than a Catholic stronghold.

One can just imagine what would have happened, if already in 1990 the German Government had began the move to Berlin, and if at that time many of the former *Junkers* had received their properties back. The *Junkers*, with their innate patriotism and their loyalty to German tradition, would now certainly be fulfilling a political role that would be considerably more independent from Allied policy and the Church of Rome. [5]

In connection with the Bonn allegations that at first the Russians, and then the Americans had insisted upon the permanence of the confiscations of the immediate postwar years, it may be mentioned that at least since the mid-1960s, the various administrations of the *Bundesrepublik* had frequently claimed that "now, Germany is again sovereign." Counterclaims by persons such as myself that this was an outright lie were dismissed as mere insults.

As I write this, it is 1997, fifty-two years since the armistice was signed. Armies from former enemy states, among them American, English, French and Belgian troops, are still occupying German soil.

Yes, certainly, it is claimed that they are there as "friends and Allies." Of course the cover story is put forth that it is their duty to retain that "wonderful peace" that has kept Europe "free and democratic" since 1945.

But I would like to ask the question, what would happen if a new German government were elected that insisted upon the withdrawal of all foreign forces and their secret services within the shortest time? Would the "friends" leave forthwith and without threats, as befits the demands of a sovereign nation?

Knowing these "friends" well, I would be inclined to doubt it.

---

[5] My criticisms here are not intended to be religious or sectional. I am a critic of Vatican policy and not of individual Catholics, among whom one finds some of the great men of our time, including the heroic "radio priest," Fr. Charles Coughlin. Catholic Bavaria produced outstanding leaders, not the least of whom was the much maligned Rudolf Hess, perhaps the most committed peace ambassador of the 20th century, who paid for his peace overture with life imprisonment and then assassination by Allied captors impatient for his death.

At any rate, Germany is not sovereign, even at this late date, no matter how often Bonn insists that is is otherwise.

Perhaps the most flagrant of the Bonn lies occurred in May of 1995. On the 8th of that month, the Allied victors congregated in their capitals and in a last spasm of their vanishing glory, celebrated the 50th anniversary of the defeat of the Reich with all the pomp and circumstance available to them.

Following in the footsteps of the disintegrated DDR (Communist "East" German) regime, which had organized pompous, May 8 commemorations ever since 1949, the Bonn rulers decided to attach themselves somewhat belatedly to the victors, and with a stroke of the pen, May 8 now became a *Tag der Befreiung* (a Day of Liberation) for the Germans also.

That most Germans did not feel too well about this complete turnabout (many of them remembered their fathers and grandfathers who had given their lives for their country), did not faze the Bonn rulers. People like Kohl and Kinkel obviously basked in the reflected glory due to "victors who had won a great war."

In Berlin an official memorial service commemorating the defeat of the Reich was held. The Bonn Government had invited dignitaries from among the major victors, and they all came. A sour note occurred when President Lech Walesa of Poland complained that he had not been asked to attend, although it had been a Polish division that was among those Soviet forces which had conquered Berlin.

At the *Staatsakt* (an official, government-sponsored memorial service), British Prime Minister John Major made a short speech in which he stated the following:

"*Fifty years ago Europe saw the end of the 30 Years War: 1914 to 1945.*

"The slaughter in the trenches, the destruction of cities and the oppression of citizens: all these left a Europe in ruins *just as the other 30 Years War did three centuries before."*

As is usual in such instances, the "German" Government translated the addresses of the British Prime Minister and the other guests, and published them in the official government bulletin.

This is how they printed the preceding passage: "*Vor fünfzig Jahren erlebte Europa das Ende der dreissig Jahre, die nicht einen, sondern zwei Weltkriege beinhaltet hatten.* Das Gemetzel in den Schützengräben, die Zerstörung der Städte und die Unterdrückung der Bürger hinterliessen ein Europa in Trümmern, gerade *wie es einige Jahrhunderte zuvor der Dreissigjährige Krieg getan hatte.*"

Now the translation of this German text--Bonn's version of Major's speech--and the reader will observe just how willing the Bonn bureaucrats are to falsify even a speech by the Prime minister of Great Britain: "*Fifty years ago Europe saw the end of the thirty years which experienced not only one but two world wars.* The slaughter in the trenches, the destruction of the cities, and the oppression of citizens: all these left a Europe in ruins *just as the 30 Years War did centuries ago.*" (Emphasis supplied).

Note the emphasized sentences. While John Major had spoken of two Thirty Years Wars that had destroyed Europe in the course of centuries, the Bonn liars mention only one (1618 to 1648). They insisted upon altering Major's speech in regard to the era 1914 to 1945, where the Englishman spoke of a second Thirty Years War, while the Bonn rulers unethically pronounced the *two world wars.*

Why would they do that? We may assume that John Major's

words were well chosen, and we may also assume that the Bonn translators were well aware of their falsification. (Falsifications like this are expected from the dictatorial rulers of Communist regimes or Third World tyrants but never from governments that claim to be free and democratic. We know of no prior instance of such a falsehood by a legitimate German government).

No doubt the Bonn rulers will excuse themselves by pointing out that the designation of the two world wars (World War I, 1914 to 1918, and World War II, 1939 to 1945) is common usage, while so far, few people in Germany would agree with the British Prime Minister.

However, what really bothers "Bonn" is the fear that Major's speech could exonerate Adolf Hitler. For, is it not a fact that one cannot start a war that is already being fought?

If, as John Major said, the second Thirty Years War in European history had begun in 1914, and not ended until 1945, then Hitler cannot be accused of starting a war. The worst offense for which he might be accused in this regard, would be to blame him for breaking an armistice that had barely lasted twenty years. But the last thing the Bonn vassals would want at this time is an absolution of the German Führer of the Third Reich.

The entire existence of the *Bundesrepublik* is built upon the demonization of Hitler, the criminalization of National Socialism; the fable of an unjust war that was fought by the Germans and the tall tales of the gas chambers. The removal of even one pillar of this house of lies would cause the entire edifice to come crashing down.

Shenanigans

In some of the other chapters I have alluded to the trickery with which the Bonn regime tried to make my incarceration as cruel as possible.

It would be amiss if I did not describe some of these occurrences in detail. However, before I go into this dismal situation, I would like to emphasize that the civil servants at the Bützow prison with whom I had constant dealings, and who at times were the executors of the chicaneries, namely, the block warden and the guards, *bear absolutely no guilt in the matter*.[1]

Several times during my incarceration at this old penitentiary I was visited by police detectives from the city of Schwerin; usually a young man and an equally young woman, who, obviously on special request, wanted me to make a deposition on this or that question relating to my case.

As a matter of principle I *always* refused to say anything pertaining to the questions at hand on the grounds that my lawyer was not present.

But after we had taken care of this formality, we usually had interesting private conversations that, hopefully, enlightened these young people about the state of Germany today. In retrospect I can only say that these detectives were very professional and respectful. It was a pleasure to converse with them.

Apart from behind-the-scenes powers whose ethnicity I can only guess, the ultimate responsibility for most of the chicanery I had to deal with at the Bützow penitentiary lay with the prosecutor, Mr. Kollarz, and the young (all-too-young) female Judge Freitag.

---

[1] For instance, when for more than two months they could not allow me to use the telephone to call either my wife or my mother.

Both of these persons reviewed every written request I had forwarded to the court, and invariably it was they who, for whatever asinine reasons, denied them.

Following in the sequence I had written in my sparse diary notes, I shall provide an overview of the unnecessary chicaneries with which I had to contend.

From the prison diary of Hans Schmidt:

September 9, 1995: One month has passed since my arrest. Still no news from America. I am completely in the dark about what is happening there relating to my case.

So far I have no response from the court to my written requests that I may either call my wife in Pensacola or my mother in the Saarland.

September 11. The block warden informs me that my wife and others from the United States have called the prison and wanted to talk to me on the phone. All such requests were denied since no permission from the court had been obtained.

September 13. Nearly five weeks after my incarceration I received notice that the approximately 1,400 *deutschmarks* I had on my person at the time of my arrest, were booked on my prison account.

That meant I was finally able to purchase some of the items I was in desperate need of, particularly writing paper, stamps and vitamin pills.

It is incomprehensible why in today`s computer age it should take five weeks for a simple transfer of money.

Personally I believe that some bureaucrat or high official in charge of *all* cash of *all* persons arrested in Germany, enriches himself through kick-backs from banks for the undoubtedly large sums of *deutschmarks* that are permitted to "rest" in some central account for more than a month.

September 14. After five weeks, I was finally able to mail confidential letters to my lawyer, Mr. Herrmann, with the envelopes sealed by me.

Up to this day a legalistic subterfuge had been used by the "authorities" on insisting that *all* my envelopes were to be open and unglued when I gave them to a guard, during the morning check. I was certain that the prosecutor used the opportunity to read the letters before they were sealed and mailed to my attorney.

September 20. Exactly six weeks after my arrest I finally received a letter from home! Knowing that air mail from the United States to Germany usually takes a week, I was able to deduct that this letter (written in German) had purposely and without due cause been held in the judge's offices for about five weeks.

My request to make a short phone call to the United States and confirm the receipt of this first letter was denied.

September 26. It had been three weeks since the *"Haftprüfung,"* (the examination for continued reasons of detention) and I was still not in possession of the indictment in spite of the prosecutor's assurances that we would have it by that time.

October 2. I received 25 pieces of mail all at once.

This was the start of the avalanche of nearly 700 letters and postcards which I received during my imprisonment, from numerous family members, friends, associates and even people that I don't know.

Had the German authorities kept me any longer, the number may well have reached into the thousands. There was no abatement until I was back in America.

Almost without exception the letters had been written a month or more earlier. Some of them are in English, and obviously had to be translated for inspection.[2]

October 6, 1995. Another hurricane created havoc on Florida's Gulf Coast. Pensacola is prominently mentioned in German television programs reporting on the destruction. My request to make an emergency call home is denied. I am wondering whether my family is safe, and whether our house is still standing.

October 13. I received notice today that I may soon make telephone calls to my mother and my wife (but to the latter only if we use the German language), and that a typewriter and a radio had been delivered for me. In order to receive these items, I had to give permission that 50 *deutschmarks* be withdrawn from my account so that these items could be thoroughly inspected for hidden contraband.

October 16, 1995. After having been incarcerated for nearly ten weeks I was finally able to call my wife on the phone, and speak to her for a few minutes. Knowing that someone was listening in, we conversed guardedly.

Subsequently, I put in a request for telephone calls to our house in Florida every week, and as time permitted, these always too-short telephone conversations usually took place on Thursday or Friday afternoons. Some of the guards went out of their way to see to it that I could call home. During an initial

---

[2] Even in retrospect, I am puzzled as to why the German authorities felt the need to read my incoming and outgoing correspondence. Mine was not a criminal case and I had not hidden away millions of stolen *deutschmarks;* nor was it my intention to coax friends on the outside in arranging for my escape. There was also nothing to discover about the state of my mind. Most certainly I was not going to change my opinion about matters of race, Hitler, WWII propaganda, the illegitimacy of the Bonn regime or the inordinate power of the Jewish lobby.

call to my mother in the Saarland I noticed that it upset her too much (she could only envision the worst), and I decided to restrict our frequent contact to letters. [3]

October 20. I was able to go to the prison warehouse and there take possession of the manual typewriter, a ream of paper and the radio that had been delivered for me a month ago. I was now able to answer in earnest the many letters I was receiving from supporters all over the world, and also write letters to the editors of the German newspapers and magazines that I felt deserved my comment.

October 23. I read in the press that the Jew Schalck-Golodkowski, one of the notorious architects of the former "East" German Communist regime, who is under criminal indictment in the *Bundesrepublik* for some of his nefarious actions, was allowed to travel to China on business.

Markus Wolf, another DDR Jew currently under indictment for his role as the former head of the "East" German secret police organization, also seems to have special privileges, for he travels about the world promoting a new book.

Are comparisons with my case permitted, or does the mere mention of these facts constitute "anti-Semitism"? One ought to remember that these two Jews committed *real* crimes, crimes of violence that ought to be severely punished under the statutes of every civilized nation.

U.S. Consular officials from Berlin who visited me and asked about my well-being were not permitted to leave newspapers and magazines in the English language for me to read. What if I were not able to read German?

---

[3] With hindsight it is now clear that both my mother and my wife suffered far more from my ordeal than I did.

October 26. This morning the 29-page indictment was handed to me. Now I was able to prepare myself for the upcoming trial.

November 11. Due to the kindness of one of the prison employees, I had a very long meeting with Mr. Herrmann and my new, additional lawyer, Dr. Eisenecker. We are able to decide on the strategy to be used at the trial.

November 15. A new judge has been appointed to handle my case, Mr. Heydorn, a former judge of the juvenile court system. I notice an immediate increase in the speed of my incoming mail. Letters from home are getting into my hands after two weeks instead of after four weeks or more, as before. Up to now, it took more than two months for me to receive an answer to a question I mailed to associates of my organization in the United States.[4]

I am running low on typewriter paper, and will have a contact person in Germany deliver another ream for me. Hopefully, I am going to get it soon.

December 16. Both of my lawyers are scheduled to visit me. It will be our last conference before the trial is to take place soon after Christmas. However, on this day I am waiting in vain for my visitors. Later I discover that the front office of the penitentiary had used a rather flimsy (and untrue) reason for not permitting my attorneys to see me. Allegedly because they had not properly requested this Saturday visit, they had been turned away at the main gate. This was especially hard on the octogenarian Hajo Herrmann, who had had to travel a great distance for nothing. I wondered who was behind this mischief?

---

[4] In arranging for these particular shenanigans, did those who were ultimately responsible for my arrest hope that these obstructions would bring about the destruction of our German-American organization?

Christmas 1995. In spite of all my hopes, I was forced to spend the holidays in prison. Two packages with Christmas cookies were handed to me but an unknown number of others (perhaps as many as twenty, according to a prisoner), were returned to their senders. One American fruit cake was even shipped back to the United States. I complained, telling the prison authorities that I did not want all the goodies for myself, I was not even insisting that I open the packages myself. But why couldn't they permit me to give the "surplus" packages to other prisoners and make those happy, who do not get anything at Christmas? In this one instance a female employee at the prison front office was very haughty and displayed a complete lack of understanding. Was she envious?

By Christmas, a month had passed since the extra typewriter paper was delivered by my German contacts at the front gate, but not to me personally, and since then I had written numerous requests for it. But somehow it didn't reach me. I had to curtail my writing. [5]

In the matter of the more than forty *Beschlüsse* (decisions) by the Schwerin court to withhold incoming mail from me until my discharge, or giving the order to photocopy, before forwarding to the addressee, those of my letters that contained statements inimical to the interests of the Bonn rulers, I shall provide an overview of some of the more interesting, or more ludicrous, instances where the judges saw fit to make their presence felt:

Court decisions regarding mail to and from Hans Schmidt:
November 15, 1995:
"The letter by Professor Robert Faurisson to Hans Schmidt

---

[5] On the day of my release I discovered this ream of typing paper in my luggage. On its wrapping was written a note to the effect that this paper hand not been handed to me, "or else the prisoner is going to write even more than he does."

dated August 29, 1995 is excluded from delivery to the prisoner because the contents of the missive and the enclosed printed matter refer to "Simon the liar" and "Jewish militias". It is felt that these remarks could create an anti-Jewish attitude, and may disturb the order inside the prison." [6]

October 17, 1995. "The postcard from Gerda B., stamped on September 25, 1995 in San Antonio, Texas, shall not be given to Hans Schmidt but instead will be held in the *Habekammer* (where the personal effects are kept). The forwarding of this card to the prisoner may disturb the order in the institution."

What did Mrs. Barker write in the German language that was so dangerous? Judge for yourself:

"Dear Hans Schmidt!

"I am mailing you this postcard to make things easier for the people who control your mail in our, ah so free, Germany. It is certainly regrettable that native Germans such as you, who defend our fatherland, are being thrown into prisons, and worse yet, when they are citizens of the United States. You, as well as my late husband who died in 1941 on the Russian front, have fought and sacrificed for Germany. What would our dead heroes say now if they were to return to Germany and could see how those parasites (the so-called asylum seekers) are more important than honest Germans, and where the Communists and other leftists have more rights than German patriots? I would like to mail you cassettes with patriotic contents but I am sure these would not be delivered to you. Be brave, eventually things will turn right again." Gerda B.

The following *"Beschluss"* is of special interest since it really

---

[6] It should be noted that Dr. Robert Faurisson's letter to me probably arrived in Schwerin on the first of September. This means it took the court more than ten weeks to consider the matter of releasing this correspondence to me--par for the course of the Bonn judiciary.

concerns a recently published letter about me to the editor of an American Establishment newspaper (i.e., the photocopy mentioned).

In other words, even written material that can be found in U.S. daily newspapers or magazines is considered dangerous in the *Bundesrepublik*. I find it interesting to note how those of the brainwashed generations of Germans who have made it to the top, also seem to have the finely tuned political antennae usually found only among Jews. They know what seems harmful to their masters, but they have no inkling as to what is good or bad for their own people. They are mind-controlled zombies.

Nov. 21, 1995:
"From the letter by Professor Robert H. Countess of the State of Alabama, USA, dated November 4, 1995, to Hans Schmidt, a photocopy of a letter to the editor written by R.H. Countess will be removed, and excluded from forwarding to the prisoner. The piece in question contains crude insults of the German judiciary, and may harm the peace at the institution."

November 20, 1995:
"The letter by Hans Schmidt, dated November 6, 1995, to Samuel Francis of the *Washington Times*, is in lieu of confiscation being photocopied, and placed into the files of the accused. The contents of this letter have a bearing on the investigation against Schmidt."

November 20, 1995:
"The letter by Hans Schmidt dated November 5, 1995, and addressed to Mike Royko of the *Chicago Tribune*, USA, is in lieu of confiscation, being photocopied and placed into the files

of the accused. The contents of the letter have a bearing on the investigation against Schmidt, and provide proof of his attitude toward the Jews."

November 15, 1995:

The *Hoskins Report* from Lynchburg, Virginia, USA, dated October 26, 1995, and addressed to Hans Schmidt, will not be forwarded to the prisoner because its contents might disturb the peace at the institution. The forwarding of this piece of literature to the prisoner might by itself constitute a transgression against existing laws."

November 23, 1995:

"The letter by Mrs. Radtke-Schoone dated 15 November 1995, to Hans Schmidt, will not be given to the prisoner since this might disturb the peace at the institution, and because the forwarding might constitute a criminal offense. The letter contains many insults against the Jewish people."

November 23, 1995:

"The book *Bonn's Zwing-Herren* (Bonn's Real Masters), by H. Kardel, Hamburg, which on November 17, 1995 was mailed by the author to Hans Schmidt, will not be given to the prisoner because it contains insults against the German justice system and against Mr. Wolffsohn, who is one of the witnesses in the case against Schmidt. The forwarding of the book might disturb the peace at the institution."

November 24, 1995:

"The letter by Hans Schmidt to Friedrich Karl Fromme of the *Frankfurter Aligemeine Zeitung* dated November 20, 1995, is to be copied and be placed into the files of the accused because its contents might have a bearing in the case. The letter relates to the accusations against Schmidt, and his attitude concerning the proceedings against him."

November 15, 1995:
"The anonymous letter to Hans Schmidt dated November 5, 1995 will not be forwarded since its anti-Jewish sentiments might endanger the peace at the institution."

November 14, 1995:
"The request by the prosecutor in Schwerin (to confiscate a piece of mail) has been rejected by the court. Instead, the letter by Hans Schmidt dated September 20, 1995, to his brother Richard Schmidt, will be copied and placed into the files of the accused. Its contents may be of importance in the investigation. Schmidt's letter proves that his *USA-BERICHT* is still being mailed with his knowledge and connivance."

November 13, 1995:
"The request by the prosecutor in Schwerin dated October 30, to exclude the letter by E. Kemper dated October 4, 1995, to Hans Schmidt from forwarding to the accused has been denied.
In this case the forwarding of this letter does not constitute a new transgression against the law, especially as far as paragraph No. 189 (defamation of the dead) is concerned. The mere statement not to believe certain historical facts does not by itself constitute the crime of defaming the dead, as long as it is not connected with words that can be considered insulting."

November 14, 1995:
"The court has decided to reject the request by the prosecutor in Schwerin to confiscate the letter by Hans Schmidt, dated

September 1, 1995, to E.T. Herndon in Washington, D.C., USA. The request is reasonable and permissible, but not germane. There is no question that the above-named letter could be used as proof of the opinion of the accused concerning the proceedings against him. A confiscation of this letter, however, would go too far since the attitude of Mr. Schmidt is clearly discernible from the many other letters and written matter in his files, and since it may be assumed that the accused will not deny his stance."

November 15, 1995:
"The letter by Wolfgang Juchem of Aktion Freies Deutschland dated 3 November 1995, to Hans Schmidt, will not be forwarded to the prisoner, because its contents can be used to blame the Jews for historical events, and this might endanger the peace at the institution."

November 14, 1995:
"The request by the prosecutor in Schwerin to confiscate the letter by Hans Schmidt, dated November 1, 1995, and addressed to Patrick Buchanan in Virginia, USA, is being denied. Instead it is ordered that the contents of the letter be copied and placed into the files of the accused because it may be of importance in the investigation. The contents provide an insight into the attitude of the prisoner regarding the proceedings against him."

November 14, 1995:
"The request by the prosecutor in Schwerin to confiscate the letter by Hans Schmidt dated November 1, 1995, and addressed to Roswitha Schmidt, has been denied with the exception that only the proposed text for future *GANPAC-BRIEFS* and *USA-BERICHTE* be withheld. The pages containing personal

messages to Roswitha Schmidt, Lucille Saunders and "Freda" may remain in the envelope, and be sent to the United States. The text for the newsletters may be of importance for the investigation in the case."

Author's comment: I find it very interesting that my proposed text for future newsletters in English and in German was confiscated rather than just photocopied and then forwarded.

This act proves my contention that the supposed, "non-existent" behind-the-scenes powers controlling Germany were anxious to stop the publication of the newsletters. Obviously, they didn t succeed. The *GANPAC-BRIEFS* appeared without interruption throughout my incarceration at Bützow, although certain delays could not be avoided. The *USA-BERICHTE* experienced a lapse of a few months: my attorney had suggested that we not mail them as long as I was out of circulation.

Although I did not agree with the lawyer's underlying reasoning for this advice, we nevertheless heeded it. This attorney and his colleague who joined our team later, had a much more difficult court fight on their hands than we can imagine, and I did not want to exacerbate the situation. In the final analysis, we did more right than wrong.

All the mail that had been withheld from me through the *Beschlüsse* of the court was given to me by Judge Heydorn at the time of my release. As far as I could ascertain, nothing was missing, although, obviously, some letters had been returned to the senders. I am still wondering what effect all our letters had on the civil servants whose job it had been to read or translate them. I cannot imagine that they all were immune to the truth.

In relation to the preceding, I interject the following humorous interlude:

At the very time I was incarcerated in Bützow the German Postal System issued the postage stamp extolling Freedom of Expression reproduced here.

When I saw it for the first time, I really had to laugh. Buying as many of the stamps as I could afford at the time, I showed them to the other prisoners and told them, in jest of course, that the Post office had issued this stamp especially in my honor!

Then, as long as my supply lasted, I used these stamps on my outgoing letters, taking care to paste them on the envelopes in such a fashion that the words *"Freiheit der Meinungsäusserung"* ("For Freedom of Expression"), were horizontally at the very top.

Then, drawing an arrow pointing toward this sentence I wrote next to it, on the front of the envelope, "Commemorative Stamp in honor of Hans Schmidt." And, what did the prosecutor's office do?

Not having the appropriate sense of humor, these petty bureaucrats photocopied one of my handiworks and placed it as incriminating evidence in my file: proof of how the prisoner ridiculed the *Bundesrepublik* and its "democracy."

The Trial and Our Defense Strategy

January 4, 1996. The day of reckoning had arrived. I entered the courtroom at exactly 9:30 a.m., in the custody of two guards and my two lawyers, Hajo Herrmann and Günter Eisenecker. We seated ourselves, and waited for the proceedings to begin.

To our left in front of high windows looking out onto the street, and on a platform not higher than a step, was a long table with four chairs set for two judges and two jurors.

At one end of the table sat a young woman, seemingly a judge's assistant. Opposite us, across the courtroom, sat Mr. Kollarz, the prosecutor, all by himself, and to our right were the benches for the press and onlookers. I noticed a few familiar faces among the spectators and waved to them, but I was disappointed by the lack of news coverage and at first I did not know what to make of it.

Surprisingly, there was no court reporter, nor did I see any recording equipment. It seemed that unlike the practice in Anglo-Saxon countries, no verbatim record of court proceedings is made. Neither was I formally sworn-in and admonished to tell the truth.

The absence of the world press bothered me. From my jail cell I had suggested to friends on the outside that we should make the most of my trial, and that they should inform all the major news outlets of the upcoming proceedings. I knew that had been done. Therefore, one should have assumed that the courtroom would be swarming with reporters. Instead, I noticed but a few local media people, including a television cameraman, and I knew that the British news agency *Reuters* and the German press agency *dpa*, (*Deutsche Presse Agentur*), were represented. Inasmuch as I was the very first American citizen before a

German court to face charges of "crimes" that under the Constitution of the United States, do not exist, my case logically should have warranted greater exposure. [1]

Then it dawned on me: the absence of the world media was actually a good sign! It was obvious that things like that (i.e., the coverage or non-coverage of certain events), is in today's 'free' world never happenstance. Depending on the whims and wishes of behind-the-scenes rulers, the most insignificant occurrences may make headlines all over the world, while truly important events may be relegated to the back pages or not publicized at all. It follows that the absence of major news coverage of my trial had been ordered *from above.* I only had to figure out why.

I was in the hands of the Bonn political system. I knew that these Allied vassals were in a deep dilemma because of me, and I assumed that they would be quite happy to get rid of me quickly and soon.

Had I possessed U.S. citizenship alone, they might have called me before a single judge amenable to them, given me a quick sentence, and deported me forthwith. But since I was at the same time still a German citizen, the Bonn Government was not able to do that.

From the time my arrest had become known, an ever increasing torrent of letters and other messages had descended not only on Bonn and Washington, but also had gone to important international organizations like the United Nations, the European Parliament at Strassburg, and the agencies presiding over the Helsinki accords.

---

[1] Fred Leuchter, the outstanding American expert in execution apparatus, had been arrested in Germany several years before and also had been accused of violating Paragraphs 130 and 131. But when he was released on bail after a four week stay at a West German prison, he fled to the United States before his trial could commence.

There was no doubt that the self-proclaimed image of the Bonn republic as a democratic state was being damaged as a result. Major news coverage of my trial would have exacerbated this situation.

It follows that *in my case* Bonn did realize that it had made a mistake in following the dictates or suggestions of the *Oberjuden* in New York. Certainly, the German vassals did not want to make the situation worse than it was already, and I believe I was not wrong in assuming that the trial would be short, low-key and resulting in my speedy release.

That the trial dates had been set for four successive Thursdays in January of 1996, namely, the 4th, the 11th, the 18th and the 25th of that month, sounded impressive, but could, in my estimation, have been made to placate the real overlords of Germany. [2]

Having received the indictment at the end of October, I had hoped that the trial would take place sometime at the end of November, so that I could be home in America for Christmas. I had no doubt that however much the *Oberjuden* and their German stooges would want to keep me out of circulation for as lengthy a period as possible, my case was so strong that I would

---

[2] The fact that I had spent the first days of January preparing for my release, sorting my "office" work, and packing the things I was not going to leave behind in Bützow, supported my premonition. When the other prisoners noticed what I was doing, they naturally wanted to know why. When I told them of my intuition that my days at the penitentiary had come to an end, but that I really had no definite proof for this contention, they merely laughed. They had seen it all before. On the other hand, this generation of prisoners had never had any dealings with a political prisoner either.

When I left my cell on the morning of January 4th, I left with the feeling of not returning. I even apologized to the other prisoners in our "compartment" for not being able to leave them more of the goodies which we normally purchase in the commissary; due to staff shortages during the recently past holidays it had been three weeks since we were able to replenish our stock.

not be held long after the trial.

My assessment of the situation changed somewhat when my lawyers informed me in November that a new judge had been named to preside at the trial, and that the case was moved from an *Amtsgericht* (District Court) to a higher level, namely to a *Landgericht* (Superior Court), where normally, crimes of greater importance were dealt with.

I have mentioned before that I had absolutely no experience with any courts in either Germany or the United States. Each new development forced me to ask my lawyers or other prisoners of the possible meaning of the change of judges. As expected, the prisoners saw everything connected with the judicial system in the bleakest of terms. My lawyers and I weren't so sure; we knew that in my case many other factors played a role of which ordinary prisoners could not possibly have an inkling.

I regarded the change from a lower court to a higher one not as a sign of an increase in the seriousness of my "crime" in the eyes of the court, but of a greater awareness on the part of the Bonn system that my arrest had become an embarrassing international incident (due in part to the avalanche of mail from all over the world written on my behalf).

Also helpful in coming to a correct judgment about every new development in my case, was a brochure published by the U.S. Government that is given to American citizens which have been incarcerated in foreign countries. I received one titled "Information for Citizens of the United States of America imprisoned in the Federal Republic of Germany," soon after my arrest, and found it very useful.

Soon after we had taken our seats, I noticed the judges and jurors entering the court room. Everybody rose for a moment, but sat down almost immediately again as the officials took their places.

My interest was focused intently on Judge Horst Heydorn, a pleasant-looking man in his fifties. I had learned that before he was appointed to handle my case he had been a judge in a juvenile court. I also was informed that he was a West German jurist sent to help establish in the former "East" Germany a replica of the allegedly better judicial system of the west, and I had been told that he knew little or nothing of my case, or of the "Holocaust", the Jewish question, and the behind-the-scenes powers holding sway over Germany.

Judge Heydorn opened the proceedings by asking me to state my name, my date and place of birth, and where I reside---both in Germany and in the United States. He then permitted the prosecutor, Mr. Kollarz, to read the 29-page indictment.

Earlier I mentioned that I was almost certain that I would not be returned to the Bützow penitentiary. In other words, I was quite confident of being released on the first day of the trial. I only hedged somewhat because I had no idea how long it would take the prosecutor to read the indictment. Therefore I did acknowledge the possibility that the following Thursday, the 11th, would be the day of my release.

Had I been the prosecutor, and had I intended to paint the accused in the worst possible light, I would have read the indictment slowly and distinctly, emphasizing the "crimes" attributed to the man I was prosecuting.

Instead, Mr. Kollarz read the indictment very quickly, in a monotonous and almost inaudible voice. In short, he couldn't have done me a greater favor (although I suspect that may not have been his intention.)

While the U.S. State Department deserves a tremendous amount of blame for the sinister role it played in my case (as well as in helping to ensure that journalist Gerhard Lauck of

The Trial and Our Defense Strategy

Lincoln, Nebraska, received a four year prison sentence in Germany), I have nothing but praise for the American consular officers I dealt with in Hamburg and Bützow.

Without going into detail, I can only say that within the framework of what these admirable people were permitted to do and to say on my behalf, they were very helpful.

Every three weeks or so someone from the U.S. Embassy in Berlin visited me and inquired about my well-being. It was obvious that these State Department employees could not go further in assisting me within the parameters set by their Jewish boss in Washington (at the time, Mr. Holbrooke assisted by Mr. Kornblum). Especially thoughtful was the gift of home-baked Christmas cookies sent to me by the ladies of the U.S. Embassy.

Due to Prosecutor Kollarz' perfunctory rendition of the indictment, the court was able to call a short recess much sooner than expected, and we quickly began the main part of the trial, which consisted of my interrogation by the two judges, with Mr. Heydorn doing most of the talking, and with only occasional interjections by either one of my lawyers.

I found it all very interesting, and at times I forgot that it was me about whose person revolved the entire matter. For myself the scene was much more like a political discussion group where political innocents were asking the questions which experts were able to answer coherently and in detail. Most certainly the theatrics did *not* in the least affect me emotionally.

With some recesses included, the entire proceedings lasted until about four o'clock in the afternoon. During most of this time, in other words, for at least the three or four hours that I was "on the stand," I had ample opportunity to present the case of Germans and German-Americans in the contemporary political world.

In order to do this I at times had to reach back into history, and speak of past events, for instance, the persecution of Americans of German descent in the United States during World War I.

I shall forever be grateful to Judge Heydorn for permitting me to speak so openly and without either interruption or chastisement. Frequently, it was the judges' or jurors' questions that enabled me to explain certain situations in detail.

"Mr. Schmidt, could you tell us whom you regard as the behind-the-scenes enemies of the German-Americans?"

Certainly, I could. I explained that it had always been, almost since the inception of the United States, the leadership of the Anglo-Saxon monied elite of America, namely, the "Old Establishment," and ever since World War I, also those whom I call the *Oberjuden,* namely, the Head Jews, mostly the Zionist activists with headquarters in New York.

Judge Heydorn's questions about GANPAC and how we operate were also intriguing and provided me with the opportunity to relate the specifics of the silent but pervasive persecution under which Germans suffer in the United States. I was able to mention the torching by arsonists, ostensibly still unknown, of our offices in Santa Monica ten years ago, and of the never-ending threats German activists like myself have to endure at the hands of those who consider themselves harmed by our advocacy of the truth.

At one point, Mr. Kollarz, my lawyers and I were summoned to the judge's table, to verify whether I had written certain notes and letters that were part of the indictment.

Here too, at this juncture, the judge was meticulously fair. However, the fact is that I had never denied writing the letters in question (to the journalist Martin Klingst, to the Israeli professor Michael Wolffsohn, and to foreign minister Kinkel), and I acknowledged the accuracy of the versions reprinted in the indictment.

But I was unable to state precisely to whom in Germany these missives had been mailed. I explained that the number of the German newsletters we mailed each month to Europe was entirely dependent upon the availability of funds, and we had priority address lists to that effect. Sometimes the money was only sufficient for a few dozen *USA-Berichte* (USA-Reports) to be mailed to Europe; at other times many more persons *sympathetic to our aims* could be considered. But as a rule we did not mail our newsletters to persons whom we considered adversaries, such as the Mecklenburg interior minister Rudi Geil, who was ultimately responsible for my arrest.

Judge Heydorn wanted to know how many GANPAC-BRIEFS we mailed out each month, a question I respectfully declined to answer. It wasn't germane to the matter at hand. But I did explain to the judge that as a result of the anti-German actions by the *Oberjuden,* and the constant spying on us by such Jewish thought police organizations as the A.D.L. and the Simon Wiesenthal Center, we were compelled to use extraordinary measures to safeguard our interests, and this included what I call *Auslagerung.* [3]

Sometime during the court session I also brought forth the fact that *all* of my many Open Letters written from the United States to such persons as Professor Wolffsohn, Martin Klingst, foreign minister Klaus Kinkel, and many others, were *always* written in defense of what is German. I pointed out that, due to the protection of the First Amendment to the Constitution of the United States, I was one of the few German writers in the world

---

[3] A World War II term signifying the tactic of not leaving all of one's important possessions in one place, so that in case of destruction through Allied firebombing air raids, at least a portion of vital documents and valuables would be saved.

who had the knowledge and the ability, to answer in kind, and that this had obliged me to assume a special duty toward my homeland.

It was clear that any German residing in Germany who had dared to write as openly and freely as I did would be jailed. I also explained that I used these Open Letters in my newsletters only when, after a few months of waiting, I had not heard from the person I had previously addressed. On some occasions the writers of articles did answer me and a cordial written discussion ensued. At that point, I regarded all such correspondence as private.

It was the prosecutor, Mr. Kollarz, who inadvertently blundered so badly near the close of the first day's court session that he gave us a smashing victory so overwhelming that it also presented Judge Heydorn with a reason ---which, following guidelines from above, he may have been seeking--- to set me free.

After an hour of monotonous legalistic procedure, Mr. Kollarz attempted to convince the court that all evidence pointed to the fact that even after a half-century absence:

a) my German was still so excellent that there was absolutely no question as to my clear understanding of every word I was writing or saying, and b) that I was undoubtedly intelligent enough to know exactly what word, phrase or statement was legally *verboten* in *Deutschland*.

Mr. Kollarz was not finished with his deliberations on these points when I interrupted him and, directing myself to Judge Heydorn, asked him whether I was permitted to address the prosecutor directly. The Judge said that was in order.

"Herr Kollarz," I began, "earlier I had mentioned the Israeli Professor Wolffsohn at the *Bundeswehr Universität* in Munich, and that my letter to him was the eighth Open Letter I had mailed this gentleman, without ever receiving a response.

"It so happened, that Professor Wolffsohn had inexplicably been chosen to be the main speaker or main preacher to the German nation on the German Memorial Day, last November 19th, a task he performed in his usual style by reminding the German people of their eternal responsibility to the Jews, a responsibility arising from the what I call the 'mythical' Holocaust.

"Listening to Wolffsohn's speech on television, I knew that I had to write a ninth letter to this man again, once I was back in the United States. And, as usual, my missive will probably contain some rather strong and clear language, unusual for Germany, and it will undoubtedly consist of six or seven tightly typewritten pages.

"When I write this letter, I obviously want to stay within the legal parameters set in Germany. In other words, I would not want to transgress against the very laws under which I am on trial today.

"Now I have a question. What if I mail the finished text of this ninth Open Letter to Professor Wolffsohn to you for legal review before either sending it to the recipient, or using it in my newsletter? You being my prosecutor today, certainly must know the laws of the *Bundesrepublik,* and especially those which I am most likely to break.

"Therefore I am asking you, whether in such a case you could assure me one hundred percent, with absolute certainty, that after removing all offending passages suggested by you, I could or would not be apprehended in Germany in the future for writing this letter, and for transgressing against such paragraphs as 130 and 131?"

Kollarz fidgeted a moment and then answered in approximately this way: "I am sorry, Herr Schmidt, but in such legal matters there can never be a one hundred percent certainty. Even for someone in my position, it is not possible to give you the assurances you ask for..."

When Kollarz had said that, I heard a little commotion among the people in the press and visitors' gallery. I immediately pressed my advantage:

"In other words, Herr Kollarz, you, the well-educated jurist, cannot tell me what in this regard is legal or illegal in Germany today, but you expect me, a layman, to know it and always act accordingly?"

I believe Kollarz still said "*Ja!*" but his words went unheard amidst the laughter and the sounds of incredulity heard in the court room.

When things had quieted down a bit, Herr Herrmann stood up and addressing Judge Heydorn, asked that due to what we just had heard, and considering the fragile state of my health, I should be immediately set free.

Against rather meek protest by Mr. Kollarz who claimed to have much more evidence against me, the judge thereupon granted the motion, saying, "Herr Schmidt, you are free to go. I herewith adjourn the court until next Thursday, the 11th of January."

There was no talk of bail, or of leaving my passports in the custody of the court (they were in any case deposited at the penitentiary).

I was free again!

Before I left the court room, the judge asked me to wait for a minute, as he had to go to his chambers and bring me a stack of letters from all over the world which the court and other censors had not been able to read and review as yet. When he gave me the letters, Judge Heydorn asked an interesting question heard by a number of my supporters:

"Herr Schmidt, where should we mail the letters for you that will undoubtedly be arriving here, to your German address or to Pensacola?"

At another time during the proceedings Judge Heydorn had made the remark, "We were surprised at how many friends all over the world you seem to have."

During the four months when I had normal mail contacts, I had received about 450 pieces of mail (not counting newspapers). To these one must add about 50 pieces that had been withheld from me due to their incriminating or offensive (to the Bonn system) contents, and in the pouch which I had received from Judge Heydorn, there were an additional 150 letters and postcards.

In response I myself had written about 500 letters, many of them as letters-to-the-editor to German newspapers. [4]

Someone told me that in the 160-year existence of the Bützow penitentiary, no prisoner had received as much mail in such a short time.

I had undoubtedly become a burden for the poverty-stricken

---

[4] I wrote the letters to the major German newspapers with the intent of driving both the editors and the court's censors a little crazy. Since I was in jail already and because I knew that there were at least twelve file folders containing proof of my literary transgressions in the hands of the prosecutor, I believed that I really couldn't make matters much worse for myself by additional writings. I chose subject matters at hand (gleaned from the newspapers), and as a rule I chastised the editors for falsification through obfuscation or through the purposeful withholding of essential facts. Someone like myself who is used to reading U.S. or British newspapers is amazed to discover how inadequately the German media informs the public of the *Bundesrepublik* of important developments.

For instance, few Germans have a coherent picture of the seriousness of the racial situation in America. German reporters have been trained to obscure the truth by editing facts to conform to the notions of a post-war *Volkspädagogik*, a system of selective popular education devised by an arrogant self-styled 'elite,' often extreme leftists who create lucrative state-subsidized careers for themselves out of serving their anti-German ideological slop to the people, whose government deprives them of alternative sources of information.

Mecklenburg judiciary. Not only had they been forced to read all incoming and outgoing letters, some of them very long, but much of the mail had to be translated from several languages, not just English.

Many of our supporters are excellent writers who knew how to enlighten the employees of the German judiciary who were intercepting my mail. They also managed to stay within the guidelines of laws and common decency, while doing so.

Again, I was not surprised to find myself released on the first day of the trial. Already during the lunch recess one of my supporters came to me (at the same time being gently admonished by one of my guards), and stated that we undoubtedly had won the case. A reporter for the British news agency Reuters said, "Herr Schmidt, after what I have heard up to now, they simply have to set you free!" I answered, "Don't bet on it!"

Leaving the courtroom after the session had ended, many people congratulated me. I do not remember whether all were supporters or whether even court employees had the courage to express their opinion.

During a last glance into the courtroom I noticed the thick file folder with the letters from the A.D.L. lying prominently atop the huge stack of documents that were supposed to have been used against me.

Gladly I took leave of Hajo Herrmann who was able to board an early train back to Düsseldorf. After I had made a few telephone calls from the justice building, including to my wife in Pensacola; my other lawyer, Dr. Eisenecker, drove me back to Bützow in order to retrieve my personal belongings.

Upon our arrival, I noted that some of my belongings had already been placed in the reception area and the discharge paper was also awaiting me. Unusual for Bützow's typical

The Trial and Our Defense Strategy

prison protocol, however, was the fact that I, the discharged prisoner, was escorted back to my cell, accompanied by a guard, where I picked up the possessions in my cell. This enabled me to say good-bye to several of the fellows who had always tried their best to take care of me while I was incarcerated.

In the meantime, German television had broadcast the news of my release world-wide, and the reporters naturally did not forget to mention the immediate protest by Jewish organizations and activists. In Bützow nearly everybody had heard of my good fortune and when I slowly walked out of the penitentiary, past the cells of block B, which was already closed for the night, I noticed nearly everywhere the mail slots opening, and from hundreds of the prisoners best wishes for my future were extended.

I was elated when the heavy steel doors of the Bützow penitentiary were finally shut behind me. Although the prison was undoubtedly harmful to my health and I was much bothered by the tremendous waste of time I had experienced, I was certain that in the long run my imprisonment was beneficial for our cause, for our enemies had gained nothing.

Soon after Judge Heydorn freed me, friends and supporters suggested that I immediately and without fail take the first train or car to Frankfurt, and there board the very first flight back to the United States. My friends didn't trust the German justice system and were fearful that I might be re-arrested before sunrise of the next morning.

I assessed the situation differently. I was sure that the Bonn regime wanted to be rid of me, even without having brought the trial to a satisfactory conclusion. I did not think that the system would dare to compound its errors by starting all over again.

There is a German saying, "*So schnell schiessen die Preussen auch nicht!"* (The Prussians shoot fast, but not quite that fast!), meaning of course, that officials and others need time to react to certain unexpected developments. So I decided to play another game.

By the time all the commotion surrounding my release had subsided, it was already late in the evening. I had a hearty meal in a nice restaurant with one of my acquaintances, and after five months of enforced abstinence, accompanied it with a good German beer. Then I took a room for one night in a pleasant hotel in Schwerin, and slept well.

The next morning, I rented a car, and soon I was on my way home to the Saarland, about 700 km (400 miles) away. The weather was good, traffic relatively light, and I made it home soon after nightfall. My mother was very glad to see me. Naturally, she had expected me for Christmas and I also regretted not having been able to make her holidays more enjoyable. But for nearly a week at least one of her six children could be with her again.

For a week I pretended to everybody whom I met or with whom I spoke by phone, including my mother and my wife, that I would be in Schwerin on Thursday the 11th, for the continuation of my trial. This gave me a week of rest and quiet at my boyhood home, while at the same time a chance to prepare myself for the trip back to America.

My lawyers received my notice that I would not be in Schwerin a few hours before the second period of the trial was to commence. I told them that I considered it best to return to America forthwith, but I also asked them to continue the trial in my absence, and defend me as if I were there. In Germany (and, I suppose in the United States also), trials can be continued even if the accused is not present in the courtroom, but as long as lawful persons represent him.

At the very time when a plane with me on board was winging its way to the United States, Judge Heydorn adjourned my trial until further notice; until the "culprit" could be apprehended again.

Later I also heard that Judge Heydorn had been compelled to re-issue an arrest warrant for me. (I do not blame the judge; after the Jewish outcry about my "premature" release, he had no choice but to act as he did). There is a chance that the reissuance of the warrant was mainly done in order to prevent my return to Germany soon. Does the Bonn regime consider me that dangerous? I assume we will never find out.

The first day of my trial was undoubtedly a great success for both of my lawyers and myself. I am certain that the second day of the trial, if there had been one, would have ended similarly. Only this time it would have had to end in an acquittal; and that was something the Bonn judicial system could not afford. The eye-ball rolling and garment rending of the *Shoah*-biz professionals (Jewish merchants of "sacred" propaganda), reflects the atmosphere in which further proceedings would be held.

Had there been a second day of the trial, and had there been a victory for us similar to the one on the first day, or even greater, then my life would have been in peril. Those whom we must consider our enemies cannot endure the truth, and anybody who wins in behalf of the truth is considered a mortal danger to their designs. It was mainly for this reason that I could not take the risk of being in the Schwerin court on January 11, 1996.

I would have been happier if the trial had come to a proper conclusion. On the other hand, there is also the possibility that the Bonn regime might have invented another set of accusations for which to re-arrest me the moment I was acquitted of the Schwerin charges. The fate of Günter Deckert provides proof for such a contention.

Lastly, a few comments about the strategy which this writer and my attorneys, Messrs. Herrmann and Eisenecker, employed. Obviously, we did everything right, but it nevertheless bears mentioning that other options for a good defense had been possible. As a matter of fact, other persons, some of them well intentioned, had warned me not to take the route that eventually led to my release and freedom.

Immediately after my arrest at the Frankfurt airport I assessed my situation as unemotionally as I could, and my first reaction was that I would fight the German authorities on grounds that everything I had written had been put to paper in the United States by an American citizen, where such writings fell under the protection of the First Amendment. I thought that it would be best if we fought the matter on the basis of what I considered cynical German transgressions against international laws and treaties, to which the German *Bundesrepublik* was a signatory.

Apart from that I saw three other possible defense strategies: an open attack on the entire "Holocaust" edifice, the allegations of which constitute the foundation of the alien system on German soil; the demolition of the claim that I had "incited to hate," "defamed the dead," and "insulted and denigrated Jews and Freemasons" (as stated in the arrest warrant), by mailing to Germany a minuscule number of newsletters and Open Letters that contained some impermissible truths.

Thirdly, exposing the inordinate power of those whom I call the *Oberjuden* in Germany and the United States.

Why didn't I use my trial as a platform to make an issue out of my skepticism toward the gas chamber claims? I regard myself as a historical revisionist, with emphasis on World War II and its aftermath. While I can not, and do not pretend to be on the same level with revisionist titans such as Paul Rassinier, Robert

Faurisson, Austin App, Arthur Butz, David Irving, and Ernst Zündel, among others of that extraordinary caliber, I am at least competent enough to articulate the multitudinous inconsistencies, contradictions, vagaries, and absolute impossibilities of what Professor Butz of Northwestern University rightly terms, "the Hoax of the Twentieth Century."

In fact, I discovered some of the holes in the hoax for myself, which, in view of their infinite number and size, was not all that hard to do. My inquiries, investigations, and research had shown that it would be a waste of time to visit the sites of former internment and labor camps, Auschwitz, Majdanek, Treblinka, for example. Either they had been falsified for propaganda purposes as in Auschwitz where the museum curator admitted to the Jew David Cole that the "killing" gas chambers on display were really built after the war by the Communists, or the labor camps had been razed, so that the Allies and certain Jews, among other German-hating, congenital liars, could call them "death camps."

However pointless from a forensic viewpoint visits to these New World Order, *holohoax* tourist spots would have been, failing to have visited them could be a potentially major psychological gap in my position, in the eyes of a court, where I would be confronted by "Survivors" and other "Holocaust" industry professionals who had in fact, "been there." [5]

An added reason for my never seriously considering a

---

[5] I doubt that even an impartial judge like Justice Heydorn would have been permitted (by the hidden elite) to allow me to call expert witnesses such as historians and chemists, who would have overturned many of the Allied/Zionist, homicidal gas chamber claims. In my opinion the judge would have had no other recourse but to cite the official *Offenkundigkeit* (the "judicial notice," i.e. declaration of the courts, that the wildly exaggerated "Holocaust" tales were beyond dispute), and that therefore no defense witnesses pertaining to this matter would be allowed. Also, even if the judge had permitted me my choice of defense witnesses, I had neither time nor money enough to enlist in my defense, experts who had been to the labor camps. In consequence I decided to forego the "revisionist" defense.

revisionist defense is based upon my conviction that the "Holocaust" hoax is essentially doomed.

Revisionists like the aforementioned academics and many others, have discovered and brought forth the essential truth and it is there in the open, available on the Internet and in books, for any objective seeker after truth to discover. Certainly, as time goes by, more interesting facts about this "big lie" will emerge.

Furthermore, in examining the performance of the Bonn courts over the past half-century, we see that truly neutral and independent specialists have not been allowed to testify.

In addition, I thought that revisionist testimony, and a defense based on it, to be unnecessary. Revisionist giants, like the men named above, and many others on all continents, by now had detected a huge number of flaws, probably including all the major ones; enough to cause this ugly "beast" to die of exposure if these lies were uncovered. That they have not yet been uncovered sufficiently before the eyes of the populace, is due to the fact that the Zionist-dominated mass media--print and electronic—have been keeping a very tight lid on them. However, here and there, the lid has begun to rust.

The allegation that I had been able to influence the German public through the few dozen, or occasionally few hundred, newsletters that were being mailed to Germany every month, came up during the trial, but was never seriously pursued by either the two judges or the jurors. We did, however, spar about the meaning of certain words, and whether they could have "incited to hate," "defamed the dead," and "denigrated" certain protected groups, as the prosecution alleged.

But in the end we did not put much emphasis on such nonsense. Any fair-minded person who reads my writings will know that such allegations are far-fetched. I believe that eventually the court agreed with us, even though my lawyers and I did not think it worthwhile to dwell on the matter.

Actually, it was the prosecutor himself who showed the defense the best way to win this case. In trying to put as much blame on me as possible, Mr. Kollarz was forced to use most of the text that I had written for Germany (as in the Klingst and Wolffsohn letters), and in the indictment there is a repetition of almost identical charges that could be easily refuted or explained by me.

If anything, I am very consistent in my writings. I am the first to admit that I harp on the all-too-great power a tiny ethnic/religious minority has in the two nations that interest me most, Germany and the United States. I think this inordinate power is fundamentally wrong and, all too often, destructive. Although I often point out that the great majority of Jews are ordinary people who just want to be left alone, there is no question that frequently I honestly do feel compelled to use the general term "the Jews," in my writing, for it is a fact that without the backing of the mass of the Jews, and without the wholehearted support of the Aryan Zionists (Anglo-Saxon, old Establishment types), the Jewish activists could not retain the powerful position they are holding in Western society.

My letters to Wolffsohn and Klingst concerned mainly this overbearing Jewish power, and its harmful results. Thankfully, Judge Heydorn gave me ample opportunity to explain how this power is gained and misused. I was also in a position to mention that the Jews in America have usurped the power that rightfully belongs to the largest ethnic group of the United States, the German-Americans who helped to build America.

As to the accusation of "inciting hate" against the Jews, I could tell the judge and others that in my nearly half century in the United States I have had almost daily dealings with Jews, and that I have met too many nice ones to "hate" or even dislike all of them. Clearly seeing what is going to happen in the future because of the obvious transgressions of a few *Oberjuden,* I was able to express feelings of sympathy and pity for the many Jewish innocents who, in the end, will suffer most.

There was another reason why I did not want to put too much emphasis on the fact that I was an American citizen, and had written all of the offending material in the United States. For all these decades I had also retained a German passport. A remark on the first page of the indictment shows that for whatever reason, the Bonn government did not want to acknowledge this fact. [6]

I assume that this was done at the behest of the Jews in New York who through such court cases as those involving Leuchter, Lauck and my own, would like to establish the precedent that anybody whom they consider an "anti-Semite" (anybody who looks askance at Jewish depredations), may well be immune to Jewish persecution in the United States, but the safeguards of the First Amendment are invalid outside of American borders, where in some countries, Jewish power is more blatant.

Had the German court actually acknowledged both my German citizenship and the fact that I am still registered in the town of my birth, this precedent would have been invalid.

Americans who are justifiably wary of officials and political activists with dual citizenship (and, hence, dual loyalties), may want to ask why I am still holding a German passport, and, to make matters worse, a passport issued by a government with which I am constantly feuding and which I regard as alien-imposed.

---

[6] There is a certain irony connected with this point. Immediately after my arrest, all my personal papers, including my two valid passports, were taken from me, and enclosed in a pouch with other valuables. There is no question that the agents of Bonn's Secret Police who went through these papers, also viewed the passports, and took note of their dates of expiration. In other words, the German judiciary was well aware that according to law I was (also) a German citizen.

The Trial and Our Defense Strategy

Being asked to elaborate on this point, I usually laugh and merely state that, "what is good for the *Oberjuden,* is also good for Hans Schmidt."

I may mention that so far I have used my German passport only once in all these years. Shortly after the opening of the Berlin wall the "East" German border patrols demanded 15 *deutschmarks* from foreigners entering East Berlin, while West Germans could pass for free. Naturally, I thought of a better way to spend 15 *marks,* and for the occasion I placed my BRD (*Bundesrepublik Deutschland*) passport on the counter.

Sometime in November, during my incarceration, I was visited by a gentleman who had connections in both Germany and the United States, who asked me on behalf of himself and others, whether I would seriously consider a defense based upon the tenets of international law.

By that time however, I was in possession of the indictment, and our minds were made up as to the course to take. Not having been willing to take the man's advice, I could see that he was quite disappointed about what he considered my unjustified stubbornness in this regard.

I think he meant well, but after he had visited me, he wrote a letter to the highest court in Germany that was clearly against my wishes and interests. He told the court that, actually, my German citizenship was invalid because U. S. law allegedly did not permit the retention of an earlier citizenship by immigrants, once they had opted for the United States.

This argument was ludicrous. One only had to look at the automatic dual citizenship granted to immigrants from Switzerland and to American Jews who had never even set foot on the soil of the Jewish state in occupied Palestine, but chose to request an Israeli passport anyway.

Viewing the first day of my trial from the distance of nearly a year, I must say that the judges and jurors were fair, and properly attentive. For me it seemed as though Judge Heydorn and Prosecutor Kollarz, acted in some manner on behalf of higher-ups, although not for the same people!

Judge Heydorn's job may have been to make it possible for me to leave Germany as I did, whereas Mr. Kollarz could have been under orders to see me convicted come what may. If I am correct in this assumption (and I must state that I have no proof of it), then this shows that not everybody in the *Bundesrepublik* is pulling on the same strings.

One could only wish that the same forces were at work when other German nationalists are being persecuted for the same alleged offenses for which I was put on trial.

Statement to the Court

[The following statement would have been read in court at an appropriate opportunity during one of the final trial sessions, had I not been released on January 4, 1996, and used the first opportunity to return to the United States. My words speak for themselves].

As a journalist and publisher, I am defending the freedom of the press. As a human being, I feel justified in expressing my opinion openly and without restraint, and to search for the truth about matters of historical importance wherever they can be discovered, even if the sensibilities of some who cling to transient dogmas are hurt. When new historical discoveries are made, I take the right upon myself to disseminate them to the unenlightened, for only the truth shall set us free.

This trial is not about "incitement to hate", or whether I insulted a politically, ethnically and religiously active minority. It is a trial about the right to free expression and about the discovery of the truth concerning certain historical events.

I am writing monthly newsletters about world events in both the English and German languages, whereby the German publication is sent to only a relatively small number of select people in Germany. No matter what I am writing, one can never claim that I am inciting "the people" to hate since *"volk"* (as in *Volksverhetzung*), means "people", i.e., the masses, and I have never tried to reach the masses of any nation.

It is a fact that before my arrest at the Frankfurt airport on August 9, 1995, I was totally unknown to anybody in Germany except to a few patriotic stalwarts, and--obviously--the political police. Although I have been politically active abroad for all-German interests for more than four decades, before my incarceration I was only once mentioned in a German major publication, namely, in *Der Spiegel* magazine of December 1994. Furthermore, the average German, i.e., the folk, never had the opportunity to read any of my views and conclusions in the German press. One can assume that as a result of the recent mention of my name in the *Schweriner Volkszeitung* on September 6, 1995, in connection with the printing of excerpts from my indictment, a thousand times more Germans were able to read some of my writings, a feat that I myself could never have accomplished on my own. Will the *Schweriner Volkszeitung* now be accused of disseminating alleged "hate propaganda"?

I can prove my prior reticence by stating the fact that in the past thirteen years I have only given two interviews to the media; one to the Bonn correspondent of the Moscow newspaper *Isvestiya,* the other to a female reporter of the *Washington Post*. It is also true that since my arrest I have refused to meet with members of the establishment press.

In my writings I sometimes use rather blunt and sarcastic language. However, I do feel that this is necessary in order to get my point across. Especially the German press is very irresponsible and inefficient in its reporting about political events in the United States. Its analyses are clouded by ideology, and totally insufficient if one assumes that it is the duty of journalists to keep the German public informed.

For instance, while the German media do tell their readers and listeners that the American elections of November 8, 1994 were a "political earthquake," and that a "right-wing revolution" has occurred, there is not one German foreign correspondent who dares to break the existing taboos, and tell the average Germans who were the true losers of the 1994 elections in the United States. If he were to do that, he would have to tacitly admit who

--what behind-the-scenes-powers--had ruled the U.S. for the past thirty years. When I tried to make up for this failure, I ended up in jail.

We have to assume that in the light of laws such as the paragraphs 130 and 131, even German diplomats assigned to foreign duty dare not write in their official reports that it was the "Israeli Lobby" in America, in other words, the most active political arm of the top Jewish leadership in the United States, that was the big loser in November of 1994. It was then that "these people" lost their stranglehold over the U.S. Congress, a position which they had held since the administration of Lyndon B. Johnson in the 1960s.

In the light of this political defeat, it is not too far fetched to assume that the 1996 Congressional elections may further dent the over-representation of this tiny ethnic and religious group, and also the Democratic Party, fifty percent of whose finances come from the aforementioned group), with great consequences for all the world. Alas, the Bonn foreign office may be unaware of this because it is afraid to call a spade a spade.

Unfortunately, it is essential that a clear and concise, future-oriented German foreign policy, the main aim of which ought to be the preservation of peace in Europe, be based upon *Realpolitik*.

This, however, cannot be attained if German diplomats are *verboten*, by outdated taboos, to think, write and act strictly according to the facts at hand. Due to the fact that paragraphs 130 and 131 run counter to the principle of equality, a crime is being committed against the very interests of the German people, since only actions based upon the truth and undeniable facts can prevent Germany from once again being pulled into the maelstrom of a world-wide catastrophe. For this reason alone, the paragraphs 130 and 131 ought to be eliminated.

Regarding the accusations against me, I am astounded to see how a few words among thousands in my articles and Open Letters have been removed from their larger context, and thereby have gained an importance far above my original intent. When a German newspaper uses a headline that says, "Serbs bombard Sarajevo," nobody in his right mind will think that all Serbs are meant by this. But when I write, "Jews in America are too powerful," then everybody automatically seems to assume that I am writing of all American Jews, and therefore I am attacking and insulting all of them. This distortion occurs even though in my writings I make a determined effort to show a difference between the (relatively) few Jewish "hyper"-activists and their more docile masses.

Besides, apart from the fact that I can prove all the things that I am putting on paper, facts usually found in articles and books written by my political adversaries, there can be no doubt that in America I am probably the only nationalistic ("right-wing") writer who frequently comes to the defense of the average Jew.

Today it is within the realm of possibility that the ethnic minority that in Germany receives special privileges and safeguards through the implementation of paragraphs such as 130 and 131, might begin to lose the final vestiges of its supremacy in the United States by 1997.

This will have great repercussions in Germany also, for under the motto, "til death do us part," the Bonn system seems to have allied itself with this still powerful minority. For the supporters and beneficiaries of the Bonn system, it might be wise to consider the possibility of total defeat, and remember the fate of that other German vassal state, namely, "East Germany", and those who were its main standard bearers.

Nearly 150 years ago, my very own great-grandfather, Hannes Schmidt from Wuppertal-Barmen in the Ruhr Valley, found himself in a situation similar to the one in which I find myself today. He, along with others, among them his neighbor and acquaintance, Friedrich Engels (the collaborator of Karl Marx), was accused by the Prussian monarchy of taking part in sedition, and inciting people to riot in the revolution of 1848. Engels was acquitted; my ancestor spent four years in jail, and lost all his possessions, leaving him and his family utterly destitute.

Today the Prussian monarchy is no more. The descendants of Hannes Schmidt, however, prospered and are spread over two continents. The valid question remains: who won in 1848, the Prussian justice system or the accused Schmidt?

In early September of 1995, a Congress of the world's women took place in Peking, China. At this Congress, Hillary Clinton, the wife of President Bill Clinton of the United States, said the following:

"Freedom means the right of people to assemble, organize and debate freely. It means respecting the views of those who may disagree with the views of their governments. It means not taking citizens away from their loved ones and jailing them, mistreating them, or denying them their freedom or dignity because of peaceful expression of their ideas and opinions."

It is my belief that many Germans ought to read these words carefully, and consider them in their actions.

My trial proves that the idea of freedom needs a better explanation. Here in Germany we are seeing almost daily that persons in public life who do not have the slightest idea what the word "freedom" really means are constantly using such phrases as "the Bonn Republic, which is the most free state that has ever existed on German soil," or, "Bonn--the *Rechtsstaat*" (i.e. *the* government imbued with justice).

The fact is that politics and the media have rarely ever been so suppressed and *gleichgeschaltet* (being "equalized" through political correctness) as in the Bonn Republic, which is itself a creature of the enemies of Germany. One only has to read German news papers from before World War I to see proof of this.

In the German *Bundesrepublik* it is frequently claimed that their system of justice is independent of politics. Unfortunately, nothing is further from the truth. Especially the incarceration of Günter Deckert, the head of a legal German, albeit patriotic and therefore "rightist" party, disproves this claim.

Another clear case of political interference into the judicial process is that of the four young Germans who in the fall of 1995 received harsh prison sentences for their alleged participation in the attack on a house occupied by the families of Turkish "guest" workers in Solingen. Even the German establishment press found many flaws in the trial procedures and wrote of the fact that the judges had been forced to come to a political solution of the matter.

I am convinced that paragraph No. 130, for which I am standing trial here, is a strictly political law that was passed in the interests of a small, albeit powerful ethnic (non-German) minority. I am therefore insisting that this is a political trial, and that the judgment to be expected can only be a political one, far removed from any sense of true justice.

Finally, I would like to quote a few words from a verdict by a higher court in Berlin that was pronounced in December of 1993 in connection with the sentencing of former Communist German judges, who had used their power to persecute German patriots:

"Transgressions against the most basic human rights occurred when the harsh punishment meted out showed an unacceptable relationship to the crimes committed."

Last but not least, I do see a certain humor in the fact that I find myself now, at an age nearing 70, and without any prison experience in either the United States or Germany, indicted for offenses which I have committed all my life --including during the Third Reich--namely, for expressing myself freely.

Furthermore, I see persons sitting in judgment over me who know well that in 1945 the Allied victors over Germany had instituted the so-called "reeducation" (brainwashing), in *Deutschland*. But they, the true targets of this brainwashing, are unable to acknowledge that they themselves, and their families, were in reality the major victims of this outrageous postwar crime, and that therefore all of their personal judgments are clouded by irrational prejudices.

A Report on Hans Schmidt
by "American authorities," namely, the ADL

On page 24 of the indictment against me (the German original, as reprinted in the appendix), there is a curious sentence:

"Aufgrund einer vom Bundeskriminalamt in dem Verfahren 45 Js 352/91 Freiburg veranlassten Erkenntnisanfrage an die Botschaft der Vereinigten Staaten von Amerika gab die Botschaft die bei *den amerikanischen Behoerden* bestehenden Erkenntnisse ueber den Angeschuldigten wie folgt an das Bundeskriminalamt weiter (Band I, Bl. 12ff.):

(Emphasis mine, HS)

Translation:
"In the course of the proceedings regarding case No. 45 Js 352/91 [1] of the prosecutor's office at Freiburg, the Federal Criminal Police Office (in Bonn? HS) sent an inquiry to the American Embassy, which provided the following information (on Hans Schmidt) as kept by **American authorities** (v. 1, p.12ff.).

Then follows a one page write-up about me that is full of errors and some nonsense (which is being dealt with elsewhere in this book, in conjunction with an analysis of the indictment), and which I immediately recognized as coming from the notorious "ADL," the "Anti-Defamation League of B'nai B'rith," which is, according to the American media, a benevolent "public service organization" and "a civil rights institution."

According to American law, no U.S. Federal Agency is

---

[1] This file number indicates that already in 1991 some German authorities began proceedings against me, at least, opened a file and asked the American Embassy in Bonn for information.

allowed to provide information regarding an *innocent* U.S. Citizen to any foreign government, especially in cases where the alleged wrongdoing is not considered a crime in the United States.

If the U.S. Embassy in fact supplied this information to the Freiburg prosecutor, then it acted against U.S. law.

We surmise, however, that the erroneous ADL information provided to the Freiburg prosecutor was, surreptitiously and without higher approval, obtained from the ADL by a Jew working in the U.S. Embassy in Bonn.

No law will stop certain Jews from acting in what they consider the interest of their group.

Remember Jonathan J. Pollard, Julius and Ethel Rosenberg and so many others.

A letter by the (Bonn) German Department of the Interior pertaining to the ADL and this writer is reprinted in its original on page 320. On page 319 you will find my translation:

DEPARTMENT OF THE INTERIOR (BONN)

File No. IS 2 - 612 280 USA / 1

August 23, 1995

Bundesministerium des Innern, Postfach 17 02 90, 53108 Bonn

(To) Prosecutor in Schwerin

(via)

Department of the Interior

and

Department of Justice of Mecklenburg-Vorpommern

19048 Schwerin

regarding information by

Mr. Elliot Welles

Associate Director of European Affairs

Anti-Defamation League

823 United Nations Plaza New York, N.Y. 10017 USA.

Re: Rightwing-Extremism in the United States here:
Proceedings 111 Js 826/95 against Hans Schmidt due to suspicion of transgressions against §130 No. 3 StGB (incitement to hate).

Mr. Elliot Welles, the associate director of European Affairs of the Anti-Defamation League, 823 United Nations Plaza, New York, NY, 10017, USA, telephone: (212) 885-7789, FAX (212) 867-0779, has informed the Department of the Interior by telephone that he would like to support the German prosecution in the proceedings mentioned above with documents which are in his possession. Therefore, I would like to ask you to get in touch with Mr. Wells.

On orders: signed, Willerscheidt

BUNDESMINISTERIUM DES INNERN

Geschäftszeichen (bei Antwort bitte angeben)

IS 2 - 612 280 USA/1

Bundesministerium des Innern, Postfach 17 02 90, 53108 Bonn

Staatsanwaltschaft Schwerin

Ü b e r
Innenministerium des Landes
Justizminister des Landes
Mecklenburg-Vorpommern

19048 Schwerin

nachrichtlich:

Mr. Elliot Welles
Associate Director of European Affairs
Anti-Defamation League
823 United Nations Plaza
New York, NY 10017
USA

Rechtsextremismus in den USA
hier: Verfahren 111 Js 826/95 gegen Hans Schmidt wegen des Verdachts
der Volksverhetzung (§ 130 Nr. 3 StGB)

Herr Elliot Welles - Associate Director of European Affairs der Anti-Defamation League, 823 United Nations Plaza, New York, NY 10017, USA, Tel.: (212) 885-7769, Fax: (212) 867-0779 - teilte dem Bundesministerium des Innern fernmündlich mit, er möchte die zuständige deutsche Strafverfolgungsbehörde im vorgenannten Verfahren mit in seinem Besitz befindlichen Beweisunterlagen unterstützen. Ich bitte deshalb, mit Herrn Welles in Verbindung zu treten.

Im Auftrag

Willerscheidt

Note the childish signature of "Willerscheidt". One can assume that a lowly, underpaid German office girl, possibly even an apprentice, was ordered to write this letter. This leaves the question open as to who spoke to the ADL, and who ultimately bears responsibility for this anti-German action.

I term it anti-German, because what I do is for German culture here and in Germany, for the German people and for the Reich. The continued existence of neither is of interest to the ADL and much of world Jewry generally.

Could we assume that the absence of the name of the person ultimately responsible for this transgression against German interests indicates a fear of the unknown future? Do people like this know, or guess, that eventually they may be called to account for such actions, and that therefore they prefer to remain anonymous? Certainly, "Willerscheidt" bears no guilt or responsibility.

The matter of ADL official Elliot Welles' having contacted German authorities to assist them in prosecuting and persecuting an American citizen for actions which in the United States (and in the opinion of most people in the world), are neither criminal or wrongdoing, and, as a matter of fact, are protected by the U.S. Constitution, bears closer scrutiny.

I have no doubt that Elliot Welles left himself wide-open to a lawsuit that may eventually cost him and his group millions of dollars. I see the day coming when new, younger American lawyers will have the courage to take on the ADL and its Orwellian dealings, and administer to this group the legal defeats that are long overdue. Obviously, it also takes independent judges (judges not bound by allegiance to Zionism or Freemasonry) to provide the chance for a fair trial in such a case.

But what is the "ADL" really?

Before I go into the story of the part played by the world's *Oberjuden* and their ADL in my arrest and imprisonment in Germany, it is appropriate, I think, to offer a brief run-down on the origin and activities of that remarkable organization that calls itself the "Anti-Defamation League of B`nai B`rith" or, for short, ADL.

It has been observed that when an American comes into wealth, he buys a yacht. When a Jew comes into wealth, he buys a newspaper or two, or three, or a periodical or two, or three. The Jewish masonic lodge B`nai B`rith organized itself in the previous century in Philadelphia. Its purpose was to penetrate and dominate the opinion-molding American news media. As we see, that purpose was achieved to a remarkable extent.

In 1913, B`nai B`rith which –like Jews, who in the previous century generally had been called "Israelites" (cf. Mark Twain, *Life on the Mississippi*) – had not evoked universal admiration or approbation, set up what might be termed an "enforcement" arm. That was the ADL.

The ADL is based on two conspicuous--some would say the two most conspicuous--traits of what we might term "the Jewish character." [2]

The one is an overwhelming predilection for lying, the other a manic hatred of, and compulsion to destroy everything they themselves have not created, and that which they cannot dominate. If the Old Testament, or Torah does not offer sufficient evidence of this, though it should be more than ample, the skeptics may look into the Talmud, which has virtually superseded the Torah and its Ten commandments.

The ADL's founding lies are manifest in its name and in its professed objective. It is not constituted to protect Jews against a "defamation" that is mostly imaginary, or concocted by the ADL to demonstrate its reason for existing, but to defame

---

[2] Once again these are general observations on human nature, a way of speaking which, prior to the imposition of Marxist categories of "wrongthink" constituted the proverbs and folk wisdom of all peoples. I am describing a psychological type. It goes without saying that I am not claiming every Jew fits the category outlined.

everyone else.

As for the ADL's assertion that it fights "anti-Semitism," that is so transparently phony that it should be apparent even to Jews who are not totally paranoid. In fact, the ADL lives and thrives on and through "anti-Semitism." The ADL knows that where there are Jews, there is anti-Semitism; that the two are inseparable. It always has been so. It always will be so. The ancient Romans noted it. The intensity of anti-Semitism fluctuates with the behavior of the Jews among their host peoples. When Jewish depredations became too excessive, the host people were driven to defend themselves.

Among the Slavic peoples such self-defense at times took on an active if equally excessive character, what are called "pogroms."

Despite manifold provocations, there was never a pogrom in Germany. The unending tales of the *Kristallnacht* – in which, depending on the source -- 91, or 36 Jews lost their lives, was a 100 percent Jewish production. [3]

When Jewish depredations became intolerable, Jews were expelled. Notable mass expulsions of Jews occurred in Rome (with Jews expelled to Sardinia in the 4th century, which later served as a model for the frustrated French, then German, "Madagascar solution" of the present century); by the English in the 13th Century, and by Portugal and Spain two hundred years later. [4]

Never, in the two thousand years during which the Jews say they have suffered discrimination and "anti-Semitism", and

---

[3] Cf. The writings of Ingrid Weckert.

[4] The edict of expulsion by King Edward I of England has never been revoked. Legally all Jews residing in England today are illegal aliens, subject to immediate expulsion at any time. Edward I, like Hitler and Haman, is a ritually denounced and hated figure among the *Oberjuden*. It was interesting to note that in the movie *Braveheart,* which garnered Academy Awards from Jewish Hollywood, the villain was none other than the Jews' old tribal nemesis, King Edward I.

were "forever persecuted," did it ever occur to their leaders to modify their behavior and make themselves tolerable to the host peoples, in order to obviate "anti-Semitism" and its occasional unpleasantness.

Instead, Jews have tried to change the natural thought processes of peoples among whom they have inserted themselves. Gentile thought control is a major activity of the ADL. When it pleads for "tolerance," for instance, what it has in mind is deferential acceptance of intolerable Jewish outrages.

Despite their age-old hysteria about "persecution" and "anti-Semitism," Jews have flourished to an extraordinary, virtually unbelievable extent wherever they chose to settle.

Particularly, and especially, in the United States and Germany which is still occupied militarily —for which beneficence the German taxpayers, willy nilly, pick up the tab—and under the thumb of the United States, which, in turn, is under the thumb of the Zionists.

It is necessary to take inventory of the Jews' staggering power over our lives; their current, apparently impregnable political position, their decisive domination of the judiciary and in academe, their ownership of almost the entire entertainment industry and most of the mass media, and their astronomical wealth. Was all this acquired honestly? I think not.

It seems incongruous and inconsistent with reality that *all* those who battle against overpowering Jewish influence are afflicted by "hate" and suffer from "anti-Semitism." But the ADL doesn't balk at incongruities and inconsistencies. It feeds on "hate" and "anti-Semitism," as I have pointed out.

Where opposition to Jews is hardly noticeable and where the Jewish community is not troubled in the least, critics of the organization have alleged that the ADL invents and exaggerates anti-Semitic "incidents" so as to have the "mortally menacing monsters" without which it would soon be be out of business.

The ADL allegedly does this to stampede its Jewish herd into paying it ever more protection money and to panic politicians, or give them pretexts, to enact more, and more virulent "hate" laws for the suppression of freedom of speech.

The ADL swims in a sea of hate produced by a Satanic symbiosis with Zionism, promoted by the Zionists' all-encompassing communications, educational, and media conglomerates.

In this environment of hate, the ADL pursues the primordial *Oberjuden* objective, to destroy the societies of their host peoples.

The ADL has inexhaustible sources of funds. There are the Zionists billionaires, and the hundreds upon hundreds of Jewish organizations; there is that portion of the American taxpayers' annual tribute to the Israelis that is funneled back to the ADL to enable it to keep up and heighten the pressures on U.S. politicians to continue, and to increase that tribute. (This reminds me of a very clever sort of financial *perpetuum mobile.*)

The ADL possesses a nearly bottomless personnel pool. In addition to its own professional spies and the police on all levels that it can suborn; a majority of Jews and Jewesses in the Jewish community are potential snoopers and saboteurs for the "Jewish Agenda" as the ADL calls it. Not all of them will go along, of course, but many do. These are called, endearingly, "warm Jews." (Note my personal experience with such a "voluntary ADL operative," as related at the end of this chapter).

Exploiting such resources, the ADL has built the largest, most insidious and pervasive interior espionage and surveillance apparatus ever known anywhere, not excluding the former

Soviet Union. For this reason the Jewish, anti-Zionist M.I.T. scholar Noam Chomsky, has termed the ADL a Stalinist organization.

The ADL spies and collects information on every individual, every commercial and professional entity, every publisher and every publication, every educational institution, every fraternal and patriotic association, every social group, every religious sect, every politician in the United States that catches its all-seeing eye.

Each clutch of information is put through an exceedingly fine sieve. If there appears a trace of what the ADL interprets as opposition to excessive Jewish power ("hate" or "anti-Semitism"), the information is skillfully edited and handed to the attorney general of the state in which it was gathered, for prosecution under the local "hate" laws. Simultaneously, the ADL cues in the media to make sure the attorney general, and the prosecutors on his staff, know what is expected of them. Confronted by such highly organized pressure, it is a rare attorney general who will decline to take seriously even the most absurd charge brought by the ADL.

In this manner the ADL applies coercion against politicians, including the judiciary, as well as public and private bodies, to attain its objectives. This practice has brought the ADL virtually incontestable influence and power, which it exercises ruthlessly, without the least accountability or responsibility to anyone.

The ADL's true objectives are manifold, but may be summarized as promoting everything that fosters Israeli interests, and the disintegration of America as a nation.

Consequently, they include, in addition to what has been mentioned, the defamation of Arabs, "justification" of the slaughter of Palestinians, spurious "terrorism" scares, sex education for six year olds, "affirmative action" to stigmatize

Blacks as inherently inferior people and thereby inciting hatred between black and white Americans, "gun control" laws to disarm citizens and make them defenseless against attack in their homes, on the streets and in public conveyances, to the end of making them amenable to accepting an even more obtrusive police state; "rights" of sexual perverts throughout society and the armed forces; "feminism" including entry into all levels of all branches of the military, weakening of the armed forces still further.

The ADL promotes the misnamed "Civil Rights" movement that agitates against a healthy progression in race relations and incites resentment between the races. The ADL advocates "human rights" for child molesters, rapists, serial murderers and the like against execution and even against prosecution; it incessantly hammers on the gas chamber hoax in order to poison the minds of Americans from kindergarten on, to defame Christians in general, and Balts, Germans, Poles, Russians, and Ukrainians in particular, and wring further billions from American taxpayers to "compensate" Jews.

The ADL has fought for abolition of prayer in public schools to steal Christian children's faith in their Creator; suppressing Christian holidays while emphasizing, to the point of nausea, Jewish ones. It has fought to ban crosses from public places, while flaunting menorahs.

The ADL has used its influence to help abolish patriotic holidays. Washington and Lincoln's birthdays are no longer celebrated as individual holidays, but merged into a generic and meaningless, "President's Day," thereby turning the most respected and revered personages in the nation's history into "non-persons."

The ADL curtails, when not suppressing entirely, the teaching of genuine American history in the public schools in favor of inculcating perverse, Old World hatreds which the Jews keep alive via their wildly exaggerated "Holocaust" tales.

This group is also implicated in the absolute silencing of any mention of the major part played by Jews for over two centuries, in the grisly African slave trade.

The ADL is also sluicing into America, clandestinely, hundreds of thousands of their Jewish brethren from Moscow and other Russian cities, and endowing them with benefits and privileges withheld from ordinary Americans—though Americans pay the tremendous cost of this chicanery. These "Russian immigrants" constitute an ominous, new criminal element in American society, as shown by reports of crimes that the Zionist media could not suppress, though it attributed them, deceptively, to the "Russian" mafia --which fooled only the most stupid--since this is a Soviet-Jewish mafia now terrorizing America.

The quality of these Jewish "imports" is well known to the Jewish importers. In part, in an attempt to reconcile Americans to this outrage, the ADL propounds the "benefits," invisible to normal Americans of "multiculturalism" and "ethnic diversity" for the *goyim*.

Then there is miscegenation. As anyone who can stomach Hollywood films, or TV "sitcoms," "or "documentaries"--or otherwise monitors the revolting, anti-American, anti-God behavior of the ADL-backed media must conclude, miscegenation is the ADL's most consistently high priority.

But not for Jews, of course. The ADL is made up exclusively of members of that ethnic group, --the only one to do so --and boasts loudly: we will not assimilate!

I have alluded to the ADL's criminally excessive influence and abuse of power, and remarked on its spying and surveillance practices. The distinction I want to make is that

ADL surveillance is carried out over a broad area, with a widespread net, in the hope of dredging up something that it could grind in its "anti-Semitism" mill. Spying is directed against specific targets for a special purpose.

One ADL spy mechanism is its "Cult Watch" (one among many of its "watchdog" groups). The Branch Davidians, in Waco, Texas, were a target of the ADL's "Cult Watch" and paid the ultimate price, after having been demonized as a cult instead of being presented as they were, a church, which was no more strange or dissident than the dozens of new and experimental churches which have historically arisen in the fertile soil of American liberty--from the Shakers to the Mormons.

The ADL has an iron grip on the granting, or the withholding of "tax exemption from Federal income tax." No American association, foundation, or organization can obtain tax exemption without the assent of the ADL. No entity can keep its tax-exempt status over objections of the ADL.

Exemption from Federal income tax is worth millions or even billions of dollars annually, according to the scope of the beneficiary.

The ADL sees to it that only those groups who serve its purpose obtain this huge advantage. That such largess, or bribery, which costs the ADL not a penny, while broadening its leverage vastly, increases immeasurably the financial burden of Americans who must make up for the revenue of which the ADL has deprived the government, means less than nothing to the ADL.

A case in point: a year or so ago, the ADL contrived to obtain a tax exemption for a notorious, pseudo-religious sect that carries in its name a false pretense of scientific knowledge. This sect, banned in even liberal European countries as a brainwashing racket that exploits its adherents; is the object of criminal suits by former members in the United States.

This outfit repaid the ADL for its vicarious generosity by taking full-page advertisements in the establishment media to denounce and deride Germany. It will not be overlooked that as enormous as the benefit of tax exemption to the ADL's collaborators is, so too is the crippling handicap represented by its refusal or withdrawal from those whom the ADL regards as enemies.

These are truly noteworthy "achievements," especially for an organization which a national weekly newspaper, *The Spotlight*, calls, "an illegal unregistered agent of a foreign government."

Among the more prominent personages bedeviled by the ADL is the exceptionally competent, contemporary revisionist historian, David Irving, a London-born Englishman.

In an address at the International Historical Revisionist Conference at Anaheim, California, in September of 1983 —at which I was present— Mr. Irving recounted experiences in relation to the publishing of several of his books.

"I am beginning to come under fire; the fact that the ADL has now seen fit to put out a defamatory leaflet attacking me (and who knows to whom it's going?), means that the boycott is beginning to start against my person. I ought to tell the ADL that in this country your laws of libel are very lax. It's just unfortunate that in this country you cannot proceed against well-funded, well-organized smear campaigns. Particularly when they are concealed smear campaigns."

Mr. Irving goes on to voice his suspicion that a defamatory leaflet circulating about him by the ADL was intended to intimidate his publishers into canceling publication contracts. He refers to his book on the 1956 Hungarian revolution, *Uprising*, which was due to be published around the world.

"It was published in England by Hodder and Stoughton, a

very respectable old company and it was going to be published in the United States by Putnam's. It was published in Germany, and in Italy, France, and many other countries.

In the United States, two weeks before publication date, Putnam's canceled the contract. They gave no explanation; they just quite simply swallowed the losses they had sustained, and Peter Israel, the managing director of Putnam's, telephoned me to say that the deal was off, they weren't going to publish. Now we don't know what kind of pressure, if any, was put on Putnam's. It is something very close to a boycott... a boycott is the cruelest and most dishonest weapon to use."

The ADL is essentially a terror organization. It employs the weapons of economic, psychological, and, it has even been alleged by its critics, of physical terror, often concurrently.

To illustrate: a person describes holohoaxer Elie Wiesel as a psychotic liar and a professional hate-monger. It's perfectly true but telling that truth makes the truth-teller into an "anti-Semite." He may be visited by a delegation of Jews, including the inevitable rabbi, bearded or not. They will cajole, and attempt to persuade him to recant, publicly.

If that fails, the delegation shifts gears to coercion. If the offender is a publisher, his advertisers will be harassed until they stop advertising with him; his periodicals will be torn from the news stands, his books will not get into the book stores.

If the offender is a manufacturer, his customers will be set upon until they stop buying from him; his products won't get into the stores, or if they should slip through here and there, those stores will be picketed viciously and vociferously by well-practiced ADL goons, in a manner to drive shoppers from them.

If economic terror does not bring supplication for forgiveness, the *Oberjuden* crank out psychological terror, in which, as in the economic, the synagogue network has a major rôle. Whispering campaigns are organized, hate ads are placed in major papers, the Jewish press inflames its readers even beyond their normal paranoia.

If the author is a professional, he will be denounced to his professional organization, and his clients pursued. If the target is an academic, he is trapped in a special hell, made by his colleagues, Jews and *goyim*, and by ubiquitous Zionist student associations and by other Jewish "watchdog" outfits; a boycott of his classes will be the least of his torments. "Boycott" is the operative word. We remember it in world Jewry`s Declaration of War against Germany on March 24, 1933, which brought the world its present ills. To boycott means to kill one's economic life and this can lead to physical death as well.

But what if the so-called "anti-Semite" is a private person, or otherwise not susceptible to boycott? The ADL has provided for that eventuality in the form of "hate laws." These are one way instruments that empower Jews to continue to spew their anti-German hatred, while criminalizing any expression the Jewish groups like the ADL, do not like. This perverse and destructive legislative swill, like so many other laws, was (admittedly) drafted by the ADL.

"Hate" can mean anything the ADL wants it to mean. A person charged with a "hate crime" is in a dangerous, potentially fatal situation. He is at an overwhelming disadvantage vis-a-vis whomever brought the charge. If, aggravating the slanted legal condition, he should find himself in a state where the presiding judge is a Zionist Jew (as is all-too-frequently the case), the attorney general is a Jew, the local court judge is a Jew, and the prosecutor is a Jew —increasingly a probability—the chances of being cleared are about the same as being struck by a meteorite.

But let us assume —though it would conflict with reality— that our "anti-Semite," "neo-Nazi," or "Fascist" were in the most equitable of courts, in the fairest of states; he would still be facing a vast prosecutorial apparatus--supported in part by his taxes—endowed with inexhaustible resources and endless time.

The court will be belabored by batteries of ADL shysters presenting briefs to "assist" the prosecution. Against all this, the victim fights alone. If he loses, he goes to prison. If he beats the charge, he can go home. In either case, the proceedings have bankrupted him. It's a win-win situation for the ADL. Its prey is dead economically, and perhaps also socially.

In case neither economic blackmail or psychological aggression can be brought to bear sufficiently to bring down its victim, the *Oberjuden* or those psychologically attuned with their general aims, move on to raw physical terror through their front groups.

Organizations like the misnamed "Jewish Defense League" (JDL), are uniquely well-equipped to instigate violent intimidation, and do so by crude means, like the pre-dawn obscene or threatening phone calls, beatings, slashing car tires, smashing windshields, fire bombings, that sort of thing.

In the southern California area these thugs operate with impunity. A recent illustration of the JDL's methods may be glimpsed in the case of the actor Marlon Brando.

When Brando articulated the painfully obvious fact that the entertainment industry is run by Jews; the Jews, for reasons that might be ascertainable by a forensic psychiatrist, frothed in fury. When the actor stood his ground, Irv Rubin (Irving Rubinstein), a psychopath who seemingly permanently heads the JDL (my family and I already had some "experiences" with him as far back as 25 years ago), told Brando in public, "we will make the rest of your life a living hell!"

Rubin knows that the ADL has so arranged matters that Rubin is able to not only make this disgusting threat, he can carry it out without fear of opposition. Other vulgar, JDL-type penny ante criminality –like toppling tombstones in Jewish graveyards or spray painting swastikas on synagogues--is done in secret in order to deflect attention from the latest Zionist atrocity in Palestine, or from some other Jewish abomination elsewhere, and to give the media hounds a pretext to howl for more, and more stringent "hate laws."

When even this covert provocation is insufficient to silence an anti-Zionist heretic, the *Oberjuden* are prepared to annihilate their perceived enemy in more sophisticated ways. In such situations they call on none other than Israel's high-tech assassination arm, the Mossad. [5]

This gang was given a license to kill, renewed by successive U.S. administrations who allow it, armed to the eyebrow, to move about our country, picking off its targets at will, and to move out again, with equal freedom.

I speak from experience. I was an early member of Willis A. Carto's Institute for Historical Review (IHR), which was in the vanguard of historical revisionism in the United States. In fact, it introduced the term into current usage. The IHR was eminently successful in researching and publishing historical truth that refuted Jewish lies, in particular, the gas chamber fraud. It attracted respected scholars from around the globe. It

---

[5] Cf. Victor Ostrovsky, *By Way of Deception: The Making and Unmaking of a Mossad Officer* (New York: St Martin's Press Paperbacks, 1991). A New York judge actually ordered the publisher not to print this book, but he was overturned on appeal. It is worth noting, in confirmation of my assessment of the "unlimited personnel" available to Jewish terror groups, that on p. xi of the paperback edition, Ostrovsky states: "The Mossad--believe it or not--has just 30 to 35 case officers, or katsas, operating in the world at any one time. The main reason for this extraordinarily low total, as you will read in this book, is that unlike other countries, Israel can tap the significant and loyal cadre of the worldwide Jewish community outside Israel. This is done through a unique system of *sayanim*, volunteer Jewish helpers."

sponsored international historical revisionist conferences (almost all of which suffered from Jewish "protest" measures as described above.)

The IHR built up a flourishing book publishing and distribution business. Of course, the ADL spotted, and "monitored" the Institute--at times employing moles or traitors—from its inception.

The IHR's spectacular progress, year upon year, ever more inflamed the hatred of the *Oberjuden*. The repulsive antics of the cretinous JDL--tire slashings, windshield smashings, four a.m. phone calls, picketing--we know the routine--did nothing to hamper the Institute--perhaps rather to the contrary.

Then, before dawn, on July 4, (note the significance of the date!) of the year 1984, there was a shattering event. A fire destroyed the IHR.

Its offices, warehouse, equipment, book inventories, files, records, all were consumed by a chemical arson attack carried out with consummate skill. As soon as the ruins cooled enough, Irv Rubin pranced and crowed about them like a berserk rooster, as though he had engineered it - and had his picture taken to accompany the stories written about it.

But the sophistication of this crime of arson was far beyond the skill of a semi-moronic humanoid like Irv Rubin.

Not astonishingly, no perpetrator ever was caught. Furthermore, and again not surprising to anyone who can tell time, this worst act of terrorism in America since World War II, well publicized in California newspapers, went missing from the FBI files. That was my first experience of the JDL-ADL-MOSSAD connection, as I call it. The second came exactly a year later.

Some years before, I had organized a "German American National Political Action Committee" (GANPAC).

Unbelievable as it may sound, GANPAC was, and still is, the *first ever* organization in the United States to speak politically (only) on behalf of America's most numerous, and most productive ethnic group, the German-Americans, who are second to none in American patriotism.

There were, and are, no "dual loyalists" among them. They were also a truly liberal, live and let live, minority; liberal in the classic sense of the word, before Jewish "intellectuals" made it a euphemism for social corrosion. The Germans who came to America in the 17th Century did not enslave the native Americans. Even less did they exterminate them, on the English model.

As can be learned from impartial histories of the era, such as Brand's fascinating *Fields of Peace*, the German settlers' relations with the native Americans around and among them were, uniquely, on a basis of mutual esteem and respect, and an acknowledgment of common humanity. The German settlers' view of slavery was of similar character. The first communal voices raised against black slavery came from Germantown (Philadelphia) in 1688.

A half century later in New York City (the British having euchred the Dutch out of New Amsterdam), a German newspaper publisher was jailed for writing anti-slavery articles. There were no German slave ships. There were no German slave traders. If there were German slave holders, they must have been much fewer than black slave holders.

And yet, although the German minority furnished disproportionately large numbers of soldiers to the Union armies, we see, for example, in a classic book on the American Civil War, (or 'War between the States'), *The Crisis,* by Winston Churchill (the American writer, not the English war criminal), that entire regiments, as in Missouri, were exclusively German.

These Germans never really acted against the South with the sanctimonious, fanatical frenzy demonstrated by Anglo-Abolitionists.

These Anglo-Abolitionists, having beaten down the Southerners after the Confederacy's four years of heroic struggle against tremendous odds, (much like Germany in 1918, and again in 1945), imposed on the helpless Southerners a savage "reconstruction" that was a foretaste, though a comparatively mild one, of what would be inflicted on the helpless German people in the next century.

In order to inform politicians, academics, editors, and ordinary Americans about the factual history of Germans in America, GANPAC began publishing a newsletter, the *GANPAC BRIEF*.

Among its objectives is to make Americans aware of the nature and the objectives of the cynical British, "hate-the-Hun" atrocity propaganda that began in 1914 to poison the minds of Americans against everything German, and succeeded in destroying German culture in America, while destroying also the lives of millions of Americans. The hundreds of thousands who were killed and maimed on distant battlefields to which they had been freighted, to fight young men of their own blood whom they didn't know, for the interests that were not America's, is a direct result of this propaganda.

The anti-German big lie grew louder and more multifarious - it cannot be said that it became also cruder and filthier; since the English, and the French, already had touched bottom in those categories - as Jews, smelling booty, joined in as the "Great War" went on.

The hate-the-Hun propaganda subsided after that, then roared into fresh flame for another dozen of years after the mid 1950s, then subsided once more.

However, as those who watch BBC TV presentations, or read British newspapers or periodicals can testify, the "hate-the-Hun" stuff is still very much there, ready to burst into full fetid flower at any time.

Jewish Germanophobia did not subside until Hollywood's Hun-atrocity films no longer sold tickets. In the early 1930s it resurged with a new manic fury. It hasn't stopped--it hasn't even paused—since then.

In the mid-1970s, with their coining of the "Holocaust" word as applied exclusively to their ordeal in WWII, and the Kabbalistic "6,000,000" figure, the *Oberjuden* moved falsehood into a new dimension, it became a dogma.

The shameless exaggerations represented by the "Holocaust" tales have poisoned relations between kindred peoples, especially of Americans and of Germans, throughout the western world.

They have cost, and are costing these nations untold billions of dollars, with the end nowhere in sight.

The "Holocaust," which, before the top Jews decreed otherwise, used to be known as "the genocide of the Six Million," is put forward to "justify" every Zionist mass butchery of Palestinians, every Jewish crime and corruption anywhere.

The Six Million swindle, incorporating the gas chamber extermination hoax and the deceitful Jewish Newspeak imposed on these matters, (the neologism "Holocaust" which came into popular use, as applied exclusively to Jewish troubles, only after the mid-1970s), makes clear to Americans, black and white alike, that they have a common enemy.

The excision of the cancer represented by the Six Million swindle, is a primary concern for Americans and Germans.

Never before have Americans and Germans, and all men of good will, in their own interest, and, much more importantly, in that of their children, had more in common against a common enemy.

It is GANPAC's task, through the *GANPAC BRIEF,* to make this clear. GANPAC is neither large nor lavishly funded. It is very far from being an AIPAC (American Israel Public Affairs Committee). I don't think the circulation of the *GANPAC BRIEF* equals that of the *ADL Bulletin,* or, for that matter, the scores of Jewish newspapers and other publications around the country.

But GANPAC and its *Brief* have influence, and that influence was growing, so much so that the *Oberjuden,* through which the ADL and other Jewish spy organizations had been tracking me from the start, felt impelled to act.

Thanks to an America that had given me the opportunity to work hard, I had made myself independent financially, and could not be boycotted or otherwise have my livelihood destroyed. As a twice-wounded World War II combat veteran, I am impervious to aggression. There was but one way, short of assassination (always a possibility), by which I could be hurt:

In June of 1985, GANPAC's west coast headquarters were in an office building in Santa Monica. I had chosen the location for tactical reasons. An office in a commercial building is not readily accessible to a Jewish goon squad. Unless the ADL emulated Menachem Begin, who dynamited the King David Hotel in Jerusalem shortly after World War II, killing about a hundred people in the process (among them a number of Jews), in order to get some British documents, a task that failed.

Being surrounded by other businesses in the middle of downtown Santa Monica, I felt relatively safe. But a few hours after midnight on June 5, 1985, I received a telephone call on my private, unlisted telephone number that was known only to a few intimates and--obviously—to some "watch dog" organizations.

A caller whose voice had that certain inflection primarily found among Jews, told me that our office was burning and that I should immediately get there. At the time I lived about ten miles from the heart of Santa Monica, and in order to get there I would have had to drive through an area where I could have been easily waylaid. Besides, if the building was really burning, there was little I could do about it. So I stayed in bed for several more hours, and drove into the city only after the sun had risen, and most businesses prepared to open their doors.

It was obvious what had taken place--during the night an arsonist had managed to get into the locked building (no forcible entry was discovered), and had tried to set our office ablaze. Due to the fact that we had the only suite with a fully enclosed ante room, something the terrorist probably did not know, the fire was not able to penetrate my inner sanctum. It spread to neighboring offices instead.

Tragically, the facilities of an amiable Jewish gentleman and a Polish immigrant who had just started an electronics business, suffered the greatest losses. Ours were inconsiderable. I had learned some time ago (during the air raids of World War II) under more difficult circumstances, to disperse my assets.

As in the 4th of July arson attack against the Institute for Historical Review in the previous year, the criminal who burned the GANPAC offices was never apprehended.

I find it highly irregular that the FBI did not enter the investigation of this terrorist arson attack. Our organization was, after all, a federally charted PAC (political action committee), and the arson did fall under federal jurisdiction. It is hard to avoid the suspicion that the arsonist was never really sought. (Only the fact that we did not have any insurance on our furnishings and equipment saved me from being investigated as the potential pyromaniac.) But for a minor incident cited below, this was the last experience I had with the world's *Oberjuden* until the summer of 1995.

This, in short, is the impact of the ADL within the context of political life in the United States as well as on the international scene.

The ADL is a semi-official spy agency, an illegal court, a brutal police force, a gigantic documentation center and a mendacious propaganda ministry, all in one. It is the all-seeing eye of Judaism, and its leaders take their job very seriously.

In the late 1970s, at a time when I was preparing myself for the retirement that never came, I lived in Palm Springs, California. One day I read in the *New York Times*, that in New Jersey three white teenagers had to appear before a judge because of some swastika-connected vandalism. The judge, according to his name an Irishman, sentenced the boys to some community work, and to the reading of three books with a "Holocaust" theme, the titles of which were given.

Knowing these books, and, as a matter of fact, having them in my own library, I knew that their contents were "full of holes." At any rate, they contained so many obvious incongruities that anybody with some amount of intelligence, and still left with the power of independent reasoning, could see through the scam.

I wrote this to the judge. I added that I too was against any and all vandalism and graffiti, whether with or without swastikas, and whether directed against Jews or anybody else, and that I believed that young perpetrators should be called to account. I further explained in my letter to the judge, that in my opinion other books written by Jews would provide a truer picture of what happened in World War II, and I gave the judge the names of such books I was able to recommend. Then I forgot about the matter.

It must have been a few months later when one day the door bell rang, and a small, elderly, well-dressed gentleman of obvious Jewish racial heritage, asked whether he could speak to me. He introduced himself, and added that he was a retired judge from New York City, now living in southern California. I saw no reason to distrust the man, and invited him in.

Mr. Jacobsen was his name. He first expressed his admiration for the the many books that framed my entrance hall. He was quite impressed by the many books which I possessed with Jewish and "Holocaust" themes. Then he came to the point. Because I had written that letter to the Irish judge in New Jersey, the ADL offices in New York City had contacted him to get more information on me, and to discover whether I was one of those notorious anti-Semites that from time to time make themselves known.

If I recollect correctly, Mr. Jacobsen and I had an interesting, and varied conversation for nearly two hours. He was intelligent but tremendously naive about the position of Jewry in American society. For instance, he had no idea (and I know he didn't fib on this), why it was that the Jews had been persecuted for thousands of years, while other nationalities or "ethnic" groups usually fared much better.

One slight disagreement arose when Jacobsen asked me whether I ever wrote letters to the editors under a pseudonym, which I readily admitted (as a matter of fact, I had used a Jewish-sounding alias at times). He thought that this was unethical, whereupon I showed him a book about currently well-known American Jews who had changed their names so that the gullible American public did not recognize them as

Jews.

Still, he wanted to impress on me that it was O.K. for Jews to change their names into Gentile-sounding ones, whereas he considered it the height of infamy for someone like myself to choose a Jewish-sounding pseudonym when writing to newspapers. I took this all as good sport and smiled at the old man's consternation.

I discovered in the course of our conversation that the ADL had not received a copy of my letter from the Irish judge himself. I had to assume that this Irishman had a Jewish legal assistant who, on his own, acted as a spy for *Eretz Israel*.

Upon leaving, Judge Jacobsen thanked me profusely for my kindness and hospitality (I had given him a Coca Cola). Then he added an interesting remark:

"You know, you are the very first person whom I have met under such circumstances who was nice and polite to me."

Acting dumb, I asked him what he meant by this.

"All the other times when the ADL send me on a mission like this, I am either being treated very impolitely, or even threatened with bodily harm..."

We parted with the usual (American?) promise to keep in touch, and to soon get together again for a cup of coffee. Alas, I never heard from Judge Jacobsen again, although I remained in southern California for another five years or so.

That is the way the ADL works. Twenty-eight well-funded and well-equipped offices across the country. Spies everywhere, agents everywhere and almost every single Jew a potential collaborator, all in the interest of the Jewish agenda of course, whatever that may be!

Once again I have to ask the question, "How would Americans react if the German-Americans were to have such a spy organization, and it dealt in exactly the same manner as the

ADL does?" To this I have to add that the German-Americans, with nearly 25 percent of the American population, would be far more justified in having their own "ADL," than that small minority of Jews in our midst who allegedly constitute a mere 2.5% (or thereabouts) of the American population.[6] Furthermore, no other ethnic group in America has a lower crime rate than have the Germans and the other Nordics.

This fact, plus their discipline, tolerance, work ethic, honesty, fairness, intelligence and talent for organization would qualify them for the position of power and influence in this country which the Jewish leaders of the United States are now holding by virtue of the psychological and physical terror emanating from organizations such as the ADL.

How does the ADL see itself? The write-up below was written by the ADL staff for the Encyclopedia of Associations, and is from the current listing.

ENCYCLOPEDIA OF ASSOCIATIONS - 1996
Anti-Defamation League (ADL)
823 United Nations Plz. New York, NY 10017 Abraham H. Foxman, Dir. Ph. (212) 490-2525 FAX (202) 867-0779 Founded: 1913. Staff: 400. Budget: $28,000,000. Regional Groups: 28. Nonmembership. Multinational. To stop the defamation of Jewish people and to secure justice and fair treatment to all citizens alike. Educates Americans about Israel; better interfaith and intergroup relations; works against anti-Semitism; counteracts anti-democratic extremism and strengthens democratic values and structures. Maintains: Jewish Federation for Christian Rescuers, Braun Center for Holocaust Studies (see separate entry). Hidden Child Committee, and A World of Difference educational project. Sponsors the Janusz

---

[6] Jewish estimates of the Jewish population of the U.S. as of this writing are a total of approximately six million.

Korczak Literary Competition for the best books about children written for children and adults.

Maintains speaker's bureau and 30 regional offices. Libraries: Holdings: articles, books, periodicals. Subjects: anti-Semitism, holocaust denial, first amendment, racism, extremism, hate groups, american democracy and pluralism. Awards: America's Democratic Legacy Award. The Courage to Care Award. Hubert H. Humphrey First Amendment Freedoms Prize. Joseph Prize for Human Rights.

Divisions: Civil Rights; Community Service; Development; Intergroup Relations; International Affairs; Leadership; Marketing and Communications. Absorbed (1965) Institute for Democratic Education. Also known as: Anti Defamation League of B'nai B'rith. Publications: *ADL on the Frontline,* monthly. Price: $12.00/year *Dimensions*, 3/year. *Facts,* quarterly. *Latin American Report,* quarterly. *Law,* quarterly. *Law Enforcement Bulletin,* semiannual. Price: free. *Middle East Insight*, quarterly. *PLO Watch*, periodic. Also publishes monographs, articles, and teaching materials. Conventions/Meetings: annual National Commission (exhibits).

Thus, the ADL about itself. But what do we see? What do we know? It's horrible that such an organization that snoops into the lives of millions of Americans, and misuses its power and influence to such an extent, exists. It is criminal. What if everybody, the Blacks (Louis Farrakhan?), the Asians, the Hispanics and all the other various European-American groups would do likewise?

Even if it were true that the Jews were always--throughout their history--innocent victims of the hate and the malice of the others, then there would still not be a good enough reason for the existence of something like the ADL here in the United

States. I maintain that except for Native Americans ("Red Indians" as they are known in Europe) and Blacks, most other large ethnic groups had roughly equal chances for progress once they arrived on these shores, and there is no justified reason for anybody to bring their Old World gripes and troubles along. The very idea of the ADL is criminal since it can only be directed against Gentile ("non-Jewish") members of society.

(The term "non-Jewish" itself is a denigration of all others. A sentence speaking of "Jews" and "non-Jews" contains the inference that the Jews are the measure of all things. Therefore the designation "non-Jews" should never be used. I consider it a personal insult.)

As I copied the ADL report about itself from the pages of the *Encyclopedia of Associations*, I purposely did not correct certain typographical errors. I am not sure whether, for instance, the word American as in "american democracy" was spelled purposely with a small a.

Apart from the tyrannical actions of the ADL with which I have become familiar over the years, I do know two things that ought to be mentioned. For an organization that loudly proclaims its wholehearted support of "democracy," and a policy of inclusion and diversity, the top echelon of the ADL is oddly bereft of directors that are not Jewish. The fact is, a Gentile would not even come close to having a say in the affairs of this organization. Compare this to the many German-American societies that have Jewish directors, and sometimes even presidents.

The other interesting fact about the ADL seems to be its immunity from any IRS audits. One should assume that a "benevolent" group with a yearly budget of $28 million per annum would at least once every ten years come under close scrutiny by a federal agency.

Where does the $28 million come from? Is part of it a payback from Israel for services rendered in helping to obtain at least $3 billion in financial assistance from the U. S. for the Jewish state year after year? If this is true, does the ADL qualify as a registered agent of a foreign nation?

Ironically, I am also on the ADL mailing lists, and therefore I was the recent recipient of an A.D.L. solicitation, so that I may help fight:
Farrakhan
Ku Klux Klan
Neo-Nazi Skinheads
White Supremacists
The Militia Movement, and
Religious Right Extremists
(as stated on the outside of the envelope).

I noticed that the ADL paid 8.6 cents for a letter that would cost us 55 cents. But this is the same group that a few years ago was able to have the non-profit status removed from a German-American society because of alleged political activity. The *Oberjuden* obviously do know that money is an integral part--often the most important part--of any political battle, and they never miss an opportunity to keep the opposition from financial spigots.

Note that apart from Louis Farrakhan, all other groups mentioned in the mailing are white, Aryan and usually Christian. Even a blind man ought to be reading from this what is the general direction of the Jewish agenda as promoted by the Anti-Defamation League. Will it soon (again, as in Gerrnany before 1933) be regarded as an anti-Semitic act if one speaks up against Communism or Bolshevism?

The way it acts (and in this regard the Germans were perhaps not too wrong after all), the ADL seems like an official United

States Government agency (i.e.,"*eine amerikanische Behörde*".) Therefore the question arises, whether the ADL's budget of $28 million per year may be somewhere hidden in the yearly budget of the U. S. Government?

At any rate, the ADL, Inc. was created under the auspices of President Wilson shortly before World War I, soon after he took office (Wilson's term lasted from 1913 until 1921). Both the ADL as well as the B'nai B'rith, Inc. received federal charters. [7]

In 1993, the Anti-Defamation League made national news when it was discovered that it had an extensive spy network all over California. According to newspaper articles of the time, the ADL had on its payroll a San Francisco policeman (and former CIA operative) named Tom Gerard who provided the Jewish organization with files on as many as 12,000 persons deemed "noteworthy".

First there were indications that the entire matter would blow up in the faces of the Jewish spy masters, but these hopes were soon squashed. The Zionist infiltration in all reaches of American public life was then, and is still now, so great as to prevent a serious investigation and prosecution of ADL wrong doing. When all was said and done, the ADL received not only no punishment for clear transgressions against existing laws, but it was even patted on the back for its efforts to "assist" law enforcement agencies. [8]

It must also be mentioned that the so-called "anti-hate" laws now being passed by many state legislatures have been patterned after model legislation written and proposed by the

---

[7] Readers of this book are advised to check into the facts surrounding President Wilson's dependency upon Jewish largess. There was the matter of a mistress, a $40,000 canceled debt, and Wilson's "friendship" with the extemely powerful Jewish "financier" Bernard Baruch.

[8] In the Fall of 1996 the ADL was successfully sued in civil court for $200,000 in damages for defaming a number of anti-Zionist groups. But the government refused to *criminally* prosecute the ADL.

ADL. That this model legislation is clearly directed against the articles of the United States Constitution, obviously bothers few people. Needless to say, in every instance it will be elite Jews among the regional directors of the ADL, who will make the decision as to what constitutes hate. For sure, everything that has been written here about the ADL is considered "hate."

How dare anybody question the noble motives of this gigantic "service" organization whose major purpose is allegedly the furtherance of "democracy"?

As the ADL takes on all the various groups and individuals mentioned previously, it may have swallowed more than it can chew. Louis Farrakhan, for instance, is now the unquestioned leader of American Blacks. Ever since the well-organized March on Washington by nearly a half million black men, all the other leaders of African-Americans have been relegated to the sidelines. It is doubtful that the Jews will still be able to alter this fact before the entire nation erupts into violence. Worst of all in Jewish eyes: Louis Farrakhan "knows the score," and does not hesitate to say so.

Certainly, the "Neo-Nazi Skinheads" and the KKK do not by themselves present a political force. But as times worsen, and as racial friction increases, both groups will see their memberships grow, and one can surmise that they will remember the ADL (and other, similar organizations) actions against them. This may backfire against Jews in general.

For the ADL to throw "white supremacists" (whatever that may be), the Militia Movement and all religious right (wing) extremists into one pot is the height of political folly. [9]

Don't Jews have enough enemies as it is? The ADL

---

[9] It is beyond my understanding how a white separatist who wants to live as far away as possible from colored people (of whatever race) can at the same time be denigrated as someone who wants to be "supreme" over the coloreds. It just doesn't make sense. Yet the American news media persists in using the "supremacist" designation for true separatists.

solicitation letter I received obviously went to hundreds of thousands of people, and many of these letters must have gotten into the wrong hands. What do Messrs. Foxman and Co. think "Rightists" of any hue will do? Throw these missives away? Or will they first show them around at Militia meetings or Christian get-togethers?

In my case, the letter by Elliot Welles of the ADL to German authorities, proves without a shadow of a doubt that people like him do not have the slightest idea as to the nature of the American ideals of freedom and justice. In fact, if the ADL were such a benevolent social service organization as it pretends to be, it would have taken my side in my fight for freedom of speech in Germany. Isn't that what America is all about?

Over the past three centuries, seven million Germans did not all just immigrate to these shores to improve their economic situation. A large number of them came in order to flee the feudal system that had enslaved them and their forefathers.

Jews who claim to have been more oppressed than others (a claim that is easily disproved), ought to be more, rather than less, anxious to preserve the freedoms guaranteed by the American Constitution.

But what does the ADL, a U. S. federally chartered institution, do? It takes actions that could have led to the imprisonment abroad of an American citizen for up to five years (without the possibility of parole!) for merely speaking his mind. Is the furtherance of the "Jewish agenda" so important to Welles and Foxman that with a stroke of the pen they forgot why they live in America and not --for instance--Israel?

As this story is being written, another ADL campaign of psycho-terrorism is making news:

In the spring of 1996, the aforementioned, best selling English historian David Irving completed his biography on Dr. Joseph Goebbels, the propaganda minister of the Third Reich. St. Martin's Press, one of the most prestigious publishing houses of the American literary establishment, announced that it would publish this book in May of that year.

Mr. Irving is known not only for his meticulous research but also for his ability to make pre-publication statements about the contents of his new books that are bound to generate controversy, and therefore publicity. Not surprisingly, this also occurred with his latest volume, *Goebbels, Mastermind of the Third Reich.*

In this tome Irving is supposed to have written that it was Dr. Goebbels, and not Adolf Hitler who must bear the greater responsibility for the German persecution of the Jews between 1933 and 1945.

Hearing of this, the *Oberjuden* were up in arms. There is little they fear more than the rehabilitation of Hitler. He simply has to remain the ogre, the monster, the second personification of Haman (the counselor to the Persian king in the Book of Esther).[10]

If Hitler were placed into the proper historical context, like, for instance, Napoleon, this could do inestimable harm to the internationalist, One World cause.

Almost immediately after the announcement by St. Martin's

---

[10] The authenticity of the Book of Esther in the Bible has been challenged by many Christian scholars, including no less a figure than the German theological genius, Martin Luther. The whole tale is too suspiciously focused on themes of Jewish blamelessness and revenge not to have been superimposed by scribal deceit. Even in the Old Testament the Israelites are often depicted as perpetually prone to sin and wrongdoing. But "Esther" reads like a propaganda-piece. It is from "Esther" that the annual Purim ritual commemorating grisly Jewish vengeance, is derived. The courageous journalist Julius Streicher, condemned by the Nuremberg court to the gallows solely for *writing articles critical of world Jewry* (he had been excluded by Hitler from all National Socialist government policy and decision-making and therefore, could not be reponsible for any so-called "war crimes"), declared, as he marched up to the scaffold, that it was "Purim-fest 1946."

Press of David Irving's new book, the Jewish censorship network went into overdrive. It might be unavoidable, in Jewish eyes, for Irving to self-publish his Goebbels biography in obscurity in England, and probably try to deal directly with the bookstores in that country, thereby limiting its sales, but it becomes a problem for the *Oberjuden* when a major American publishing house brings this book out, and thereby gets it into the major American bookstores practically overnight. This had to be prevented!

We know that the ADL executives always use the most benign language when writing letters to the editor, for instance. These missives ooze tolerance, justice and understanding. The ADL bosses never fail to express their wholehearted support for "democracy and freedom of expression."

The only time they get really nasty is when they attack the penchant of white, "racist" Americans for keeping weapons in their homes. But it is one thing to write letters to the editor in order to befuddle the masses, and another to work behind the scenes in gangster fashion to demand that no book can be published by a major publishing house in the United States that was not approved by our Jewish overlords.

And so it happened that early in April 1996, St. Martin's Press announced that it was canceling the publication of *Goebbels: Mastermind of the Third Reich.* Just as happened with David Irving's *Uprising* more than a dozen years ago.

The reason given? Thomas McCormack, the Jewish head of the publishing house, had allegedly finally gotten around to reading the manuscript, and he had found David Irving's book "an insidious piece of anti-Semitic propaganda." While canceling the project (no doubt while the printing presses were already running), Mr. McCormack "generously" permitted David Irving to keep the $15,000 advance royalties which he had received for it.

I am sure all Americans are grateful to this gentleman for saving them from such an evil book. How horrible would it be if we did not have such upright, tolerant and understanding publishing executives who take such good care of our mental well-being!

But, not to forget: it was mainly through the efforts of the ADL and other major Jewish American organizations that made St. Martin's Press drop David Irving's book and renege on its contract with him. In publishing this is called, "self-censorship."

Therefore, in closing this chapter, I will ask the question, What if the German-Americans had such power and used it against, for instance, Daniel Jonah Goldhagen's racist, anti-German hate propaganda, *Hitler's Willing Executioners,* in a similar fashion? [11]

Would we then hear protests by American advocates of the First Amendment? Naturally--and rightly so. But where are these defenders of the U S Constitution now, when we need them so desperately?

---

[11] For those who desire proof of the extent to which Goldhagen's book is part of a malignant trend toward a growing genocidal hatred for Germans, I furnish the statement of historian David Neal Miller, who has spoken out prominently in defense of the Goldhagen book. In an Internet newsgroup, Miller gleefully applauded the mass murder of defenseless German civilians at Dresden:

"Better to apprehend the destruction of Dresden as a small moment of exemplary rightness in the massive wrongness of which Dresdeners were co-authors . . . (W)e children of the victors might be permitted something akin to joy at the thought of Dresdeners and Germans as a whole getting the bombing they so ... richly deserved... I do not predicate my satisfaction with the bombing of Dresden on a theory of collective guilt, but on the certitude of the *actual* guilt of a near-totality of the German people--women, grandparents, non-combatants...a well earned death sentence indeed." (Documented by Ingrid Rimland, cf. *ZGram*, Feb. 13, 1997).

The Sickness that is Germany Today

"If Deckert's opinion of the Holocaust is correct, then the Bundesrepublik's existence is based upon a lie. Every speech by a German president, every official minute of silence, everything that is now printed in our history books would be lies. Because Deckert denies the (systematic, planned) murder of the Jews, he also questions the legitimacy of our state. Because a court of this republic asserted that Deckert was somehow justified in engaging in his endeavor (of questioning the gas chambers) he triumphed."

The preceding paragraph is an excerpt from a lengthy editorial by Patrick Bahners that appeared in the *Frankfurter Allgemeine Zeitung* of August 15, 1994.

It was part of an incredible, nationwide media campaign against the decision of a court in Mannheim that ascribed other than base motives to Günter Deckert, a former school teacher and head of one of the small nationalist parties in Germany, the NPD (*Nationaldemokratische Partei Deutschlands*).

The court sentenced him to only two year's probation for the horrible crime of not believing all the World War II propaganda stories of the victorious Allies.

What follows is a reprint of an analysis of the case, excerpted from a booklet on this and similar excesses of the judicial system of the "free" world, issued by Ernst Zündel, the German-Canadian freedom fighter who was tried twice in criminal court in Toronto for publishing a revisionist pamphlet. He was ultimately acquitted by Canada's Supreme Court.[1]

I am republishing these things here since they and my case are intimately linked.

---

[1] Ernst Zündel, 206 Carlton Street, Toronto, Ontario M5A, 2L1 Canada

German Laws Against Holocaust Revisionism

In 1991, Fred Leuchter, an American authority on execution technology and an expert witness at Zündel's 1988 "false news" trial in Toronto, went to Germany and gave a lecture on his findings regarding the alleged homicidal gas chamber installations at the concentration camps of Auschwitz and Majdanek. His forum was provided by the National Democratic Party headed by Günter Deckert. Deckert, who is bilingual, translated Leuchter's English-language lecture for the benefit of the German-speaking audience and subsequently sold videos of the event. For this deed, Deckert was later charged with inciting racial hatred and propagating "Holocaust" revisionism.

In October of 1993, ten minutes before Leuchter was to appear as an invited guest on one of Germany's most popular television talk shows, he was arrested at the TV studio, on charges of contravening the Auschwitz law and agitating the people. The police making the arrest told the show's shocked producer that, *"the decision to arrest Leuchter was political because his appearance on television would have damaged Germany's image."*

In March of 1994, Germany's Federal Court of Justice overturned Deckert's conviction, holding that doubting the gassings did not by itself constitute incitement to racial hatred. The court ordered a new trial for Deckert to determine whether he sympathized with Nazi beliefs. However, in April of 1994, the Supreme Court of Germany gave a contradictory ruling in another case stating that gas chamber skepticism *did* fall within the purview of the law.

In the meantime, Deckert was tried again by a three judge panel which held that he was a Nazi sympathizer. However, the court sentenced Deckert to only a *suspended* one-year jail sentence and a small fine. The judges demonstrated unprecedented courage and resistance to political interference by furnishing as grounds for their comparative leniency, the fact that Deckert had merely expressed a sincere opinion based on his conscience; that he was a good family man, and that he was trying to strengthen German resistance to incessant Jewish demands.

Thereupon the Deckert case created a storm of controversy in the media which even caused the formation of a new word in the German language: *'Richterschelte,'* (the act of admonishing a judge for wrongful sentencing.)

Two of the judges were immediately relieved of duty because of alleged 'long-term illness.' This was the only way the Bonn regime was able to remove these honest jurists from their posts. Prior to the Deckert case, it was extremely unusual, if not illegal, to intrude into the judicial process in this way because German judges were supposed to be free from political interference.

As a result of the artificially-generated media hysteria, the Federal Court of Justice, on appeal, quickly overturned the lenient decision of the three judge panel and ordered yet another trial for him.

In 1994, in response to the Deckert case and the pressure exerted by the Federation of German-Jewish Communities, the Bonn parliament passed a new law making doubting the gas chambers in and by itself a criminal offense.[2]

A spokesman for the Federation, Michael Friedman, expressed the motivation for the law:

---

[2] This is a reference to statute 130, the law concerning *Volksverhetzung,* namely, 'incitement to hate,' and statute 131, relating specifically to *Rassenhass* ("racial hate"), both of which were enacted into law in Germany at the end of 1994. These laws, specifically legislated to protect sacred Jewish *Shoah* theology (the "Holocaust"), from critical scrutiny, contravene Article 3 of the Bonn Constitution which guarantees that "no one can expect preference on the basis of religion or heritage. "

"It was a highly symbolic move in the democratic Germany that was established under the condition that it would accept responsibility for the history of the Third Reich and the Holocaust."

Friedman was dismayed that "Holocaust" revisionism was not illegal in Canada, thus allowing Zündel to send revisionist information into Germany. (*Globe & Mail*, May 21, 1994).

International human rights groups have protested the anti-revisionist laws in Germany. The distinguished legal authority on human rights, Ronald Dworkin, wrote an article titled, "The Unbearable Cost of Liberty" published in the *Index on Censorship* in 1995, dealing with the Leuchter and Deckert cases. He wrote:

"The German Constitution guarantees freedom of speech. What justifies this exception? It is implausible that allowing fanatics to deny the Holocaust would substantially increase the risk of fascist violence in Germany. Savage anti-Semitic crimes are indeed committed there, along with equally savage crimes against immigrants, and right-wing groups are undoubtedly responsible for much of this. But these groups do not need to deny that Hitler slaughtered Jews in order to encourage Hitler-worshippers to attack Jews themselves. Neo-Nazis have found hundreds of lies and distortions with which to inflame Germans who are angry, resentful and prejudiced. Why should this one be picked out for special censorship, and punished so severely?"

"We must not endorse the principle that opinion may be banned when those in power are persuaded that it is false and that some group would be deeply and understandably wounded by its publication. The Muslim fundamentalists who banned Salman Rushdie were convinced that he was wrong, and they, too, acted to protect people who had suffered deeply from what they took to be outrageous insult. Beware principles you can trust only in the hands of people who think as you do."

Human Rights Watch/Helsinki condemned the German anti-revisionist laws in its 1995 publication, *Germany for Germans: Xenophobia and Racist Violence in Germany*. After reviewing Germany's laws and recent cases such as that of Deckert and Zündel ally Ewald Althans, the organization wrote:

"Human Rights Watch/Helsinki acknowledges that the tragedy of the Holocaust is the historical context in which such laws were adopted. We also recognize that, by more rigorously enforcing these laws, the German government has underscored the seriousness with which it views the danger posed by right-wing extremists.

"Nevertheless, Human Rights Watch/Helsinki believes that such measures seriously restrict the protected right to freedom of expression, association and assembly. We are mindful of the fact that international human rights laws provide different and conflicting standards in this area and base our opinion on a strong commitment to freedom of expression as a core principle of human rights.

"Our own research has shown that such restrictions are often misused by majority governments against minorities. It is our view that it is inherently dangerous for governments to have the power to determine which political philosophies are 'threatening'; for this is a power that invites abuse against political foes."

It would take an entire book, not just a chapter, to properly describe the situation that exists in Germany today. However, inasmuch as I, Hans Schmidt, was held for five months in a

German prison precisely because Germany is not free, or, better yet, because "Germany is not in German hands," I will have to describe the situation as I see it in a somewhat anecdotal form. The matter of the legitimacy of the Bonn regime is explained elsewhere.

A week after I had returned to the United States from my incarceration in Germany, arson destroyed an apartment building in the German city of Lübeck. This building had mainly been used to house so-called "asylum seekers," namely people from all over the world who came to Germany to take advantage of its excellent social services. In this fire ten persons, most or all of them foreigners, and among them several children, died, and many others suffered injuries.

Ever since Germany was reunited (partially) as a result of the fall of the Berlin Wall on November 9, 1989, the world media have made much of so-called anti-foreigner attacks in Germany that have allegedly been committed by "neo-Nazi skinheads," and in which asylum seekers have come to harm.

While it is true that in *some* of these cases young Germans had attacked houses occupied by foreigners for their own good reasons (for instance, because some of the unassimilable strangers had accosted German girls), I can state emphatically that few if any of these young people really had an inkling of what National Socialism, or Hitlerism (Nazism), really is.

The frequent use of the swastika and other N.S. symbols can be ascribed to the fact that these symbols are *verboten* by law in the Bonn Republic, and it is known that youth everywhere love nothing more than to twist the noses of a disdained political system by doing things that are forbidden.

In my well-researched opinion, the great majority of significant incidents where foreigners came to harm in Germany were incited, or perpetrated directly, by non-German secret services, such as the Israeli Mossad, the CIA, the British Secret Service and similar agencies. The resulting prosecutions such as in Solingen, Mölln and elsewhere were nothing but political show trials where the Bonn system simply had to find young Germans to scapegoat as guilty "culprits" in order to satisfy the demands of foreign powers.

The Solingen trial of three German youths for allegedly causing a fire that resulted in the deaths of five Turkish females, was so obviously rigged that even many of the establishment newspapers in Germany questioned the validity of the sentences meted out.

Not quite coincidental is the fact that the (planned) anti-foreigner attacks and the associated outcry by the internationalist media usually occurs when someone --anyone-- makes special, extortionist demands on Germany. Either the Israelis need more money or Germany's enemies want more draconian laws (such as "my" §130) passed or strengthened, or NATO wants Bonn's assurances of German military participation in coming undertakings; or, worse yet, some major Jewish organization in New York expects to place even more international Jews under the umbrella of the German social services. Bonn will *always* cave in, and do the bidding of those who hate a free, healthy and independent Germany.

Within hours after the Lübeck fire that had caused the death of the ten people became known, the *entire* German media condemned all rightists ("Nazis", nationalists, patriots, skinheads, right-wing radicals, and whatever other terms one can use), and held them *collectively responsible* for this crime, pretending to believe that the arson had "once again" been the result of persons from this quarter.

When the Lübeck police managed to arrest three young men who wore typical skinhead paraphernalia, nobody belonging to the Bonn system had any doubts as to their guilt.

Michael Bouteiller, the ultra-liberal mayor of Lübeck, made a tearful appearance on German TV that could not have been better rehearsed by the most famous actor in the country, and began by pleading (like Rodney King of Los Angeles), "Why can't we all get along?"

German president Roman Herzog, one of the Bonn politicians usually traveling about the world wearing a black rabbi's hat, was quoted as saying that "his patience (with German nationalists) is coming to an end." The foreign press naturally reported as a fact that the fire had been started by the three alleged skinheads who had been taken into custody.

And, not to forget, thousands (or was it tens of thousands?) of people all across Germany prepared to take part in the ubiquitous *Lichterketten-Demonstrationen* (candlelight demonstrations) against "hate", and "intolerance," and for "love" of all human beings--whereby they would spew out their hatred of patriotism and demand totally open borders for Germany, so that everybody can gain the benefits of "diversity" and Germany can become the dumping ground for the unassimilable peoples of the entire "Third World."

Then the bottom fell out. After a thorough investigation, the police arrested a young Arab from Lebanon who lived in the burned-out apartment building and who seemingly had started the fire as a result of a fight with other "asylum seekers." (There were far more foreigners living in this building than were either allowed by law, or known to the authorities in question).

The three German youths were cleared of the arson charge, after the police admitted that all along they had only been under surveillance as common car thieves. This did not sit well with the Bonn establishment that simply loves to dwell on German guilt, shame, penance and "wickedness." One establishment newspaper complained that, "incredibly, it had to be the police that exonerated the three (assumed) culprits". Seemingly, it would have been better to release the true arsonist, and pin the blame on innocent Germans in order to satisfy "Germany's friends abroad."

Mayor Bouteiller remained stubborn, still pinning the major blame on German society because "things like this would not happen if Germans were to embrace the foreigners living in our midst."

President Herzog was also adamant: "The mere fact that people like myself had to think immediately that the crime had been committed by Germans (against foreigners), points to a sickness in German society." Herzog`s paradoxical statement is of course correct, albeit for all the wrong reasons.

Perhaps the best tell-tale reaction are quotes from a letter from ZDF, (the major German-government sponsored T.V. channel), to a German patriot who had complained about the anti-German bias which was obvious in a special report concerning the arson attack. A ZDF executive wrote:

A few hours after the fire in Lübeck, ZDF had decided to create and broadcast a special report about this crime. Because there were so many casualties, there was the justified expectation that once again it had been anti-foreigner elements in the German population that could be held responsible. After the many similar occurrences in the past this was a logical conclusion.

As a valid excuse we may mention that even President Herzog had immediately after the fire assumed that it was right wing-radicals who could be held responsible for this dastardly deed. Furthermore, nearly all national and local newspapers and T.V.

stations had reached the same opinion.

The preceding is an excerpt from a letter by ZDF written on February 1, 1996, and signed by a Dr. Thomas Bellut, no doubt one of the Germans whose mind-set is the result of the Allied imposed "re-education" of the German people after the war. Instead of being sorry that his organization had broadcast a program that was insulting to the German people as a whole, Bellut still believed that the contents of the report were justified. It is interesting to note that this gentlemen uses the "everybody did it" claim as an excuse. One must wonder if he realizes that with this claim he confirms the brainwashing of all major persons connected with the German media.

Several times before this arson attack of January 18, 1996, Lübeck had received similar media attention: in April 1994, someone threw Molotov-Cocktails into the Lübeck Synagogue, causing minor damage. In September of 1995, an apartment house in Lübeck mainly occupied by Turks had burned down, resulting in the death of a German woman.

The alleged culprits for the attack upon the Synagogue--four young Germans--were caught a year later and received sentences that were not overly severe. In the case of the arson against the house occupied mainly by Turks, three men from Lebanon were arrested and charged but, just as with the Lebanese perpetrator of the January 18, 1996 fire, I do not know the outcome.

The incidence of house fires in Germany is far greater in the case of dwellings occupied by foreigners than in dwellings where the native population lives. This is partly the result of a cultural pattern (similar conclusions can be drawn in the United States).

Other reasons are the reluctance by Germans to set fires in

order to cheat insurance companies, a reluctance not necessarily imbued in some Third World people whose main quest is often to become rich as fast as possible. One added point to be mentioned as a frequent cause for both arson fires and physical attacks, is the "short fuse" characteristics of some men of certain Third World nationalities. Tragically, they often insist on having retractable daggers on their person, and many do not seem to have any scruples against using them.

In connection with the fact that in two Lübeck arson attacks the culprits were men from Lebanon, I would be remiss if I did not point out that the Israeli Mossad secret service has been known to use Lebanese for much of its dirty work and the Israeli army operates in southern Lebanon in alliance with a renegade, mercenary Lebanese unit (the SLA).

One must take into consideration that at the time of both incidents in Lübeck, Israel, respectively New York based international Jewry, had made demands on Germany that even Bonn had been unwilling to accommodate. After the attacks all demands were quickly met.

Furthermore, how could the attack on the synagogue have occurred without the police being able to arrest any culprits immediately? In Germany all synagogues and other Jewish institutions are under 24-hour surveillance by the local police. It is likely that the Mossad would know when the guard was down.

It is now thirty or forty years since Germany was the recipient of frequent world-wide attention by the "Democratic" press, when (usually unknown) vandals daubed Jewish institutions in the *Bundesrepublik* with swastikas, destroyed gravestones at Jewish cemeteries, or painted anti-Semitic graffiti on railroad overpasses.

Then, as now, these incidents usually occurred in connection with something important going on in Germany that had to do with World War II; either an Auschwitz trial was being held (and someone wanted to put the judges under pressure), or foreign elements wanted the German parliament to pass legislation such as removing the statute of limitations from laws pertaining to war crimes. Or else, Israel and Bonn were in a state of negotiations about the continuing tribute the Germans were ordered to pay to the Jewish state.

Today we know that these "neo-Nazi" incidents had been planned and organized abroad (there is a sufficient number of books available to give names and places), and that generally the headquarters of these anti-German actions was at the main offices of the then Jewish-led Stasi in Communist East Berlin, or at Czech secret police office located in Prague. An apology *by anyone* was never extended.

Even the Israeli Professor Michael Wolffsohn, who is frequently mentioned in this book, and who describes himself as a "German-Jewish patriot," wrote in his book *Die Deutschland-Akte* ("The Germany File") of such nefarious doings. Wolffsohn reminds his readers of the anti-German world-wide outcry of 1959-60.

On Christmas Eve 1959 someone had daubed the synagogue in Cologne with swastikas, and then, as now, so-called "neo-Nazis" had been considered the only likely culprits. The entire Bonn political system seemed upset and since the media demanded immediate action, this "serious incident of resurgent anti-Semitism" in Germany had to be countered. The result was the passage of a law that made the yearly issuance of the *Verfassungsschutzberichte* (reports on "hate crimes" by the

Office to Safeguard the Constitution) mandatory.[3]

Henceforth *every* assertion of patriotic or nationalistic (i.e., pro-German) sentiment in Germany was considered a "hate crime" and thus reported.

Wolffsohn points out that in early 1960 a secret cabinet meeting about the Cologne incident was held, and that Adenauer was informed of the likely Communist secret police connection. This "Chancellor of all Germans" nevertheless decided to play along with this anti-German charade, and leave the guilt for the synagogue attack on his blameless compatriots.

According to Wolffsohn, at another time in the early 1960s, the Communist Stasi mailed crude, anti-Semitic literature to Jews all over West Germany, and then the Communist (and, naturally, "liberal") press complained loudly that now even the few Jews who had returned to Germany, were once again so afraid that they were thinking of leaving the country. Wolffsohn does not elaborate, but I assume that this resulted in the German Jews being the recipients of more security for their institutions, and additional financial inducements to make them change their minds about leaving the "land of the murderers."

The question may be asked why the Jewish Wolffsohn would publish information that actually may harm the image of the Bonn system. My assessment is that he is attempting to bolster his self-promotion as a "German-Jewish patriot," and no doubt many genuine, albeit gullible German patriots are deceived by Wolffsohn's "courage." They do not realize that this is an

---

[3] As a result of demands by the ADL and the American Jewish Committee, U.S. police forces must also compile and report "hate crime" statistics. The FBI recently issued its report which was of course top heavy with incidents of "attacks on Jews" and Blacks. The role of Jewish fabrication is disregarded in these reports. Most bias-related assaults by Blacks against Whites are dismissed as "economically motivated." These reports are issued in the hopes of making White gentiles feel guilty and masochistic. The psychological warfare perpetrated against Germans is rapidly spreading to other White nations.

iniquitous game. It proves that Jews, due to their exalted position, may do and write things forbidden for average mortals.

If Wolffsohn were a true German patriot he would try to delve seriously into the matter of the "gas chambers," the tales of "millions of Jews killed by Germans" and uncover incongruities connected with these stories. Instead he misses no opportunity to sicken the souls of the German people, by increasing false guilt and self-hate, which is a type of mental genocide.

In light of the preceding revelations by Wolffsohn, one should assume that the German media and politicians such as President Herzog would be hesitant to forever jump on the anti-German bandwagon and immediately point the finger of blame at young German patriots. Do these politicians know better? I surmise that they do, but their job is to keep the Germans in a permanent state of submission through manufactured guilt and obviously, they do their job well.

The fact is, they benefit from this state of affairs. If the remnant of German nationalism which is undoubtedly still simmering beneath the surface, were allowed to assert itself, most Bonn bureaucrats and politicians would lose their positions of influence and many would find themselves on trial for treason.

The German Memorial Day is commemorated every year in November. It is called *Volkstrauertag,* and is generally less martial than the American Memorial Day. Although Germany and its neighboring countries--with the exception of Switzerland--are seeded with war cemeteries from the many European conflicts, few Germans and even fewer German organizations, try to remember those who made the ultimate sacrifice for their country.

This too is the result of Allied indoctrination. Many Germans now seriously believe that those who fought and died in two world wars had somehow fought for the wrong side and the wrong ideals.

Last November 19th, while I was in Bützow prison, I had the opportunity to see a television program transmitted directly from the Berlin cathedral. For the occasion of the 1995 *Volkstrauertag* that seems to have been organized by the group that in is charge of the German military graves everywhere, a solemn memorial took place, attended by the German president and other dignitaries. Apart from a sermon and the music, there were two main speakers, President Roman Herzog, and Professor Michael Wolffsohn, the man who played a prominent role in my prosecution.

It was clear that President Herzog had learned from his predecessor, Richard von Weizsaecker, that his first duty was to uphold Allied propaganda and the inculcation of guilt in his people, and he chose the "high moral road" of admonishing the Germans, advising them of their (eternal) responsibility toward others.

Herzog used but one line to commemorate the millions of German soldiers who died in the two world wars for Germany, while he alluded to the Jewish dead of the same era with three lines, and those (relatively few!) who betrayed Germany in World War II, he praised with five sentences.

At the end of his sermon (for, that is what it sounded like), he cautioned the Germans concerning their responsibility for retaining the peace at home "and in the world," obviously preparing them for the international military missions to come, such as defending Israelis on the Golan heights.

What was left unstated was Herzog's and Bonn's thinking that Germans fighting for defense of German interests is now and in the future totally out of the question.

I am still wondering what German nincompoop was responsible for inviting Michael Wolffsohn to make the major address to the German people on this solemn occasion. [4]

Would not an old, decorated war veteran from World War II have been a better choice?

Wolffsohn spoke for about a half hour. I will only translate some of his most abrasive sentences. In general, this Israeli used what I call typical Jewish gobbledygook: words and sentences that sound right but are actually without serious content. Naturally, Wolffsohn's address was recited with the intent to confuse the poor Germans even further.

The very first sentences of Wolffsohn's address give an inclination of what he was up to:

"*On this Memorial Day Germans ought to ask themselves two questions: Who are the Germans, and who mourns in Germany for whom?*

Then Wolffsohn provides his (typically Jewish) answers:

"The German people are, just like any other people, a community of people living together, a society that communicates (assumably in the same language, HS), with each other, and it is tied by mutual responsibility. The children

---

[4] It would be interesting to discover who was responsible for Wolffsohn's appointment to his sensitive position at the *Bundeswehr Universität*. To have a (Zionist) Israeli professor teaching modern German history, including the Third Reich era, to forthcoming generations of officers of the German Army, is tantamount to having a P.L.O. operative teaching Israeli history to Jewish cadets at the military academy of the "Zionist entity," as the Arabs call the Jewish state. On the other hand, we ought not to be surprised by Michael Wolffsohn's appointment. In a secret Department of Defense memorandum which in January of 1996 was leaked to the press by someone from the Pentagon, Israel is mentioned as the major recipient of stolen American secrets. One sentence in this memorandum is noteworthy, and I am sure it applies to Germany (and the Wolffsohn appointment?) as well: "Placing Israeli nationals in key positions... is a technique utilized (by the Israelis) with great success." (*Washington Post,* Jan. 30, 1996)

of the Turks or other foreigners who have lived in Germany for decades are undoubtedly not German citizens but they do belong to the German 'communications society' because they live with and amongst us. Background, language or mutual history are nowadays here in Germany, as in other European countries, not anymore the criteria of belonging to the community in the state. But in spite of all our international interdependence this state is still the major fulcrum of communications.

Every community based upon communication and living together in the same land, in other words, each people, is at the same time a community that bears mutual responsibility. As long as things go well, nobody is bothered by that; if our team wins the Soccer world cup, we are all happy, but when it comes to accepting real responsibility then problems arise, even here in Germany.

Once a teacher asked me, 'How can I explain to my Turkish or even Jewish students that as German citizens they also bear part of the German responsibility?'

"My answer was simple: Spiritually, and according to his family and ethnic background, the German of Turkish or Jewish background naturally does not bear any responsibility for the murder of millions of Jews by the Germans. However, by virtue of their citizenship, German Turks and Jews are politically part of the German mutual responsibility. For instance, German Jews do pay taxes, and part of this money is being paid as restitution to the Jews outside of Germany."

So much for the first portion of Wolffsohn's lecture or sermon. Note that he assumes the right to speak as "we," thereby speaking "as a German." But he is no German!

In one of my letters to Wolffsohn I wrote him that one can

board a brood of Belgian mares for ten generations in the same stables with an equal number of thoroughbreds, and after all this time nothing will have changed. The Belgian horses will still be best qualified for pulling a plow, while the thoroughbreds will itch, so to say, to show their best at the race track. It is the genes that count. Now more than ever.

It is horrible that such a character as Michael Wolffsohn has the audacity and on such an occasion, the means, to impose a guilt complex and responsibility for the "millions of Jews" allegedly murdered by the "Nazis" in World War II, on young Germans that were born fifty years after that war had (also allegedly, HS) ended.

For, nothing else can be read from his words about making a distinction between native German and so-called "Turkish German" and "Jewish German" students.

At the end of his address Wolffsohn continues on this theme of guilt and responsibility:

"Did we in Germany, in Europe, and, as a matter of fact, in the entire world, really learn from our past history? No! The Germans watched, as did all others in the last few years how in Bosnia aggression and genocide took place. Nevertheless, we all had a good conscience. But in fact we all were callous. How can we have a good conscience when watching the genocide in Bosnia, Rwanda, Burundi, Sudan and Chechnya right before our eyes on television, while we sit and do nothing? How can we accuse the parents and grandparents who did nothing against injustice in the Third Reich, while we act similarly today?"

The correct answer to Wolffsohn's soliloquy is to tell him that he is plain nuts. How can any normal citizen, here or there, do anything at all about what is happening in foreign countries? Go on the street and protest? Write the president? Begin a hunger strike? *Complain to the United Nations?*

Not even a United States Senator, one of the most influential people in the U.S., could have stopped the wholesale murders in Rwanda. Were not the Dutch "peace keepers" only a mile away while the Bosnian Serbs murdered thousands of Bosnian Moslems last summer? If *they* could not interfere, what was a German *hausfrau* to do?

Wolffsohn conveniently forgot to mention that overpopulated Germany took in nearly half a million Bosnian refugees, most of them ethnically, linguistically and religiously quite different from the Germans, and sheltered them at tremendous cost, while at the same time a country such as Poland, far less populated and culturally much more akin to Bosnia, refused to help.

This Jewish professor knows these facts just as well as this writer does. But his main aim was not to remind the Germans of their humanity (and their responsibility resulting therefrom), and to uplift their spirit, but rather it was to once more inject the "millions of Jews killed by the Germans" into a speech, and for that he had to use some (phony) reason.

If Michael Wolffsohn were truly an honest man then he would accept his own guilt and responsibility for his *voluntary participation* in the Israeli Six-Day-War, during which, according to recent reports, thousands of Egyptian POWs were murdered in cold blood by Israeli soldiers.

Wolffsohn cannot claim not to have known of these atrocities. According to assumptions formed after the Nuremberg trials, every soldier of every army knows everything that is happening within the realm of their forces, or at least has hearsay knowledge of it, and therefore can neither claim innocence by virtue of being uninformed, nor evade responsibility.

Once again we see the covert agenda of Jewish racism corrupting, like a cancer, all sincere dialogue. Wolffsohn is speaking on the occasion of the German Memorial Day, where for once the suffering of the German people is supposed to be considered. Instead he twists the focus onto the WWII-era Jews with clever cover provided by lectures about what happened to Muslims in Bosnia etc. But what happens to Muslims in Palestine is not mentioned.

Another fixture of Jewish racism is the Talmudic idea that only Jews are really human. If this is not the case, why then does Wolffsohn give Jewish suffering predominance over German suffering?

The obsession with the forever-repeated stories of "millions of Jews who were murdered" carries with it a racial assumption: that the murder of millions of Germans by the Allies, instigated by the *Oberjuden* in Washington, London and Moscow, is unworthy of consideration or reparation.

Who is accusing American, British or Russian grandparents and elderly of "not doing enough" in the 1940s to stop the murders of German civilians or of "remaining silent" in the course of it?

At the Potsdam conference, the Allies ordered the forced expulsion of all the Germans in the east:

"In what was once eastern Germany, an anguished tide of humanity, one of the greatest mass movements of Germans in history, flowed toward the borders of the shrunken Reich. At least 10 million hungry Germans were being uprooted from their old homes in East Prussia, Pomerania, Silesia (and) Sudetenland by the new Polish, Czech and Russian owners.

"The wanderers choked the roads in Russian-occupied Germany. Ragged, barefoot, with children in their arms and the shabby remains of homes stacked on perambulators, carts and wheelbarrows, they trudged westward." [5]

Upwards of fifteen million Germans were rooted out of ancestral homes and forced to march on a genocidal "trail of tears," and this *after all hostilities had concluded*. At least three million German civilians were murdered by this means.

Where is the Jewish and American and Russian guilt for the murder of these millions of Germans? How can any self-respecting German feel guilty about anything, knowing what the Allies did to his people in *peacetime*, when there was absolutely no military necessity, to people who posed no threat to anyone?

Michael Wolffsohn is an unabashed promoter of a so-called "multi-cultural, multi-racial" society for Germany. In other words, he would like to see the German people with its God-given ethnicity and culture, destroyed; drowned in an amalgam of unassimilable foreigners from the Near East, Asia, Africa and Third World nations. Not surprisingly, Wolffsohn is a supporter of the laws that make it impossible for patriotic Germans to defend their culture, their heritage and their traditions.

As of the writing of these lines (January, 1997), Günter Deckert is incarcerated in a prison near Bruchsal, West Germany, and suffers from similar chicaneries as I did: interference in his communications with family and friends through inordinate delays of his mail; restrictions on the publications he can receive, restrictions on the number of visitors who may see him.

While Deckert has many supporters in Germany, he is not so well known abroad, and therefore the groundswell of protests from foreign countries that helped to get me free is missing. My

---

[5] *Time Magazine*, August 13, 1945.

guess is that he will have to serve the entire two-year sentence plus an additional 20 months meted out later, since part of the reason for the sentence was the Jewish quest to have him out of circulation. [6]

(That Deckert is not really out of circulation just as I was able to keep up with my contacts, is another matter. Oppressive systems never learn.)

Another person who has to be mentioned in connection with the Bonn suppression of all non-Marxists is Gerhard Lauck, an American citizen from Lincoln, Nebraska.

For years, Lauck had been a thorn in the eyes of the German authorities because he had mailed to Germany large quantities of books, brochures, newspapers and newsletters with National Socialist themes and insignia.

Considering that both National Socialism and the swastika were an integral part of Germany at a time when the Reich fought perhaps its most important battle in its 1000 year history, and realizing that millions of Germans gave their lives for this ideology, it is ludicrous that now laws exist which prohibit both.

Gerhard Lauck had undoubtedly been a great problem for the Bonn vassals. One can only imagine how many complaints arrived in Germany's ersatz capital from Jews when they saw themselves confronted with swastika or SS insignia sported by young so-called skinheads and others in the former Reich.

For a couple of decades, Bonn could do nothing about Lauck until after January 1993, when Bill Clinton became president of the United States, and the *Oberjuden* openly assumed their rule over this nation. It was then that the administration, from the presidency on down, and including the State Department, the CIA and the FBI, were able to give the Bonn Germans

---

[6] Günter Deckert Freedom Committee, c/o G. Coletti, Box 61221, Pasadena, California 91106.

assurances that it was okay for them to arrest U. S. citizens for such crimes as expressing their opinion.

This resulted in the arrest of Gerhard Lauck *in Denmark* for thought crimes in March of 1995, and his extradition to Germany months thereafter.

In August of 1996 Lauck was sentenced in Germany to four years in prison for printing and mailing from the U.S. publications which are perfectly legal to produce and possess in America.

In a press release dated Aug. 22, the ADL, which has semi-official status with the U.S. government, stated:

"Lauck's conviction and sentencing puts all neo-Nazis around the world on notice that their anti-Semitic and racist hate propaganda will not be tolerated by a democratic Germany."

In other words, the ADL is applauding what would be a flagrant violation of the Constitution in the U.S. The ADL thereby reveals how anti-American it really is, as well as what it is working to achieve behind the scenes in the U.S.--the enactment of similar laws for the imprisonment of publishers and writers who offend Jews in America.

On May 7, 1996, fifty-one years to the day after the German capitulation, another important German trial against "Holocaust" revisionists began in the city of Tübingen.

This time, the accused were the writers, publishers and distributors of an anthology on the "Holocaust" titled *Grundlagen zur Zeitgeschichte.*

This had been published by the Grabert-Verlag in Tübingen in 1994. [7] According to the prosecutor, this large size, superbly-written book, incites hate against the Jews, insults all Jews world-wide, and defames their dead; even though it is merely an anthology of now generally accepted historical corrections

---

[7] Grabert-Verlag, Postfach 1629, 72006 Tübingen, Germany.

The Sickness that is Germany Today

about the "Holocaust".

But in today's Germany it is forbidden even to state that the original lie of "four million Jews killed at Auschwitz," for instance, was a propaganda lie. The fact is that this book does not contain any polemics at all but merely reports the results of scientific research into the unsolved problems connected with the gas chambers.

Although the book appeared under the pseudonym of one "Ernst Gauss," I know that it was written by a young (31 year old) German chemist, Germar Rudolf-Scheerer, who has already been sentenced to fourteen months in prison for his courageous efforts in behalf of the publishing of scientific truths which are not politically correct.

Rudolf-Scheerer was a research chemist working toward his doctorate at the prestigious Max Planck Institute when he became interested in unsolved questions regarding the homicidal gas chamber claims. As a result, he traveled to the former German concentration camp of Auschwitz in Poland, where he removed samples from the bricks of the alleged gas chambers, and upon his return to Germany, had them tested for traces of Zyklon-B poison, *without informing the testing laboratory where the samples came from.*

The tests determined there were no traces of the gas. When Germar published his findings he was dismissed from his position at the Max Planck Institute, prevented from completing his work toward his doctorate, and he and his wife and young children were evicted from their apartment, *even though he had never even given permission for the results of his research to be publicly disseminated.*

In the appendix are reprints of two letters pertaining to Germar Rudolf's firing from the Max Planck Institute.

Following is the translation of excerpts from a letter Germar

377

Rudolf wrote to Matthias Wissmann, the Minister of Transportation in the Kohl administration. I have also reproduced some material on both Germar Rudolf and General Otto Remer (who had first published Rudolf's research), taken from a newsletter written by the general's wife. Both these missives provide an interesting insight into the status of the German judiciary at the moment.

Germar Rudolf's letter to Mr. Wissmann is both an answer and a follow-up to a note to the minister that had been written in behalf of the young scientist by a German couple who will remain anonymous but who are residing in North America.

From: Germar Rudolf, 71141 Steinenbronn, Germany.
August 25, 1995
Dear Mr. Wissmann:

Although I know neither you nor Mr. and Mrs. -- personally, and I have no idea as to the relationship between this couple and you, permit me to send you herewith a few comments regarding their letter.

I am writing you under the assumption that you do not recognize my name. In the current Registry of active Members of Fraternities you will discover my name among those belonging to AV Tusiconia Königsberg at Bonn. However, it is unlikely that I will be mentioned in the next issue, for I was officially excluded from this academic society following a session of its Court of Honor which accepted as true the most outrageous lies about me.

Nevertheless, personally I shall always regard myself as a member of AV Tusiconia Königsberg, of which I know you are an honorary member.

A few points regarding my case, as brought forth in the letter by ---- to you, deserve correction:

In 1992 I had submitted expert testimony about the "gas chambers" of Auschwitz. In the following year this testimony was copied without my permission by the former *Wehrmacht* general Otto Ernst Remer, and mailed along with the general's personal commentary to the media, judicial authorities, politicians and members of academia in Germany.

As a result, not only General Remer but I too was formally accused in criminal court of "incitement to hate" by the "High Society" of the *Bundesrepublik*. The prosecutor accused me of having secretly worked together with General Remer all along, and he arranged that I be hauled before a level of court where no appeal is possible.

Even before my trial began, this court asked the highest judges in the *Bundesrepublik* for advice on how to deal with the situation, and they mentioned the Deckert case as an example to be followed.

As a result, I was sentenced to fourteen months in jail without the possibility of parole. The court also found it necessary to claim that all our defense arguments were either false or dishonest and it did not shy away from claiming that witnesses in my behalf had also lied. Due to the fact that there are no court reporters present in German courts, and because no records are made of what is said, and furthermore, because in such cases an appeal is precluded from the start, obviously no revision of such goings-on is possible. There is no level of court that would try to discern the facts in my case.

In present-day Germany it is obviously impossible for the accused to defend himself properly in some cases, and to appeal unjust sentences. This is especially bad when, as happened in my situation, the defendant is fighting for his livelihood.

Due to the immense political pressures under which German judges have to labor, and because there are no records made of testimony, it is easy for an unethical judiciary to belatedly assert that statements had been made which bear no resemblance to the truth.

In the light of this I came to the conclusion that Germany is, and never was, a land of justice. For, is it not true that it is the mark of a strong system of justice when a single, almost defenseless defendant can fight and win a case, against the power of the state that bases its persecutions not on the quest for justice, but on the alleged necessities of society, and is wholeheartedly supported by the media and a great array of special interest groups?

I feel I have the right to judge the justice system of the *Bundesrepublik* so harshly because a defendant like myself has no recourse to appeal, and, as a result of the lack of official record keeping in the courtrooms, he is at the mercy of manipulative prosecutors who retroactively claim assertions that had never been made.

Viewing this matter one step further, I would like to say that it does not even matter whether my declaration of innocence was truthful or not, because in my opinion even a guilty person should have the right to appeal, and most definitely there ought to be a proper keeping of records of what was said in the courtroom so that later falsifications are impossible.

These shortcomings of the German judicial system become especially apparent in so-called "Holocaust" trials. For it is there where judges and prosecutors are immediately put under immense political pressure, and a guilty verdict is a foregone conclusion. Should the jurists in question fail to follow the dictates of the *Zeitgeist,* then they themselves will become the victims of the medieval inquisition. The reason for this is the fact that the "Holocaust" has become the pre-eminent taboo of present-day German society. The following statements bear witness to this:

"Whosoever denies the truth about the National Socialist death camps shakes the foundations upon which the German Bundesrepublik *is built. This state must remain a belligerent democracy that will fight back when anti-democrats try to weaken it."*

--Rudolf Wassermann, a former high judge, as quoted in the newspaper *Die Welt*, April 28, 1994, after the famous judgment against Günter Deckert became public.

In other words, according to Judge Wassermann, anybody who disagrees with some historical allegations must be an anti-democrat. The judge does not say where the borderline between historical assertions and political opinion can be found. Another example:

"Whosoever denies or belittles the National Socialist mass murder, namely, the Holocaust, must realize that he shakes our democratic foundations."

These words were spoken by the socialist *Bundestag* representative Dr. de Wirth during the debate about new and stronger amendments to the "Holocaust law" on May 18, 1994. He was heartily applauded.

Other quotes in the same vein:

"Whosoever denies Auschwitz...shakes the foundations which are taken for granted in our society. (*Die Welt*, March 16, 1994)

"The moral foundations of our republic are endangered." (*Die Zeit,* December 31, 1993, in calling for measures to silence "Holocaust" revisionists.)

"If Deckert's (revisionist) beliefs about the Holocaust were true, then there is only one conclusion possible: The Bundesrepublik *is founded upon a lie. Then every speech by a president, every minute of silence, every history book would be a lie. Whosoever denies the truth of the mass murder of the*

Jews questions the legitimacy of the Bundesrepublik." (*Frankfurter Allgemeine Zeitung,* August 15, 1994, also in connection with the Deckert judgment.)

"In his understanding for the *raison d'etre* of the *Bundesrepublik*, President Richard von Weizsaecker is closer to the Green party than to Chancellor Kohl: it is not NATO but Auschwitz!" As quoted by Joschka Fischer, a Green party *Bundestag* representative, after a visit to the German president. (*Der Spiegel*, No. 28, 1987).

Such quotes could be continued for many pages. The fact is that most members of our "elite," almost without exception, believe that it is in the interest of state and society that the generally alleged tales of the homicidal "gas chambers" are accepted as the absolute truth, and may not be debated.

I cannot accept this dictate by our "elite," and furthermore, the moral foundation of a nation cannot and ought not to depend on whether we accept the official version of the "Holocaust." It is the basic principles enunciated in our Constitution, especially those concerning human and international rights, and how we abide by them, that are the pillars on which our nation should rest.

Obviously, this cannot remove the fact that in this republic we have all been taught that the 'Holocaust' as alleged is the moral equivalent of the north star, in accordance to whose position we all have to define our moral bearings.

The result of this insanity is the fact that all those who question any tenets of the gas chamber stories, will suffer from a persecution that can only be compared to the burning of the witches in earlier times. The incredible public outcry that was purposely instigated by the media after the results of the Deckert trial had been announced, and which generated a general hysteria in our people about the matter, resulted in the fact that any further "Holocaust" trials in Germany are now outrageously simple, because no fair trial is possible.

In such situations one can clearly notice the difference between a state of justice and one whose existence is based upon terror. A nation where justice prevails will always also safeguard the rights of dissidents; a nation where terror rules denies such rights. In the *Bundesrepublik* the rights of German dissidents and patriots have been negated through the new additions to criminal law, and the entire media applauds this injustice.

When my trial was held, there was never any argument about the real facts of the case. In German 'Holocaust' trials the establishment of the facts is from the start prevented through the expedient use of a so-called 'judicial notice.'

At my trial, prosecutors and defense argued merely about the political commentaries of General Remer, and whether I had a hand in composing them or not. And since the state's attorney had not been able to prove that I had known of these commentaries before their publication, falsifications were used to establish such an allegation. [8]

Mr. Ignatz Bubis, (the titular head of the German Jewish community of less than 100,000), did not threaten my employer, the Max Planck Institute. But his firm expectation, as expressed in a letter to the Institute, that my expertise should not be further used, certainly was clearly understood by the people in charge of the Institute.

Currently, I am facing another trial because I was the author of a book titled *Grundlagen zur Zeitgeschichte, Ein Handbuch*

---

[8] In the spring of 1996, a book titled, *Hitler's Willing Executioners* by Harvard professor Daniel Goldhagen, made world news. The resulting argument centered on whether during World War II the German people as a whole participated in the "genocide of the Jews" or not. The real argument, namely, whether the "gassing of millions" had actually taken place or not, was, in the course of the fracas, forgotten (as was intended from the start?).

über strittige Fragen des 20. Jahrhunderts, ("Foundations of Modern History: An Anthology of Unsolved Historical Questions Relating to the 20th Century").

It was published in 1994 by the Grabert Verlag, Tübingen. At the time I had used the pseudonym Ernst Gauss. It was one of four books by the same publishing house that in 1994 fell victim to the wrath of German government censors. This publisher is but one of many who year after year have to battle this sort of censorship.

In today's Germany one does not argue; inconvenient books are simply confiscated and burned. Yet at the same time the ruling system assumes an attitude of moral superiority toward the Third Reich, whose leaders were at least honest enough to admit that censorship existed.

Those who defend censorship in the *Bundesrepublik* are using the argument that this is preventive censorship, something the Constitution allegedly permits.

Certainly one could defend censorship in cases of pornography and graphic depictions of brutality, but in these areas precisely no censorship exists, as one can discover on any German newsstand, including those easily accessible to minors.

But all politically inconvenient and dissident writings are successfully censored. Once such intellectual books or pamphlets are *verboten,* they are usually confiscated and burned by the government. Nowadays patriotic publishers, writers and printers are supposed to censor themselves before bringing out new publications. If they do not, they may find themselves in court.

In the Third Reich there were special offices where the manuscripts of new books had to be read and censored before they saw a printer. Today writers and publishers have to do that themselves, often at great cost for lawyers, or for other

The Sickness that is Germany Today

professional reviewers. Officially the government has clean hands in the matter, and still can insist that no censorship exists (as it is stated in the Bonn Constitution).

I prefer a government that is honest enough to admit to censorship, and sets the parameters for it, than one that preaches liberty but stabs its innocent citizens in the back, as the German *Bundesrepublik* does. However, I really would prefer a system such as exists in the United States, where no state censorship of scholarly writings exists.

I am not going as far as Mr. and Mrs.---in distancing myself from the political system of the *Bundesrepublik*. For instance, I realize that in spite of your own prominent position in the government you cannot alter the situation as it exists. But perhaps you ought to think about the effects the 1994 amendments had on the German set of laws, and you may consider approaching other important persons about an introduction of laws that guarantee the right to appeal in every case, and that assure that in all trials court reporters are used.

--Sincerely, Germar Rudolf

In my opinion, the implications of Germar Rudolf's case, as outlined in his eloquent letter, is of special significance for the understanding of the present German situation, because before 1992 this young scientist was a total unknown in revisionist *and* political circles.

Rather inadvertently he came into contact with "matters pertaining to the Holocaust," and it is clear that at first he did not have an inkling as to the significance of his research work relating to Auschwitz. I am not even certain whether he knew of Fred Leuchter's earlier investigation of alleged homicidal gas chamber residues. Following, I have translated and reprinted a short summary of the Germar Rudolf situation as it was presented in a newsletter by the wife of General Remer from that couple's exile in Spain (Rudolf is himself, as of this writing, in exile in Great Britain).

From Mrs. Remer's Newsletter
For a clearer understanding:

The Superior Court of Stuttgart headed by Judge Maier had sentenced Germar Rudolf-Scheerer to fourteen months in prison without the possibility of parole because the judges were convinced that it was Mr. Rudolf, and not General Remer, who had organized the mass mailing of his expert findings (on the gas chambers of Auschwitz).

This assumption by the court is false and without foundation. It is a complete reversal of the facts. Already in January of 1995, Mrs. Remer had stated under oath at a court in Marbella (Spain), that her husband had acted purely in self-defense when he used Germar Rudolf's Auschwitz findings *without permission of the research scientist.*

The general saw no other way to defend himself because a court had sentenced him to 22 months in prison for questioning Allied postwar claims, and the judges had not permitted the testimony of a single defense witness who would support the general's allegations regarding certain historical facts.

Particularly, Judge Siebenbürger of the Superior Court in Schweinfurt denied all proposed expert defense witnesses to testify, among them Germar Rudolf. It was for this reason that General Remer mailed copies of Germar Rudolf's Auschwitz findings to all parliamentarians of the *Bundesrepublik*, to all chemistry professors in Bonn, to all professors of modern history, to many chief executives of corporations, to high

The Sickness that is Germany Today

church leaders and others.

General Remer asked all recipients of this expert testimony to review Germar Rudolf's findings, and test them for accuracy. The chemistry professors especially could have verified whether Mr. Rudolf's statements were correct or not. But so far there has been no claim that Germar Rudolf's discoveries were erroneous.

On the contrary, Mr. Rudolf's findings had been tested for their accuracy by the number one research institute in the world. The Max Planck Institute admitted that the young scientist did not make even one error in coming to his conclusions. In spite of this, Germar Rudolf was not allowed to speak in behalf of the defense at General Remer's trial, even though he was present in the courtroom.

Then the German prosecution-democracy reached its zenith of hypocrisy. At the conclusion of Remer's trial, our expert witness Germar Rudolf was himself persecuted and punished, even though he had no hand in disseminating his findings to the persons mentioned above.

The moment Germar Rudolf had heard of General Remer's action, he went to the general and asked that the mailings be stopped. This was done immediately. It must be mentioned, however, that General Remer had never believed that the government would prosecute a young scientist who had traveled to Auschwitz at his behest and there made his chemical tests. But in spite of testimonies by Mrs. Remer and others, the Superior court in Stuttgart came to the conclusion that the general's assertion that he acted without Rudolf's permission, had been false. This in spite of the fact that several witnesses had under oath confirmed the sequence of events.

Still lacking proof for its contention, the German judiciary tried to use the ruse of an alleged civil suit in order to get Mrs.

Remer to change her testimony. That is why she was called before judges in Spain and asked to again testify about the matter. Mrs. Remer however, recognizing the intent of this infamy, merely confirmed under oath what she had earlier stated in Germany.

(Here concludes the statement from the Remer newsletter).

Ironically, in August of 1995, General Remer received from the prosecutor in Schweinfurt, where his own prosecution had been held, a bill for more than 13,000 *deutschmarks* for costs of expert witnesses that were supposed to have been used at his trial.

This in spite of the fact that no such witnesses had been called. I count this deed by the Schweinfurt prosecutor as one of the typical chicaneries the Bonn justice system uses to make life unbearable for those who disagree with its political (anti-German) stance, as I personally have also experienced.

General Remer assumes that the prosecutor placed so-called expert testimonies after the fact into the files of his trial, so that in later years everything will look proper. Since no court reporter was ever present, who can later swear what was or was not said at the trial? Certainly, the words of judge *and* prosecutor together would count more than those of a convicted defendant and his defense lawyer.

The general also has reason to believe that the two copies of Rudolf's testimony about the non-existence of Zyklon-B residue in areas of Auschwitz claimed to have been homicidal gas chambers, which had been presented to the court (even though the witness was not allowed to testify in behalf of the accused), are now missing.

On June 24, 1995, the *Pensacola News Journal* published the following item regarding Germar Rudolf and General Remer:

"Stuttgart, Germany (Associated Press). A chemist who produced a scientific paper claiming the gas chambers at Auschwitz were a Jewish hoax was sentenced Friday to fourteen months in jail for incitement to racial hatred.

"Otto Ernst Remer, 82, a former general and Hitler loyalist, paid Germar Scheerer to test brick in the Auschwitz gas chambers for a deadly cyanide compound used in the Holocaust gassings. Scheerer's 1991 report asserted that since he found none, it couldn't have been used to kill Jews.

"The cyanide compound Zyklon B was used to kill hundreds of thousands of the 6 million Jews slain during the Nazi Holocaust.

"Scientists say the compound quickly decomposes and disappears. In addition, some gas chambers at former death camps were destroyed and have been rebuilt with new bricks by curators of the historical sites.

"In his ruling, Judge Dietmar Mayer called Scheerer an anti-Semite fanatically committed to denying the Holocaust.

"Remer, who rounded up dozens of people involved in the July 1944 assassination attempt against Hitler, was sentenced to 22 months in prison for incitement to racial hatred in 1992, and lives under house arrest in Malaga, in southern Spain." [9]

(Here ends the *Pensacola News Journal* article).

---

[9] On July 20, 1944, after the assassination attempt on Hitler, Remer, then a highly decorated major who had been badly wounded on the Eastern front, was the commander of the German Army's "Guards battalion" in Berlin. It fell upon him to arrest, on Hitler's personal orders, the conspiratorial officers of the Wehrmacht at their "Home Army" headquarters in the Bendler-Strasse. This is something for which the Bonn regime hasn't forgiven Gen. Remer to this day. During World War II, Remer had been wounded eight times. He had been decorated with the Oak leaves to the Knights Cross of the Iron Cross, with the German Cross in Gold, and with the rare Close Combat Clasp, for 48 days of hand-to-hand combat. It may be mentioned that already years ago the Bonn Government stopped paying the pension to which Remer, as a former professional officer, is entitled. And, although he is quite sick now and needs constant supervision, the German (public) medical insurance system refuses to pay his medical bills.

For the Tübingen trial of all the persons connected with the publication of Germar Rudolf's book *Grundlagen zur Zeitgeschichte*, it was assumed that the defense would ask high-ranking representatives of major Jewish organizations in Western Europe to testify. They were supposed to confirm that Jews in general do not feel insulted or defamed when controversial results deriving from revisionist research are published. It was also assumed that these prominent Jews would not be permitted to testify.

Furthermore, the defense had reason to believe that the court would not allow the testimony of expert witnesses whose discoveries might help demolish the tenets of the gas chamber allegations.[10]

Unquestionably, such actions by German courts damage the human dignity of researchers and historical revisionists willing to bring proof of certain impossibilities, and they thereby obviously transgress against Article 1 of the German Constitution, and Article 19 of the U.N. Charter guaranteeing freedom of expression.

At the moment, political persecutions in Germany have reached epidemic proportions. A claim in the indictment of the Tübingen defendants that all the accused had cooperated in the "erection of a building based upon doubt" cries to high heaven, since it makes doubt a punishable offense in Germany.

At the same time a great *public* argument about the "Holocaust" has also reached a fever pitch in France. Abbé Pierre, hitherto a beloved and respected icon of the left, has

---

[10] It is a common occurrence at German "Holocaust" trials, i.e. at trials where doubters of the gas chamber tales are being prosecuted, that the court does not allow expert witnesses to testify. As a matter of fact, since the end of World War II no German court has allowed any forensic evidence about concentration camp deaths to be presented, obviously for fear that it may demolish the gassings dogma. The judges usually hide behind the smoke-screen of *Offenkundigkeit* (judicial notice).

publicly demanded that so-called 'Holocaust' revisionists be allowed to debate their issues. He stated, "I was in Auschwitz, and I saw the memorial stones inscribed with the four million dead claim. Now one speaks of one million..." (*Frankfurter Allgemeine Zeitung,* April 30, 1996). Abbé Pierre asks that everybody have the right to freedom of expression, including those who question the official depiction of historical events.

As a result of the (mainly) Jewish attacks against him, and because of threats against his life, Abbé Pierre was forced to leave his homeland and seek refuge in a monastery in Italy. Does anyone doubt that we have returned to medieval times when heretics were haunted to death and forced to seek sanctuary in foreign lands?

1996 also witnessed the debut of David Irving's biography of Goebbels, which has been lauded by the British press and even by two leading American periodicals (*The New York Review of Books* and *Vanity Fair*). Yet in Germany, anybody who would dare to either translate or publish Irving's book would be incarcerated. [11]

A preview of how the Bonn system views Mr. Irving and his monumental (and unsurpassed) research into World War Two and especially Third Reich history, can be gleaned from the following excerpt taken from the acknowledgements of Irving's *Goebbels* book:

"Even more lamentable have been the actions of the German government's federal archives, the *Bundesarchiv*, to which I also donated many Goebbels documents, including a set of all the diaries I retrieved in Moscow. On the instructions of the

---

[11] *Goebbels: Mastermind of the Third Reich,* Focal Point Publications, 81 Duke Street, London, W1M, 5DJ, England. On the symbolic date (for Germans) of November 9, 1996, the government of Australia, at the behest of Jewish groups, once again banned Irving from entrance to Australia, where he had intended to conduct a university lecture tour.

Jailed in 'Democratic' Germany: The Ordeal of An American Writer

minister of the interior, on July 1, 1993 the archive banished me forever from its halls, without notice, two hours before the conclusion of my seven years of research on this subject. It had earlier provided a hundred photos at my expense—but on the minister's instructions, it now refused to supply caption information for them.

"When I requested the Transit-Film Corporation, which inherited the copyrights of Third Reich film productions, to provide still photographs of the leading actors and actresses who play a part in the Goebbels story, the firm cautiously inquired of Professor Friedrich Kahlenberg, head of the *Bundesarchiv,* whether 'special considerations' might apply against helping me! (A copy of this letter fortuitously came into my hands, but not the pictures I had requested.)

"The background can only be surmised. Professor Kahlenberg had hurried to Moscow in July 1992—too late to prevent the Russians from granting me access to the coveted microfiches of the Goebbels Diaries.

(There was no reason why the Russians should have denied me access: several of my books, including those on Arctic naval operations and on Nazi nuclear research, have been published by Soviet printing houses.)

"The Bundesarchiv has justified its banishment, which is without parallel in any other archives, on the ground that my research might harm the interests of the Federal Republic of Germany.

"The ban has prevented me from verifying my colleagues' questionable transcriptions of certain key words in the handwritten diaries. I had a list of twenty such words which I wished to double-check against the original negatives; pleading superior orders, the *Bundesarchiv's* deputy director, Dr. Siegfried Büttner, refused to allow even this brief concluding labor.

"As one consequence, evidently unforeseen by the German government, the *Bundesarchiv* has had to return to England its "Irving Collection," half a ton of records which I had deposited in its vaults for researchers over the last thirty years.

"These include originals of Adolf Eichmann's papers, copies of two missing years of Heinrich Himmler's diary, the diaries of Erwin Rommel, Alfred Jodl, Wilhelm Canaris, and Walther Hewel, and a host of other papers not available elsewhere."

Irving's statement that "The *Bundesarchiv* has justified its banishment, which is without parallel in any other archives, on the ground that my research might harm the interests of the Federal Republic of Germany," says it all.

Bonn fears the truth and will do everything in its power to uphold the WWII myths.

In Sweden, the well-known historian Lennart Lundmark demanded in *Svenska Dagbladet* (April 10, 1996), that the Royal Academy of Sciences in Sweden should take it upon itself to arrange for a neutral investigation into the "Holocaust" claims and counterclaims.

Precisely this was demanded by the defense lawyers for the persons accused by the court in Tübingen.

The final judgment in the Tübingen trial (that in the opinion of this writer should have received as much publicity in the United States as do Chinese human rights violations, but instead has been blacked out by the entire American media), was handed down in June of 1996.

At its conclusion, a Belgian human rights organization, *Stiftung Frij Historisch Onderzoek*, (Postbus 60, 2600 Berchem 2, Belgium), issued the following report:

Scientific Book to be Burned!

Starting with the 7th of May, Judge Burkhardt Stein of the district court in Tübingen sat in judgment of the publisher, editor and writers of a historical work titled *Grundlagen zur Zeitgeschichte*.

Immediately after the beginning of the trial, the cases of the writers were separated from the main accusation for various reasons. Then the matter of the accused Germar Rudolf-Scheerer (alias Ernst Gauss), the editor of the work, had to be set aside because he had fled outside of the jurisdiction of German courts. Instead, the judge issued an arrest warrant for Mr. Rudolf.

During the trial, both the judge, and prosecutor Susanne Teschner, accused Mr. Wigbert Grabert, the publisher, of transgressing against existing laws, because the book can be considered incitement to hate. This could be clearly seen by the frequent use of such adverbs as "allegedly", "assumably", and "supposedly" in connection with the "Holocaust".

However, the defense attorney for the publishing house claimed that a careful reading of the book proves that every single statement indicating doubt or open questions had been extensively explained in the footnotes, and must be regarded from a historical and scientific point of view. At any rate, the sources for all statements are meticulously listed. The various requests by the defense, to permit the testimonies of expert witnesses, and the use of existing documents proving the veracity of the book's statements, were flatly turned down by the court.

Also denied was the request by the defense to stop the entire proceedings since the prevailing situation in Germany has made impartiality by the judge impossible, because in the event of an acquittal of the accused, the judge would be severely chastised by the present-day German society, and he might even have to face disciplinary procedures as could be seen in the outcry following the so-called Deckert judgment.

The court agreed that Dr. Joachim Hoffmann, a well-known historian at the German Military/historical Research Institute, would be allowed to present his testimony as to whether *Die Grundlagen zur Zeitgeschichte* satisfied the demands for a well-researched and thoroughly documented historical work. Some of Dr. Hoffmann's findings are:

"The various contributions to the book come from experts in the field, and are generally written in a style that is commensurate with serious research in any matter. The footnotes are so well explained and contain so few unanswered questions that little improvement can be expected. Particularly someone who wants to discover new findings in this field will be amply rewarded since the authors have not been reticent about mentioning all available counter-literature.

"The various contributions of the work are put together logically and expertly. Its essential character as a work of serious scientific research cannot be questioned. This is especially true since extensive use of counter arguments and counter literature is made.

"The general impression of this work is that even though it is written with criticism in mind, it ought to be taken as seriously as is the case with all other 'official' Holocaust literature. And, it is known that the latter is usually uncritically acclaimed and never hindered in its distribution.

"An official suppression of this excellent work would be tantamount to a brutal attack against legitimate research into any scientific field of endeavor. After all, it is clear that our

knowledge of nearly everything is constantly changing. It is a sad fact that errors and exaggerations are to be found in nearly every scientific controversy. The state ought not to take it upon itself to assume that it has a better critical judgment than free and sovereign researchers. Usually it is not very far from the suppression of unwanted literature to the burning of the books. And, if we permit that ,we would be back exactly there, where it all had started..."

The report of the Belgian human rights organization, *Stiftung Frij Historisch Onderzoek*, continues:

The witness Hoffmann personally did not like adverbs such as "allegedly" and "assumably" but they did not alter his opinion about the scientific value of the book.

At last the prosecutor made her presentation. She put the emphasis on such "horrible" wordings as "supposed gas chambers," "alleged death camps," "the Auschwitz bludgeon," "Holocaust Religion," "identity-creating group fantasies," "alleged genocide,","established Holocaust scene," "to claim *ad absurdum,"* even though, in part, these phrases were derived from establishment sources.

The female prosecutor claimed that taken together, the use of these words prove that the National Socialist murder of the Jews was being put in doubt, and that this therefore proves the crime of inciting to hate.

According to the prosecutor, the expert witness, Dr. Hoffmann, was no more competent to give testimony in the matter than any jurist, and therefore his assertions ought not be taken into consideration. In light of this, the publisher of the book, Mr. Grabert, ought to be sentenced to 9 months in prison, the prosecutor said.

The defense refuted the argument by the prosecutor that the book is a pseudo-scientific invention of the worst kind. The lawyer pointed out that such talk is pseudo-judicial talk without content or definition. The defender also alluded to the fact that it took a tremendous effort to create such an extensive scientific work as *Grundlagen zur Zeitgeschichte*.

Lastly, the defense attorney stated that in his opinion, paragraph No. 130, article 3 (concerning incitement to hate) is unconstitutional since its main purpose seems to be to justify the burning of books with despised contents.

At the conclusion of the trial, the judge sentenced the publisher Grabert to a fine of 30,000 deutschmarks. He further ordered the confiscation of the remaining stock of the book, and the original manuscript and plates needed for the printing, and their subsequent incineration.

In his opinion, the judge wrote that words like "allegedly," "assumably," "sacrifice by fire of the Jews," "supposed planning," "furious fantasies," were obviously designed to deny the "Holocaust," and that this therefore proves the allegations of incitement to hate.

(Here ends the Belgian report).

In this chapter I wrote of the unjust persecutions of generally well-known persons: Deckert, Remer, Grabert, Christophersen, Rudolf(-Scheerer), and others.

In closing I would like to present the case of an elderly German lady whose treatment at the hands of a German court presents an instructive picture of how the brainwashed judiciary of the *Bundesrepublik* deals with average citizens who do not toe the Bonn propaganda line.

On February 7, 1996, a court in Landsberg on the Lech, in Bavaria, (the same city where Adolf Hitler spent his nearly one year imprisonment in 1924), issued a *Strafbefehl* (writ of penalty), for a Mrs. B.C. According to this order, the accused had committed the following offenses:

1. She had mailed a letter written by a presently incarcerated, octogenarian German patriot containing his testimony before a court, and his treatise "39 points of evidence against the usual Auschwitz allegations," to a prosecutor in northern Germany, and a similar letter to another prisoner of the German political inquisition, named Bela (Ewald) Althans. In the treatise about the "39 points," the imprisoned elderly German patriot had doubted the mass murder of Jews in the gas chambers, and had questioned the alleged systematic extermination of the Jews.

2. During a search of the home of the accused lady, the police had discovered 25 copies of the letter by the octogenarian German patriot to a prosecutor in Osnabrück, and this proved, in the eyes of the court, that the lady had intended to mail these letters to others.

Because the "39 points" are considered an attack against the dignity of others (i.e., of the Jews), and because of the letter that was assumed to be mailed out along with these "39 points," the court had no recourse but to find that these acts proved the woman's continued identification with the National-Socialist ideology.

She was therefore found guilty of being in possession of written matter that incites to hate against national, racial, religious or *identifiable "successful" groups*, [12] of treading on human dignity, and of defaming others. Her crimes fall under

---

[12] This is a new one. The German courts are, on their own, constantly broadening the paragraphs under which the Jews can maintain their domination.

the paragraphs No. 130 and 53 of the German criminal code.

Without ever having seen her, or giving her a prior notification of a court date, the judge ordered her to pay 3,000 *deutschmarks* (about $2,000.00), or, if she cannot pay the fine, to a sentence of 30 days in jail.

Just as with a traffic ticket, she was notified where she could mail a check. And, also as in traffic cases, the woman was notified that she did have the opportunity to appear in court, and contest the case.

Mrs. C. thereupon wrote to the judge, informing him that certainly, she disagreed with the court.

She also pointed out that according to the detective with whom she had spoken after her house was searched, as a result of the confiscation of the offending 25 letters, the case had been resolved.

Mrs. C. furthermore explained that she had never mailed the "39 points" to the prisoner Bela (Ewald) Althans.

She had merely told him that this essay exists, and that he might be able to use it in his legal defense. She had also told Althans that he might request the "39 points" from the prosecutor in Osnabrück.

She had no knowledge of any *recorded* testimony in any German court.

In her letter, Mrs. C. pointed out to the judge that the real attacks against human dignity are directed against the German people, for the Allied war propaganda still being used against Germans--claims of brutality and crimes of which Germans are incapable.

She then asked that the writ of penalty be withdrawn.

Instead, she received the notification that her trial date was set for May 2, 1996.

Unfortunately, for quite some time before that date it had been arranged that just then the lady was supposed to be a speaker at a ceremony where her late father, a well-known poet, was to be honored. She therefore requested a new trial date.

This request was cursorily rejected by the court, with the remark that the planned event was not of sufficient importance to be grounds for a delay.

Three weeks later, on May 22 the court mailed Mrs. C. a judgment, *Im Namen des Volkes*! ("In the name of the people"), informing her that the judgment was correct, that the fine stands, and that she now also has to pay the court costs. [13]

Tragically (for the sense of justice pervading the German "justice" system), the court also informed Mrs. C. that it considered her absence on May 2nd as a "vacation" not allowed by law.

The rare occasion of the public honoring of her late father was, according to the court, not a valid reason to miss the session.

(Reading this we must remind ourselves that this legal matter did not even concern anything resembling a crime. It certainly cannot count more than a simple, non-accident related traffic ticket in the United States.)

The government of Helmut Kohl knows full-well that it transgresses against the most basic human rights and that it demeans human dignity while allowing the persecution of German dissidents, revisionists and patriots to continue.

Kohl's own assistant and vice chancellor, Wolfgang Schäuble, had this to say about the so-called *"Auschwitz Lüge"* law that provides legalistic underpinnings to this persecution:

"In the matter of the prosecutions regarding the Auschwitz

---

[13] Reading this I remembered that before May 8, 1945 the words "Im Namen des *deutschen* Volkes" were used. Slowly but surely they are trying to eradicate Germanity from the German people. How long will the words *"Dem deutschen Volke,"* chiseled above the entrance to the Reichstag in Berlin, remain?

lüge (lie),[14] *I will say only the following: Certainly, if we are speaking in an abstract sense, we would assume that from a judicial point of view it is nonsense to restrict freedom of opinion. But for us here today it is important and just that (this restriction of the freedom of opinion) is correct, even if from a strictly legal point of view one ought to regard the matter with skepticism."* (FAZ, April 24, 1996, page 41).

The Minister of Justice in the Kohl Government in 1996, Dr. E. Schmidt-Jortzig, admitted on television (channel 3--SAT, March 10, 1996, 7:10 pm), that his government transgresses against human rights:

"I find it rather depressing that we will soon receive from the United States government, and presented through the United Nations, not a formal complaint but a reprimand because of our punishing people as a result of the so-called Auschwitz lie, since obviously we are restricting freedom of expression this way."

In the summer of 1996 the German translation of the book *Hitler's Willing Executioners* by Daniel Jonah Goldhagen, was published, a book that spews incredible hate, lies and defamation against the German people.

Upon reaching the European market, we know that nothing was done by the Bonn authorities to prohibit the publishing or distribution of this work of pure sectarian hatred.

It is obviously permissible for Jews to print the most sinister

---

[14] In a manner reminiscent of George Orwell's book *1984*, German politicians do not mean the swindle of the "four-million-Jews-killed at Auschwitz" (that has now been admitted to have been false), when they use the term, *Die Auschwitz Lüge* ("The Auschwitz lie"). Quite the opposite, they claim that it is a lie not to believe this fantastic four million figure and associated falsehoods about the Auschwitz labor camp.

"blood libels" about the Germans, but Germans are not allowed to defend themselves and their parents and grandparents with alternative facts, contrary testimony and healthy skepticism.

Commenting on Goldhagen's book, the British newspaper *The Observer* wrote: "And thus this work is a single hymn of hate against the Germans."

Americans may wonder why so many Germans gave up on fighting against the blatant hate and insults that are *daily* directed against Germany and that are largely based upon the propaganda lies connected with the Second World War.

It bears remembering that in 1945 Germany was forced to capitulate *unconditionally,* and was thereafter totally at the mercy of the victors.

The millions of German war veterans who returned from the Allied POW camps had no greater desire than to rebuild their country and go on with their normal lives.

But the victors had no intention of letting "Germans be Germans," and instead, embarked on the greatest brainwashing scheme the world has ever seen.

This "re-education" (as the elaborate and totalitarian process of implanting into German minds an artificial and fabricated account of the war and its causes, was deceptively termed), forced the Germans to accept as true a type of Allied propaganda that they themselves, as still living witnesses of the war era, knew was utterly false.

In other words, the people who were the actual authorities on the war, the German combat veterans and the German civilians who had survived the savage fury of the Allies, were now rendered into "students" who must accept their former (?) enemy's version of events as the actual "reality."

If, for instance, a returning German soldier wanted his old teaching job back, he had to accept and teach the victors' fairy tales of what had transpired.

If the German veteran even once tried to tell his side of the story, he was foregoing all his chances for advancement or even employment. [15]

This occurred in all professions and trades but especially in the media, in academia, in politics and in religion. And thus, the Germans of the succeeding generations were indoctrinated into believing that things like the "gas chambers" happened exactly as depicted.

The present crop of prosecutors, judges, journalists and other public persons who are such staunch defenders of the 'Holocaust' religion are pitiable creatures in that they are German by blood and language *only*, but spiritually they can be called Jews.

They have accepted the anti-German and un-Christian hate standard of "Never forget, never forgive," as well as the concept of "The end justifies the means."

Their spirit has been captured by aliens. They are sick and therefore self-destructive. This sickness has been deliberately instilled in them. As a direct result, Germans have among the lowest birth-rates and highest abortion rates of any nation on earth. Many more Germans die every year in Germany than are

---

[15] Since I arrived in the United States but four years after the war had ended, I did not realize for a long time the extent of the brutal psychological methods used by the Allies (mainly under U. S. and Jewish tutelage), to brainwash the German people. As late as the 1960s I was dismayed that no German who had been a guard or even a kitchen chef in one of the major concentration camps came forward to tell the world what had really happened there. I did not know at that time, that even the most innocent German veteran, who would step forward and tell the world what he really saw and experienced, would, as punishment for his truth-telling, immediately have been accused of some horrible war crime (such as killing a sweet Jewish child with his bare hands). In his own defense, he would then have been forced to conform to the "Holocaust" story.

The fate of the Auschwitz agricultural expert Thies Christophersen, is a prime example of how an honest witness who spoke out against the lies, was mercilessly hounded and who today lives in exile in poverty, his health deteriorating.

born there. This is a pathological form of *genocide* that has been psychologically inculcated by the Allied/Jewish powers. It is the fulfillment of the American Jew Theodore Kaufman's extermination plan, as clearly outlined in his infamous 1941 book, *Germany Must Perish*.

As stated before, the German *Bundesrepublik*, one of the two original vassals of the Allied victors over the Reich, (the other having been the *Deutsche Democratische Republik* – Communist "East" Germany), was founded in 1949. Almost from the start it presented an aura of legitimacy that in later years was augmented by the frequent claim that "now Germany is again sovereign."

The fact is that to this day Germany is neither free or sovereign, and the Bonn Government is, in spite of all claims to the contrary, totally bereft of any legitimacy.

In order to understand the predicament of the *few* good Germans who at this time are still working for the Bonn Government (most of the politicians and civil servants by now having totally accepted alien philosophies), I shall include in this chapter the translation of the essence of the so-called *Überleitungsvertrag* (Treaty to Transfer Power), that was signed on May 26, 1952 between the Bonn stooges and the Western occupation powers, and which is still in force today.

I shall emphasize those sentences, which I deem so important for the understanding of the present German situation, for there is no evidence that the Bonn Government has ever tried to abrogate this treaty or any part of it:

"Article 2 (1): All rights and duties that are founded upon the laws, judicial measures and administrative actions of the occupation powers are and shall remain in force as if they are part of the basic German laws and actions. This shall be so

regardless whether these laws and actions agree with other law giving procedures. These laws, measures and administrative actions (by the Allied powers) shall also remain in force in the future, and have to be considered when new German laws are promulgated. (2) All rights and duties deriving from international laws relating to Germany which were instituted during the occupation, and which were valid on the day of the undersigning of this treaty, shall henceforth also remain in force, and be treated by Germany as if a German Government had negotiated and signed them."

For instance, in 1947 the Allied powers eradicated the German empire state of Prussia from the map, (an unheard of act in the annals of modern European history). Allegedly this was done because of the inherent militarism and aggression of Prussia. The fact remains, however, that in the 200 years before WWII, Prussia fought fewer wars than either France or England (and other nations). Prussia was eliminated because it had the most incorruptible, and Protestant government, something not to the liking of parliamentary democracies and the Vatican.

As a result of the *Überleitungsvertrag,* Germans cannot reestablish Prussia even if the German people as a whole voted for it in a plebiscite. A further result of this treaty is the Allied assumption that the Germans would "forever" have to abide by the Potsdam agreement that was responsible for the theft of a quarter of German Reich territory and the expulsion of upwards of 15 million Germans from their ancient homelands. The Allies seem to have forgotten that one-sided treaties are only valid as long as the former victors have the power to enforce them.

Although the *Überleitungsvertrag* was only signed by Bonn, the U.S.A., England and France, there are now indications that since the German reunification, Russia has also become part of it. I am specifically referring to the fact that in questions of German borders and sovereignty, the U.S.Government always sides with its old ally Russia instead of with the new (alleged) ally Germany.

For the sanity of all of us it might be best if I close this chapter on the dismal situation in Germany today on a lighter note. I must caution you, however, the story I am about to tell is true and does show that many people in Germany's public life now are presently not quite rational, and really ought to assign themselves to a psychiatric hospital.

In 1924, during his incarceration at Landsberg prison in Bavaria for the attempted Munich insurrection of November 9, 1923 (the so-called "Beer Hall Putsch"), Adolf Hitler wrote his famous book, *Mein Kampf.* During the *Führer's* lifetime, about eight million volumes of the book were sold or given away (all newlyweds in Germany received a copy during the Third Reich), and there is little doubt that a huge number of these books can still to be found in German homes.

When the war was over, the rights to *Mein Kampf,* as well as those of Hitler's personal possessions that still remained in Germany, became the property of the state of Bavaria, where Hitler had his personal domicile.

As the new legal owner of *Mein Kampf,* the Bavarian government granted permission to foreigners to translate the book into numerous languages, and sell it to the general public all over the world; except in the European lands where German is spoken. A reprinting of *Mein Kampf* in German was and is to this day strictly *verboten,* and foreign-language editions may not be sold to the German public.

The Ralph Manheim translation in English can be purchased in almost any reputable American bookstore but one will not find it in the foreign language section of the major booksellers in Munich or Berlin, and elsewhere in the *Bundesrepublik*. As a matter of fact, not very long ago the Bonn Government complained to the American military authorities that *Mein Kampf* in the English language was available in the "P.X." stores of the American occupation troops in Germany, and ought to be removed.

Recently, Joachim Fest, one of the former pillars of the German liberal establishment, the author of a best-selling Hitler biography and former editor of Germany's most influential newspaper, the *Frankfurter Allgemeine Zeitung*, called upon the Bavarians to lift the *Verbot* ("prohibition") against a German edition of *Mein Kampf*. The decision, under the jurisdiction of the finance minister of Bavaria, a politician named Georg von Waldenfels, was to deny Joachim Fest's request that Hitler's book be published in the *Bundesrepublik*.

Herr von Waldenfels claimed that *Mein Kampf* was spiritual nonsense, difficult to understand, and hard to read. He also stated that Hitler's work was now more useless than a cheap novel.

Using the Bavarian finance minister's reasoning, would it not make sense to print *Mein Kampf* by the millions and give it away for free so that the bulk of the Germans living now could fast recognize the falsity of the National Socialist ideology and become immune to it?

One must also wonder whether Mr. von Waldenfels has read the books written by Lenin, Stalin, Mao Tse Tung and the Communist dictator of "East" Germany, Erich Honnecker, that are freely available in Germany today. Are they *all* better written and of greater social value? Were the crimes of these political leaders less abhorrent than those of the "Nazis"?

Mr. von Waldenfels also claims that there is no demand for a

German reprinting of *Mein Kampf.* If that is so, then would it not make sense to permit a reprinting, at least in the interests of freedom of speech, and thereby show the world through a clear expression of non-interest, what the present-day Germans really think of the dead German *Führer?*

The Bavarian minister furthermore argues that a reprinting would certainly entail the necessity of advertising, and how would it look to the world if all over Germany one could suddenly see display cases showing a huge Hitler poster surrounded by copies of *Mein Kampf?*

This last claim by Von Waldenfels proves that he has not visited a bookstore for a long time, for there can be no denying that in German bookstores Hitler is well represented in both word and pictures. So-called Hitler literature fills book shelves everywhere, and year after year there are new additions to it. The appearance of a swastika on a mass market volume that has been approved by the kosher authorities, is routinely used as a promotional tactic to increase the profile and "visibility" of the book they seek to market.

Probably no other statesman of this era and our immediate future provides as many writers, publishers, and printers with work as does Adolf Hitler. This is especially true for professionals who belong to ideological circles where the questions, "What made Hitler possible?" and "How is it that so many Germans fell for his siren song?" are constantly being regurgitated.

Perhaps the most amusing aspect of Georg von Waldenfels' reasoning, and one that proves his and his cronies shortcomings and mental problems, is the one where he argues that *Mein Kampf* "is a symbol of National Socialism and as such must be withheld from the German public."

He claims that re-publication of the book in Germany would

awaken bad memories among the victims of the Third Reich still living there. Negating his own words, this Bavarian politician then permitted a Tel Aviv publisher to translate *Mein Kampf* into Hebrew, and sell it to the Israeli public, among whom are a greater number of so-called Nazi victims than anywhere else in the world!

Asked about this incongruity, Mr. von Waldenfels merely stated that, yes, he knows he is not very consistent in his decision but that there was certainly room for argument about it...

This can be said about nearly everything the *Bundesrepublik* servants of the Allies are deciding at present. They are the cause, not the symptom, for the sickness that pervades Germany right now.

Epilogue

This then is the story of my arrest and incarceration in allegedly 'free' Germany, for the crime of writing of things in the United States that Germans are not supposed to read about. Even in retrospect the entire matter conveys an aura of pure idiocy; of a government gone crazy in masochism, false and unwarranted guilt complexes, and the obvious desire to serve alien masters.

Apart from damage caused to my health as a result of five months of physical inactivity and the lack of sunlight, I came out all right. Now I am busier than ever and we have gained not only public recognition, but additional friends and supporters all over the world.

Furthermore, my own personal goals and aspirations are now more clear than ever; the enforced five months' contemplation accomplished wonders.

Officially, I cannot now visit Germany. The trial is merely being held in abeyance, and my lawyers are not permitted to continue the case in my absence, something done frequently in other judicial proceedings.

Allegedly, there is again a warrant out for my arrest should I set foot on German soil.[1]

I do not believe that the Bonn system is intent on going through the same shameful episode --so harmful to the image of this "most free state that ever existed on German soil"-- for a second time. If suddenly I should appear again at

---

[1] After I had flown back to the United States, leaving the matter "up in the air," some newspapers reported that the Germans were going to ask the U.S. Government to extradite me. I doubt that anyone in his right mind would want to do this after such a debacle for the system. But much more important is the fact that my "crimes" are not crimes in America (or in many other countries in the world), and therefore any talk of "extradition" either now or in the future is simply nonsense.

Frankfurt/Main airport, or any other German entry point, it is not at all certain that I would be imprisoned.

However, I do not see a need to make a test of it. The current political developments demand that I retain my freedom of movement under all circumstances.

Furthermore, indications are that the *world* political situation is now in such a flux that we may expect a blow-up of greatest dimensions (whether strictly political or mainly economic is immaterial) within the next couple of years.

If such a *world* catastrophe should occur then it will likely result in the collapse of the German political system as it was instituted by the victors of 1945 and it will free patriotic Germans from the bondage under which they have been held ever since. Obviously, this will affect my situation also.

Interestingly, numerous papers and memoranda issued by internationalist organizations such as the European Union, NATO, the Council of Foreign Relations, other sundry, and various governments, have fixed upon 2002 as the year when their ultimate goals shall be reached.

As a firm believer in the eventual victory of truth and justice, and being mindful that the groups working toward a one-world government have been building their entire artificial edifice on lies and deceit, I am convinced that the latter shall not win, and, furthermore, that their own timetable for victory will in fact be a terminus of defeat.

How dangerous is it for Americans to travel to Germany at the moment?

Perhaps the best answer would be: one simply doesn't know. In their fight for survival, and undoubtedly at least subconsciously being aware that the tide has already turned against them, the enemy vassals and beneficiaries of the Bonn system will undoubtedly employ even more repression to keep the German masses down.[2]

And, since by their own admission the *raison d'etre* of the *Bundesrepublik* revolves around the "truth of the Holocaust," we can expect that *to the very last minute of the system* everything will be done to uphold the myth. In other words, any writing or utterance that casts doubt on either the gas chamber tales, or on the alleged criminality of the Third Reich, will be persecuted to the fullest.

The fact that American citizens such as Fred Leuchter, Gerhard Lauck and Hans Schmidt were jailed in Germany, and American historian Richard Landwehr was fined without his knowledge, by Bonn, proves that no American citizen is safe from prosecution by the Bonn authorities. This is particularly true for Americans who work in publishing and other fields of mass communication.

The German computer magazine *Gateway* reported in its July 1996 issue, that Internet service providers have been ordered by the authorities in Bonn to censor all politically incorrect material that is being sent through their equipment. Should they be remiss in fulfilling this dictate, they face fines ranging between DM 200,000 and DM 3,000,000 ($130,000 to $2,000,000).

Already the Bonn government holds the world record in phone and computer tabs: they are used ten times as often as in the United States. The massive police raids against the German offices of CompuServe and America Online prove that

---

[2] One of the facts speeding the collapse of the Bonn system will be the spiritual confrontation arising from the difference in *Weltanschauung* between the West and "East" Germans. According to the New York Times of 6 May 1996, the entire Bonn establishment was a big loser a day before, when 6 million "East" Germans went to the polls. On that day, the inhabitants of the province of Brandenburg surrounding the capital of the Reich refused to see their state being combined with the city of Berlin, which contains 2 million West Berliners and innumerable foreigners. Personally, I regard this vote as a clear vote of non-confidence in the Bonn vassal system.

American companies are not immune from this repression. German courts would not hesitate to order the arrest of highly placed U.S. executives of companies that did not abide by Bonn's arcane laws that have no place in a civilized society.

In the appendix, the reader will find facsimiles of both an order for the opening of an investigation, as well as the court order for a house search, with the intent to confiscate the computer hardware and files of historical researcher Norbert H. Malzahn, who studies revisionist subjects. Bonn claims that this study constitutes an "incitement to hate."

In a letter from the Minister of Justice of the State of Mecklenburg-Vorpommern dated October 20, 1995,[3] to the prosecutor handling my case in Schwerin, reference is made to five thick file folders on me that were being mailed from the German Consulate General in New York to the court where I was scheduled to go on trial.

In this letter it is alleged that this writer (or in the case of our German-American organization, "we"), had advertised in publications such as *Jew Watch*, as well as a Ku Klux Klan magazine, and the *Sharkhunters* journal.

The fact is that neither Hans Schmidt or the organization he heads, have ever advertised in small publications. When we did advertise, our ads appeared in major newspapers such as the *Washington Times* and the *Washington Post*, for the express purpose of setting the record straight. As mentioned earlier, before major newspapers accepted our advertisements they scrutinized every word of our text, and we practically had to bring documentary proof of every statement we made. One could only wish that the establishment press were as vigilant with the ads and announcements of the "Holocaust" lobby and liberals.

---

[3] Reprinted in its original in the appendix.

The mention of the small magazine *Sharkhunters*[4] in conjunction with the (seemingly negative) file on me deserves closer analysis.

Sharkhunters is a publication solely geared toward fostering comradeship among former enemies, and for exchanging information among former veterans of all nations who served in their countries' submarine services.

Due to the fact that the Germans had one of the largest submarine fleets of World War II, and because they were most active in all the oceans, it follows that *Sharkhunters* prints more articles on the German U-Boats and their men, and on those Americans who had to deal with them during the war, than on any others.

But this seems precisely the reason why *Sharkhunters* found itself on the hit list of the ADL and other special interest, private eye outfits. According to the latter, it is a serious crime to regard World War II German soldiers in any other way but as criminals. For, did they not wear swastikas on their uniforms and enable Hitler to murder the mythical figure of six million Jews?

The fact that *Sharkhunters* is an absolutely apolitical publication, and that neither Hitler nor the Jews were ever mentioned either directly or by allusion, did not keep the ADL from professing alarm at the appearance of this specialized historical journal. For the ADL, and others like it, it is already a catastrophe when normal human beings view wars from the moral perspective of Christian civilization, in which hate ends when the shooting ends. This runs counter to the Old Testament "Eye for an Eye," and Talmudic "Never forget, never forgive" hatred.

---

[4] *Sharkhunters* magazine, Harry Cooper, publisher, P.O.Box 1539, Hernando, Florida 34442 USA

With *Sharkhunters* smeared as a "hate sheet" by the ADL and its sycophants who presume to dictate the norms of present-day social discourse, it follows that even the inadvertent possession of a copy of this magazine in Germany by an American citizen may lead to his or her arrest.

Or, if a former German submarine officer seeks to visit the United States, he may be turned away at the border because the Jews of the OSI (Office of Special Investigations of the U.S. Justice Department), have entered his name in the computers of the INS (Immigration and Naturalization Service of the United States), an agency that is currently also under Jewish control, simply because in World War II he fought on the losing side.[5]

What can we learn from my experiences? That the battle for freedom, of which the freedom of expression is an integral part, is never ending. There are always those who, for reasons of greed or lust for power, are trying to make the masses subservient to them. They clothe their purpose in the noblest of words, and they use unsavory laws and methods, outrageous lies, and devilish cunning to bend people to their will. Unfortunately, they often succeed, and then an era of darkness descends upon man and beast.

Nevertheless it is also a fact that in some people neither greed nor lust for power knows any limits, and this is usually their undoing. Eventually, as a result of the misuse of power, and the ever increasing brazenness of the liars, even the most blind among the masses sees through the lies and deceit, and

---

[5] Every German arriving in the United States for a visit has to sign a statement that in the time from March 23, 1933 (the very day when Judea declared war on Germany), to May 8, 1945, he did not participate in the persecution of the Jews. Idiotically, this statement also has to be given by persons born decades after the war. No such statement is required of those Russians who were alive during the era of the Soviet Red Army's persecution of Germans and Christians. This shows to what extent the United States has become an instrument in the execution of policies that are presumed to lead to the *pax judaica* in the world.

miraculously, as if God or nature has waved a wand, the truth prevails.

But Satan does not like to lose the prey he has pursued for so long and so avidly. Before he descends again into Hell, he will wreak such chaos and destruction that it will take mankind decades, if not centuries, to return to normal.

As this manuscript was being written, a prejudicial news item appeared in the *Toronto Sun* of June 22, 1996, and was brought to our attention. Additional jail time had been meted out to Günter Deckert, the German patriot, for merely *translating* a public oration by Fred Leuchter. This additional punishment, coming shortly after his new sentence was imposed, is just about the "best" news reporting about the Deckert case that one could wish for, in order to make clear to American readers of this book what our fight is all about.

The *Toronto Sun* headline referred to Deckert as a "Neo-Nazi". Apart from the question of what really constitutes a "Neo-Nazi," I can emphatically state that Deckert is first and foremost a German patriot, and neither he or millions of other German patriots want to turn the clock back.

Germans are not like the Jews who seem to thrive on recalling the past (real or imagined). For the *Toronto Sun* to use this terminology is simply insidious. One must wonder, for instance, how many times this same newspaper had used the designation "terrorist" for either Yitzshak Shamir or Menachem Begin when they were in the public eye.

The article states quite clearly why Deckert received an additional sentence of 20 months in jail (allegedly for "inciting racial hatred"), unfortunately, no American or Canadian newspaper will print an article spelling out what really occurred, and what Deckert truly had said or written.

The judge in Weinheim, Dieter Herbig, claims that Deckert

"was no martyr, but rather someone who plays fast and loose with historical truth." I wonder how this judge might someday react if he is accused for malfeasance in office (as a result of this case), and in defense of his life, may have to prove all the historical facts which at this time he believes to be true.

Would Judge Herbig be able to document six million Jewish dead, and killings in gas chambers at Auschwitz, or a determined attempt by the National Socialist Government to exterminate all the European Jews in a court of law where normal judicial procedures were followed and *forensic* evidence of the alleged genocide was demanded? Will the judge be able to prove the collective innocence of the *Oberjuden* after Israel becomes the first country since 1945 to unleash nuclear weapons on innocent civilians? I doubt it.

Lastly, this additional sentence for Günter Deckert (and the heavy sentence of four years meted out to the American Gerhard Lauck) also prove that I did right in not waiting for my second trial date that was supposed to have taken place on January 11, 1996.

While it is true that all indicators pointed to the fact that Judge Heydorn would have had to either acquit me or let me off with a slap on the wrist, and it is doubtful that I would have been remanded to the Bützow penitentiary; I am also certain that by that day our greatest enemies would have taken notice of the fiasco for them that had occurred on the first day of the trial, and they would have been better prepared. There was a better than even chance that I would have been re-arrested on other trumped-up charges, by another German jurisdiction upon leaving the court room as a free man on January 11th, and that is something that I could not afford.

For the time being Germany has to get along without my presence. But I am also convinced that I shall be seeing a truly free and sovereign *Deutschland* much sooner than any of the Allied vassals in Bonn, and their henchmen, expect today.

Patriots and revisionists are putting their very lives on the line every day in this struggle against the annihilation of the German people (for that is the ultimate goal of the constant defamation of all things truly German).

79 year old German author Thies Christophersen, who had been hounded from his homeland by the Bonn renegades, because he had been one of the very first eyewitnesses to term the homicidal gas chamber allegations, "the Auschwitz lie," returned to Germany in 1997 after years in exile, that he might die on the soil of his beloved homeland.

Even though he was dying, Helmut Kohl's merciless bureaucrats still sought to jail him. Only reluctantly was Christophersen allowed to go free, after being medically certified as having terminal cancer, with only two weeks to live.

On Feb. 13, 1997, fifty-two years to the day on which the British commenced the deliberate firebombing of the undefended city of Dresden, Thies Christophersen, who had been present at that inferno, died in Kiel, Germany, having spent his life in service to his people.

With calculated malice, the "German" authorities forbade the last honors to be given in the hometown of the deceased, and when a memorial service was held in Kiel, the officials demanded a list of those in attendance, the text of the eulogies, and they ordered that only prescribed funeral music be played.

Let us also remember historian Udo Walendy and writers Günter Deckert and Gerhard Lauck who, as this book goes to press, continue to languish in Bonn's dungeons.

We are the vehicles who bear within us the spark of a truth that will not die. This struggle is eternal. Let us be worthy of it by our sacrifice and our loyalty.

Appendix I: Revisionists and the Internet

The anti-Germans and their Bonn stooges are redoubling their efforts to stifle free speech, and prosecute those who question their motives.

For Americans, the following is of special interest because it concerns the ultimate instrument of free expression, namely, the Internet, and because it crosses international boundaries.

Shortly after the Los Angeles-based Simon Wiesenthal Center sent out a fundraising letter explaining that the Center now devotes 80 percent of its time trying to stop "hate propaganda" on the Internet, Ernst Zündel, the indefatigable German-Canadian freedom fighter, received notice from the German Government's official censorship office that no fewer than eight of Zündel's postings on his Internet "Zündelsite," had been placed in the index of forbidden literature.

Of course what the Simon Wiesenthal Center calls hate propaganda is typically little more than criticism of and skepticism toward the unrelenting World War II-era tall tales the Wiesenthal Center still spews out from its various offices throughout the world.

Dated August 15th, 1996, and emanating from Bonn's Orwellian "Federal Office for the Censorship of Literature that is harmful to Youth," (*Bundesprüfstelle für jugendgefährdende Schriften*), with offices at Kennedyallee 105-107, 53175 Bonn, Germany, the following text was mailed in eight separate letters to Zündel's Toronto address, letters that arrived after the time for objection had passed:

Indexing (of forbidden literature) according to the law against the dissemination of writings harmful to youth.

It is herewith proposed that the following matter which has been disseminated over the Internet Zündelsite be placed on the index of writings that are harmful to youth. (refer to the eight titles below) The reason for this decision is as follows:

This program available through Internet is according to

Statute 1, Article 1, Sentence 1 of the GjS (Law for the censoring of writings harmful to Youth) and in agreement with prior decisions of this office, considered dangerous to youth and children, and can lead to disorient them ethically.

This program propagates national-socialist and right wing extremist ideology by denying the crimes of national-socialism, thereby restoring the reputation of the Hitler regime. At the same time it leads to a restoring of the National Socialist ideology through the dissemination of historical falsehoods, and this can lead to the creation of false goals in young people.

(signed) Dr. Schulz

The titles of the indexed books appearing on the Zündelsite (http://www.webcom.com/-ezundel/english) programs are as follows:

THE LEUCHTER REPORT: END OF A MYTH
AUSCHWITZ: MYTHS AND FACTS
INSIDE THE GAS CHAMBERS
A PROMINENTLY FALSE WITNESS: ELIE WIESEL
NOT JUDICIAL NOTICE BUT JUSTICE
HOLOCAUST DENIAL: WHAT IS IT?
PRESSAC'S NEW AUSCHWITZ BOOK
THE DEVELOPMENT OF A HOLOCAUST REVISIONIST

After receiving the eight registered letters from the Bonn regime, Ernst Zündel immediately contacted his German lawyer, Dr. Jürgen Rieger in Hamburg, who wrote the following to the Bonn censors:

Dear Mrs. Monssen-Engberding:

I am herewith giving notice that I am representing Ernst Zündel of Canada.

I am asking you to withdraw your office's intention to place the named Zündelsite programs on your index.

My reasons are as follows:

Your office has no jurisdiction, since its function is merely to concern itself with printed literature, and audio and visual tapes.

Your reasons for indexing are so scant that it is impossible for me as a lawyer to comment on the matter. Not one sound reason is presented why Zündel's writings are supposed to be harmful to youth.

You may contact my office with your final decision.

In addition, I would like to add the following comment regarding your actions:

Seemingly, it is sufficient for you to mention that a person is a historical revisionist. This provides you with the grounds for placing his statements on your index.

I would like to point out that the European Union has refused to acknowledge and accept the German laws upon which your actions are based, and there are indications that at the United Nations an official reprimand will be issued against the *Bundesrepublik* because its laws pertaining to the prohibition of the questioning of the gas chamber are clearly against the basic human right to freedom of expression.

It seems that the *Bundesrepublik* is ever more moving backwards into the dark ages, and that the restrictions against free speech become ever more stringent. In doing so, the *Bundesrepublik* constantly moves further away from the judicial standards prevailing elsewhere in the world.

May I suggest that in the future you do not give people accused by you only one week to respond to eight different charges; why not just wait until you have a dozen accusations for any one person, and then mail them together with the admonition that the accused has but one day to respond, especially if he is located overseas. This way you would still have fulfilled your obligations, and satisfied the letter of the law.

Sincerely, J.Rieger, Esq.

P.S.: And come next (and every following) month of May, please do not forget to express your abhorrence about the "evil Nazis who burned books!"

With regard to Attorney Rieger's letter, the question must be asked again, what are the Bonn stooges and the Simon Wiesenthal Center afraid of? Isn't the truth as to what happened in World War II strong enough to stand on its own feet?

What kind of truth is it that has to be safeguarded by law? How many Americans know that in Germany the "genocide of the Six Million" must be believed under pain of fine and imprisonment? Doubting any part of it will be punished with up to five years in jail without the possibility of parole.

It appears that the anti-Germans are going to have their hands full in the years ahead, attempting to police "cyberspace" and obstruct the Internet, which was initially designed to withstand a nuclear war. The Bonn regime is a System built on lies. No wonder they are so desperate to censor truths transmitted by means of the Internet.

Readers who have Internet access may wish to consult the

following revisionist sites:

The Zündelsite:
http://alpha.ftcnet.com/~freedom/cfsl/index.html

Bradley Smith's Committee for Open Debate:
http://www.codoh.com

The Campaign for Radical Truth in History:
http://www.hoffman-info.com

Appendix II: Documents

ZENTRALRAT DER JUDEN IN DEUTSCHLAND
Körperschaft des öffentlichen Rechts

An den
Präsidenten der Max-Planck-Gesellschaft
zur Förderung der Wissenschaft e.V.
Herrn Prof. Hanns F. Zacher
Hofgartenstr. 2

8000 München 2

SEKRETARIAT
Neue Postleitzahl: 53173
5300 Bonn 2 - Bad Godesberg
Rüngsdorfer Straße 6
Telefon 02 28 / 35 70 23-24
Telefax 02 28 / 36 11 48

22. Juni 1993

Sehr geehrter Herr Prof. Zacher!

Der Vorsitzende des Direktoriums des Zentralrats der Juden in Deutschland, Ignatz Bubis, hat Ihnen in einem Telefonat am 16.04.1993 seine Besorgnis über die Wirkung des "Gutachtens ..." des Dipl.-Chem. Germar Rudolf mitgeteilt.

Der Verwaltungsrat des Zentralrats hat sich eingehend mit den Unterlagen und der Wirkung des Gutachtens auseinandergesetzt. Er teilt die Sorge des Vorsitzenden, daß dieses "Gutachten" nur allzu leicht als pseudowissenschaftlicher Nachweis für die Leugnung des Massenmordes an den Juden benutzt werden kann. Dies ist - wie bekannt - durch die Verwendung durch O. E. Remer geschehen.

Der Zentralrat der Juden in Deutschland erwartet von Ihnen, sehr geehrter Herr Prof. Zacher, daß geeignete Maßnahmen seitens der Max-Planck-Gesellschaft und des Max-Planck-Institutes ergriffen werden, die weitere Betätigungen des Gutachters verhindern.

Die Presseerklärung des Pressereferates der Max-Planck-Gesellschaft vom 21.04.1993 ist ausführlich, verhindert aber keine weitere Betätigung des Dipl.-Chem. G. Rudolf.

Mit freundlichen Grüßen

Heinz Jaeckel

Appendix II: Documents

DER PRÄSIDENT
DER MAX-PLANCK-GESELLSCHAFT
ZUR FÖRDERUNG DER WISSENSCHAFTEN

POSTFACH 101062 – RUF 2108212
RESIDENZSTRASSE 1A · EINGANG HOFGARTENSTRASSE
8000 MÜNCHEN L 14. Juli 1993
BI/Wi

Herrn
Heinz Jaeckel
Zentralrat der Juden
in Deutschland
Rüngsdorfer Str. 6

5300 Bonn 2 - Bad Godesberg

Sehr geehrter Herr Jaeckel,

für Ihren Brief vom 22. Juni danke ich Ihnen. Ich darf Ihnen mitteilen, daß die Max-Planck-Gesellschaft das Dienstverhältnis mit Herrn Rudolf mit Schreiben vom 7.6.93 fristlos gelöst hat.

Weitere Möglichkeiten, das Verhalten von Herrn Rudolf in Zukunft zu kontrollieren, hat die Max-Planck-Gesellschaft nicht. Ich nehme an, daß Sie darin mit mir übereinstimmen.

Mit schönen Grüßen
Ihr

Hans F. Zacher

Proof of how the Bonn Government lies to the German people:

On the occasion of the 50th anniverary of the capitulation of the German armed forces of World War II on 8 May 1995, British prime minister John Major was invited to Berlin, to take part in the German ceremonies marking the end of the war. Below is the reprint of an important paragraph of Major's speech, as it was given to us by the British Government:

Fifty years ago Europe saw the end of the 30 Years War, 1914 to 1945. The slaughter in the trenches, the destruction of cities and the oppression of citizens: all these left a Europe in ruins just as the other 30 Years War did three centuries before.

We translated this statement correctly in the sense as it was meant thusly:
"Vor 50 Jahren erlebte Europa das Ende des dreißigjährigen Krieges 1914-45. Das Gemetzel in den Schützengräben, die Zerstörung der Städte und die Unterdrückung der Bürger hatten Europa genau so in Ruinen gelassen, wie in dem früheren Dreißgjährigen Krieg, der vor drei Jahrhunderten geschah."

The Bonn vassals, however, purposely mistranslated this paragraph this way:

Vor fünfzig Jahren erlebte Europa das Ende der dreißig Jahre, die nicht einen, sondern zwei Weltkriege beinhaltet hatten. Das Gemetzel in den Schützengräben, die Zerstörung der Städte und die Unterdrückung der Bürger hinterließen ein Europa in Trümmern, gerade wie es einige Jahrhunderte zuvor der Dreißigjährige Krieg getan hatte.

Note John Major's first sentence. It says: "Fifty years ago Europe saw the end of the 30 Years War, 1914 to 1945." "Bonn" translated this as follows: "Fifty years ago, Europe saw the end of the thirty years that contained not only one but two World Wars."

This raises the question, why would the Bonn people purposely mistranslate this? Since they are constantly ruining the German language with unneeded Anglicisms, one cannot assume that they don't know English well enough for correct translation. Regretably, their motives are much more sinister.

John Major's sentence, read correctly, means that Adolf Hitler cannot be solely blamed for starting World War II, since a war already being fought (i.e., a war that began in 1914) cannot really be started. Unfortunately for Bonn however, the foundations of this postwar "German" republic are based upon the demonization of Hitler, and the neverending acknowledgement of German guilt, including full responsibility for starting the war. Without this dishonest foundation, Bonn is doomed. Therefore, all efforts are being made to keep the knowledge of such facts from the German people; - - - if necessary with obvious lies such as this.

GANPAC, P.O.Box 11124, Pensacola, FL 32524-1124 USA

Appendix II: Documents

ANTI-DEFAMATION LEAGUE
130 N WELLS ST., SUITE 1418
CHICAGO, ILLINOIS
PHONE FRANKLIN 2247

December 13, 1933

TO THE PUBLISHERS OF ANGLO-JEWISH PERIODICALS

Gentlemen:

Scribner & Sons have just published a book by Madison Grant entitled "The Conquest of a Continent." It is extremely antagonistic to Jewish interests. Emphasized throughout is the "Nordic superiority" theory, and the utter negation of any "melting pot" philosophy with regard to America.

Scribners, in a sales circular concerning the book, points to Herr Hitler as the man who has demonstrated the value of "racial purity" in Germany. The author insists that American development depends upon the elimination of unassimilable alien masses in our midst. This book is considered by some as even more destructive than Hitler's "Mein Kampf." Mr. Grant also avers that "national problems are in the end racial problems."

We are interested in stifling the sale of this book. We believe that this can be best accomplished by refusing to be stampeded into giving it publicity. Every review or public criticism of a book of this character brings it to the attention of many who would otherwise know nothing of it. This results in added sales. The less discussion there is concerning it, the more sales resistance will be created.

We therefore appeal to you to refrain from comment on this book, which will undoubtedly be brought to your attention sooner or later. It is our conviction that a general compliance with this request will sound the warning to other publishing houses against engaging in this type of venture.

Sincerely yours,

Richard E. Gutstadt,
Director

REG:EF

THIS LETTER IS PROOF THAT THE ADL HASN'T CHANGED IN SIXTY YEARS.

Jailed in 'Democratic' Germany: The Ordeal of An American Writer

Justizvollzugsanstalt
Bützow

Buchnummer
1708/95

Einweisungsbehörde — Geschäftsnummer
AG Schwerin-34 Gs 350/95

Tag
04.01.1996

Entlassungsschein

Familienname (ggf. auch Geburtsname) — Vornamen
Schmidt, Hans

Geburtstag — Geburtsort — Kreis
27.04.1927-Völklingen

Beruf
Kaufmann

Wohnort / letzter Aufenthaltsort
66333 Völklingen/Luisenthal, Parkstr. 1

Haftdauer von/bis
09.08.1995-04.01.1996

Entlassungsgrund (z. B. Strafende, Aufhebung des Haftbefehls)
Haftentlassung

Personalausweis vorhanden (ja/nein)

Auflagen und Bedingungen (ggf. Name und Anschrift des Bewährungshelfers)

Teilnahme an berufsfördernden Maßnahmen während der Haft (Art und Dauer)

1. Entlassen nach (Ort, Straße): **w.o.**

2. Unterkunft — nach seiner Angabe — durch Vermittlung der Anstalt — bei:

3. Arbeit — angebahnt — vorhanden — nach seiner Angabe — durch Vermittlung der Anstalt — bei:

4. Eigene Kleidung a) Umfang: **reichlich**
                    b) Zustand: **gut**

5. Bei der Entlassung sind folgende Bekleidungsstücke gegeben worden:

6. — Gutschein für — Fahrkarte nach _____ wurde — nicht — ausgehändigt.

7. Bei der Entlassung erhalten:
   a) Vorhandenes Guthaben   **1423,75** DM
      davon Überbrückungsgeld bzw. als solches zu behandeln ____ DM
      (besonderer Pfändungsschutz: vgl. § 51 Abs. 4 und 5 StVollzG)
   b) Beihilfe zu den Reisekosten   ____ DM
      (besonderer Pfändungsschutz: vgl. § 75 Abs. 3 Satz 1 StVollzG)
   c) Überbrückungsbeihilfe   ____ DM
      (besonderer Pfändungsschutz: vgl. § 75 Abs. 3 Satz 2 StVollzG)
      Summe   ____ DM

   Abzüge für Fahrkarte / Kleidung   ____ DM

   Summe   ____ DM

   Davon überwiesen an _____   ____ DM

   in bar wurden ausgezahlt   **1423;75** DM

Nachträgliche Fürsorgemaßnahmen und
Zuwendungen bitte auf der Rückseite vermerken

Der Anstaltsleiter
I.
(Unterschrift, Amtsbezeichnung)

VG 44 Entlassungsschein - Nr. 54 VGO - gen. 10. 1990
       JVA Rheinbach Preisklasse 12

Appendix II: Documents

Landgericht Schwerin
Große Strafkammer 3

19053 Schwerin, Demmlerplatz 1-2
Telefon: 74150
Telefax: 7415 183

Herrn Rechtsanwalt
Haja Hermann
Friedrichstraße 11

40217 Düsseldorf

Geschäfts-Nr. (bei allen Schreiben angeben)	Strafkammer	Zimmer d. Gesch.Stelle	Fernsprecher (Durchwahl)	Datum
33 Kls 51/95	3	107	0385/7415 110	24.10.1995

Strafsache

gegen   Hans Schmidt

Sehr geehrter Herr Rechtsanwalt,

Auf Anordnung des Gerichts wird Ihnen anliegend die Anklageschrift zugestellt.

Falls Sie die Vornahme einzelner Beweiserhebungen vor der Entscheidung über die Eröffnung des Hauptverfahrens beantragen oder Einwendungen gegen die Eröffnung des Hauptverfahrens vorbringen wollen, so muß diese binnen **2 Wochen** nach Zustellung dieser Anklageschrift unter Angabe der Gründe schriftlich in deutscher Sprache oder zu Protokoll der Geschäftsstelle erfolgen. Die Tatsachen, die Sie beweisen wollen, und die Beweismittel hierfür (Urkunden, Zeugen, Sachverständige, Tatortbesichtigung) müssen genau angegeben werden.

Zusatz: Die formelle Zustellung ist an Ihren Mandanten erfolgt.

Wendt
Justizangestellte

Staatsanwaltschaft Schwerin

Aktenzeichen: 111 Js 826/95

An das
Landgericht Schwerin
Große Strafkammer 3
Demmlerplatz 1-2

19053 Schwerin

Schwerin, 18.10.1995
ko-eh

HAFT!
Haftprüfungstermin
gem. §§ 121,122 StPO
am 08.02.1996

Anklageschrift

Den Kaufmann
Hans Schmidt

geboren am 27.04.1927 in Völklingen,
wohnhaft 32504 Pensacola/Florida/USA,
Amerikaner und nach eigenen Angaben zugleich deutscher Staatsbürger, verheiratet,

- in dieser Sache festgenommen am 09.08.1995 (Bd.I Bl.74 d.A.) und seit demselben Tage aufgrund des Haftbefehls des Amtsgerichts Schwerin vom 28.03.1995 (Bd. I Bl. 33f. d.A.) - 34 Gs 350/95 - in Untersuchungshaft, zur Zeit in der JVA Bützow zu Gefangenen-Buch-Nr. 1708/95;
Haftbefehl abgeändert durch Beschluß des Amtsgerichts Schwerin vom 05.10.1995 (Bd. II Bl. 152ff. d.A.) -

<u>Verteidiger:</u>
Rechtsanwalt Hajo Hermann,
Friedrichstraße 11, 40217 Düsseldorf (Bd. I Bl. 83 d.A.)

klage ich an,

in Schwerin und anderenorts,
in der Zeit vom 23. Dezember 1993 bis 25. April 1995,

durch 12 Straftaten,

in den Fällen 1. und 5.

in einer Weise, die geeignet ist, den öffentlichen Frieden zu stören, die Menschenwürde anderer dadurch angegriffen zu haben, daß er sie beschimpft, böswillig verächtlich gemacht und verleumdet hat,

Appendix II: Documents

und durch dieselbe Handlung,

Schriften, die zum Rassenhaß aufstacheln oder die grausame oder sonst unmenschliche Gewalttätigkeit gegen Menschen in einer Art schildern, die eine Verherrlichung oder Verharmlosung solcher Gewalttätigkeiten ausdrückt, oder die das Grausame oder Unmenschliche des Vorgangs in einer die Menschenwürde verletzenden Weise darstellen, hergestellt, in den räumlichen Geltungsbereich des Strafgesetzbuches eingeführt und verbreitet zu haben,

in den Fällen 2. - 4., 6. - 8. sowie 10. - 12.

in einer Weise, die geeignet ist, den öffentlichen Frieden zu stören, die Menschenwürde anderer dadurch angegriffen zu haben, daß er Teile der Bevölkerung beschimpft, böswillig verächtlich gemacht und verleumdet hat,

und hierbei jeweils

tateinheitlich

Schriften, die zum Haß gegen Teile der Bevölkerung oder gegen eine religiöse Gruppe aufstacheln und deren Menschenwürde dadurch angreifen, daß sie beschimpft, böswillig verächtlich gemacht und verleumdet werden, hergestellt, eingeführt und verbreitet zu haben,

wobei sich die Tathandlung in

den Fällen 2. - 4. und 6. - 8.

jeweils auf solche Schriften bezog, in welchen eine unter der Herrschaft des Nationalsozialismus begangene Handlung der in § 220a Abs. 1 StGB bezeichneten Art geleugnet oder verharmlost wurde

sowie in den Fällen 1. - 9.

jeweils zugleich

das Andenken Verstorbener verunglimpft zu haben.

Der Angeschuldigte ist Verfasser und Herausgeber der Druckschriften "USA-Bericht", "GANPAC-Briefe" sowie von ihm so überschriebener "Offener Briefe", die er in den Vereinigten Staaten herstellt und dort von verschiedenen Orten aus in nicht näher bekannter Anzahl auch in die Bundesrepublik Deutschland versendet.
Soweit es sich um Schriften sowie um Briefe strafbaren Inhalts handelt, werden dem Angeschuldigten folgende Tathandlungen zur Last gelegt:
Zu 1.:

(Hauptakten Bd. I):

Mit Poststempel vom 04. November 1994 versandte der Angeschuldigte aus Burke, Virginia (USA) die Schrift "USA-Bericht, November 1994" an die Adresse "Land Mecklenburg, Bundesrat CDU: Rudi Geil, Karl-Marx-Straße 1, 19055 Schwerin", welche im Innenministerium des Landes Mecklenburg-Vorpommern am 09.11.1994 einging. Bestandteil dieser Schrift ist ein "Offener Brief" des Beschuldigten vom 08.05.1994 an den Journalisten Martin Klingst, der zu dessen Artikel "Neuer Terror" in der Wochenzeitung "Die Zeit" vom 17.12.1993 Stellung nimmt. In diesem "Offenen Brief" ist unter anderem ausgeführt:

"Aber jedesmal, wenn ich mich an meinen Computer (EDV-Gerät) setzte, um die Sache so eingehend wie möglich zu behandeln, machten mir die amerikanischen Oberjuden einen Strich durch die

Rechnung. Offensichtlich sind diese nun wegen des sich in den USA breitmachenden Zweifels an der Holocaust-Geschichte und wegen der offenen polemischen Angriffe gegen sie seitens der Neger in einer derart panischen Stimmung, daß kaum ein Tag vergeht, an dem sie nicht ein neues "Holocaust"-Märchen in die Welt setzen, das natürlich von jemandem wie mir, der sich seit fast einem halben Jahrhundert in den USA politisch aktiv für die Belange unseres deutschen Volkes und unserer deutschen Nation einsetzt, berichtigt werden muß.

Ihren Brief lesend fällt einem auf, daß auch Sie unter einem vielleicht unbewußten Angstzustand leiden. Sie erwähnen nämlich gleich am Anfang Ihres Artikels mit offensichtlichem Schrecken, daß ein kleines, rechtes Magazin eine Liste von sage und schreibe 250 Menschen - Politiker, Juristen, Schriftsteller, Bürgermeister, Sozialarbeiter, Journalisten, Lehrer, Unternehmer - veröffentlicht hat, die wegen ihrem "mutigen Eintreten für eine liberale Ausländerpolitik" und ihrem "beherzten Widerstand gegen rechtsextremistische Umtriebe" als Feinde Deutschlands von den Rechten auszuschalten seien.

Als ich dies las, mußte ich lachen. Wissen Sie, wieviele Deutsche <u>meiner Ansicht nach</u> nach dem kommenden Umsturz in Deutschland aus dem öffentlichen Leben unserer Nation entfernt werden müssen? An die 100 000! Und gerade in den von Ihnen genannten Berufen (man vergaß Professoren und Fernsehlügner auf der Liste). Ich gehe bei dieser Zahl von der Anzahl der von den Alliierten und ihren Helfershelfern ermordeten französischen Kollaborateure aus, die 1944/45 wegen ihrer Freundschaft oder Zusammenarbeit mit Deutschland ihr Leben lassen mußten. Um aber nicht falsch verstanden zu werden: Ich schlage nicht vor, daß die ca. 100 000 schlimmsten deutschen Handlanger <u>unserer</u> Feinde hingerichtet werden sollen.

Tatsächlich bin ich der Meinung, daß nur ganz wenige der ärgsten Vaterlandsverräter ihren Kopf verlieren sollen, und wenn eine derartige Hinrichtung stattfindet, so soll sie, wenn auch hunterprozentig rechtens, doch wegen der Stellung der betreffenden Person einen erheblichen symbolischen Wert haben.

Der Hauptgrund, warum ich gegen viele Hinrichtungen bin, hat nichts mit Pietät zu tun, die verlor ich nach dem Krieg, als ich sah, wie die Alliierten mit den unsrigen umgingen. Ich denke aber, daß wir für Jahrzehnte nach dem Umsturz (bis 2033, da dieser Zeitpunkt vom 9. November 1989, dem Tag der Wende, genau so lang entfernt ist wie der 8. Mai 1945) Prozesse abhalten müssen, in denen man im Interesse der Wahrheitsfindung und geistigen Gesundung Deutschlands alle diejenigen zur Rechenschaft zieht, die sich so sehr an unserem Volk und unserer Nation vergangen haben. Und für derartige Prozesse braucht man, um der Wahrheit zu dienen, lebende Zeugen. <u>Wen meine ich?</u>

Die Politiker, die seit Kriegsende unser Volk nach Strich und Faden belogen und betrogen haben. Ich brauche dabei keine Namen der jetzt noch Lebenden zu nennen, die kürzlich bekanntgewordenen "Geheimnisse" über verstorbene Politiker wie Brandt, Wehner und Strauss sollten genügen. Gibt es überhaupt noch Deutsche, die annehmen, daß die gerade jetzt in Bonn herrschenden Feindvasallen anders sind? Über deren Lügen und Missetaten werden wir, wie gewöhnlich, erst nach ihrer Verhaftung oder ihrem Tod unterrichtet werden. Ich hoffe, daß dies bald unter der Schirmherrschaft eines ordentlichen deutschen (Reichs-)gerichtes geschehen kann.

Die Staatsanwälte und Richter, die entgegen ihrem eigenen, von unseren Feinden eingeführten Grundgesetz das Recht der Meinungsfreiheit mit den Füßen treten. Besonders hinsichtlich des sogenannten "Holocaust" erlassen sie (wohl aus religiösen Gründen, die aber in offensichtlichem Konflikt mit dem Deutschsein stehen) sich auf eine angebliche "Offenkundigkeit" berufende Urteile, die allem Recht Hohn sprechen. Später, wenn diese Menschen zur Rechenschaft gezogen werden, soll man an das Schick-

Appendix II: Documents

sal deutscher Patrioten wie Ernst Zündel, Erhard Kemper, Günther Deckert, T. Rudolph usw. denken und genau so viel Mitleid mit diesen dann vielleicht alten Juristen haben, wie sie es derzeit für General Remer, einen deutschen Helden, bezeugen."

Weiter ist ausgeführt:

"(...) Historiker wie Eberhard Güchel, der als sogenannter Holocaust-Experte eifrig dabei ist, im Interesse unserer Feinde die Sechsmillionen-Mär aufrechtzuerhalten."

Weiter heißt es in dieser Schrift:

"...mein Gott, was haben Leute wie Sie sich eigentlich gedacht? Es waren die Linken, die Chaoten, die juden- und freimaurerverseuchten politischen Systemparteien und die Lizenzpresse, die seit Jahrzehnten Jagd auf alles Nationale machten: brutal, intolerant, unnachgiebig, haßerfüllt".

Zu 2.:

(Fallakte 1):

Mit Poststempel vom 19.12.1994 versandte der Angeschuldigte aus Burke/Virgina (USA) die Schrift "USA-Bericht, November 1994" mit dem unter Ziffer 1. genannten Inhalt auch an die Staatsanwaltschaft Kiel, bei der dieses Schreibem am 09.01.1995 einging.

Zu 3.:

(Fallakte 2):

Mit Poststempel vom 19.12.1994 versandte der Angeschuldigte dieselbe Schrift - wiederum aus Burke/Virgina (USA) - auch an die Adresse "Staatsanwaltschaft, Westring 8, 4630 Bochum 1", wo das Schreiben - welches dort nicht mit einem Eingangstempel versehen wurde - spätestens am 29.12.1994 einging.

Zu 4.:

(Fallakte 3):

Ebenfalls mit Poststempel vom 19.12.1994 übersandte der Angeschuldigte ein ebensolches Schreiben an die Adresse "Staatsanwaltschaft Bochum, Reitzensteinstraße 17, 4350 Recklinghausen, wo das Schreiben - welches ebenfalls nicht mit einem Eingangstempel versehen wurde - spätestens am 04.01.1995 einging.

Zu 5.:

(Fallakte 4):

An einem nicht genau bekannten Zeitpunkt zwischen dem 08. Mai und dem 08. Juni 1994 übersandte der Angeschuldigte einen mit 08. Mai 1994 datierten Brief mit dem unter 1. beschriebenen Inhalt an die Adresse : "Martin Klingst, DIE ZEIT, Postfach 10-6820, 2000 Hamburg 1".

Zu 6.:

(Fallakte 5):

An einem nicht genau bekannten Zeitpunkt zwischen dem 09. März und dem 21. März 1995 übersandte der Angeschuldigte ein Schreiben mit folgendem Inhalt an Professor Dr. Michael Wolffsohn in München:

Jailed in 'Democratic' Germany: The Ordeal of An American Writer

"Hans Schmidt

9. März 1995

P.O.Box 11124
Pensacola, FL 32524-1124
USA
FAX (904) 478-4993

Herrn Professor Dr. Michael Wolffsohn
Professor für Neuere Geschichte
Bundeswehr-Universität
Werner Heisenberg-Weg 39
85579 Neubiberg   Germany

OFFENER BRIEF

Lieber Michael!

Ich hoffe, Du hast nichts dagegen, wenn ich nach amerikanischer Art das "Du" gebrauche. Immerhin haben wir uns schon einmal in Washington kennengelernt - sogar kurz gesprochen - und außerdem haben wir eine ganze Anzahl von gemeinsamen Bekannten (hier wie da). Vielleicht gelingt es mir, Dich durch den Gebrauch der persönlichen Anrede dazu zu bringen, Deine angeborene Scheu abzulegen und mir diesen nun achten Brief zu beantworten. Immerhin behandle ich in diesen Schreiben das wohl wichtigste Problem unserer Ära, nämlich das deutsch/jüdische oder arisch/jüdische Verhältnis. Für einen Kenner der Lage wie Du einer zu sein scheinst, sollte es doch ein Leichtes sein, etwaige bei mir feststellbare Fehlansichten klarzustellen. Ich erhalte viele Deiner in deutschen Zeitungen veröffentlichten Artikel und kann daraus ersehen, wie "mahnend" Du wirken kannst, wenn Du schriftlich zu der anonymen und in diesem Fachgebiet zumeist unwissenden deutschen Masse sprichst. Für Dich gilt es, das Judentum zu verteidigen!

Es tut mir leid, daß nichts aus Deinen Plänen wurde, nach den USA umzusiedeln. Unsere gemeinsamen Bekannten in den Vereinigten Staaten können immer noch nicht verstehen, was Dich letzten Endes doch in Deutschland hielt. Besonders, nachdem gewisse Leute in Neubiberg Dir das Leben so schwer gemacht hatten. Deine (deutschen) Rentenansprüche waren geregelt, und soviel ich weiß, hattest Du sogar schon eine gute Anstellung in Amerika in Aussicht. Trotzdem hielt Dich irgendetwas im "Reich der Mörder" fest. War es ein ausdrücklicher Befehl seitens Deiner höhergestellten "Glaubens-"genossen in Tel Aviv oder New York, Deinen für das Internationale Weltjudentum äußerst wichtigen Posten in Deutschland nicht aufzugeben?

Ich kann mir nicht vorstellen, daß die ungewisse Ruhe, die in Neubiberg jetzt um Deine Person herrscht, für Deinen Entschluß des weiteren Verbleibens bei der BW-Uni ausschlaggebend war. Du und ich, wir wissen besser als viele andere, daß die Dir von Deinen Kollegen jetzt entgegengebrachte Freundlichkeit zum größten Teil unecht ist.
Nachdem es Dir gelungen war, sogar die Entfernung eines Dir unangenehmen Präsidenten der Lehranstalt zu erreichen, und weil es die Spatzen von den Dächern der Uni pfeifen, daß Deutsche, die Dir einen wahrheitsgetreuen, aber Deiner Meinung nach beleidigenden Brief schreiben, schwer bestraft werden, herrscht in Neubiberg Friedhofsruhe. Aber wie lange noch? Berichte, die man mir zukommen ließ, sprechen davon, daß es besonders Deine neueren, jüngeren Kollegen und viele der jetzigen Schüler sind, die sich (wie nicht anders zu erwarten) hinter Deinem Rücken über Dich und Deine salbungsvollen Worte und ernste Miene lustig machen. Und gegen so etwas helfen alle Gesetze und Mittel des Psychoterrors nichts. Aber, ich weiß, im Interesse Israels nimmst Du das gern hin.

Auch wenn Du Dich oft nicht klar ausdrückst (typisch jüdische Verschleierungsversuche), so bleibt beim Lesen Deiner Artikel

doch immer der Eindruck zurück, daß für Dich die ganze
Holocaust-Anklage gegen das deutsche Volk ein religiöses Dogma
geworden ist, an dem man nicht rütteln darf. Indem Du Dich so
einstellst, bist Du praktisch zu einem Priester der neuen
Holocaust-Religion geworden, der jeden (auch den leichtesten)
Zweifler zum Ketzer erklärt. Demnach kannst Du unmöglich ein
derartiger "Deutsch-jüdischer Patriot" sein, wie Du selbst
vielleicht glauben magst. Wer die Wahrheit nicht an die erste
Stelle setzt, ist kein guter Geschichtsprofessor. Er hat sich
selbst zum finsteren Agenten einer mehr als zweifelhaften Sache
gemacht. Wie sagten die Engländer beim rücksichtslosen Aufbau
ihres rassistischen, von Hitler so bewunderten Empires?
Right or wrong, my country. Ja, man fällt so leicht (aus Liebe
zu einer Sache) in diese moralische Falle. Es wird der Tag kommen, an dem Du Dich vor den Kopf schlägst und schreist: Wie
konnte ich nur so dumm sein?

Im übrigen hast Du echt jüdisch gehandelt, als Du die deutschen
Briefschreiber anzeigtest. Bevor ich ein ähnliches Beispiel aus
Amerika bringe, möchte ich erwähnen, daß mir so etwas nie ein-
fallen würde. Das liegt aber sicher daran, daß wir (Deutsche
und Juden) genetisch eben total unterschiedlich veranlagt sind.
Demnach ist es das in uns befindliche Erbgut, das verhindert,
daß ich je ein Jude sein kann oder Du Dich in einen echten
Deutschen verwandelst. (Mir ist bewußt, daß es in Deutschland
gegenwärtig eine größere Anzahl von waschechten Deutschen -
besonders in wichtigen Stellen - gibt, die dem Holocaust-
Glauben verfallen sind und sich anderweitig typisch jüdisch
benehmen. Abgesehen davon, daß dies hauptsächlich aus opportu-
nistischen Motiven geschieht, möchte ich behaupten, daß die
jüdische Weltanschauung dieser Noahiten nur hauchdünn ist und
in dem Moment verfliegt, wo es keine jüdische Weltmacht mehr
gibt. Wäre ich Jude, dann würde ich mich nicht auf die Treue
und Standhaftigkeit dieser Typen verlassen: sie werden die ersten sein, die sich gegen ihre jetzigen jüdischen Gönner und
"Freunde" wenden.)

In Deutschland hat man sicher über die "Proposition 187" gele-
sen, einem Volksentscheid, bei dem die Wähler in Kalifornien
mit überwältigender Mehrheit dafür stimmten, daß illegale (also
durch ihr Einschleichen gesetzübertretende) Einwanderer nicht
mehr in den Genuß von öffentlichen Leistungen wie Fürsorge,
Schulbildung für ihre Kinder und kostenlosen Krankenhausaufent-
halt kommen. Der Grund war die Tatsache, daß inzwischen Millionen von Mexikanern ihre "Zelte" in Kalifornien aufgeschlagen
haben und den dort lebenden Menschen ungeheure Kosten aufbür-
deten. (In Los Angeles gibt es ein Kreiskrankenhaus, in dem die
Entbindungsabteilung für "normale" Amerikanerinnen nicht mehr
benutzbar ist, da sie immer von Mexikanerinnen belegt ist. Ver-
irrt sich einmal eine schwangere weiße Mutter in diese Abtei-
lung, dann wird sie von den Braunhäutigen mit Absicht hinausge-
ekelt.) Wir zweifelten nie daran, daß "Liberale" unter jüdischer Führung alles daran setzen würden, diesen Volksentscheid
unter Berufung auf von Juden erlassene oder verdrehte Gesetze
auszusetzen. Das geschah dann auch. Gegenwärtig ist die Sache
noch in der Schwebe, und wenn es so weiter ginge wie bisher,
dann brauchte es Jahre, um die Sache zur Zufriedenheit der
Mehrheit zu klären. Inzwischen verdienen die jüdischen Rechtsanwälte **beider** Seiten beim Scheinfechten Riesensummen, für die
die Mehrheit aufkommen muß.

Nach der Wahl war kein Monat vergangen und schon erklärte die
jüdische Richterin Mariana Pfaelzer (na, wer denn sonst?), die
mit dem jüdischen Hollywood-Produzenten Frank Rothman verheiratet ist, den Volksentscheid für ungültig. Kurz danach schrieb
ein legaler Einwanderer aus Argentinien der Richterin einen
Brief, in dem er sie fragte, "wie ist es möglich, daß Juristen
wie Sie es überhaupt wagen, illegale Einwanderer zu unterstützen, deren Anwesenheit einen Gesetzesbruch darstellt?" Der Ar-
gentinier erwähnte auch, daß er zwei Jahre warten mußte, bis er
die Einwanderungspapiere erhielt. Drohungen irgendwelcher Art
enthielt der Brief jedoch keine. Was tat die liebe Mariana?

Anscheinend unter der auch bei Dir verbreiteten Annahme, daß man Juden nicht kritisieren darf (das ist immer antisemitisch!) übergab sie den Brief den Behörden und eines Tages erhielt der argentinische Einwanderer den Besuch von zwei Beamten des "U.S. Marshal's Service", einer der amerikanischen Bundespolizeibehörden, und wurde von einer Frau namens Aschbrenner verhört...

Der Grund, warum ich Dir heute schreibe, hat mit dem erstaunlichen und für mich erfreulichen Wahlergebnis zu tun, mit dem die amerikanischen Wähler am 8. November 1994 (der beim Schließen der Wahllokale in Kalifornien schon der symbolträchtige 9. November in Deutschland war!) der jüdischen Allmacht über den amerikanischen Kongreß ein Ende bereiteten. Du mit Deiner überempfindlichen jüdischen Antenne wirst sicher erkannt haben, was dieser Tag bedeutete. Da Du aber nicht hier lebst, werden Dir manche Anzeichen dieser "Revolution" entgangen sein, und ich will Sie hier kurz beschreiben.

Amerikanische und deutsche Patrioten in den USA geben sich keinen Illusionen hin, daß sich mit der Wahl nun alles sofort zu Gunsten des Staatsvolkes (eben der arischen Amerikaner) geändert hat. Noch sitzen Deine Glaubensgenossen in der Clinton-Regierung fest im Sattel, und es gibt keinen Zweifel darüber, daß sie sowohl die Medien wie auch die Finanzen des Landes völlig in den Händen haben. Selbst die Hauptsprecher der "Revolution", also Newt Gingrich (der übrigens nicht deutscher Herkunft ist, da sein Geburtsname McPherson war) und Robert Dole sind treue Diener des Internationalismus und weiß Gott von wem noch, und sie haben es seit dem November schon mehr als einmal bewiesen. *Das macht aber nichts. Wir, die wir sowohl in den USA wie auch in Deutschland zur Rechten gehören, betrachten den gegenwärtigen Zustand lediglich als ein Interregnum, das möglicherweise schon 1996 sein Ende finden wird. In anderen Worten, besonders Gingrich kann als der amerikanische Gorbatschow angesehen werden, der lediglich den Übergang zur neuen Zeit erleichtert. Es ist gut möglich, daß er schon 1996 seinen großen Einfluß verlieren wird.

*)Die Frau von Gingrich erhielt vor einigen Monaten eine Anstellung bei einer jüdischen Firma, die sich um die Verbesserung der Handelsbeziehungen mit Israel kümmert. Ich hörte, es sei eine MOSSAD-Scheinfirma. Außerdem ist Gingrichs engster Berater ein Jude, und seit der Wahl stellte er noch einen anderen Mann als politischen Berater ein, der bisher ein hoher Angestellter der AIPAC (Israel-Lobby) war.

Ich selbst nehme an, daß die an sich konservative Masse der weißen Amerikaner nun Blut geleckt hat und nicht zufrieden sein wird, bis die Übermacht der hiesigen demokratischen Diktatur, mit der die Macht des Judentums heutzutage untrennbar verbunden ist, gebrochen ist. Was uns noch bevorsteht, kann man aus Ziffern des vergangenen Wahlergebnisses ersehen: 37 % der Wahlberechtigten gingen zur Urne. Lediglich 2 % dieser 37 %, fast ausschließlich weiße Männer, waren für das allerseits überraschende Ergebnis ausschlaggebend. 78 % der jüdischen und 90 % der schwarzen Wähler stimmten für die Verlierer und haben sich damit selbst kaltgestellt. Mein Hauptaugenmerk ist auf die 63 % der Wahlberechtigten gerichtet, die zu Hause geblieben waren. Da in den USA aus verschiedenen - besonders rassischen - Gründen oftmals völlig andere Verhältnisse herrschen als in Deutschland, nehme ich an, daß man mit ca. 20 % Wahlberechtigten (zumeist Schwarzen) rechnen muß, die immer zu Hause bleiben. Demnach muß man die Frage stellen, wer die 43 % der Nichtwähler sind, die aus anderen Gründen diesmal nicht mitmachten.

Ich glaube, daß es sich um arische Amerikaner oft deutscher Herkunft handelte, denen der ganze (bisherige) "demokratische" Schwindel zum Hals heraus hing. Das oben dargestellte Beispiel der vorläufig durch die Juden zur Entgleisung gebrachten kalifornischen "Proposition 187" sollte als Beweisgrund für den berechtigten Wählerunmut genügen. Jetzt war es aber so, daß man nach dem 8.11.1994 zum ersten Mal seit über 40 Jahren feststel-

Appendix II: Documents

len konnte, daß grundlegende Änderungen durch Wahlen zu erreichen sind. Demnach rechne ich 1996 mit einer erheblich höheren Wahlbeteiligung und zwar von Leuten, die so denken wie wir.

In anderen Worten, die Demokratische Partei (die als Judenpartei bekannt ist, weil man zugibt, daß über 50 % ihrer Einnahmen von Juden und deren Vereinigungen kommen) hat nicht nur keine Möglichkeit, den Kongreß wiederzuerobern, sondern sie wird auch das Weiße Haus verlieren. Allerdings: Nach der ungeheuren und unerwarteten Niederlage des 8. November werden die Oberjuden alles daran setzen, eine Umkehr in ihrem Sinn zu erreichen.

Aus diesem Grund werden die End-Kandidaten beider Parteien und vielleicht sogar einer schnell ins Leben gerufenen dritten Partei fast bestimmt treue Gefolgsmänner Eretz Israels sein. Ein Patrick Buchanan wird 1996 noch keine Chance haben, Präsident zu werden. Erst nach 1996 wird der Niedergang jüdischer Macht für jedermann ersichtlich sein und die zu erwartenden Folgen zeigen. Gegenwärtig tippe ich auf Dole als Präsidentschaftskandidat der Republikaner, der mit seiner Frau, die Präsidentin des amerikanischen Roten Kreuzes ist (ein pay-off-Posten der Internationalisten), zu unseren Gegnern gehört.

Eines der klassischsten Beispiele dafür, wie sehr sich seit dem 8. November alles verändert hat, war die Sache mit dem Kollaps des mexikanischen Peso. Diese Währung wurde im Dezember 1994 gegenüber dem Dollar plötzlich stark heruntergesetzt, was amerikanischen Investoren schweren Schaden zufügte. Clinton ging beinahe nichtsahnend zum Kongreß und beantragte die Bereitstellung von Anleihengarantien im Wert von 40 Milliarden Dollar für den südlichen Nachbarstaat, angeblich, um dessen Währung zu stützen und das Land vor einer wirtschaftlichen Katastrophe zu bewahren. Es gibt keinen Zweifel darüber, daß <u>vor der Novemberwahl</u> alles wie am Schnürchen geklappt hätte, und der Präsident die Garantien innerhalb von Tagen bekommen hätte. Plötzlich aber war alles anders. Sowohl im Kongreß als auch in den Medien wurde offen davon gesprochen, daß es sich bei der Anleihenversicherung hauptsächlich um eine Rettungsaktion für die "Wallstreet-Finanziers" handelte, und manche der Kommentatoren gingen sogar so weit, Alan Greenspan (von der Bundesbank) und den Schatzminister Robert Rubin für das Fiasko verantwortlich zu machen, wobei kein Zweifel gelassen wurde, daß man "Juden" meinte.

Jedenfalls geschah das fast Unglaubliche: Nach fast 2 Wochen mußten Dole und Gingrich (die <u>natürlich</u> für die Sache waren, da doch die Hintergrundbosse davon profitieren sollten) Clinton mitteilen, daß es angesichts der Dickköpfigkeit besonders der neuen Kongreßmitglieder nicht möglich war, genügend Abgeordnetenstimmen für die Angelegenheit zu gewinnen. Clinton blieb nichts anderes übrig, als einen möglicherweise ungesetzlichen und bestimmt gefährlichen Schritt zu tun.

Er nahm 20 Milliarden Dollar aus einer noch aus Roosevelts Zeiten stammenden Schatulle, die dazu bestimmt war, den Dollar zu stützen, falls er im internationalen Handelsverkehr zu sehr an Wert verlieren würde. Außerdem versprach er den Mexikanern riesige Dollarbeträge aus dem IFM-Fund und anderen internationalen agencies, über die er gar kein alleiniges Verfügungsrecht hatte, was zu Unstimmigkeiten besonders mit Deutschland und Frankreich führte. Die fehlenden 20 Milliarden werden natürlich den eventuellen Kollaps des Dollars beschleunigen.

Kommt er, dann wird es hier eine Wirtschaftskatastrophe ungeahnten Ausmaßes geben. Die amerikanische Bevölkerung wird sich dann der Namen Greenspan und Rubin erinnern, was furchtbare Wirkungen für das gesamte amerikanische Judentum haben kann, da besonders die Judenvereinigungen fast geschlossen hinter diesen Beiden (und anderen ähnlichen jüdischen Verbrechern) stehen und jede Kritik an deren unlauteren Machenschaften als Antisemitismus ahnden. (Diesbezüglich sei erwähnt, daß die große Verbreitung von Computern in Amerika <u>jetzt schon</u> das jüdische Machtmonopol über die Medien gebrochen hat. Selbst 80jährige Greise in den Altersheimen sind durch Internet und andere Programme untereinander verbunden. Der Druck auf ein paar Tasten genügt, um einem Abgeordneten klarzumachen, daß "man" die finanzielle Unterstützung Israels, oder die Rettung jüdischer Wallstreet-Finanzierer ablehnt. Außerdem werden jetzt schon die Leute besser informiert als je. Auch die Radio talk shows tragen ihr Übriges zu diesen veränderten Verhältnissen bei.)

Daß die ultrareichen Juden von Anfang an schwer in die Peso-Sache verwickelt waren, konnte man an dem Eifer aller wichtigen Juden (inbegriffen der vielen jüdischen Journalisten) erkennen, die Anleihenversicherung durch den Kongreß zu bringen. Auch ist es hier kein Geheimnis, daß es hauptsächlich jüdische Investoren und *investment* companies waren, die in letzter Zeit am meisten in Mexiko investiert hatten. Ich nehme an, daß Deine wie die Kletten zusammenhängenden Rassengenossen ein zweites Mal innerhalb eines Jahrzehntes erreichen wollten, daß sie sich auf dem Rücken der amerikanischen Steuerzahler schlagartig noch mehr bereichern konnten, wie sie es Tag für Tag sowieso tun (vielleicht benötigte man auch mehr Geld als bisher für den Parasitenstaat). Der erste große Raub, der an die Missetaten der "deutschen" Treuhandgesellschaft erinnert, geschah mittels der S&L (Sparkassen)-Machenschaften, wodurch die amerikanischen Völkerschaften um annähernd 500 Milliarden Dollar betrogen wurden. Es gibt Anzeichen dafür, daß man die Weichen für das mexikanische Fiasko schon vor über einem Jahr, also vor der überraschenden Novemberwahl, stellte. Man arbeitete also unter der Annahme, daß der damals noch in den Taschen der "Finanzierer" befindliche Kongreß "selbstverständlich" die Anleihenversicherung genehmigen würde, und dann hätte der Diebstahl vonstatten gehen können. (Ich glaube nicht, daß es in Deutschland bekannt ist, daß die Großanleger in mexikanischen Anleihen bis zu 23 % Zinsen erhielten. Dies für Milliardenbeträge. Dieses Geld wollte man durch U.S.Steuern absichern. Kein Wunder, Mexiko ging bankrott.) Es ist auch wahrscheinlich, daß man nach dem absichtlich herbeigeführten Kollaps des Peso Mexiko billig aufkaufen wollte.

Nur diesmal mit dem Unterschied, daß der mexikanische Staat auch PEMEX, die staatliche Ölfirma, hätte "privatisieren" sollen, ein Ziel, das die Internationalisten (One-Worlders) in New York schon seit Jahrzehnten verfolgen. (Die im Februar ausgehandelten Verträge zwischen den USA und Mexiko erinnern mich sehr an die amerikanische "Großzügigkeit" gegenüber dem Deutschen Reich nach dem Ersten Weltkrieg (Dawes-Young Plan) als praktisch ganz Deutschland an die Gauner in Übersee verpfändet wurde. Sicher ist, daß nun die mexikanischen peons noch ärmer dran sein werden, als bisher.)

Die für das gesamte Judentum klar erkenntlichen Niederlagen des 8.11.94 und von der Peso-Geschichte, Niederlagen, die auch durch den größten Einsatz aller noch vorhandenen Kräfte nicht wieder gutgemacht werden können, erlauben meine Feststellung, daß die Führung zumindest der amerikanischen Juden gegenwärtig total vermessen ist. Anstatt endlich das zu tun, was ich schon ungefähr 1987 vorschlug, als das Judentum den größtmöglichen Höhepunkt seiner Macht in diesem Land erreicht hatte, nämlich endlich die Gürtel enger zu schnallen und mit dem Eroberten zufrieden zu sein, verbreitete man seitdem noch die Machtbasis und trat notgedrungen immer mehr in den Vordergrund. Meiner Ansicht nach gibt es für die Juden nichts Schlimmeres, als "Aufdeckung", ganz gleich, ob diese durch Arier geschieht oder selbstverschuldet ist. Jetzt gibt es kein Zurück mehr, und das schreckliche Schicksal wird seinen unabänderlichen Lauf nehmen. Tatsache ist nun einmal, daß kein Volk, keine Nation es sich leisten kann, auf die Dauer von einer kleinen, fanatischen, immer auf selbstgewählte Absonderung ausgerichteten, aber mit Sonderprivilegien ausgestatteten rassisch-religiösen Minderheit regiert zu werden.

Daß die Oberjuden jetzt zumindest unterbewußt erkannt haben, daß sich ihre Macht im Endzeitstadium befindet, kann man an einem z. Zt. überall in der Welt erkennbaren Phänomen feststellen: Ob nach Befreiungsfeiern in Auschwitz, Terrorangriffen gegen jüdische Institutionen in Argentinien, England und sonstwo, "Kamikaze"-Attacken gegen jüdische Soldaten in Israel, oder amerikanischen "Holocaust"-Festlichkeiten, immer und immer wieder zeigen Presse und TV Bilder von weinenden Juden. Da man das gleiche nicht mit Bildern von Bosniern in Sarajewo, Frauen in Grossny, Überlebenden israelischer Angriffe im Libanon oder zerhackten Menschen in Ruanda tut, muß man annehmen, daß hinter der Kampagne eine Absicht steckt. Aber welche? Ich muß da an Kinder denken, die etwas angestellt haben, wofür sie mit Bestimmtheit bestraft werden. Sie weinen schon bevor sie die Prügel erhalten, manchmal aus Angst vor den zu erwartenden Schmerzen, zumeist aber um Mitleid zu erregen. Will man durch die propagansistische Ausnutzung von Bildern weinender Juden jetzt schon das bei der hiesigen arischen Masse nicht mehr vorhandene Mitleid wiedererwecken? Das mag sein. Jedenfalls haben die Juden als Gesamtheit zumindest in den USA den seit 1945 auf lange Zeit existierenden good will schon längst selbst abgebaut. Selbst das tägliche Zeigen von weinenden, trauernden, hilflosen und ach so empfindsamen ("menschlichen") Deiner Rassengenossen wird nichts mehr an den gegenwärtigen Tatsachen ändern. Man hat Judäa durchschaut...

Diesbezüglich begehen Juden wie Du, Bubis, Friedman, Gysi u. a. einen schweren Fehler im Interesse Eures Volkes, indem Ihr Euch in Deutschland, dem Land das einzig und allein dem blutsmäßig deutschen Volk gehört, in Stellen eingeschlichen habt, die Ihr meiner Ansicht nach unter den gegebenen Verhältnissen einfach nicht einnehmen dürftet. Auch wenn es nur 60 % der Deutschen sind, die jedes Mal, wenn sie einen von Eurer Sorte am Fernseher erkennen, "Jude" denken, dann kann das später gefährlich sein.

Es ist nicht so, daß ich eine pogromähnliche Reaktion gegen den (gegenwärtigen) Mißbrauch jüdischer Macht erwarte, die gab es auch während des Dritten Reiches nicht. Was aber damals geschah und jetzt schon in den USA der Fall ist, wird auch in Deutschland stattfinden: es werden sich nur wenige Leute finden, die sich im Notfall vor bedrohte Juden stellen (auch die Lichterkettenhelden werden schön zu Hause bleiben und die Rolläden herunterlassen). Der Grund dafür ist einfach: Wenn die Juden (wie seit 1945 gesehen) die Macht haben, dann kennen sie in ihrer Anmaßung keine Grenzen. Es gibt keinen Tag, an dem sie sich nicht neue Feinde schaffen (was Du bei der BW-Uni tatest, ist ein gutes Beispiel dafür). Eines Tages verschiebt sich dann die Waage wegen Übergewicht, und wie schon seit Jahrtausenden immer wieder geschehen, ist plötzlich der Traum jüdischer <u>Allmacht</u> aus.

In einem meiner vorherigen Briefe schrieb ich schon einmal, daß mich bei Deinem Volk nichts so sehr stört, wie die oft ersichtliche, tiefgründige Unehrlichkeit. Heute kann ich wieder einmal ein klassisches Beispiel bringen: Zu den Gedenktagen um Auschwitz im Januar dieses Jahres, brachte die in jüdischem Besitz befindliche Washington Post* am 26.1.1995 einen langen Artikel der Jüdin Sharon Waxman, worin sie in Anbetracht der nun nicht mehr behaupteten 4-Millionen-tote-Auschwitzhäftlinge-Ziffer diesen Satz schrieb: "Der Westen hatte diese Ziffer nie geglaubt." So eine Frechheit, so eine Unverschämtheit, so eine Lügnerei! Wieviele Leute wurden in Deutschland seit Jahrzehnten bestraft, weil sie die Lügenziffer von 4 Millionen (und die damit direkt verbundene Zahl der "6 Millionen") öffentlich bezweifelt hatten? Wieviele Amerikaner wurden als "Antisemiten" von dem angeblich so machtlosen Völkchen kalt gestellt und um Stellung und Ehre gebracht, nur weil sie auf die mit der 4-Millionen-Ziffer verbundenen Unwahrscheinlichkeiten hingewiesen hatten? Und nun kommt diese Jüdin daher und behauptet frech, daß "der Westen" den Unsinn nie geglaubt hat. Wird sie das bald auch - mit gleicher Unverfrorenheit - über Gaskammern in Auschwitz schreiben?

439

*) Unsere Nachforschungen haben ergeben, daß jede einzelne der ca. 1600 amerikanischen Tageszeitungen und fast alle Wochenzeitungen und andere Veröffentlichungen zu der Zeit einen Auschwitz-Bericht brachten.

Im Zusammenhang mit der Holocaust-Geschichte muß ich Dir persönlich einen schweren Vorwurf machen (den ich allerdings gern zurücknehme, falls Du Dich tatsächlich schon öffentlich mit dieser Sache befaßt hast): In der Washington Jewish Week vom 2.2.95 konnte man einen kleinen Bericht über den Holocaust-Suchdienst des amerikanischen Roten Kreuzes lesen, der vor ein paar Jahren in Boltimore, Maryland, eröffnet wurde, nachdem die beiden Hauptalliierten (USA und ex-UdSSR) endlich die sorgfältig geführten deutschen Namenlisten (über Transporte, Tote, Arbeitseinsätze und dergl.) des Konzentrationslagerwesens freigegeben hatten, Listen, die schon 1945-46 bei dem Nürnberger Prozeß verwendet worden waren. Jedenfalls kam es laut dem Artikel in den vergangenen paar Jahren zu 260 Familienzusammenführungen.

Dies nach fast 50 Jahren. Was aber konnte z. B. die Amis dazu bewogen haben, diese ungeheuer wichtigen Listen fast ein halbes Jahrhundert lang geheim zu halten?

Ich habe nur eine Erklärung dafür: Je mehr Juden es nach 1945 nicht gelang, ihre Lieben zu finden, desto besser konnte die Holocaust-Mär aufrechterhalten werden. Also aus politisch motivierten Gründen starben inzwischen Millionen von Juden überall in der Welt, ohne geahnt zu haben, daß Eltern und Geschwister, Großeltern und andere Verwandte die Kriegswirren, Hunger und Durst, Typhus, Cholera und die Flächenbombardierung der Alliierten überlebt hatten. Ich selbst kann beschwören, daß schon 1949 die zionistischen Vereinigungen in den USA den Juden, die nach dem Verbleib ihrer Lieben forschten, die Pauschal-Auskunft gaben, daß man diese in Auschwitz' vergast hätte. Danach suchten nur die wenigsten weiter. Darf man ihnen das übel nehmen? (Laut einem in der New York Times am 19.2.1995 gedruckten Bericht leben jetzt immer noch 70 000 "Holocaust-Überlebende" in den USA.) Du aber, ein jüdischer Geschichtsprofessor, der auch politisch sehr rege ist, müßtest es als Deine Pflicht betrachten, endlich einmal dieser Sache nachzugehen und die Schuldigen für dieses in der Menschheit unvergleichbare Verbrechen anzuprangern. Ich glaube, das wärest Du Deinem Volk und seinen echten Opfern schuldig. Auch die Juden können auf die Dauer kein Staatswesen aufrechterhalten, das auf Lügen aufgebaut ist. Die Suchdienst-Telefon Nr. in Baltimore ist 800-848-9277 (unentgeltlich i.d. USA).

Erinnerst Du Dich, als ich in einem meiner Briefe über das OSI schrieb, das Office of Special Investigations im amerikanischen Justizministerium, das beinahe den Justizmord an dem unschuldigen Iwan Demjanjuk auf dem Gewissen hatte? Wie Du weißt, wurde das OSI durch ein von jüdischen Gruppen vorgeschlagenes, von der jüdischen Abgeordneten Elizabeth Holtzmann eingebrachtes und durch den damals jüdisch kontrollierten Kongreß eingeführtes Gesetz ins Leben gerufen. Nun, laut Washington Jewish Week vom 26.1.95, existiert es nach 15 Jahren immer noch. 32 meist jüdische Personen (darunter mindestens 12 jüdische Rechtsanwälte), arbeiten in dem Amt, es hat ein Jahresbudget von 3,5 Millionen Dollar und konnte im vergangenen Jahr sage und schreibe 7 neue Fälle eröffnen, zumeist über ehemalige, einfache Soldaten, die aus den osteuropäischen Ländern stammten und auf deutscher Seite kämpften. M.E. wäre es einfacher, jedem dieser alten Männer 500 000 Dollar mit der Bedingung zu geben, sich wieder in Europa anzusiedeln. Aber das würde ja jüdische Rachegelüste unbefriedigt lassen, nicht wahr? Neil Sher, der Jude, der lange Jahre Leiter des OSI war und jetzt der Hauptmann von AIPAC, der Israel-Lobby, ist, meinte, daß das OSI für die Juden Amerikas sehr wichtig ist und besonders jetzt, wo es so viele Revisionisten gibt, die nicht mehr an den Holocaust glauben, eine besondere Bedeutung gewonnen hat.

Appendix II: Documents

Zum Schluß dieses Schreibens möchte ich noch kurz auf ein Thema zurückkommen, das auch Dich sicher interessiert: Die immer noch bestehende Kontroverse um den Mord des amerikanischen Präsidenten John F. Kennedy vor nun über 3 Jahrzehnten.

Damals, als die Mordtat geschah, hatte ich nicht einen Augenblick geglaubt, daß es sich um die Handlung eines einzelnen, eines zunächst immer als etwas verrückt dargestellten Attentäters gehandelt hatte. Ich erinnere mich auch noch gut daran, daß "man" (mit Hilfe der hörigen Medien) zunächst versucht hatte, amerikanische Rechte als die Hauptverantwortlichen hinzustellen. Dieser Punkt allein hätte mir schon damals einen Hinweis auf die wirklichen Hintergrundmächte geben sollen, die an der Entfernung Kennedys interessiert waren. Jedenfalls glaubte ich seither nie die Geschichte eines Einzeltäters und ich ließ die Frage über die wirklich Verantwortlichen offen.

Am 31.1.1995 entdeckte ich in der m.E. nicht von Juden kontrollierten (der Mun-Sekte gehörenden) Washington Times, <u>aber sonst nirgends</u>, einen Bericht über einen Dr. Charles Crenshaw, wonach sowohl das Journal der größten amerikanischen Ärztegemeinschaft (AMA) wie auch die Dallas Morning News mit diesem ehemaligen Arzt des Parkland-Krankenhauses in Dallas, in dem sowohl Kennedy wie auch Oswald nach ihrer Erschießung behandelt wurden, einen Vergleich anstreben mußten, bevor es zu einer Gerichtsverhandlung kam. Dr. Crenshaw hatte 30 Jahre nach dem Mord in einem Buch geschrieben, daß er als behandelnder Arzt vom ersten Augenblick an erkannt hatte, daß Kennedy von vorne und demnach nicht von Oswald erschossen worden war. Aufgrunddessen hatten die AMA und die DMN (beides Systeminstitutionen) öffentlich Zweifel an seinen medizinischen Fähigkeiten geäußert. Daß es nun zum Vergleich in der Höhe von etlichen hunderttausend Dollar zugunsten von Dr. Crenshaw kam, spricht Bände. Interessanterweise war diesmal auch wieder ein Jude namens David Belin in die Sache verwickelt. Er war schon 1963-64 einer der Rechtsanwälte der Warren-Commission, die die "Einzelgänger-Theorie" (Lee Harvey Oswald als Attentäter) amtlich verankern wollte.

Inzwischen ist viel Wasser den Rhein hinuntergeflossen. Jetzt, nach so vielen Jahren, sieht man plötzlich viel klarer, und ich glaube nun besser ahnen zu können, wer - oder welche Gruppe - den Tod Kennedys wollte oder brauchte. Jedenfalls lamentieren hauptsächlich Juden seit dem 8.11.1994 immer wieder, "daß die Republikaner jetzt das ganze amerikanische soziale Gefüge zerstören wollen, welches in den Lyndon B. Johnson-Jahren so sorgfältig errichtet worden war". Damit meinen diese Juden die verheerenden Gesetze, die das seit Anbeginn der Nation bestehende System zerstörten. In anderen Worten, unter LBJ fand eine Revolution im jüdischen Sinn statt. Hätte Kennedy überlebt, dann wäre es nicht dazu gekommen. Ein weiterer Hinweis, daß Kennedy womöglich auf jüdische Initiative hin ermordet worden war, lag die ganzen Jahre direkt vor meiner Nase, ich erkannte dies aber erst vor kurzem: Seit 1964 wurde eine Unmenge von Büchern über den Kennedy-Mord geschrieben, viele von jüdischen Schreiberlingen, alle mit einer anderen Theorie über die möglichen Hintermänner.

Da in den USA kein Buch von einem "renommierten" Verlag verlegt wird, von einem Buchkritiker wichtiger Zeitungen besprochen wird, und in die Auslagen der meisten Buchgeschäfte gelangt, das jüdischen Interessen widerspricht, muß man annehmen, daß der Ausstoß der vielen Mutmaßungen im Interesse des Judentums war. In anderen Worten, die wirklichen Attentäter von Kennedy wollten ihre Spuren mittels der oft gebrauchten Verschleierung verwischen und die Massen in der Suche nach der Wahrheit verwirren. Heute jedenfalls gibt es keine Zweifel darüber, daß die Ermordung von JFK den Weg für Lyndon B. Johnson (der m.E. nicht an dem Attentat beteiligt war, aber doch "ahnte", daß er bald an die Macht kommen würde) frei machte, und dies wiederum ermöglichte die jüdische Revolution in Amerika, die dieses Land bis zur Unkenntlichkeit veränderte.

Ich weiß, dies ist ein schwerer Verdacht gegen Dein Volk. Aus diesem Grund müßtest Du es wegen Deiner herausragenden Stellung in Deutschland als Deine Pflicht betrachten, etwaige Unrichtigkeiten in meinen Gedankengängen und Ausführungen zu finden und zu verurteilen. Tust Du es nicht, dann weiß ich, daß Du mir innerlich zustimmst, aber aus Loyalität und Pflichtgefühl beschlossen hast, die Wahrheit zu verschweigen.

Viele Grüße

gez. Hans

P.S. *Laut Süddeutsche Zeitung vom 20.1.1995 drückte sich der französische Jude Michel Friedmann, der gegenwärtig als Vorzeigejude im CDU-Bundesvorstand sitzt, bezüglich der Unterwanderung Deutschlands durch Fremdrassige so aus: "Dabei gehört doch niemandem dieses Land. Und dabei ist doch die nationale Identität a priori das Recht des Individuums, nicht das einer Nation..." Gilt dies auch für Israel? I wonder...*

Zum Kennedy-Mord möchte ich folgendes hinzufügen: Ich schrieb schon einmal, daß während der Amtszeit von LBJ ein jüdisches Ehepaar namens Krim Dauerbewohner im Weißen Haus war. Und im Februar d.J. starb in Dallas, Texas, der von LBJ ernannte jüd. Richter Irving L. Goldberg, der lt. NYT (13. Feb. 95) "am 22.11.1963, wenige Stunden nach der Ermordung von Kennedy, (aus Dallas! HS) für Konsultationen ins Weiße Haus gerufen wurde." Während des Zweiten Weltkrieges hatte der damalige "MdB" Johnson Irving L. Goldberg von der U.S. Navy zu sich in das Capitol abkommandiert."

Zu 7.:

(Fallakte 6):

An einem nicht genau bekannten Zeitpunkt zwischen Mai 1995 und dem 27. Juni 1995 übersandte der Angeschuldigte den von ihm gefertigten und herausgegebenen "USA-Bericht Nr. 6-95", der im wesentlichen aus dem in der Anklageschrift zu 6. wiedergegebenen Brief an Professor Dr. Michael Wolffsohn in München bestand, an den Rentner Werner Schulz in Bonn.

Zu 8.:

(Fallakte 7):

An einem nicht genau bekannten Zeitpunkt in der zweiten Hälfte des März 1995 übersandte der Angeschuldigte den "USA-Bericht 4-95" an die Gemeindeverwaltung in 82140 Olching. Dieses Druckwerk enthält u. a. folgende Passagen:

"(...) Die jüdische Führung nutzte die Auschwitz- und Dresden-Gedenktage, um den kommenden 50. Jahrestages des Abwurfes der ersten große A-Bombe auf Hiroshima natürlich - wie gewöhnlich - für ihre eigenen Zwecke aus. Nachdem die Gehirnwäsche der Deutschen so hervorragend geklappt hat, daß die simple Äußerung des Wortes "Auschwitz" seitens eines jüdischen Aktivisten die gleiche Wirkung hat, wie das "Sesam, öffne dich" der Märchenwelt, und sich damit alle deutschen Schatzkammern öffnen, versucht man nun das gleiche hier in den USA. (...) Außerdem gibt es jetzt noch weitere Millionen Menschen in der ganzen Welt mehr, die wissen, daß nicht jeder die Dogmen der neuen Holocaust-Religion glaubt."

Zu 9.:

Appendix II: Documents

(Fallakte 8):

Mit Poststempel vom 23. Dezember 1993 übersandte der Angeschuldigte von Burke/Virgina (USA) aus den "USA-Bericht 1-94" an den Bundestagsabgeordneten Siegfried Vergin in Bonn. Die Sendung war mit einem vom Angeschuldigten handschriftlich verfaßten Begleitschreiben mit folgendem Inhalt versehen:

"Lb. Herr Vergin -

Las Ihren Leserbrief (MA Mo 12.12.93) über Leuchter.
Wissen Sie was über Redefreiheit?
Übrigens, Leuchter ist bestimmt kein Propagandist, er half allerdings, die "H"-Mär zu zerstören.
Nur weiter so.
Ihr H. Schmidt"

Zu 10.:

(Fallakte 9):

Mit Poststempel vom 21. Dezember 1994 versandte der Angeschuldigte von Pensacola, Florida aus ein mit 01.11.1994 datiertes Rundschreiben des GERMAN AMERICAN NATIONAL PUBLIC AFFAIRS COMMITEE (GANPAC) sowie einen mit 10. November 1994 datierten "Offenen Brief" an die "Vorsitzenden des Amtsgerichts und der Staatsanwaltschaft Arnstadt-Thüringen, 99310 Arnstadt Germany". In diesem offenen Brief, der am 28.12.1994 bei der Staatsanwaltschaft Bochum einging, heißt es wie folgt:

"Ist es möglich, daß das Judentum (insgesamt, als religiöse, rassische, kulturelle und ethnische Gemeinschaft) angesichts des überwältigenden Beweises eigener selbsterwünschter Absonderung andere Ziele als die vorgegebenen hat, die Rassenmischung zu betreiben und andere Nationen und Völker durch die Zuführung unassimilierbarer Völkerschaften von innen zu zersetzen?

(Man bemerke das Asylantenproblem im heutigen Deutschland.) Es sieht so aus und ich wäre Ihnen allen, werte Herren und Damen Staatsanwälte und Richter in Arnstadt herzlich dankbar dafür, wenn Sie mir andere Beweggründe für das Verhalten der Juden in dieser Hinsicht mitteilen könnten.

(...) Nur die Wahrheit (über sich selbst) kann die Juden aus ihrem Teufelskreis bringen, aber an die kommen Sie nie heran, wenn es unwissende Staatsanwälte und Richter gibt, die verhindern wollen, daß jüdisches zersetzerisches Gebaren und andere gefährliche (kollektive) Eigenschaften dieses eigenartigen Volkes öffentlich behandelt werden."

Zu 11.:

(Fallakte 10):

Mit Poststempel vom 21. Dezember 1994 versandte der Angeschuldigte von Pensacola, Florida aus die unter 10. beschriebenen Druckwerke an die Adresse: "Staatsanwaltschaft Bochum, Reitzensteinstraße 17, 45657 Recklinghausen". Diese Schreiben gingen bei der gemeinsamen Briefannahmestelle der Justizbehörden Recklinghausen am 28. Dezember 1994 ein.

Zu 12.:

(Fallakte 11):

Mit Poststempel vom 25.04.1995 übersandte der Angeschuldigte von Karlsruhe aus den Abdruck eines ursprünglich an den Außenminister Klaus Kinkel gerichteten Briefes vom 05.07.1994 an den Bundestagsabgeordneten Peter Conradi in Bonn.

Der Briefabdruck trägt folgenden Zusatz: "Herrn Peter Conradi zur Kenntnis!
Vielleicht erkennen Sie jetzt, wer bei uns wieder zu bestimmen hat?"

Und hat den folgenden Inhalt:

"Werter Herr Kinkel!

Die in Kalifornien erscheinende deutschsprachige Zeitung "Neue Presse" druckte am 31.05.1994 einen von der dpa stammenden Artikel über Sie ab, nachdem Sie sich dahin gehend geäußert haben, daß "das Deutschlandbild im Ausland verheerend, eigentlich zum Heulen sei". In dem Bericht wird auch erwähnt, daß Ihre Botschaft in Washington Ihnen gekabelt habe, daß (in den USA) "Entsetzen in allen Medien" über den Magdeburger Rassenkrawall herrsche. Andere Stilblüten aus dem dpa-Bericht waren, daß deutsche Diplomaten und andere Vertreter im Ausland (nach Magdeburg) "weltweit einen Aufschrei" bemerkt haben und daß u. a. selbst aus Städten wir Singapur, Budapest, Kopenhagen und Sophia riesige Aufmerksamkeit gemeldet wurde." Das schlimmste Bild spiegelte (jedoch) eine vom Außenamt in Auftrag gegebene amerikanische Untersuchung sämtlicher Fernsehkanäle des Landes."

Dieser letzte Satz erlaubt meine Frage, ob Sie als "Deutscher" Außenminister denn nicht wissen, daß nicht nur die amerikanische Presse, sondern fast alle anderen Medien, inbegriffen des Fernsehens, in jüdischen Händen sind. Und ist Ihnen denn nicht klar, daß die Rassenmischung und Vernichtung der individuellen Völker ein (von den Oberjuden selbst zugegebener) Bestandteil der Jewish agenda, eben der jüdischen Zielsetzung, ist? Daß demnach jede deutsche Abwehrhandlung à la Magdeburg gegen jüdische Interessen verstößt und auch so geahndet wird? Betrachten Sie doch nur einmal die Handlungen und hören Sie die Sprüche der Hauptvertreter des Weltjudentums in Deutschland, also der Herren Bubis, Friedman, Wolffsohn, Cohn-Benndit usw. und Sie werden darin die klare Linie des Judentums erkennen. (...)

Vergehen, strafbar gemäß §§ 130 Nr. 1 und 3, 131 Abs. 1 Nr. 1 und 4 a.F. StGB;
§§ 130 Abs. 1 Nr. 2, Abs. 2 Nr. 1 Buchst. a) und d), Abs. 3, Abs. 4 n.F. StGB;
§§ 189, 194 Abs. 2, 52, 53 StGB

Beweismittel:

I. Angaben des Angeschuldigten

II. <u>Zeugen:</u>

    1. Martin Klingst, zu laden über:
       Pressehaus Speersort 1,
       20095 Hamburg

    2. Professor Dr. Michael Wolffsohn,
       zu laden über:
       Historisches Institut der Universität der Bundeswehr München,
       85577 Neubiberg

    3. Werner Schulz,
       Im Weiler 5, 53123 Bonn   (Fallakte 6, Bl. 1R)

Appendix II: Documents

      4. Frau Ruhle, zu laden über:
         Gemeindeverwaltung Olching,
         Rebhuhnstraße 18,
         82140 Olching   (Fallakte 7, Bl. 3)

      5. Siegfried Vergin, MdB,
         zu laden über:
         Bundeshaus,
         Görresstraße 15,
         53113 Bonn   (Fallakte 8, Bl. 2)

      6. Peter Conradi, MdB,
         zu laden über:
         Bundeshaus,
         Görresstraße 15
         53113 Bonn   (Fallakte 11, Bl. 1)

III. Überführungsstücke:

      1. USA-Bericht Nr. 11/94
         nebst Briefumschlag mit
         Absender:
         P. O. Box 10600,
         Burke, VA 22009-600, USA,
         adressiert an:
         Land Mecklenburg,
         Bundesrat: CDU:
         Rudi Geil,
         Karl-Marx-Straße 1,
         19055 Schwerin   (Hauptakten Bd.I, Bl.4ff.)

      2. USA-Bericht Nr. 11/94
         in 2 Stücken nebst
         2 Briefumschlägen mit
         Absender:
         P. O. Box 10600,
         Burke, VA 22015, USA,

         nebst 2 Briefumschlägen
         adressiert an:
         Staatsanwaltschaft,
         Schützenwall 31,
         2300 Kiel 1   (Fallakte 1, Bl. 2ff.)

      3. USA-Bericht Nr. 11/94
         nebst Briefumschlag mit
         Absender:
         P. O. Box 10600,
         Burke, VA 22015, USA,
         adressiert an:
         Staatsanwaltschaft,
         Westring 8, 4630 Bochum 1   (Fallakte 2, Bl. 2ff.)

      4. USA-Bericht Nr. 11/94
         nebst Briefumschlag mit
         Absender:
         P. O. Box 10600,
         Burke, VA 22015, USA,
         adressiert an:
         Staatsanwaltschaft Bochum,
         Reitzensteinstraße 17,
         4350 Recklinghausen   (Fallakte 3, Bl. 1ff.)

      5. Brief an Martin Klingst
         in Hamburg vom 08. Mai 1994   (in Ablichtung)
                                        (Fallakte 4, Bl. 4ff.)

    6. Brief vom 09. März 1995
       an Prof. Dr. Michael Wolffsohn,
       Neubiberg   (in Ablichtung)
                                          (Fallakte 5, Bl. 2ff.)

    7. USA-Bericht Nr. 6-95   (in Ablichtung)
                                          (Fallakte 6, Bl. 4ff.)

    8. USA-Bericht Nr. 4-95   (Fallakte 7,
                                          Hülle Bl. 8 d.A.)

    9. USA-Bericht Nr. 1-94 mit
       einem hierauf aufgeklebten
       handschriftlichen Anschreiben
       an den Bundestagsabgeordneten
       Vergin nebst einem Briefum-
       schlag,
       Absender:
       P. O. Box 10600,
       Burke, VA 22015, USA   (Fallakte 8, Bl. 3ff.)

   10. GANPAC-Brief vom 01.11.1994
       sowie ein "Offener Brief" an
       die Vorsitzenden des Amtsge-
       richts und der Staatsanwalt-
       schaft Arnstadt-Thüringen"
       vom 10. November 1994
       nebst einem Briefumschlag
       Absender:
       P. O. Box 11124,
       Pensacola, FL, 32524-1124, USA,
       adressiert an:
       Staatsanwaltschaft,
       Westring 8, 44787 Bochum 1

   11. GANPAC-Brief vom 01.11.1994
       sowie ein "Offener Brief" an
       die Vorsitzenden des Amtsge-
       richts und der Staatsanwalt-
       schaft Arnstadt-Thüringen"
       vom 10. November 1994
       nebst einem Briefumschlag
       Absender:
       P. O. Box 11124,
       Pensacola, FL, 32524-1124, USA,
       adressiert an:
       Staatsanwaltschaft Bochum,
       Reitzensteinstraße 17,
       45657 Recklinghausen

   12. Schreiben an den Bundestags-
       abgeordneten Peter Conradi
       nebst einem Briefumschlag
       ohne Absender, in Karlsruhe
       am 25.04.1995 zur Post gegeben.

IV. Beiakten:

    1. 1 Sonderheft mit Ablichtungen der
       Vorgänge zu 11 Js 10471/92,
       StA München I und 11 Js 14651/95,
       StA München II

    2. 1 Band Sachakten 11 Js 10471/92,
       StA München II

    3. 45 Js 352/91 StA Freiburg,
       die ich von dort zu erfordern bitte.

Appendix II: Documents

Wesentliches Ergebnis der Ermittlungen:

I. Zur Person:

Der Angeschuldigte wurde am 27. April 1927 als zweites von sechs Kindern seiner Eltern in Völklingen an der Saar geboren. Er wuchs bei seinen Eltern in Luisenthal auf, wo er in der Zeit von 1933-1941 die Volksschule besuchte. Im Anschluß daran absolvierte er eine Lehre als Kaufmann, bis er sich im Jahre 1944 als Freiwilliger zur Waffen-SS meldete, wo er bis zum Kriegsende, zuletzt in Östereich, Dienst tat. Nach Kriegsende geriet der Angeschuldigte für einige Wochen in amerikanische Kriegsgefangenschaft, konnte dort aber entweichen. In der Folgezeit beendete er in Saarbrücken seine Kaufmännische Lehre und begann seine Berufstätigkeit als Kaufmann. In der Zeit von 1947 bis 1949 hielt sich der Angeschuldigte verborgen, da er befürchtete, als ehemaliger Waffen-SS Angehöriger von den französischen Militärbehörden im Saarland zu Zwangsarbeiten verschleppt zu werden.

Im Jahre 1949 verließ er dann Europa und wanderte in die Vereinigten Staaten aus. Dort bekam der Angeschuldigte nach eigenen Angaben nach etwa fünf Jahren Aufenthalt die amerikanische Staatsbürgerschaft, will aber zugleich die deutsche Staatsbürgerschaft behalten haben. Nach eigenen Angaben war der Angeschuldigte ab Ende der 50iger Jahre mit einer eigenen Firma als selbständiger Geschäftsmann tätig. Seit 1979 ist der Angeschuldigte Rentner. Seit 1975 ist er in zweiter Ehe mit seiner Ehefrau Roswitha verheiratet (Fallakte 4, Bl. 54ff. d.A.).

Nach Erkenntnisses des Landeskriminalamtes Mecklenburg-Vorpommern (Bl. 2f. d.A.) ist der Angeschuldigte schon seit geraumer Zeit als Verfasser und Herausgeber von Publikationen strafbaren Inhalts bekannt. Nach dortiger Auskunft ist er

- Vorsitzender des "German-American-Political-Action Comitee" (GANPAC) mit Sitz in Santa Monica/Californien (USA) und als solcher auch Verfasser und Herausgeber der "GANPAC-Briefe",

- Herausgeber der "Amerika-Briefe", P.O.Box 27566 Washington D.C.20038 USA,

- Verfasser verschiedener unter dem Absender P.O.Box 10600, Burke, VA 22015, USA, herausgegebener "Offener Briefe",

- Herausgeber des "USA-Berichts", P.O.Box, Burke, Virginia 22009-600, USA, später teilweise auch unter der Absenderadresse P.O.Box 11124 Pensacola, FL 32524-1124 erschienen.

Im Jahre 1988 hatte Schmidt (Amerika Brief) Postfächer sowohl in Washinton D.C. wie auch in Virginia benutzt.
Damals wurde festgestellt, daß Schmidt in Fairfax, Virginia, wohnte.

Fairfax liegt in der Nähe von Burke, Virginia, wo der jetzt fragliche Hans Schmidt ein Postfach besitzt."

Nach Angaben, die der Angeschuldigte gegenüber dem Landeskriminalamt Saarbrücken am 21.03.1995 gemacht hat, unterhält er unter der Adresse seiner Mutter, Hilde Schmidt, in 66333 Völklingen einen zweiten Wohnsitz.
Hier halte er sich auch gelegentlich auf, wenn er in Deutschland zu Besuch sei (Bd. I, Bl. 53 d.A.).

Nach Angaben seiner Mutter gegenüber der Polizei in Völklingen, hält sich der Angeschuldigte nur "sporadisch" bei ihr zu Hause auf (Bd. II, Bl. 149 d.A.).

II. Zur Sache:

Hinsichtlich der Einzeltaten wird auf den Anklagesatz verwiesen.

Bei den dem Angeklagten zur Last gelegten Taten handelt es sich mit Ausnahme der Fälle zu 5., 6., 10. und zu 12. um Presseinhaltsdelikte. Da die vom Angeschuldigten verbreiteten Schriften jedoch nicht im Geltungsbereich des Strafgesetzbuches ihren Erscheinungsort haben, greift der besondere Gerichtsstand der Presse (§ 7 Abs. 2 StPO) nicht ein. Der Gerichtsstand folgt dem Tatortprinzip (§ 7 Abs. 1 StPO) dies bedeutet, daß bei Druckschriften, die im Ausland erscheinen, ein Gerichtsstand an jedem Verbreitungsort begründet ist (vgl. Kleinknecht/Meyer-Goßner, StPO § 7 Rn. 7).

Soweit es sich bei den angeklagten Taten um Presseinhaltsdelikte handelt, folgt die Verjährung aus den am jeweiligen Verbreitungsort geltenden Landespressegesetzen, welche in allen Bundesländern - mit Ausnahme des Landes Nordrhein-Westfalen -, wo Vergehen nach § 130 Abs. 2 und 4 StGB der presserechtlichen Verjährung nicht unterliegen - für Vergehen sechs Monate beträgt.

Soweit diese Frist bei einzelnen Presseinhaltsdelikten überschritten wurde, sind rechtzeitige Verjährungsunterbrechungen erfolgt.

Zu den einzelnen Taten ist ergänzend noch folgendes auszuführen:

Zu 1.:

Die Verjährung wurde unterbrochen durch Erlaß des Haftbefehls vom 28.03.1995 (Bd. I, Bl. 33 d.A., § 78c Abs. 1 Nr. 5 StGB); durch den Haftfortdauerbeschluß des Amtsgerichts Frankfurt am Main vom 10.08.1995 (Bd. I, Bl. 84 und 114ff. d.A.) zuletzt durch Neufassung des Haftbefehls und Haftfortdaueranordnung des Amtsgerichts Schwerin am 05.10.1995 (Bd. II, Bl. 151ff. d.A.).

Mit der im Anklagesatz wiedergegebenen Leugnung des planmäßigen Massenmordes an Juden in den Gaskammern von Konzentrationslagern während des 3. Reiches, die sich aus seinen Ausführungen zu der von ihm abgestrittenen Offenkundigkeit dieser geschichtlichen Tatsache und der Bezeichnung einer "im Interesse unserer Feinde" aufrechtgehaltenen "Sechsmillionen-Mär" ergibt, erfüllt der Angeschuldigte den Tatbestand der Volksverhetzung in Tateinheit mit Aufstachelung zum Rassenhaß und Verunglimpfung des Andenkens Verstorbener (§ 130, 131 Abs. 1 Nr. 1 StGB in der bis zum 30.11.1994 geltenden Fassung). Soweit er mit seinen Schriften hierbei den Eindruck erwecken möchte, die jüdische Minderheit in Deutschland nutze mittels einer Lügengeschichte die Bundesrepublik aus, stellt er hierdurch Juden als minderwertige Wesen, als der Achtung anderer Staatsbürger unwürdig dar und bezweckt, daß auf diese Weise die Empfänger seiner Schriften zu einer stark emotional gesteigerten feindseeligen Haltung gegen Juden aufgerufen werden (vgl. BGH NStZ 1995, 128f.).
Gleichzeitig verunglimpft er das Andenken derer, die während des Massenmordes in den Gaskammern von Konzentrationslagern ihr Leben ließen.

Soweit der Angeschuldigte die von ihm als "Systemparteien" bezeichneten politischen Parteien in der Bundesrepublik Deutschland als "juden- und freimaurerverseucht" bezeichnet, sind diese Begriffe ebenfalls gegen die entsprechenden Bevölkerungsgruppen in Deutschland gerichtet und stellen eine besonders üble Form des Beschimpfens bzw. böswilligen Verächtlichmachens dieser Gruppen dar. Sie sollen ihnen ihr ungeschmälertes Lebensrecht in der staatlichen Gemeinschaft absprechen bzw. sie als minderwertige Wesensgruppe darstellen (vgl. hierzu OLG Hamm, NStZ 1995, 136ff.)

Die verschiedenen in der Druckschrift verwendeten volksverhetzenden und verunglimpfenden Bestandteile ergeben ihr diskriminierendes Gesamtbild und stehen zueinander in natürlicher Handlungseinheit (§ 52 StGB).

Der Strafrahmen wird nach der Neufassung des § 130 durch das Verbrechensbekämpfungsgesetz vom 28.10.1994 mit Wirkung vom 01.12.1994 der Vorschrift des § 130 Abs. 2 zu entnehmen sein, auf die auch § 130 Abs. 4 hinsichtlich der Leugnung des planmäßigen Massenmordes an Juden durch Schriften (§ 11 Abs. 3 StGB) verweist.

Zu 2. - 5.:

Soweit der Angeschuldigte die im Anklagevorwurf zu 1. beschriebene Schrift jeweils mit Poststempeln vom 19.12.1994 versandt hat, ist hinsichtlich des Eingangs bei der Staatsanwaltschaft Kiel am 09.01.1995 die presserechtliche Verjährung zunächst durch Anordnung der verantwortlichen Vernehmung des Angeschuldigten durch die Staatsanwaltschaft Saarbrücken am 11.05.1995 unterbrochen worden (Fallakte 1, Bl. 24R, vgl. auch Vermerk zu Ziff. 1 auf Bl. 28 der Fallakte 1).
Eine erneute Verjährungsunterbrechung ist durch die Erweiterung des Haftbefehls auf die den Gegenstand der Fallakte 1 betreffende Tat durch Beschluß des Amtsgerichts Schwerin vom 05.10.1995 erfolgt.

Hinsichtlich der Fälle 3 und 4 handelt es sich um Taten, deren Verjährung sich nach den Vorschriften des Pressegesetzes für das Land Nordrhein-Westfalen richtet, nach dessen § 25 Abs. 1 Satz 2 bei Vergehen nach § 130 Abs. 2 und 4 StGB die Vorschriften des Strafgesetzbuches über die Verfolgungsverjährung anzuwenden sind.

Im Fall 5. handelt es sich um eine Zuschrift an eine Zeitungsredaktion, die, da sie volksverhetzendes Inhalts ist, einen Angriff im Sinne des § 130 StGB (alter Fassung) darstellt, der geeignet ist, den öffentlichen Frieden zu stören. Denn eine Eignung zur öffentlichen Friedensstörung kann bei einer Zuschrift an eine Zeitungsredaktion (oder einen Redakteur) auch dann gegeben sein, wenn der Einsender zwar nicht mit einem kommentarlosen Abdruck als "Leserbrief" rechnet, sondern, wie hier nach den Umständen allenfalls zu erwarten, lediglich mit einer Berichterstattung rechnen kann, die dem volksverhetzenden Angriff kritisch-ablehnend gegenüber tritt und in der möglicherweise vor den Gefahren der in ihm zum Ausdruck kommenden politischen Bestrebungen nachdrücklich gewarnt wird (vgl. BGH 29, 26ff.).

Zum Presseinhaltsdelikt ist dieser an den Journalisten Martin Klingst gerichtete "Originalbrief" dann allerdings mangels eines durch diesen veranlaßten Abdrucks des Schreibens nicht geworden, so daß insoweit die Verjährungsvorschriften des StGB in Anwendung kommen.

Zu 6. und 7.:

Gegenstand des Verfahrens ist der in der Anklageschrift vollständig wiedergegebene Text eines Schreibens an den Historiker und Publizisten Prof. Dr. Michael Wolffsohn in Neubiberg, deren Charakter als volksverhetzende Schrift im Sinne von § 130 Abs. 2 Nr. 1 (neuer Fassung) sich aus den im Gesamtzusammenhang zu sehenden, in diesem Schreiben enthaltenen zahllosen Diffamierungen von Menschen jüdischen Glaubens ergibt. Sie gipfeln darin, daß nicht nur die planmäßige Tötung von Juden in Gaskammern des 3. Reiches in Abrede gestellt, sondern dem "Judentum" auch die die Ermordung des amerikanischen Präsidenten John F. Kennedy angelastet wird.

Zu 8.:

Aus dem Gesamtzusammenhang des im Anklagesatz näher beschriebenen Druckwerkes und die Bezeichnung der planmäßigen Vernichtung von Juden während des 3. Reiches als "Dogma der neuen Holocaust-Religion" in Verbindung mit der Behauptung, daß die Äußerung des Wortes "Auschwitz" seitens eines "jüdischen Aktivistens die gleiche Wirkung hat, wie das Sesam, öffne dich, der Märchenwelt" ergibt sich auch hier das Vorliegen der sogenannten "qualifizierten Auschwitz-Lüge" einer Darstellung, die den Zweck hat, die während des 3. Reiches erfolgten Massentötungen als ein zum Zwecke der Stellung von materiellen Forderungen an die Bundesrepublik erfundene Unwahrheit zu abzuqualifizieren.

Hierdurch sind gleichzeitig die Straftatbestände des § 130 Abs. 1 Nr. 1, Abs. 2 Nr. 1 sowie Abs. 3, Abs. 4 erfüllt.

Zu 9.:

Durch die (vor der Reformierung des Tatbestandes des § 130 StGB erfolgte) Bezeichnung der planmäßigen Vernichtung von Juden während des 3. Reiches als "Holocaust-Mär" ("H-Mär") ist der Tatbestand des Verunglimpfens des Andenkens derer, die während der Zeit der nationalsozialistischen Gewaltherrschaft als Juden Opfer der Massenvernichtung wurden, erfüllt (§ 189 StGB).

Zu 10. und 11.:

Die im Anklagesatz zu 10. in ihrem wesentlichen Inhalt wiedergegebene Schrift des Angeschuldigten, in welcher er "das Judentum" bezichtigt "andere Nationen und Völker durch die Zuführung unassimilierbarer Völkerschaften von innen zu zersetzen" und "jüdisches zersetzerisches Gebaren und andere gefährliche (kollektive) Eigenschaften an den Tag zu legen, wird der Zweck verfolgt zum Haß gegen eine religiöse Gruppe aufzustacheln bzw. die Menschenwürde dieser religiösen Gruppe angehörenden durch die in der Schrift enthaltenen besonders groben Beleidigungen anzugreifen (§ 130 Abs. 1 Nr. 1, Abs. 2 Nr. 1 StGB n.F.).

Zu 12.:

Die Bezeichnung der rassistischen Ausschreitungen in Magdeburg im April 1994 als "deutsche Abwehrhandlung" die gegen jüdische Interessen verstoße und deshalb von den "in jüdischen Händen" befindlichen Medien als gegen jüdische Interessen verstoßend "geahndet" werde, verfolgt ebenfalls den vorbezeichneten Zweck und unterfällt dem Tatbestand des § 130 StGB neuer Fassung.

III. Strafzumessung:

Bei der Strafzumessung wird zu berücksichtigen sein, daß nach der Rechtsprechung des Bundesgerichtshofes zur Strafzumessung bei Volksverhetzung durch politische Überzeugungstäter (vgl. BGH NStZ 1995, 128f.) die Verhängung einer empfindlichen, nicht zur Bewährung auszusetzenden Freiheitsstrafe geboten sein dürfte.

Strafschärfend werden in diesem Zusammenhang auch die sich aus Beiakten ergebenden verjährten Taten des Angeschuldigten (vgl. hierzu BGH StV 1994, 423; Foth in NStZ 1995, 375f.) zu berücksichtigen sein.

IV. Zuständigkeit:

Die Zuständigkeit des Landgerichts zur Aburteilung der angeklagten Taten ergibt sich aus § 24 Abs. 1 Nr. 3 GVG. Es handelt sich insoweit um Straftaten von besonderer Bedeutung, was sich aus dem Ausmaß der Rechtsverletzung und den Auswirkungen von Straftaten der dem Angeklagten zur Last gelegten Art ergibt, die neben der Herbeiführung eines aufgeheizten Klimas in der Bevölkerung in der jüngeren Vergangenheit auch stets geeignet waren, den Boden für rassistische, ausländerfeindliche und religiös-diskriminierende Taten bis hin zur Begehung von Brand- und Mordtaten zu bereiten.

Zudem haben sowohl die Straftaten des Angeschuldigten als auch seine Verhaftung ein besonders großes Presse-Echo im In- und Ausland hervorgerufen. Auch rechtfertigt die zu erwaretende lange Verhandlungsdauer die Durchführung des Verfahrens vor dem Landgericht unter dem Aspekt des § 24 Abs. 1 Nr. 3 GVG (vgl. Kleinknecht/Meyer-Goßner, StPO, 42. Aufl., § 24 GVG Rn. 6).

Ich beantrage,

        a) das Hauptverfahren zu eröffnen,

        b) den Haftbefehl nach Maßgabe der Anklageschrift zu erweitern und Haftfortdauer anzuordnen.

Kollorz
Staatsanwalt

Jailed in 'Democratic' Germany: The Ordeal of An American Writer

January 12, 1996 — Pensacola News Journal

Local anti-Semite flees Germany to U.S.

By Rick Barrett
and Mary Grunwald
News Journal staff writers

Hans Schmidt of Pensacola has fled his native Germany and returned to the United States to escape trial on charges that he incited racial hatred through his German-American newsletter.

Schmidt, 68, is not disclosing his location, his wife Roswitha said Thursday.

A NEW ARREST warrant has been issued for him in Schwerin, Germany, where his trial was scheduled to continue today.

If convicted, Schmidt faces up to five years in prison.

German officials said he is a fugitive but they did not yet know whether he could be extradited from the United States.

SCHMIDT, A retired accountant who has lived here two years, was arrested Aug. 9 while visiting relatives in Frankfurt because German authorities had found copies of an anti-Semitic newsletter he publishes from Pensacola circulating in the country.

Articles in the newsletter referred to the German government as "Jew- and Mason-infested."

IN OTHER writings he refers to the Holocaust as "fairy tales."

In a signed news release faxed from a Pensacola telephone number, Schmidt wrote that he returned to the United States because he had received threats and that he was concerned about his health.

"I HAD HOPED that the trial would continue without my being present. The German judiciary system has a way of finding people guilty — and sentencing them — without their being present. I therefore saw no problem for them to continue my trial."

Schmidt was freed on his own recognizance last week, over the objection of prosecutors, after defense lawyers argued he was too ill to remain in jail.

The court ruled there was no danger of flight and ordered Schmidt to appear in court Thursday.

He did not show up and left a taped telephone message with his German lawyer saying he didn't feel well and couldn't make it.

Roswitha Schmidt said she expects her husband to be back in Pensacola soon.

"I FEEL WONDERFUL that he's back in this country," she said.

Schmidt has directed his lawyers to appeal his sentence if his trial continues without him.

"Rather than alter my stance or my defense, I chose the only way out of this dilemma. I returned to the land of the free," he wrote.

Monday, February 5, 1996 — Pensacola News Journal

Schmidt: I'm defending free speech

Here we go again: Would you please be so kind, and tell me what, in your opinion, is an anti-Semite?

In two articles you used that designation for me, but for the life of me I can't imagine that it is I you are writing about.

Is it because I am against the more than $3 billion tribute (of taxpayers' money) the U.S. pays to Israel each year?

I admit I am against the inordinate power the top Jews are wielding in/over the United States at this moment in history. I think it is plainly wrong for a tiny ethnic and religious minority to be as influential as American Jews are right now. An ethnic group consisting of but 3 percent of the population occupying about a third of the cabinet posts in the U.S. government looks wrong not only to me, but to millions of other Americans.

It can only backfire!

Put in perspective, this means that American Jews have a thousandfold influence above that which they are really (only) entitled to.

HANS SCHMIDT

But I will be honest: I would be equally opposed if "my" German-Americans were to hold more than the approximately 25 percent power and influence in U.S. society they ought to be allowed by population count.

While my real battles are about truth and justice, and for the honor of my Germans here and in Deutschland, by reading your articles one cannot avoid the feeling that all I do is concern myself with matters of Jews and the "Holocaust."

Actually, I consider myself a free speech advocate. Nothing more, nothing less.

Even during the Third Reich I was able and willing to openly debate Communists and anti-Hitler people, and it never entered my mind to tell someone to "shut up" for this or that reason.

So the more surprising I find it that an American paper such as the PNJ at least tacitly supports those hysterical "ethnic" fanatics who want to do away with the constitutional guarantees of freedom of expression as stated in the cherished First Amendment (that, by the way, was largely the result of the court battles of John Peter Zenger, a German immigrant to this country).

At any rate, I do think you are wrong when you use such obviously misleading designations as shown in your articles about me. As an American newspaper, you ought to support me, even if you do not agree with many things I say or write.

It is incomprehensible to me that you can state without further comment that in Germany, I, an American citizen, could have been put in jail for five years for merely expressing my opinion, something that is "free" in America.

You may scoff at this, but I am fighting my battles also for you and your readers.

Hans Schmidt, of Pensacola, faces charges in Germany for his views on the Holocaust.

Appendix II: Documents

GERMAN INFORMATION CENTER (GIC)

Pr 312 SE

New York, March 1, 1996
pü/-

Hubert H. Brockhues

Dear Hubert H. Brockhues,

Your letter addressed to the German National Tourist Office has been forwarded to us for further attention.

The Holocaust is a generally acknowledged historical fact that is well established through reports of eyewitnesses and documents. If the denial of this fact is only directed at historiography, accusing it of falsity, this is not a punishable offense under German law.

If, however, the denial of the holocaust is aimed at the dignity and self-respect of our Jewish fellow citizens, it is a punishable offense.

An inseparable part of a person's dignity may also be the singular circumstances of his or her death. Had he or she - like the Jews murdered in the concentration camps - come to a violent and cruel death through state-organized and directed violence due solely to his or her descent (race), this tragic fate is imprinted on his or her individual dignity and thereby onto his or her memory among the living as well.

Compared to the severity of defamation, the restriction of the freedom of expression in this partcular area is considered less serious.

Sincerely yours,

Marianne Purtinger

Index

Aachen, 154
Abbé Pierre, 390-391
Abendland, 153
Address lists (of GANPAC), 125-128
Adel, 267
Adenauer, Konrad, 257, 267-268, 366
ADL-AntiDefamation League B'nai B'rith, 65-68, 317-353, 427
  and all-seeing eye of Judaism, 341
  as "American authorities," 26, 199, 232
  bulletin of, 339
  budget of, 344, 347
  collaborators with, 330
  creation of, 322
  cult watch and, 329
  documents at H.S. trial, 299
  entrapment of President Wilson, 348
  exclusively Jewish leadership, 346
  fighting "anti-Semitism," 323
  five thick file folders on H.S., 413
  funding of, 325
  impact on American society, 341
  IRS relations with, 346
  "Jewish thought police," by Village Voice, 27, 294
    psychoterror, 331
  San Francisco Spy scandal and, 27, 348
  spying, 325
  statement after Lauck's arrest, 376
  symbiosis with Zionism, 325
  terror organization, 331
  true objectives of, 326
  unregistered agent of Israel, 232
  visit by Judge Jacobsen, 351-353
  write-up in Encycl.of Assn., 344-345
Advance to Barbarism by F.J.P. Veale, 47
Affirmative action programs, 326
Africa, 328, 374
African-Americans, 211, 233, 349
Africans, 102, 211
AIPAC (American Israel Public Affairs Committee), 179, 188, 339, 436
AJC (American Jewish Congress), 210
Aktiengesellschaften, 159

Index

Aktion Freies Deutschland, 284
Allied:
  death figures for concentration camps, 208
  dictate of, 267
  eradication of Prussia, 405
  friends of the Germans, 157
  indoctrination by, 367
  military units, 229
  nations, 157
  occupation troops, 269
  postwar claims, 386
  propagandists, 229, 354
  scheme re missing Jews, 228-230
  terror bombings, 47
  vassals in Bonn, 418
  vengeance of, 214
  war aims, 259
  war crimes, 7
  Zionist gas chamber claims and, 304
Allies, and French collaborators, 172, and the Reich, 250-256
Althans, Ewald (Bela), 358, 398
AMA (American Medical Association), 189
America Online, 15, 28, 412
American
  archives, 229
  army (duty of, in Germany), 22
  attorney, 127
  authorities (the ADL), 26, 199, 232
  bayonets, 23, 73
  bill of Rights and, 247
  Day of Remembrance, 186
  captivity under, 198
  Constitution, 353
  Consulates:
    Berlin, 277, 292
    Hamburg, 56, 292;
  developments, after arrest, 64
  elections 1994, 311
  election statistics, 180
  embassy--in Berlin, 89; in Bonn, 24, 164
  First Amendment, 71
  freedoms, 73
  friends, 74
  friendship with Germans, 157, 231

friendship with Israel, 157
G.I.s, 74
guilt for murder and expulsion of Germans, 374
hierarchy, 40
Indians, 221
Jewry, 77
lawyer, 127
media, 14, 45
Mein Kampf and, 407
newsletters, 44
newspapers, 244
occupation of Germany, 58, 73, 269
patriots, 131
political spectrum, 120
population, one quarter German,
Red Cross, 181
school system of, 245
Tracing Service and, 187
responsibility, 74, 221
right-wingers, 189
soldiers, 213
school system, 74
support, 42
teenager (in Singapore), 41
veterans associations, 213
Amerika-Brief, 200, 237
Amnesty International, 130
Amtsgericht (District Court), 290
Anaheim, 330
Anderson, Jack, 199, 232, 234-240
Anklam, 111
Anschluss, 98, 166
AP (Associated Press), 64
App, Dr. Austin, 304
Arabs, 326, 369
Arbeitsdienst (Labor Service), 101
Argentina, 178, 184, 212
Arminius, 150
Armistice (WWII), 8 May 1945, 249
Artukovic, Andrija, 215
Aryan-Americans, 179
Aryan-Jewish relationship, 175
Aryan Zionists, 306
Aryans, 102, 185, 220, 306, 347

Aschbrenner, 178
Asia, 374
Asians, 243, 345
Assassination of Pres. Kennedy, 189-191
Asylum seekers in Germany, 62, 253, 359
Attica, 136
Ausbeutersystem, 166
Auschwitz, 439, 450
  Auschwitz-Birkenau, 13
  bludgeon (Auschwitz-Keule), 396
  Communist POWs in, 243
  concentration camp, 8, 54, 71, 107, 184, 187, 243, 304, 355
  death lists (74,000), 229
  death toll (variations of) 13, 186, 208, 240
  forever in our mind, 218
  four million deceased lie, 12, 377, 391
  gas chambers, 386, 417
  inmates' fear of Jewish psycho-terror, 241
  kapos, 243
  lie, 204, 400
  museum, 304
  myth, 13
  Open Sesame and, 192
  Orwellian Newspeak and, 401
  proclamation of 4 million dead, 229
  statement by Germar Rudolf about, 379
  trial, 365
Auschwitz Lüge, Die by Christophersen, (Auschwitz Lie), 12
Auslagerung, 69, 294
Austria, 43, 164, 198, 250, 267
AV Tusiconia Königsberg, 378
Baden, 261
Bad Müritz, 48
Bahners, Patrick, 354
Barker, Gerda, 280
Basic Law (Grundgesetz), 173, 261
Bauer, Yehuda, 13
Balkans, 62
Baltic Sea, 47, 80
Baltimore, Maryland, 187, and Red Cross Tracing Service, 188
Balts, 242, 327
Baruch, Bernard, 348
Bauer, Yehuda, 237
Baumann-Hendricks, 252

Bavaria, 225, 230, 406, and Mein Kampf, 406-409
Bayern, 261
Beer Hall Putsch 1923, 406
Begin, Menachem, 339, 416
Belgian, 160, 269, 371
Belgium, 157
Belin, David, 190
Bellut, Thomas, 363
Benedictine Abbey, 114
Bertram, Günter, 14
Berlin, 89, 152, 213, 268
  cathedral, 368
  Declaration of 1945, 255
  Jews in Berlin telephone book of, 1941, 227
  wall, 258, 264
Beschlüsse (decisions by the court), 279-285
Beverly Hills, 210
Bilderbergers, 153
Bismarck, Otto von, 267
Blacks, 102, 233, 243, 345
Bochum, prosecutor's office, 174, 192, 194
Bodo, (the story of), 109-112
Bolshevism, 237, 347
Bonn (city), temporary capital, 268
Bonn (regime), 152, 192
  anti-Fascist dictatorship and, 89
  book burnings by, 394
  bureaucracy of, 258
  Catholic Republic, 267
  censorship, 384, 412, 421
  Constitution (see Grundgesetz), 50, 356
  Corporations, 162
  counter attack against dissidents, 7
  court system of, 246
  dictatorship, 262
  dishonesty of, 257-272
  ethical foundations, 381-382
  East German properties, 264
  failure to prepare for unification, 258
  financing M. Wolffsohn, 223
  forbidden books and, 99
  Government of, 244
  house searches by, 99, 398-400
  holidays, 135

holiday schedule, 135
idolizes M. Wolffsohn, 217
justice system and witnesses, 388
legality of, 404
lip service to German reunification, 257
mind-set of bureaucrats, 12
Minister of Justice, 121, 401
Ministry of the Interior, letters by, 27, 144, 250-252, 319
NATO association of, 360
number of system loyalists, 171-172
Oberjuden and, 289
parliament and the Deckert case, 356
pillars of its system, 403
parties, 38
politicians, 163
pressure on, 45
prosecutors, 245
raison d'etre of, 382, 412
regime cronies, 162
repression of German patriots, 89
Republic, 250
shenanigans of, 273
special place of Jews in, 33
speech by John Major and, 1995
suppression of non-Marxists, 375
theft of East German properties, 155
tyrants, 13
toadying to the Israelis, 85
U.S. embassy and, 164
vassals, 32, 55, 75, 81, 85, 246, 418
view of Hans Schmidt, 302
Zionist instituted system of, 19
Bonns Zwing Herren, by H. Kardel, 282
Book burnings in modern Germany, 8
Book of Esther, 351
Bosnians, 185, 371, 372,
Bosse, Georg Albert, 9
Boutellier, Michael, 361
Brackmann, Michael, 138, article on Bützow, 139-142
Branch Davidians, 329
Brandenburg, 254, 261
Brando, Marlon, 333
Brandt, Will, 172
Braveheart, 323

Bremen, 17, 261
Brighton Beach, 210
British, 150,
British Empire, 16, 176, 337, 360
Brockhues, Hubert H., 453
Brooklyn, 210
Bruchsal, 374
Bruessels, 253
Bubis, Ignatz, 185, 383
Buchanan, Patrick, 181, 284
Budapest, 54, 194
Büttner, Siegfried, 392
Buna factory (Auschwitz), 107
Bundesarchiv, 391-393
Bundestag, 152, 192
Bundesrepublik, 7, 55, 144, 152, 217, 219, 268-269, 308, 315
  basic law of, 261
  brainwashing and, 157
  Allied friends of, 157
  immigration, 256
  "most free state ever," 158
  remnant of the Reich, 153
Bundeswehr University, 176, 186
  and impact of Hans Schmidt's letters, 224
  resignation of President, 224
  Wolffsohn and:
  appointment of, 369
  influence over, 224
Burke, Virginia, 35, 170, 200
Burundi, 371
Bush, George, S., 265
Bützow prison, 26, 28, 36, 42, 47, 48, 50, 51, 58, 115, 117, 161, 163, 273, 368, 417
  books desired, 116
  Christmas at, 131
  comparison with Auschwitz, 108
  conditions at, 139-142
  cost of postage stamps at, 106
  delivery of indictment, 117-118
  description of, 82, 85, 90
  description of the city of, 84
  description of activities in, 96
  description of food, 103-104
  description of the library, 115

Index

   discharge from, 300
   distance to Schwerin court house, 146
   during the Third Reich, 137-138
   during the Communist era, 137-138
   file number (Log book), 169
   fuchs-device, 112-113
   general inspection, 134-142
   handling of prisoners cash, 105, 274-275
   handling of prisoners mail, 107, 275-276
   hostage taking, 134-142
   indictment, 117
     English, 168-246
     German, cf. Appendix II
  location of, 152, 153
  new underwear for America, 114
  personnel of, 274
  place of execution, 137-138
  politically minded prisoners in, 81
  purchases from the commissary, 106
  report on, 80-116
  searching of the cells in August 1995; 86, 134-142
  sent-off by other prisoners, 300
  torn political letter and, 89
  weekly showers at, 107
Bulgaria, 97
Butz, Dr. Arthur, 304
By Way of Deception, 334
California, 75, 177, 180, 335
Canada, 157, and Supreme Court, 235, 354
Canaris, Wilhelm, 393
Carpetbaggers, 31, 145, 158
Carto, Willis, A., 334
Catch 22, 59
Catholics, 151
Catholicism and Germany, 268
CDU (Christian Democratic Union), 31, 165, 191, 268
Celler, Emanuel, 245
Central Europe, 150, 153
Censorship of Literature, Federal Office of, 419
Central Germany, 124
CFR (Council on Foreign Relations), 153
Chancellor Helmut Kohl, 121
Chechnya, 371
Chicago Tribune, 241, 281

China, 40, 41, 64
Chinese, 40-41, 44, 64, 393
Chomsky, Noam, 326
Christian, 77-78, 121, 327, 350, 414,
Christianity, 78
Christmas, 72, 98, 131, 279
Christophersen, Thies, 12, 13, 397, 403, 418
Churchill, Winston (Prime Minister), 47
Churchill, Winston (American writer), 336
CIA (Central Intelligence Agency), 164, 348, 360, 375
Clay, Lucius D., 28, 252
Clemenceau, Georges, 48
Clinton, Bill, 41, 179, 181, 182, 226, 375
Clinton, Hillary, 314
Cockburn, Alexander, 66
CODOH (Committee for Open Debate), 423
Cohn-Bendit, 195
Cole, David, 304
Cologne (Köln), 154, 156, 365-366
CompuServe, 15, 28, 412
Communist:
  era of Germany, 47, 156
  East Berlin
  "East" German Army, 114
  judges in DDR, 315
  kapos in concentration camps, 243
  occupation of DDR, 258
  propaganda by, 156
Communism, scourge of, 17, 347
Communist Germany, 101, 250
Concentration camps, 136, 202, 240, 304
  casualty lists, 187
  Communist kapos in, 243
  death figures of, 208
  records of, 187, 228
Confederacy, 337
Congress, of the U.S., 129, 181, 182
Conradi, Peter, 194, 231, 444
Constitution, (German: see Grundgesetz)
Constitutional freedons (in the U.S.), 72
Conquest of a Continent, The, 427
Cooper, Harry, 414
Copenhagen, 194
Copernicus, Nicholas, 260

Index

Coughlin, Fr. Charles, 269
Council on Foreign Relations, 411
Countess, Professor Robert, H., 281
Crenshaw, Dr. Charles, 189, 230
Crisis, The, 336
Czech Secret Police, 365
Czechia (Czechoslovakia), 164, 250, 254, 258
Dachau concentration camp, death figures and, 208
Dahmer, Jeffrey, 91
Dall, Curtis, 116
Dallas, 189, 192
Dallas Morning News, 189
Danzig, 254
Dawes-Young Plan, 184
Day of Liberation (8th of May), 270
Day of Remembrance, 220
Day X, 258
DDR ("East" Germany), 28, 31, 47, 83, 153, 161, 167
  legal foundations of, 250-256
  final acts by, 259
  infrastructure of, 263
  death camps and, 107
Deckert, Günter, 9, 33, 173, 302, 315, 354-356, 381-382, 397, 416-418
  FAZ comment on, 354
  whereabouts of, 374
Dees, Morris, 66 (n. 1)
Deir Yassin, 218
Delta airlines, 29, 30
Demjanjuk, John, 131, 188, 213
Democratic party (in the U.S.), 180, 312
Demokratie live, 11
Denmark, 13, 14, 376
Deportation, 259
Depression, 156
Der Spiegel, 102
Destruction of Dresden, The, by David Irving, 47
Deutschland, 30, 225, 263, 417
Deutschland Akte, Die, 365
Deutschmarks, 262
Deutschtümelei, 152
DeWirth, Dr., 381
DeZayas, Alfred, 259
Dickmann, Judge, 36

Dole, Robert, 179, 182
dpa (Deutsche Presse Agentur -German Press Agency), 64, 287
  nonreporting after hostage taking, 138,
Dreibergen penitentiary (official name of Bützow prison), 84
Dresden 213, 353
Dr. X, 119-133
Dual citizenship, 232, 307-308
Dual loyalty, 307
Düsseldorf, 124
Dutch peace keepers, 372
DVU (Deutsche Volks Union), 89
Dworkin, Ronald, 357
Dyatel, Danylo, 117, 119
East Berlin, 158, 308
"East" Germans, 150-167
  border patrol officers of, 308
  Communists, 158, 263
  dissatisfaction with West Germans, 158
  factories, 160
  poverty, 159
  the better Germans, 156
  unemployment, 160
  workers, 160
"East" Germany (DDR), 28, 31, 83, 263
  condtitions (in 1996), 165
  Communist enterprises, 159
  destruction of German heritage in, 155
  Königsberg, 260
  possession of large landholdings, 158-159
  resistance to the West, 166
  theft of infrastructure by the West, 155
  visit to, 156
East Prussia, 254, 260
Edward I of England, 323
Egerton, John, 66
Egyptian POWs, 216, 372
Ehrensache, 222
Ehrenwort, 145
Eichendorff, Joseph, 260
Eichmann, Adolf, 393
Eisenach, 155
Eisenecker, Günter, 124, 278, 287-309 299
Eisenhower, Dwight D., death camps of, 213
Elbe river, 263

Index

Elite, Germans of WWII, 17
EKG, 49, 56
Empire of the Middle, 40
Engels, Friedrich, 90, 314
England, 184, 221, 405
Eretz Israel, 343
Erfurt, 155
Estonia, 71
EU (European Union), 157, 253
Euro (new European currency), 262
Europe, 6, 28, 92, 152, 155, 158, 167, 270-271
European Union (EU), 157, 253, 411
Exhorters Inc., 78
Expulsion, 259
Extradition (of Hans Schmidt), 410
Fairfax, Virginia, 200
Farrakhan, Louis, 345, 347, 349
Faurisson, Dr. Robert, 45, 279-280, 303-304
FAZ (Frankfurter Allgemeine Zeitung), 354
FBI, 66, 69, 200, 238, 335, 340, 375
Fear of the Jews-Syndrome, 78
FED (Federal Reserve Bank), 181
Federal Republic, 143
Federal Supreme Court (of Germany), 205
Feldman, Clara, 211
Fest, Joachim, 407
Filzung, 86, 134
Final Solution, 13, 218
Fire bombings, 47
First Amendment, 16, 28, 71, 79, 303, 353
Fischer, Joschka, Bonn legislator, 382
Florida, 24, 75, 77, 142, 276
Foxman, Abraham, 350
France, 154, 157, 182, 221, 232, 405
Francis, Sam, 281
Frankfurt, 80, 154, 300
  airport of, 19, 24, 29, 30, 32, 34, 105, 303, 310
  court house of, 42
  jail, 24, 42, 48, 49, 51, 52
  judge, 47
Frankfurter Allgemeine Zeitung (FAZ), 21, 23, 217, 282
  comment regarding Deckert, 354, 382
  letter to the editor (by K. Lewan), 220
  on the prohibition of Mein Kampf, 407

Freda, 285
Freimaurerverseucht, 35
Freistunde, 96, 102, 106, 117, 135
Freitag, Frau, (Judge) 143, 273
Freemasons, 33, 68, 159, 173, 215, 321
"Freemasonry infested," 35
French:
  collaborators, 172
  War Crimes Research Office, 13
  1947 kidnapping of Waffen-SS soldiers, 231-232
  Jew from, (Michel Friedman), 191
  occupation troops and, 269
  people of, 54, 159, 164
  scholar, 242
Frey, Dr. Gerhard, 89
Friedman, Michel, 185, 191, 356-357
Fromme, Friedrich Karl, 282
Führer, 101, 272, 406
Gacy, John, 91
Gannett newspaper chain, 66
GANPAC (German-American Public Affairs Committee), 32, 44, 198, 232, 236, 443, 447
  history of, 335-337
  membership, 75, 294
  Santa Monica offices torched, 293, 339
  Washington post office box of, 232
GANPAC-BRIEF, 32, 77, 197-199, 284-285, 337-338
  continuously published, 285
Gas chambers, 13, 107, 202, 204, 272, 303-304, 355, 367,
  as absolute truth, 382
  claims for, 377
  fraud of, 327, 334
  no forensic evidence of, 417
Gateway magazine, 412
Gauss, Ernst (pseudonym of Germar Rudolf), 377
Geil, Rudi, 31, 33, 35, 86, 134, 171, 209-210, 215, 294
Gelsenkirchen, 61
Generalrevision, 86, 134
Geneva Conventions, 254-256
Genscher, Hans-Dietrich, 265
Gerard, Tom,, 348
German-American
  attitude toward slavery, 336
  characteristics of, 150

Index

  families (old), 78
  Friendship Garden, 129
  German-American Day, (October, 6th, 1988), 129
  loyalties of, 336
  lobby (in Congress), 151
  media, 224
  newsletter, 77
  organization, 232, 278
  persecution in the U.S., 293
  politics and, 32, 65, 126, 151
  population of, 71
  racial attitude and, 150
  settlers, 336
  situation in the U.S., 292-293
  traits of, 150
  Union Army and, 336
  university, 68
  vs. Jews in the U.S., 344
German-Information Center, 453
Germans (postwar), 6, 218, 259, 316
Germantown, 336
Germany, 182
  anti-Jewish pogroms and, 228
  Appeal by 100, 21
  current attempt at destruction, 374
  being infiltrated, 185
  borders, 164, 258
  brainwashing by Allies, 157
  criminality, 85
  criminal nation, 229
  cultural devastation, 74
  Day of Liberation, 6
  divisions, 151
  duty toward Israel, 219
  eastern orders, 258
  feudal rulers, 20
  future actions, 172
  importance to neighbors, 164
  inner-German border 161
  new Germany, 243
  peace treaty (WWII), 249
  pogroms, 228
  prohibition of free speech, 240
  prohibition of Mein Kampf, 407

pride in, 162
Reich of the Murderers, 175
renaming of Central Germany, 152
reunification, 151
reunited, 159
safety of Americans in, 207
the sickness today, 354
sovereignty, 404
the Reich, 6,
  and 1945 capitulation, 6
suppression of free speech, 10
taxpayers, 160
Third Reich and, 10
traitors to, 172
unfree vassal of the U.S., 71
unemployment statistics, 163
Germany Must Perish, by Theodore Kaufman, 404
Gestapo, 7, 14
Gibraltar, British organized elections in, 256
Gingrich, Newt, 179, 179 (n.1), 182, 436
Gleichgeschaltet, 315
Globe & Mail, 357
Goebbels, Josef, 351, 391
Goebbels, Mastermind of the Third Reich, 351-352, 391-392
Görlitz Agreement, 251
Golan Heights, 219
Goldberg, Irving L., 191
Goldhagen, Daniel Jonah, 353, 383, 401
Gorbachev, Mikhail, 179, 229, 265
Grabert, Wigbert, 7, 376, 394, 397
Graf, Jürgen, 33
Grant, Madison, 427
Great Britain, 154, 157, 386
Greenspan, Alan, 181-182
Green Party (of Germany), 382
Grenada, 37
Grossny, 185
Grundgesetz (Ersatz Constitution), 22, 28, 50, 247, 252, 256
  creators of, 252
  disregard in Deckert case, 356
  two versions, 260-261
Grundlagen zur Zeitgeschichte, 7, 376, 383, 390, 394-397
Güchel, Eberhard, 173
Gutstadt, Richard E., 427

Gypsies, 85, 211
Gysi, Gregor, 166, 185
Habekammer, 280
Haftprüfung (examination for continued detention), 120, 275
Hague, The and the laws of war, 255-256
Haider, Jörg, 253
Halpern, Tom, 68
Haman, 323, 351
Hamburg, 14, 26, 48, 52, 80, 261
  prison, 56-63
  prison hospital incident, 59-60
  prisoner from Hamburg, 80
Hanover, 26, 52
Hans Schmidt Defense Committee (HSDC), 117-133
Hanseatic port, 47
Hauptmann, Bruno Richard, 92
Heer (German Army), 235
Heidelberg, 253
Heilbronn, 11
Helsinki Accords, 28, 288, 358
Herbig, Dieter, 416
Herndon, Edward T., 284
Herrmann, Hajo, attorney, 40, 42, 43, 44, 124, 169, 275, 278,
  asking for Schmidt's immediate release, 296
  trial and defense strategies of, 287-309
  trips to Bützow and Schwerin, 146
Herzog, Roman, 121, 152, 219, 361, 368
Hess, Rudolf, 269
Hessia, 161, 245, 261
Hewel, Walther, 393
Heydorn, Judge Horst, 278, 286, 297-298, 302, 417
Hilberg, Raul 13
Himmler, Heinrich, 393
Hiroshima, 213
Hispanics, 345
Hitler, Adolf, 48, 65, 67, 155, 157, 163, 176, 200, 215, 237, 268, 276
  1944 assassination attempt upon, 389
  demonization of, 272
  Globe & Mail article, 357
  1924 incaceration, 397
  like Haman, 323
  legal heirs, 406
  literature on (in Germany), 408

Machtergreifungí, 227
war responsibility and, 272
Hitlerism, 359
Hitler Youth, 101, 199, 235
Hitler's Willing Executioners by Goldhagen, 353, 383, 401
Hoax of the Twentieth Century, The, by Arthur Butz, 304
Hobart College, 218
Hoffman-info.com (Michael A. Hoffman II), 423
Hoffmann, Joachim, and Grundlagen zur Zeitgeschichte, 395-396
Holbrooke, Richard, C., 153, 292
Holland, 97
Holocaust, 66, 68, 171, 173, 215, 219, 237, 240, 243, 296, 303-305, 341
  as business, 225
  as religious dogma, 16, 148
  claims, 187, 393
  death figures, 186
  denial, 202
  deniers, 46
  statistics, in U.S. 210
  gassings, 389
  hoax, 305
  invention of term, 211
  Law, 381
  Mär, 210
  Memorial Day, 215
  Memorial Museum, 129, 210,
  religion, as, 176, 192, 225, 403
  revisionism and, 355, 381
  survivors, 107, 226
    fairy tales, 243
    number receiving compensation, 240
    testimonies, 241
    in the U.S., 188
  tale, 210, 338
  trial in Tübingen 1996, 376, 394-397
Hollywood, 259
Holocaust (of Germans, during WWII), 14, 47
Holtzman, Elizabeth, 188
Homer, 242-243
Honnecker, Erich, 407
Hoskins, Richard, 282
Höss, Rudolf, 13

HSDC (Hans Schmidt Defense Committee) 117-133
Human Rights Watch, 130, 358
Hungarian Jews, 54
Hungarian revolution 1956, 330
Hungary, 71, 153
Huns, 150
Huntsville, AL, 68
Hurwitz, Charles, 236
Ideologie der Neuen Weltordnung, Die, 8
IHR (Institute for Historical Review), 330, 334-335, 341
Index of Censorship, 357
Indictment of Hans Schmidt, 26
  entire text (English), 168-246
  entire text (original German), cf. Appendix II
International conventions on human rights, 14, 247
International organizations, 121
IMT (International Military Tribunal), 255
IMF (International Monetary Fund), 182, 262
INS (Immigration & Naturalization Service), 415
Internet, 15, 28, 305, 353, 412, 419, 420-422
Interpol, 8
IRS (Internal Revenue Service) and the ADL, 346
Irish, 150, 243
Iron Curtain, 151
Iron Cross, 17
Irving, David, 33, 47, 304, 330, 351-353, 391-393
  address, 391
  Collection, 393
Israel, 26, 106, 131, 164, 179, 182, 213, 222, 225, 350
  payments from Germany, 230, 365
  payments from the U.S., 347
  using Lebanese mercenaries, 364
  warning by U.S. DoD, 369
  Israel-first luminaries, 72
Israeli:
  assassination bureau, 27
  American citizens, 232, 308
  future officers, 216
  German tribute, 230
  government, 216
  military academy, 222
  need for money, 360
  occupied Palestine, 245
  soldiers, 216

war crimes, 216
Israel lobby, 188, 312
Isvestiya, 311
Italians, 150, 212
Italy, 97, 154, 212
Ivan the Terrible, 131
Jacobsen, Judge, visit to Schmidt in Palm Springs, 341-343
Jana, 94-95
Japan, 157
Japanese-American origanizations, 227
JDL (Jewish Defense League), 69, 333-335
Jaeckel, Heinz, 424
Jerusalem, 216
JFK (President John F. Kennedy), 189-191, 449
Jesus, 78, 150
Jewish:
  activists, 204
  agenda, 66, 193, 225, 325
  antenna, 179
  atrocities, 212
  attorneys, 178
  American organisations, 72
  behavior of, 205
  boy in Singapore, 120
  boycott, 332 of Germany, 1933, 332
  cemeteries, 364
  commissars in America, 224
  communists, 212
  control over the media, 120, 189
  declaration of war on Germany of 1933; 332
  dominance in Germany, 227
  double-talk, 68
  elite, 50
  extortion re 6 million, 244
  faith, 243
  Germanophobia and, 338
  hatred, 213, 306
  hoax, 389
  Hollywood and , 323
  hospital in Berlin (WWII), 227
  "infested," 35
  interests and book trade, 190
  investors, 183
  journalists, 183

judge (agent for ADL), 342
kapos, 107
legislators, 72, 245
Lobby, 72, 276
lobbyists, 72
losses in World War II, 131
mafia, 328
manipulation, 68
masses, 68
monopoly over the media, 182
newspapers, 224
Newspeak, 338
obfuscation by, 176
organizations in Berlin in 1941, 227
in the U.S., 325
overlords, 69
partisans, 212
peddlers, 72
power worldwide, 185, 213; in the United States, 32
population, 219
professors (returned to Germany), 23
propaganda, 231
race mixing and, 231
(over-)representation in the U.S. 33
revenge, 213, 351
shenanigans, 224
soldiers (in Israel), 185
subversive behavior of, 205
synagogues, 364
terrorism in the U.S., 69
thirst for revenge, 188, 213, 351
unassimilable group, 205
vengeance, view of Jews, 209
Wall Street financiers and, 182
war dead, 225
wealth, 68
writer, 69
expulsions, 323
"Jew-and Freemasonry-infested," 36, 173, 202
Jews:
  Allied scheme re missing Jews, 228-230
  and assimilationm, 329
  and German-Americans, 129,
  and freemasons in Germany, 215

allegedly being depicted as inferior, 202
allegedly hating the Jews, 306
critical comments (about), 215
deliberate mass murder during WWII, 201
differences between J. and others, 102
expulsion from England, 323
(laws protecting them), 12, 148
forced busing, 245
in Berlin in 1941, 227
mention in Klingst letter, 173
number allegedly exterminated, 240
  in the U.S.Government, 41
  in the O.S.I., 188
  in World War II, 53, 107, 108
  missing after the war, 229
  special privileges, 231
  weeping, 185, 226
Jew Watch magazine, 413
Johnson, Lyndon B., 190, 312
Journal of the AMA, 189
Juchem, Wolfgang, 284
Judeo-Christianity, 78
Judicial notice (Offenkundigkeit), 21, 304, 390
Judenverseucht, 173
Junkers, 267
JVA (Justizvollzugsanstalt: penitentiary), 93
KGB, 7
Kahlenberg, Professor Friedrich, 392
Kamikaze, 184
Kant, Immanuel, 260
Kardel, H., 282
Karlsruhe, 194
Kassel, 52
Katyn, 213
Kaufman, Theodore, 404
Kemper, Erhard, 33, 173, 283
Kennedy, John F., 189, 449
  assassination, 189-191, 230, 244
  alledgedly blamed on Jews, 204,
Kiel, 19, 149, 174, 418
Kindergarten, 226
King David Hotel (Jerusalem), 339
King, Rodney, 361
Kinkel, Klaus, 194, 231, 270, 293, 444

Klan Watch, 65, 66-67,
Klinger, Sergeant, 95
Klingst, Martin, 31, 33, 35-38, 204, 209-211, 214, 293, 306
  Jews and Freemasons, on, 173, 202
  Open letter, 171
  role in indictment, 200-204
Kohl, Helmut, 31, 81, 152, 165, 257, 264, 270, 382, 400, 418
Kollarz, Prosecutor, 143, 146, 291, 451
  blundering at the trial, 295
  conversation with Hans Schmidt, 148
  indictment of Schmidt, 168-246
  reading of, 292
  shenanigans of, 273
  Schmidt's trial and, 287-309
Koreh, Ferenc, 215
Kornblum, John, 153, 292
Kosher racket, 244-245
Kriegsmarine (German Navy), 235
Krim, Mr. & Mrs., 191
Kristallnacht, 135, 211, 218, 228, 323
Kühnen, Michael, 33
Ku-Klux-Klan, 347, 349, 413
Lady Godiva, 145
Landgericht (Superior Court), 290
Landsberg on the Lech, 397, 406
Landsleute, 154
Landwehr, Richard, 17, 18, 20, 412
Lafontaine, Oscar, 138
Las Vegas, 91
Latvia, 71
Lauck, Gerhard, 14, 20, 33, 291, 307, 412, 417-418
  reason for incarceration, 375-376
  arrest in Denmark, 376
  lawyer for, 24
LBJ (President Lyndon B. Johnson), 190
League of Nations, 48,
Lebanon, 185, 363-364
Lebed, General Alexander, 164
Les Mesonges d' Ulysse (by Paul Rassinier), 242
Le Monde, 13
Lenin, V.I., 407
Leuchter, Fred, 33, 193, 230, 288, 307, 355, 385, 412, 416
Leuchter Report, 420
Lewan, Kenneth,

Lichterketten-Demonstrationen, 361
Life on the Mississippi, 322
Lille, France, 231
Lincoln, Nebraska, 14
Lindbergh baby, 92
Lithuania, 71
Lizenzpresse, 35
London, 6, 97, 156
London Protocol, 251
Los Angeles, 178, 227
Lufthansa German airline, 123
Luther, Martin, 268, 351
Lutherans, 69
Lübeck, 58, 359-364
Lüneburg, 53
Luftwaffe (German Air Force), 42, 235
Luisenthal, 34, 169, 197, 200
Lynchburg, Virginia, 282
Maastricht, 157
Madasgaskar, 323
Magdeburg, 194, 205, 231
Mailing lists (of GANPAC), 125-129
Majdanek concentration camp, 304, 355
Major, John, speech May 8, 1995, in Berlin, 270, 426
Malaga, Spain, 389
Malzahn, Norbert H., 413
Manheim, Ralph (translator), 406
Mannheim, 15
Mao-Tse-Tung, 40, 238, 407
Marbella, Spain, 387
Mark of Cain, 218, 229
Mass murder of German women and children, 47
Marx, Karl (Das Kapital), 10, 90, 165, 314
Marxism-Leninism, 166
Marxist professors, 68, and socialists, 238
Mayer, Arno, 237
Mayer, Judge Dietmar, 389
Max Planck-Institute, 8, 377, 383, 387
McCormack, Thomas, 352
McGowan, Daniel, 218
Mecklenburg-Vorpommern (State of), 84-85, 114, 261
  interior minister of, 19, 86, 171
  minister of justice of, 413
  capital of, 30, 31, 47

summons, 80
unemployment rate, 86, 163
Medicare, 62
Mein Kampf, 43, 406-409, 427
Menschen, 227
Mexicans, 177
Mexican bailout 1995, 181, 183
Mexican peso, 181
Mike, 135
Militia movement in the U.S., 347, 349
Miller, David Neal, 353 (n.1)
Millken, Michael, 237
Missouri, 336
Mitteldeutschland, 165, 259
Mitteleuropa, 153
Mölln, 360
Mongols, 150
Monssen-Engberding, Mrs., 421
Monte Cassino, 213
Moon, Reverend, 189
Mormons, 329
Moscow, 20, 164, 391-392; Treaty (of 1990), 251
Mossad, 27, 69, 179, 334, 360, 364
Muench, Professor K., 253
Musgrove, Gordon, 47
Muslim, 357
Munich, 15, 154
Nation, The, 66
Napoleon, Bonaparte, 90, 351
National Hebdo, 13
National Socialism, 17
  and young Germans, 359
  criminalization, 272
  crimes, 221
  government, 417
  ideology, 407-408
  mass murder and, 202
  rule, 248
  tyranny and, 205
Native Americans, 346
NATO, 157, 382, 411
Nazi rocket program, 68
Nazis, 65, 357, 360
Nazi beliefs, 355, 407-409

Nazi, 102, 212, 359, 392,
Near East, 374
Nemesis at Portsdam, 259
Neo-Nazi, 46, 245, 333, 347, 349, 357, 359, 416
Netherlands, 157
Newspeak, 211
Neubiberg, 175, 204
Nevada, 91
New American, The, 27
New Amsterdam, 336
Newark, New Jersey, 121
New York City, 16, 127, 184, 225, 342
New York State, 136
New York Post, Feldman article, Nov.6th, 1988, 211
New York Times, 45-46, 188, 217, 244, 341, 412, 440
New World Order, 304
Niedersachsen, 261
Nixon, Richard, 40
NKVD, 7
Noahites, 177
Nobel Peace Prize, 218
Nordrhein-Westfalen, 261
Northrhine-Westphalia, 201, 261
Northrhine-Westphalia press law, 203
Northwestern University, 304
November 9 holiday, 135
NDP (National Demokratische Partei Deutschlands), 355
Nuremberg, 7, 69, 154, 187, 229, 231, 255, 351, 372
Oberdeutschen, 210
Oberjuden (top Jews), 31, 41, 46, 153, 245, 323, 325, 317-353
  actions of, 224
  inordinate power of, 303, 375
  reason for this designation, 209
Observer, The London, (quote), 402
October 3 holiday, 135
Oder river, 263
Oder-Neisse border, 153, 259
Offenkundigkeit (judicial notice), 21, 304, 390
Old Man of the Sea, The 243
Olching, 230
Open letters, 170
Operation Gomorrah by Gordon Musgrove, 47
Ordnungsmacht, 153
Oregon, 17

Index

Orwell, George, 211, 401
OSI (Office of Special Investigations), 73, 131, 230
  actions, 215, 414
  description, 188
Osnabrück, 398
Ossies, 153, 162
Ostdeutschland, 259
Ostrovsky, Victor, 334
Oswald, Lee Harvey, 189, 190
PAC (Political Action Committee or Public Affairs Committee), 236, 340
Pacific theatre of war, 214
Palatine, 16, 216, 218
Palestinians, 41, 227, 326, 338
Palestine, 308
Palm Springs (visit by ADL), 341
Pandora's box, 44
Paris, 6, 97, 156
Parkland hospital, Dallas, 189
Passau, 153
PEMEX, 183
Pensacola, Florida, 24, 25, 34, 114, 124, 130, 169
  hurricanes in, 65, 276
  situation there after arrest, 64,
  printer (disappointment regarding), 77
Pensacola News Journal, 37
  anti-Semitism smear, 452
  article re Remer and Rudolf, 388-389
  editorial of August 21, 1995, 70, 74, 77
  Free Speech (op-ed by Hans Schmidt), 452
  reaction following Schmidt's arrest, 66-73
Pentagon warning about Israeli spying, 369
Perpetuum mobile, 325
Pfaelzer, Judge Mariana, 178
Philadelphia, 322, 336
PLO (Palestine Liberation Organization), 369
Poland, 71, 106, 131, 153, 241, 258, 268, 372
Poles, 54, 242
Polish Administration, 250, owners of German properties, 373
Politikverdrossenheit, 151
Pollard, Jonathan, 232, 318
Pomerania, 254, 268
Portugal, 323
Potsdam, 155

Potsdam Agreement (1945), 251, 405
Pressac, 420
Priebke, Erich (SS-Captain), 212
Princeton University, 237
Progressive, The, 66
Proposition 187 in California, 177, 180, 435
Protestantism and Germany, 151, 268
Protestant aristocracy, 267
Prussia, 90, 155, 255, 262, 267, 314, 405
Prussians, 301
Psycho-terrorism, 176, 331
Purim, 351
Purtinger, Marianne, 453
Putnam's, 331,
Quedlinburg, 155
Radio Free Europe, 215
Radtke-Schoone, Hilde, 282
Rassinier, Paul, 242, 303
Reagan, Ronald, 129, 230
Realpolitik, 157, 312
Rechtsanwalt (attorney), 42
Recht und Wahrheit magazine, 9
Rechtsstaat (government with justice), 55, 314
Reconstruction period (in the 19th century U.S.), 337
Red Army, 17
Red propaganda, 156
Red Star, 17
Re-education, Allied imposed, 6, 316, 363
Rehberg, Eckhardt, 164
Reich (The German), 48, 58, 74, 153, 164, 166, 184, 210, 225, 227-228,
  allied war aims, 259
  elimination of the, 256, 262
  Government (arrest, May 1945), 255
  peace treaty between R. and Allies, 249-252
  territory, 255
  annexation of, 255
  Überleitungsvertrag, 405
Reichsarbeitsdienst, 101
Reichstag, inscription at, 400
Reitlinger, Gerald, 13
Religious Right, 347
Remer, General Otto Ernst, 33, 173, 378, 383, 397
  activities on July 20th, 1944, 389

Index

  statement by wife, 386-388
Resettlement of non-Germans (on German soil), 255
Restitution payments to Jews and Israel, 90
Reuters Agency, 64, 287
Revisionists, 189, 381
Rheinland-Pfalz, 31, 261
Richterschelte, 356
Rieger, Jürgen, 421-422
Rimland, Ingrid, 259, 353 (n.1)
Rittenhouse, Stanley, 78
Riviera, 99
Rockefeller, Nelson, 136
Roeder, Manfred, 33
Roman general Varus, 150
Rome, 156, 212, 268-269, 323
Rommel, Erwin, 393
Roosevelt, Franklin Delano, 47, 116
Roosevelt, Theodore, 256
Roper poll (re "Holocaust" belief), 210
Rosenberg, Ethel, 318
Rostock, 47
Rostock travel promoter, 97-99
Rothman, Frank, 178
Royko, Mike, 281
Rubin, Irv, 333
Rubin, Robert, 181-182
Rudolf (-Scheerer), Germar, 8, 33, 389-390, 394, 397
  letter to Minister Wissmann, 378
  statement by Mrs. Remer, 386-388
Rudolph, Thiudar, 173
Ruhr Valley, 90, 313
Rumania, 153
Rumanian criminals (in Germany), 85, 86, 134
Rushdie, Salman, 357
Russia, 20
Russian
  Administration (Königsberg), 250
  Czar, 256
  front, 280
  immigrants, 328
  mafia, 328
  museums, 262
  occupied Germany, 373
  owners of German properties, 373

POW, 42
theft of German cultural values, 262
Russians, 13, 157-158, 164, 220, 264
Rwanda, 185, 371
Saar plebiscite 1935, 48
Saarbrücken, 30, 198, 200
Saarbrücker Zeitung, 138
Saarland, 47, 48, 115, 132, 197, 198, 261, 277
Sachsen, 261
Sachsen-Anhalt, 261
Salamon, Julie, 241-243
San Antonio, Texas, 280
San Francisco, 227
San Francisco Bay Guardian, 27
San Francisco Chronicle, 27
Santa Monica, 62, 198,
  arson fire at GANPAC HQ, 69, 293, 340
Sarajevo, 185, 313
Sardinia, 323
Saunders, Lucile, 285
Sayanim, 334
Schaffer, Ronald, 47
Schalk-Golodkowski, 277
Schäuble, Wolfgang, statement about Auschwitz Lie, 400-401
Scheerer, Germar (see Rudolf, Germar)
Schindler's List, 68, 241
Schleswig-Holstein, 13, 261
Schmidt, Hans:
  American passport, 207
  against race-mixing (integration), 208
  anti-Semitism and, 226
  arrest of, 29
  arrest warrant (English), 34-36
  arrest warrant (German), Appendix II
  attitude toward others, 207
  awakening in America, 403
  captivity after WWII, 198
  citizenship, 36, 206--207, 307-308
  commentary re 8th Wolffsohn letter, 225-230
  commentary re indictment, 206 - 246,
  contents of newsletters, 207
  "crimes" committed on American soil, 145
  current legal status, 410
  Defense Committee, 117-133

Der Spiegel article and, 102
diary excerpts, 274-279,
domicile in Germany, 200
doubts about "Holocaust" tales, 202
effect on Professor Wolffsohn, 224
experiences with JDL, 333,
extent of influence, 207
feelings toward Jews, 68
fined by Kiel court in absentia, 149
flight back to the U.S., 300
foreign languages, 100
French slave labor and, 231
friends all over the world, 298
GANPAC-Brief and, 170
German-American journalist, 138
German soldier (in WWII), 68
high official of NSDAP, 100
home in Germany, 132
immigration to the U.S., 198
impact of arson in Santa Monica on, 339-340
indictment:
  English translation, 168-206
  German original, Appendix II
Kennedy assassination views, 244
life history (in indictment), 197
leaving Bützow prison, 300
letters in behalf of, 38-39
material evidence and, 196
medical condition, 26, 49
money in prison, 274
mother of, 132, 276-277
newsletters, 37
Open letters, 170, in the indictment, 168-206
passports, 207, 246, 307-308
phone calls, 274, 276
post office box in Washington, 236
prediction of coming events, 411
punishment to be expected, 36
racial attitude, 208
"racist", 102
release from prison, 289, 299
reasons for benign treatment, 145
relationship with Jews, 241
return to Saarland, 301

sentence to be expected, 205
special postage stamp, 286
statement to the court, 310-316
trial,
witnesses, 195
typewriter in prison, 100
unblemished record, 290, 316
USA-Bericht and, 170
visit by ADL agent, 341
visit to East Germany, 156
Schmidt, Hannes Johann, (ancestor of Hans Schmidt), 90, 313
Schmidt, Hilde (mother of Hans Schmidt), 200
Schmidt, Richard (brother of Hans Schmidt), 283
  letter to Dr.X, 127
Schmidt, Roswitha (wife of Hans Schmidt), 276-277
  actions of 24, 25, 42
  first greetings from, 57,
  first letter, 58
  first phone call, 276
  instructions to, 45
  return to Pensacola, 74
  treatment by Dr. X, 124-133
Schmidt-Jortzing, E., 401
Schröcke, Professor H., 22
Schulz, Werner, 192, 230
Schumer, Rep. Charles, (D-NY), 72, 245
Schurz, Carl, 116
Schwarzfahrer, 61
Schweinfurt Court, 386
Schwerin, 30, 31, 34, 42, 47, 124, 145, 287-309
Schweriner Volkszeitung, of Oct.10th, 1995; 93-94, 138, 311
  article on conditions at Bützow prison, 139-142
Scribner and Sons, 427
Serbs, 313
Sergeant Klinger, 95
Shakers, 329
Shamir, Yitzhak, 416
Sharkhunters magazine, 413-415
Sher, Neil, 188
Shyster, 333
Shoa, 229, 302, 356
Shoah-business, 302
Siebenbürger, Judge, 386
Sieg magazine, 200, 237

Siegrunen magazine, 17, 18
Silesia, 254, 260, 268
Singapore, 194
Six Day War and murder of Egyptian POWs, 372
Six Million Tale, 202, 229, 244, 338, 389, 414
Skinheads, 347
Slave labor, 69
Slavic peoples, 323
Slovakia, 153
Smith, Bradley R., 423
Soap from "Jewish fat," 237
Social Security, 62, 163
Solingen, 315, 360
Sophia, Bulgaria, 194
Soviets, 158
Soviet confiscations, 265
Soviet Jews, in America, 62, 228
Soviet soldier, 131
Soviet Union, 13, 20, 250
Spain, 8, 13, 154, 323, 386
Spanish language, 100
Speck, Richard, 91
Spotlight (newspaper), 132, 330
Spiegel, Der, (magazine), 102, 311, 382
SPLC (Southern Poverty Law Center), 65
SS, 69
SS runes (insignia), 17, 375
Staatsvolk, 266
Stalin, Josef, 158, 221, 407
Stalinist show trials, 19
Stalinists, 221
Stanislaw, 95
Status of the Reich (1997), 254
Stasi ("East" German secret police), 23, 365
Statute of limitations, 201, 254, 365
Stein, Burkhardt, 394
Stiftung Frij Historisch Onderzock, 393, and report of, 393-397
St. Martins Press, 351-353
St. Petersburg, 20
Strafbefehl. 398
Strafgesetzbuch, 247
Strassburg, 288
Strauss, Josef, 172
Streicher, Julius, 351

Stuttgart Superior Court, 386-387
Sudan, 371
Sudetenland, 250, 254, 259, 268
Suhl, 160
Süssmuth, Rita, 152
Swastika, 14, 17, 65, 334, 365, 375, 414
Swedes, 150
Swedish Royal Academy of Sciences, 393
Svenska Dagbladet, 393
Switzerland, 106, 308, 367
Syria, 216, 218
Tag der Befreiung, 270-271
Talmud, 73, 222, 322
Talmudic, 42, 113, 214, 217, 414
Tauchsieder, 113
Tel Aviv, 175
Teschner, Susanne, 394-396
Teutons, 150
Third World, 62, 245, 361, 374
Thirty Nine Points, 398
Thirty Years' War, 152, 271
This Week in Germany, 228
Thüringen, 261
Thuringia, 161, 162, 261
Toronto Sun, 416
Time magazine of August 13th, 1945, 374
Transit Film Corporation, 392
Travelers Alert flyer, 121-123
Treaty Concerning Germany, 251, 256, 264, 266
Treaty of Versailles, 254
Treblinka, 131, 304
Treuhandanstalt, 159, 162, 263, 265
Trier, 154
Trilateral Commission, 153
Tübingen trial, 384, 390, 393-397
Turks, in Germany, 63, 315, 360
Turner Halls, 150
Two-plus-Four Treaty, 251, 256, 264, 266
U-Boats, 414
Überleitungsvertrag of 1952 (Article 2) text, 404
Uhrlau, Ernst, 23
Ukraine, 228
Ukrainian-American, 131, 213
Ukrainians, 221, 242

Umvolkung, 167
Unconditional surrender, 402
Unification Treaty (of Germany, 1990), 252
United Europe, 261
United Germany, term used in 2+4 Treaty, 256
United Nations (UN), 247, 288, 372
  charter, 247, 390
  Convention, 254
United States
  actions re Hans Schmidt, 44
  acquiescence to arrest, 57
  call to Roswitha re good conduct statement, 75
  Congress, 129, 261
  citizenship, 131
  connivance re Demjanjuk, 213
  Constitution, 7, 15, 247, 349
  consulate
    Berlin, 277
    Frankfurt, 24
  Department of Defense memo, 369
  discriminationm against Germans and, 415
  "East" German properties and, 266
  election results, 180
  embassy, 26
  inaction, 14, 40-46,
  first contact by, 56
  Holocaust Museum and, 210
  Jewish power and influence over, 32, 33
  Justice Dept. (OSI), 73, 188
  occupation of Germany, 28, 157
  legal standing of citizens, 36
  Marshal's Service, 178
  State Department:
    ADL, 232, 348
    Anderson text, 235
    blame for incarceration, 291
    brochure for prisoners, 290
    change of designations, 153
    inaction of , 20, 40, 45
    Jewish control over, 40
  Supreme Court, 73, 266
Untersuchungshaft, (pre-trial detention), 51
Uprising, 330, 352
Urlaub auf Ehrenwort, 131

USA-Bericht, 32, 35, 192, 230, 283-285, 431
USSR, 187
Utah, 91
Varus, 150
Vatican, 269, 405
VEB, 161
Veale, F.J.P., 47
Verfassungsschutz (Bonn Secret Police), 23, 200, 232, 262
Vergin, Siegfired, 192-193, 230
Versailles, 254
Vienna, Austria, 154
Vienna Convention, 254
Vienna, Virginia, 78
Village Voice, 27
Villeroy & Boch china, 114-115
Vogt, Günther, 33
Volk, 310
Völklingen, 34, 169, 197, 200
Volkstrauertag (German Memorial Day), 367
Volksverhetzung (incitement to hate), 30, 55, 247, 310
Von Braun, Wernher, 68
Von Braun, Mrs., 68
Waco, Texas, 329
Von Waldenfels, Georg, 407-409
Von Weizsaecker, Richard, 219, 221, 368, 382
Waffen-SS, 17, 18, 101, 198-199, 231, 235
Wahl, Max, 33
Waigel, Theo, 152
Walendy, Udo, 7, 418
Walesa, Lech, 270
Wall Street financiers, 181-182
Wall Street Journal, 241
Wanderers, The, 259
Warren Commission, 190
Warren Court, 266
Washington, D.C., 6, 29, 129, 175, 232
Washington Jewish Week, 72, 187-188
Washington Post, 186, 211, 311, 369, 414, 439
Washington Times, 189, 211, 281, 414
Wassermann, Rudolf, 381
Waxman, Sharon, 186, 439
Weckert, Ingrid, 323
Wehner, Herbert, 172
Wehrmacht, 12, 379

Index

Weimar Constitution (of 1919), 253
Weinheim, 415
Welles, Elliot (ADL), 319-321, 350
Welt, Die, 381
Wessies, 154, 162
West Germany, 98, 250-256
West Germans stationed in "East" Germany, 89
West Point, 216
Wiesel, Eli, 331, 420
  quote about hating Germans, 218
  Simon Wiesenthal Center and, 294
Wiesenthal, Simon, 294, 419
Willerscheidt, 319
Williams, Eandall, 66
Wilson, Woodrow, Pres., 348 and the ADL, 348
Wings of Judgment, American Bombing in WWII, 47
Wisconsin, 147
Wissmann, Matthias, 378
Wittenberg, 155
Wolf, Markus, 277
Wolffsohn, Professor Michael, 174, 192, 204, 217, 225-230, 243, 293-296, 306, 434
  and anti-German propaganda, 217
  appointment to Bundeswehr-University, 369
  asset of Zionism in Germany, 225
  book, Die Deutschland Akte, 365
  Bonns Zwing Herren , 282
  comment on (old) anti-Jewish actions, 365
  effect of Schmidt letters upon, 224
  Egyptian POWs and, 372
  genetic make-up, 226
  "German-Jewish patriot," 176, 216, 365-370
  German Memorial Day speech, 368-373
  German soldiers defending Israel, 219
  gobbledygook on German Memorial Day, 369
  Holocaust religion, 225, high priest of, 225
  immunity in Germany, 226
  Israeli Zionist, 216
  "Jews and Germans tied forever," 218
  lecture in Washington, D.C., 223
  legal immunity of, 226
  letter by Hans Schmidt to, 175-191, 208
  "Mark of Cain on Germans," 218
  Weltanschauung and, 222

Woltersdorf, Hans Werner, 8
Wood, Laurie, 67
Worch, Christian, 33
World Almanac, 219
World War I, 98, 184, 293
World War II, 116, 121, 213-214, 227-228, 235, 249, 255, 276, 354, 402
Wu, Harry, 40, 41, 44, 64, 129
Wupperthal-Barmen, 313
Yeltsin, Boris, 164
Yugoslavia, 71, 153
Xenophobia, 358
Zacher, Hans F., 425
ZDF (Zweites Deutsches Fernsehen), 362-363
Zeit, Die 33, 35, 36, 171, 381
Zeitgeist, 220, 380
Zenger, John Peter, 16, 71
ZGram, 353 (n.1)
Zionism, 27, 131, 244, 321, 317-353
Zionist, 216, 187, 325, 338
Zündel, Ernst, 33, 45, 68, 173, 235-236, 304, 354, 357-358, 419, 421
Zündelsite, 421, 423
Zyklon-B poison (disinfectant), 377, 388-389

Jailed in 'Democratic' Germany

The Ordeal of an American Writer

Hans Schmidt

Guderian Books
Milton, Florida